THE MASK OF ANARCHY

STEPHEN ELLIS

The Mask of Anarchy

*The Destruction of Liberia and
the Religious Dimension of
an African Civil War*

HURST & COMPANY, LONDON

First published in the United Kingdom by
C. Hurst & Co. (Publishers) Ltd.,
38 King Street, London WC2E 8JZ
Copyright © 1999 by Stephen Ellis
All rights reserved.
Printed in Malaysia
ISBNs
1-85065-401-8 (cased)
1-85065-417-4 (pbk.)

Then they will return with shame
To the place from which they came,
And the blood thus shed will speak
In hot blushes on their cheek.

Every woman in the land
Will point at them as they stand –
They will hardly dare to greet
Their acquaintances in the street.

And the bold, true warriors
Who have hugged Danger in wars,
Will turn to those who would be free,
Ashamed of such base company.

And that slaughter to the Nation
Shall steam up like inspiration,
Eloquent, oracular;
A volcano heard afar.

And these words shall then become
Like Oppression's thundered doom
Ringing through each heart and brain,
Heard again – again – again –

Rise like Lions after slumber
In unvanquishable number –
Shake your chains to earth like dew
Which in sleep had fallen on you –
Ye are many – they are few.

(Percy Bysshe Shelley, *The Mask of Anarchy*, 1819)

ACKNOWLEDGEMENTS

I owe my deepest thanks to the many people who have helped me gather information on Liberia, or who have otherwise assisted in the production of this book. Among institutions, I would like to thank my employer, the Afrika-Studiecentrum, Leiden, and its director, Gerti Hesseling, for supporting two research trips to Liberia in 1997. Most particularly I am grateful to the staff of the Centre's library, one of the finest Africa libraries in the world. Thanks are also due to Amnesty International, which invited me to take part in missions to Liberia, Guinea and Sierra Leone in 1994, 1995 and 1998.

Individuals who have been particularly helpful in locating documentation, in sharing their knowledge of Liberia and in other ways include Els Bakker, David Brown, Jeanette Carter, Max Jarrett, Tom Kamara, Fred van der Kraaij, Carolyn Norris, Binaifer Nowrojee, François Prkic, William Reno, Irma Specht and Kofi Woods. Bart Witteveen, as well as sharing his great knowledge of Liberia and his personal memories of recent events, read earlier drafts of the text and made many helpful suggestions, as did Werner Korte. Jean-François Bayart and Béatrice Hibou were a source of constant stimulus. These, and others whose names are better left unmentioned, have no responsibility for any opinions expressed in the following pages, still less for any errors.

I have discussed many of the themes in this book endlessly with Gerrie ter Haar, whose help and support I could not do without.

Amsterdam, June 1999   S. E.

CONTENTS

Part II. AN INQUIRY

ILLUSTRATIONS

between pages 186 and 187

The NPFL leader Charles Taylor and George Boley

Leaders of the Coalition Group: Roosevelt Johnson, François Massaquoi, Hezekiah Bowen, George Boley, Tom Woewiyu and Sam Dokie

Former President Dr Samuel K. Doe at his last press conference in the Executive Mansion, Monrovia

Alhaji G.V. Kromah, leader of Ulimo-K

NPFL fighters in war attire, 1991

INPFL fighter, 1990

A NPFL girl fighter

An Ulimo-K boy soldier

The photographs are copyright © and any request for reproduction must be addressed to the publisher.

MAPS

ACRONYMS

The following is a list of the main acronyms used in the text, excluding widely-known ones such as US, UN, BBC.

AFL — Armed Forces of Liberia. The military arm of the Liberian state, descended from a force established in 1908. Loyal to Samuel Doe until 1990; thereafter, best considered a generally anti-Taylor faction with a collective leadership.

CFA — Communauté financière africaine. The financial community which issues the CFA franc, the main currency of francophone West Africa.

CRC — Central Revolutionary Council. Formed 1994 by Tom Woewiyu, Sam Dokie and other senior NPFL officials who defected to Ecomog. They participated in a coalition force which attacked Gbarnga in September 1994 but thereafter dissolved.

Ecomog — Economic Community of West African States Cease-fire Monitoring Group. Formed by Ecowas in 1990 as an intervention force in Liberia with components from several West African states, led by Nigeria. Later also included small contingents from elsewhere, including Tanzania and Uganda. Later deployed also in Sierra Leone and Guinea-Bissau.

Ecowas — Economic Community of West African States, an economic forum established in 1975 which has become of increasing diplomatic importance as a forum for the regulation of inter-state disputes.

FPDL — Front for Popular Democracy in Liberia, an armed anti-Doe group led by H. Boima Fahnbulleh in the 1980s. Apparently extinct since 1990.

IGNU — Interim Government of National Unity, the provisional government of Liberia from October 1990 to 1994, led by Professor Amos Sawyer, recognised by most West African states but never formally by the US.

INPFL   Independent National Patriotic Front of Liberia. A militia led by Prince Johnson. Created in a breakaway from the National Patriotic Front of Liberia in July 1990; dissolved 1993.

LDF   Lofa Defense Force. Established in refugee camps in Guinea in 1993-4 with support from the Poro society. Allied principally to the NPFL, although one faction also joined an anti-NPFL coalition in 1994. Its political leader was François Massaquoi.

LPC   Liberia Peace Council. Led by George Boley. Formed as a political lobby in 1991, re-emerging as an armed faction, with Ecomog and AFL support, in 1993. Mainly active in south-east Liberia.

LUDF   Liberian United Defense Force. Formed by General Albert Karpeh in Sierra Leone in 1991, later merged into Ulimo.

MOJA   Movement for Justice in Africa. A pan-African radical political group formed in Liberia in 1973, with chapters in Ghana and Gambia. The Gambian chapter supported a coup attempt in Gambia led by Kukoi Samba Sanyang in 1981. Samba Sanyang later joined the NPFL.

MRM   Movement for the Redemption of Muslims. Organisation formed by Alhaji G.V. Kromah in Conakry, 21 February 1991. Later fused with Ulimo.

NPFL   National Patriotic Front of Liberia, said to have been established by Thomas Quiwonkpa in 1985, later led by Charles Taylor. Initiated the war in Liberia in 1989.

PAE   Pacific Architects and Engineers, an American security company close to the US government, contracted to work with Ecomog.

PAL   Progressive Alliance of Liberia, a radical political group formed in 1975, led by Gabriel Baccus Matthews. In 1980 formed the Progressive People's Party (PPP).

PRC   People's Redemption Council, the military junta chaired by Samuel Doe from 1980 to 1985.

RUF/SL   Revolutionary United Front/Sierra Leone. An armed group formed in Libya in 1989 by Foday Sankoh, a former corporal in the Sierra Leonean army. Allied to the NPFL, it attacked Sierra Leone in March 1991 to begin the Sierra Leonean civil war.

TWP   True Whig Party, established 1869. The ruling party of Liberia for all but six years between 1870 and 1980.

Ulimo   United Liberation Movement for Democracy in Liberia, an armed group formed in Sierra Leone in 1991, initially under General Albert Karpeh. Subsequently split into two main factions, known since 1994 as Ulimo-K (under Alhaji Kromah) and Ulimo-J (under Roosevelt Johnson). Both factions switched alliances with other factions frequently.

Unomil   United Nations Observer Mission in Liberia, formed on 22 September 1993 by Resolution 866 of the Security Council to observe the implementation of peace accords by Ecowas.

MAPS

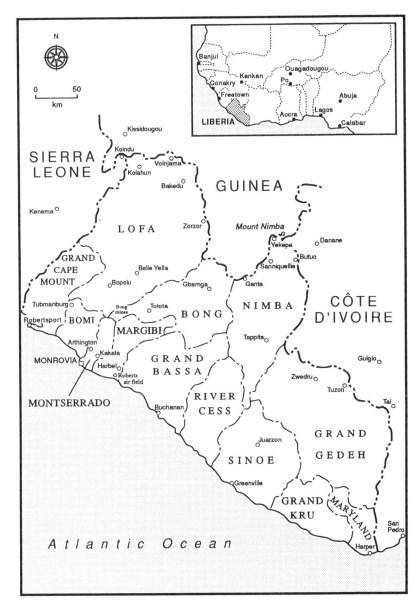

Liberia: counties and major towns

Liberia: ethnic groups

INTRODUCTION
AFRICAN WARS

A death in the night

Sunday, 9 September 1990, began amid a lull in the two-month-old battle for Monrovia, Liberia's capital city. President Samuel Doe was besieged in the Executive Mansion, the massive 1960s office-block which serves as Liberia's seat of government and presidential palace, its back to the brilliant white beach of the Atlantic Ocean at the point where West Africa comes closest to Brazil. On the day before there had been some shelling, but by Sunday morning all was quiet. The weather was hot and humid, punctuated by the heavy rains of Liberia's monsoon season.

Holed up with Doe in the Mansion were those few ministers and officials of his government who had not yet fled the country, defended by several hundred loyal soldiers of the government army, the Armed Forces of Liberia (AFL), who lived in the Mansion and its grounds with their families. At this stage, they still had a little food and abundant water. Still loyal to Doe were also the troops in the main AFL barracks at nearby Barclay Training Center, who held a few blocks of the residential district of Sinkor. The outer suburbs of Monrovia were held by the rebel force known as the National Patriotic Front of Liberia (NPFL), and another part of the city, the market area alongside the Mesurado river and all the suburbs to the west on the other shore, was held by a third armed faction led by Prince Johnson, which had split off from the NPFL a few weeks into the war. (Prince is a common first name in Liberia, and is not a royal title of any sort.) Johnson called his breakaway group the Independent National Patriotic Front of Liberia (INPFL).

Johnson's territory was also the base for an international peace-keeping force which had arrived just two weeks previously. The peacekeepers were hastily organised, largely at Nigerian behest and with some US encouragement, by the Economic Community of West African States (Ecowas). This economic cooperation body was hardly intended for military purposes but, under pressure of circumstances, its leading members had agreed to form an

1

expeditionary force known as the Ecowas Cease-fire Monitoring Group, or Ecomog for short. This force immediately became a party to the war itself. Since the war had begun in December 1989, the number of contesting groups had thus already doubled from the original two. Many more were to come and go in the next seven years of war.

For most citizens of Monrovia, food was in short supply, and an estimated fifty people were dying every day from starvation and disease.[1] Those Monrovians who had not fled when the war came to their city in the middle of the year spent their days indoors, venturing out only in search of food, avoiding if they could the attention of the hundreds of armed youths, men and women who were scavenging and looting throughout the city. No one knew how many people had been killed in the NPFL's drive from the north-east of the country to Monrovia, or in the purges launched by Doe's army in retaliation, but the figure was probably between 13,000 and 20,000 by September 1990.[2]

The NPFL had begun its campaign with an attack from neighbouring Côte d'Ivoire at a point over 200 miles from Monrovia. Its core force of about 100 fighters trained in Libya and Burkina Faso included not only Liberians but also various adventurers and international revolutionaries from other West African countries whom the NPFL had recruited in its foreign training camps. They were further reinforced by regular soldiers on loan from the government of Burkina Faso, the third country of an unlikely trio supporting the NPFL. The presence of the non-Liberians in the NPFL made other English-speaking countries in the region nervous, and this factor had helped persuade the governments of Nigeria, Sierra Leone, Gambia, Ghana and Guinea – the latter being the one French-speaking contributor – to send contingents of their own armies to form the Ecomog peacekeeping force. The troops assembled in Freetown, Sierra Leone, before embarking on the short sea voyage to Monrovia, where the peacekeepers came under shell-fire from the NPFL as they landed.

Ecomog did, however, enjoy the support of Prince Johnson's INPFL faction. Johnson, a professional soldier who had once been a junior officer in President Doe's own army before deserting in 1983, had been the training officer of the NPFL before he broke away from the organisation with a few dozens of the most experienced fighters shortly after the start of the war. By July

---

[1] Estimate by Médecins sans Frontières, reported in *West Africa*, 3819 (5 November 1990), p.2796.

[2] See Annexe A.

1990, when the NPFL seemed close to success, Johnson had a core of about 300 combatants under his orders, according to US officials, with a few civilian hangers-on.[3] Johnson's hope was to win the three-cornered battle for Monrovia and take the presidency for himself. He was counting on getting the backing of the US government, which was known to be embarrassed by Doe but also to be unenthusiastic about the NPFL, since the latter had Libyan backing and was led by a man who had once escaped from prison in the United States, Charles Taylor. In the event, Johnson was disappointed to be given only a hand-set with which to communicate with the vast, fortified US embassy in Monrovia that kept in touch with all the main players in the Liberian crisis.

Johnson and his INPFL occupied some strategic areas of Monrovia, including notably the seaport where the regular West African troops of Ecomog landed from their transport ships on 24 August 1990. He welcomed the arrival of the Ecomog peacekeepers, who set up camp in Monrovia's Freeport, an area controlled by Johnson and close to his own base. The Ecomog commanders, with virtually no intelligence on the situation in Monrovia, were so poorly prepared that, according to the peacekeepers' Nigerian chief of staff, they even had to borrow uniforms and boots from Johnson.[4] The 3,000 men of the international force consisted mostly of support staff such as drivers, cooks and clerks, with only about 1,000 infantry.[5] Some Ecowas officials arrogantly assumed that Charles Taylor's ragged NPFL fighters would melt away at the sight of a professional, mechanised army, but they were to be proved wrong.[6] More dependent on Johnson's faction than they had ever intended, and camping on Johnson's territory, Ecomog commanders developed close links with Prince Johnson and his men, who included one or two Nigerian and Ghanaian nationals who had come down from the north with the NPFL and joined Johnson when he split off from the main rebel force. Johnson took to dropping in for social visits to the Ecomog headquarters with his bodyguards, unannounced and 'armed to the teeth'. His men

---

[3] The US figure is quoted in *New York Times,* 1 August 1990. Mark Huband, *The Liberian Civil War,* London, 1998, p.116, gives the figure as 3,000 INPFL, which most commentators regard as too high.

[4] C.Y. Iweze, 'Nigeria in Liberia: the military operations of Ecomog' in M.A. Vogt and A.E. Ekoko (eds), *Nigeria in International Peace-Keeping, 1960-1992,* Lagos, 1993, p.231.

[5] Lindsay Barrett, 'General Quainoo and Liberia's Crisis', *West Africa,* 4014 (5 September 1994), pp.1545-6.

[6] Iweze, 'Nigeria in Liberia', p.220.

made themselves at home in the headquarters of the Ecomog peacekeepers and held impromptu parties, 'strumming guitars and singing'.[7] Johnson himself was particularly fond of Christian hymns. Fuelled by alcohol, he encouraged his audience to participate, and his notoriously violent temper made it unwise to refuse an invitation to sing along.

For weeks Doe was under pressure to flee the country and leave the presidency to one or other of his rivals, Prince Johnson or Charles Taylor. Most of his ministers and aides had left him and slipped out of Liberia long before September, and his wife had gone to England where her children were in school. In between bouts of fighting, the President whiled away his time playing draughts with his aides. In June four US warships with 2,000 Marines proceeded to Monrovia and stayed long enough to evacuate US and some other foreign nationals, but did not intervene either to help Doe, previously a leading ally of the United States, or to restore order to the devastated city. Every effort to mediate foundered on the intransigence of Doe and Taylor. Some people wondered whether Doe was not being prevented from leaving by his own troops, who feared for their own lives if their president were to go into exile and abandon them. Doe's continuing occupation of the Executive Mansion was only prolonging an indecisive battle and frustrating the governments of Nigeria, Ghana, and the other countries which had assembled the Ecomog peacekeeping force, not to mention the United States which supported this experiment in regional peacekeeping, the most important since the recent end of the Cold War.

Ecomog's arrival in August 1990 did stimulate some political movement. On Wednesday 5 September, Doe and Johnson signed a two-week ceasefire. The President agreed not to venture into Johnson's zone of control without asking permission, a measure of just how weak he had become. At a subsequent meeting at Barclay Training Center, the main AFL barracks just a few streets from the Executive Mansion, the two men embraced and decided to work together against the third of the warlords, Taylor. Not everyone in Doe's camp was comfortable with the arrangement. On the evening of Saturday 8 September, a woman who lived in the barracks at the Barclay Training Center had a dream so disturbing that she left her bed and ran to the AFL Brigade Headquarters. She said that she had seen angels descending from the sky and carrying President Doe away with them. 'They carried Doe-o,' she said, adding an extra 'o' for emphasis as Liberians

[7] *Ibid.*, p.227.

often do. 'The angels from heaven carried the President in the sky.'[8] Although Liberians generally pay close attention to dreams and portents, no one appears to have reported this particular revelation to Doe. On the next day, the President made his first sortie from his fortified residence to visit the Ecomog commander, the Ghanaian Lieutenant-General Arnold Quainoo.

Why exactly Doe ventured out from the Executive Mansion on that fateful Sunday remains a matter of some disagreement. Slightly different versions of events were later given by various parties. General Quainoo himself, his chief of staff Brigadier Cyril Iweze, and a subsequent Ecomog press officer all maintain that Doe left his citadel without any prior warning and drove the two or three miles to Ecomog headquarters unannounced.[9] Only one published eye-witness account, by a captain in Doe's army who was with him in the Executive Mansion on that day, differs on the reasons for his sortie, claiming that an intermediary from Doe's entourage had arranged for the President to visit Ecomog head-quarters with the full knowledge of General Quainoo.[10] The West Africa correspondent of the BBC happened to be visiting the Ecomog headquarters at the time of Doe's visit and recalls vividly that there was a relaxed atmosphere at the base. The Nigerian colonel who headed Ecomog's intelligence department seemed his usual, affable self. She sensed no particular feeling of expectation.[11] If Ecomog had no foreknowledge of Doe's visit, then it strengthens the view that subsequent events were a tragic catalogue of misunderstandings, misjudgements and coincidences, whereas many Liberians to this day believe that Doe was lured to his death as part of a conspiracy by the US and Nigerian governments to remove him from the fray and open the way for a solution to Liberia's civil war.

A former deputy minister, one of the few senior officials who had remained loyal to Doe, recalls that he was sitting on the front porch of a guest house in the grounds of the Executive Mansion at about 1:30 p.m. on Sunday 9 September, talking to the minister

---

[8] James Youboty, *Liberian Civil War: a graphic account*, Philadelphia, PA, 1993, p.399.

[9] These accounts are respectively: interview with Lieut.-Gen. Quainoo in the *Daily Graphic* (Accra), 11 May 1991, summarised by Agence France-Presse, Accra, 11 May 1991, and a later interview in Lindsay Barrett, 'General Quainoo and Liberia's Crisis', *West Africa*, 4014 (5 September 1994), pp.1545-6; Iweze, 'Nigeria in Liberia', pp.216-44; Nkem Agetua, *Operation Liberty: the story of Major General Joshua Nimyel Dogonyaro*, Lagos, 1992, pp. 48-52.

[10] 'Last Moments of Doe', *West Africa*, 3815 (15 October 1990), p.2652.

[11] Author's phone interview with Elizabeth Blunt, London, 25 April 1997.

of defence, when the President's press aide said to them 'Gentlemen, I'm going across', and went off to see the President. Fifteen minutes later the presidential motorcade came out of its garage. The two ministers got in their own cars to follow the convoy.[12] The President's twenty-car motorcade drove out of the grounds of the presidential palace with Doe's own black Mercedes stretch limousine in the middle, sirens blaring and headlights blazing. They drove along the highway over Capitol Hill, past the legislature building and across the bridge to Providence Island, the little island in the Mesurado river where the first African-American settlers, the founders of the modern state of Liberia, set up their original camp in 1822. From there they crossed a second bridge to Bushrod Island, named after Bushrod Washington, nephew of the first president of the US, a sponsor of the original venture to encourage African-Americans to establish a colony in West Africa. The motorcade sped past looted shops and houses, unburied corpses, and displaced people scavenging for food. Some people who saw the motorcade applauded President Doe as he waved from his stretch limousine. Others booed.

When the wail of sirens announced the arrival of the seventy-strong presidential party in their vehicles at Ecomog headquarters, the West African troops on guard duty, mostly Nigerians, were clearly surprised.[13] They insisted that Doe's bodyguards give up their weapons before entering the Freeport area. This the AFL men reluctantly did, leaving only Doe and a couple of others with side-arms. The motorcade drew up outside the port building where General Quainoo had his office. The Ecomog chief of staff, Brigadier Iweze, and the Deputy Force Commander, the Guinean Major-General Lamine Magasoumba, went downstairs to talk to Doe, who told them he had come to register a complaint. According to an Ecomog press officer, Doe's intention was to intimidate General Quainoo with a show of force, complaining that the Ghanaian had breached diplomatic protocol by not paying a courtesy call on the head of state.[14]

General Quainoo came down to join his officers. He saluted the President and bade him welcome. The two men shook hands and then went back upstairs to Quainoo's office with their aides. Doe complained bitterly to Quainoo that the Ghanaian had not

---

[12] Paul Allen-Wie, quoted in 'Last Moments of Doe', p.2650.

[13] The following is taken from the above accounts plus Lynda Schuster, 'The Final Days of Dr Doe', *Granta*, 48 (London, 1994), pp.41-95, and 'Doe, the Complete Story', *Newsbreed* (Lagos), 22 October 1990.

[14] Agetua, *Operation Liberty*, p.50.

come to pay his compliments to the President on arrival in Monrovia. 'As Africans', he lectured the General and his staff, 'you know our tradition; when you enter a village or town, the first thing you do is you go and call on the chief. Since you came you have not paid a courtesy call on me.'[15]

Quainoo apologised. Doe then told him that they were victims of a vast plot, hinting darkly that the Americans were at the heart of it all. Once a leading US ally, Doe now bitterly resented what he saw as American treachery and ingratitude. He reminded Quainoo of 'what happened to Nkrumah while he was preaching the unification of Africa', a reference to the belief widespread in West Africa that the 1966 coup which overthrew President Kwame Nkrumah of Ghana, a nationalist hero and an evangelist of pan-African unity, had been backed by the Central Intelligence Agency (CIA). 'The Americans do not want native Africans to do anything for their countries,' Doe told Quainoo.[16]

The President demanded a full apology, which General Quainoo was in the process of making when INPFL leader Prince Johnson appeared at the Freeport with a group of his own soldiers, no more than ten minutes after Doe's entry. The newcomers, unlike Doe's entourage, were not required to surrender their weapons. Quainoo and Doe broke off their discussion when they heard shouting outside. The Ghanaian general went downstairs and found Johnson armed with an AK-47, his favourite weapon. 'I saw it was Prince Johnson who was shouting and threatening to kill a man who was kneeling before him,' Quainoo recalled.[17]

Johnson and a squad of his INPFL troops had forced their way into the walled port area just minutes after Doe's bodyguard had surrendered their weapons to the peacekeepers. Johnson called out his war-cry 'Commando!' which drew the response from his men 'Brave! Strong! Intelligent!'[18] 'All of a sudden, all the men and women under his command reacted immediately, deploying and cocking their personal weapons,' Quainoo recollected.[19] According to Brigadier Iweze, the Nigerian chief of staff who was present throughout, a quarrel began in the compound when one of Doe's men referred to Johnson's soldiers as 'rebels' in Johnson's hearing. 'Soon after that,' Quainoo recalled, 'all hell broke loose.'

[15] Quoted in 'Last Moments of Doe', p.2650.

[16] Iweze, 'Nigeria in Liberia', p.229.

[17] Interview with Lieut.-Gen. Quainoo in the Ghanaian *Daily Graphic*, 11 May 1991.

[18] Youboty, *Liberian Civil War*, p.406.

[19] Interview with Lieut.-Gen. Quainoo in the Ghanaian *Daily Graphic*, 11 May 1991.

Quainoo ran back up the stairs and told the others 'I'm sure the situation is under control,' before disappearing once more. Meanwhile, Johnson's men were setting up a heavy machine-gun trained on the entrance to the building inside which the President was sitting. The commander of the presidential motorcade recalls that Doe's men complained about this, leading to a fierce argument. 'Fuck you,' Johnson replied, yelling further obscenities at the AFL soldiers who were remonstrating with him.[20]

Colonel Harrison Pennue, said to be a relative of Doe's, well known as the commander of a notorious AFL death-squad and a participant in the 1980 coup which had brought Doe to power, was the one who argued most strongly with Prince Johnson. 'We are here for peace, this is not called for,' he said. 'Pennue,' Johnson replied, 'who invited you into the whole show?' and he ordered his men to arrest Pennue and remove his boots. Then Johnson began issuing further orders to his men, shouting 'Gentlemen, prepare for war.'[21] Minutes later, Johnson blew Pennue's brains out with two shots to the head.

Back upstairs, Doe and his aides, still inside the office block with only a few pistols between them, were increasingly worried. Doe was constantly asking where Quainoo was. They left their meeting-room and barricaded themselves in another room on the same floor. They then heard beating on the heavy door and demands to open up. They opened the door to see a dozen armed Johnson men behind two Ecomog soldiers who promptly disappeared. 'Look,' the leader of Johnson's force told Doe, 'we all have decided to make peace, so we don't want to fight, we want your arms. Lay down your arms and we will consult our commander to see what can be done.' For five minutes the rebels argued with Doe's bodyguards. Finally Doe's group laid down their arms. Immediately Johnson's men began firing. Doe dived for cover behind a desk and was covered by a pile of bodies. The rebels pulled him out as he pleaded with them not to shoot him, but at some point he received a bullet wound in one of his legs.

By now shooting had broken out in the open space where the bulk of Doe's party had initially gathered in front of the administration building. Johnson's men began firing at the AFL soldiers as they ran for cover. Doe's men had little chance of escape in the confined space of the port. 'They were going from office to office killing soldiers in the presence of Ecomog,' recalled one

---

[20] Youboty, *Liberian Civil War,* p.406.

[21] Quoted in 'Last Moments of Doe', p.2651.

survivor.[22] Another of Doe's officers remembers standing with a Nigerian soldier and watching helplessly. 'I saw my men dying, without arms, just running from one direction to the other.'[23] Altogether, some sixty-four of Doe's men were killed in a period some recall as thirty minutes but which the BBC correspondent, trapped indoors and sheltering under a table, thinks was nearer ninety minutes.[24] Quainoo estimated that the shootout lasted about two hours. A handful of AFL men managed to survive by hiding in some empty shipping-containers, helped by Nigerian soldiers appalled by the slaughter they were witnessing.

Ecomog peacekeepers looked on as Johnson's men pushed Doe downstairs, bound him and drove off to Prince Johnson's Caldwell base, a few minutes' drive away, according to some accounts bundled into the boot of Doe's own presidential Mercedes or, according to others, in a Cherokee jeep. There he was stripped of his five-star general's uniform and shown to a crowd of bystanders. Doe begged the onlookers to pray for him.[25]

Subsequent events were captured on a video made by a Palestinian journalist, Tahseen or Tasim by name, who was filming at Johnson's headquarters on behalf of a Middle Eastern news agency.[26] Tahseen had been sent by the Palestine Liberation Organisation to cover events in Liberia in retaliation for Samuel Doe's outspoken support for Israel, one of the many diplomatic favours the Liberian head of state had performed for the US government during his days as an American ally. Prince Johnson was later to show Tahseen's video with some pride to journalists and visitors to his headquarters and copies went on general sale throughout West Africa.

One version of the video opens with a blare of martial music and white title credits set against a background of blue sky: THE CAPTURE OF SAMUEL K. DOE BY FIELD MARSHAL PRINCE YEDUO JOHNSON AND HIS GALLANT MEN AND WOMEN OF THE INDEPENDENT PATROITIC [sic] FRONT OF LIBERIA ON SUNDAY, 9 SEPTEMBER 1990. The opening shot is of the inside of Prince Johnson's headquarters, showing the tall, good-looking, thirty-eight-year-old rebel leader sitting behind a desk, a string of hand grenades around his neck and a can of Budweiser

[22] Colonel T. Gowah, quoted in *ibid.*

[23] *Ibid.*, p.2652.

[24] Author's phone interview with Elizabeth Blunt, London, 25 April 1997.

[25] 'Doe, the Complete Story', *Newsbreed*, p.23.

[26] Anthony Daniels, *Monrovia Mon Amour*, London, 1992, pp.107-17.

in his hand. He is being fanned with a towel wafted by a female attendant. On the wall behind him is a large picture of a very Caucasian Christ. Doe sits on the floor opposite the desk, his hands tied behind his back and his legs outstretched, bound at the ankle. He is wearing only his underpants and the remains of a camouflage shirt, all that is left of the five-star general's uniform which the President was wearing earlier in the day. Everywhere there are rebel soldiers milling around or lolling on chairs. One rebel plucks a strand of protective amulets from around the President's waist. Various charms had earlier been found on his body, including inside his anus. Johnson, growing steadily more drunk, makes a show of interrogating his prisoner, occasionally bellowing at Doe and at one stage bursting into a round of hymn-singing. Doe pleads for his arms to be loosened, and appeals constantly to a tall slim man, Samuel Varney, Johnson's second in command and an acquaintance of Doe's in times gone by. 'Gentlemen,' says Doe, 'we are all one.'

Johnson bangs on the desk and orders one of his men to cut off Doe's ear. The camera jerks to show the President, being held down by several men while one of them takes a knife first to one ear, then the other, as Doe struggles and thrashes around. On one version of the video, Johnson appears to be eating part of Doe's severed ear.[27]

Later the camera picks up a new scene outside the building where Doe is still sitting, half-conscious while rebels ask him about the money he has stolen from the Liberian treasury during his ten years in power, occasionally subjecting him to further brutalities. Doe can only mumble vague answers and pleas for mercy. He has a long exchange with an INPFL man called Joseph, a soft-ly-spoken, apparently gentle soul whom he seems to know. The interrogators are anxious to prevent Doe, even in this pitiable state, from escaping 'by the power of some voodoo' which they clearly believe he can use if they were to untie him.[28] On some versions of Tahseen's video footage, Prince Johnson, clearly drunk, is seen telling his men to 'take him away', often interpreted by Liberians as an order to kill the President.

Samuel Doe died at some point during the early hours of 10 September. Some people say he died of loss of blood. One account later claimed that the *coup de grâce* was administered with a bullet:[29]

27 Huband, *The Liberian Civil War,* p.193.

28 Youboty, *Liberian Civil War,* p.429.

29 Quoted in 'Doe, the Complete Story', *Newsbreed,* p.39.

[Doe] was crying and blood was running down his cheeks from his face and head. But you know how when sweat runs down your chest sometimes it collects in the centre – well, the blood was collecting and he was trying to blow on it, to make it run down. Blowing, you know? He just kept blowing. That's all he did. Then one of Johnson's men thought he was trying to do some kind of *juju*, blowing on himself to make himself disappear. So he shot him again. He was nearly dead by then, anyway, from loss of blood.

Doe's body was put in a wheelbarrow and paraded by Johnson's jubilant soldiers. His killers took his body to a clinic where a Nigerian doctor, a civilian who had been living in Liberia for years and ran a private medical practice, declared that he could not find any pulse. The corpse was put on display at the Island Clinic for two or three days to convince Monrovians that the dictator was really dead, and to ensure that no one would think he had miraculously flown away or disappeared. People came to see the body from curiosity, from satisfaction, or to confirm that the news of his death was not just another of the rumours swirling around the city. Some spat on it, some poured beer on it, and one man stubbed out his cigarette on the late President's forehead. General Quainoo sought refuge on a Nigerian warship moored in the port and shortly afterwards headed for Nigeria in search of assistance, never to return.[30] Some of the Sierra Leonean Ecomog contingent began preparing to leave Liberia and return to Freetown. It was the worst possible start to an international peacekeeping mission.

A jubilant Johnson, already self-proclaimed brigadier-general and field marshal, now declared himself acting president of Liberia and commandeered the captured presidential motorcade for his progress around Monrovia. He took to wearing the late President Doe's wristwatch and glasses. As for Taylor's forces, they began a close siege of the hundreds of AFL forces who were still holding out in the Executive Mansion, firing at the building from the University of Liberia which stands just a few hundred yards away, separated by a highway and by the Statue of the Unknown Soldier, a monument to the AFL erected by Doe after the military coup which brought him to power in 1980 as one of a junta of lower-ranks soldiers. Doe had been a humble master sergeant in those days, and was not even generally regarded as the leader of the seventeen soldiers who had overthrown the old government of the True

[30] Agetua, *Operation Liberty,* pp.51-2.

Whig Party. The Statue of the Unknown Soldier, widely believed to be endowed with strong spiritual power, was to remain standing until it was finished off by a few direct hits during heavy fighting in April 1996. The fighters who manned the front lines in 1990 would probably have been surprised to learn that their struggle for power was to turn into a war which would last for so long.

Rumours flew around Monrovia about exactly what happened on the day of Doe's capture. The Ecomog command denied having exchanged messages with Doe on the day of his visit, claiming that their only communication had been a formal diplomatic note which Ecomog had sent to the late President some days before the fatal Sunday. Ecomog chief of staff Brigadier Iweze, though, has testified that there was also a flow of verbal messages, first when Doe's own chief of staff visited General Quainoo, and once when Ecomog tried to arrange a meeting between Johnson's and Doe's camps.[31] Many Liberians are convinced to this day that Doe's trip to the Ecomog headquarters was the result of some sort of conspiracy engineered by the US intelligence services and involving Nigerian officers. While Liberians are often inclined to over-estimate the extent of US responsibility for whatever transpires in their country, it is correct that the US government contributed to the overthrow of President Tolbert in 1980 at the very least by withdrawing support from him. Many Liberians assume, rightly or wrongly, that the United States was the hidden hand behind many subsequent events too.[32] Now, after Doe's death, Liberians indulged in an orgy of conspiracy-theorising. Why did US diplomats urge the NPFL leader, Charles Taylor, not to attack the Executive Mansion, they wondered. Why did Johnson formally announce his break with the NPFL in July 1990, when it was known that the CIA was in communication with the main players? Where did Johnson get his abundant supplies of weapons? Above all, why did Ecomog let Doe die at the hands of Prince Johnson, thus depriving Charles Taylor, the main leader of the rising against Doe, of the prestige which he would have acquired, in Liberian eyes at least, by himself eliminating the incumbent president? The many Liberians who believe that some sort of conspiracy lay behind Samuel Doe's capture and murder at the hands of Prince Johnson, hatched by people determined to deprive Charles Taylor of this prize, point out that US intelligence officers were in radio communication with all sides, and could easily have offered verbal

[31] Iweze, 'Nigeria in Liberia', p.228.

[32] Bill Berkeley, 'Liberia: between repression and slaughter', *Atlantic Monthly*, Dec. 1992, p.56.

encouragement to Prince Johnson to visit the Ecomog base at precisely the moment Samuel Doe was there.[33] Their alleged motive would be to get rid of Doe, seen as the main impediment to peace, without putting power in the hands of his most formidable rival, Charles Taylor, a man distrusted by the US government and feared by Nigeria. This explanation, it must be said, is plausible in the cynical world of intelligence.

Whatever transpired exactly on Sunday 9 September, it remains the case that what people believe is a motive for their conduct at least as important as the actual sequence of events. Moreover, the way in which people form their beliefs and base their subsequent actions upon them is determined not just by the vagaries of the information they receive – which in Liberia usually takes the form of unofficial spoken communication, or rumour, when it comes to political events – but is embedded in the character of any given community or society. The cultivation of secrecy and the hiding of intention are notable features of Liberian religious culture and politics.

The supposition that verifiable facts, such as Doe's death, are the manifestation of hidden forces, and never the result of coincidence or simple bungling, has deep roots in Liberian traditions of thought, in which social action and individual agency are considered complex matters. These are philosophical traditions in which the deeper truths about the destiny of individuals and the course of events are considered to be ambiguous, ruled by forces which have their origin in the invisible world of God and spiritual beings. The workings of these invisible entities are held to be obscure by their nature, but they may be revealed to humans by signs and portents and interpreted by specialists, such as priests, prophets and soothsayers. Traditionally, the spirit world is made manifest in Liberia by various means including the use of carved wooden masks, a notable feature of cultural life in many Liberian rural communities. The use for religious purposes of masks, behind which a person becomes unrecognisable and in which a spirit is deemed to take visible form, says much about traditional Liberian attitudes concerning both the spirit world and the hidden nature of reality. The spoken word, subject to a thousand interpretations and meanings, is not regarded as the deepest level of truth, but must be sifted for clues as to the real causes of visible events. If, in the narrative of events from 1989 to 1997 which follows, we pay some attention both to rumours and to occurrences widely interpreted by Liberians as portents or as manifestations of the

---

[33] Huband, *The Liberian Civil War,* pp.191-204.

power of the spirit world, it is because many of the actors in
the war, high and low, themselves regarded these phenomena
as signs of deeper truths governing human behaviour.

Certainly there were good reasons for Johnson to announce
his break with Taylor in July 1990, as the two men had been
on bad terms for months.[34] And it was reasonable enough for
Johnson to believe that, by killing the incumbent president, he
could himself make a bid to be recognised as head of state just
as Doe himself had come to power ten years earlier, or at least
to become a king-maker who could appoint his own candidate
to the presidency. It was presumably so as to prove that he, not
Taylor, had killed Doe that Johnson permitted the video-recording
of Doe's death. A considerable number of the very West African
heads of state who organised the Ecomog intervention had themselves come to power by similar means. But, in the event, Johnson
never did become president of Liberia. He had almost no political
support other than the few hundred fighters whom he had recruited
when he defected from Taylor's NPFL, and his unpredictability
and propensity to casual violence ruled him out as a candidate
who could inspire international confidence. There were other
pretenders to the vacant presidency, almost all of them more
plausible than Johnson. Just a few days before Doe's death, a
conference of Liberian politicians meeting in Banjul, Gambia, on
27 August 1990, representing all the main Liberian political parties
but not Taylor's NPFL or Johnson's faction, had elected the
prominent academic and political activist Amos Sawyer as interim
president of the country. One disenchanted Liberian pointed out
that this meeting was of doubtful legitimacy since it was attended
only 'by a few dozen people who were invited and could afford
to attend'.[35] Within a short time, this Interim Government of National Unity (IGNU) was to be dubbed by cynical Monrovians
the Imported Government of No Use.[36] It was never formally recognised by the United States, although US district courts were to
recognise the Interim Government as a party in a number of
civil suits, while the US acting secretary of state received Amos
Sawyer in October 1991 when the latter visited America to address
the UN in his capacity as Liberian head of state. Sawyer could

[34] *Ibid.*, p.171.

[35] Carl Patrick Burrowes, 'Democracy or Disarmament: some second thoughts on
Amos Sawyer and contemporary "politicians"', *Liberian Studies Journal*, XX, 1 (1995),
p.117.

[36] K. Moses Nagbe, *Bulk Challenge*, Cape Coast, Ghana, 1996, p.12.

demonstrate that he had the support of a substantial part of Liberia's political elite. He was more acceptable to most other West African governments than the psychopathic Johnson, than Taylor who was feared to be bent on destabilising West Africa, or than yet other contenders, such as the deputy commander of Doe's army General David Nimley and, later, Doe's former vice-president Harry Moniba, both of whom were also to declare themselves president. Above all, Sawyer was the preferred candidate of Nigeria, the power behind Ecomog.

Prince Johnson's bid for the presidency did not last long. In late September 1990 the Nigerian Major-General Joshua Dogonyaro arrived from Lagos to replace the unfortunate General Quainoo as Ecomog commander. The no-nonsense Nigerian, who had an imposing, soldierly manner, immediately began to build political support behind the formation of the Interim Government under Professor Sawyer. 'Our primary aim is to end the bloodshed and to bring about a ceasefire,' a Nigerian government spokesman had claimed at the inception of the Ecomog intervention. 'We aim to make way for an interim government which will not include any of the warring faction leaders and which can prepare for elections.'[37] There was considerable irony in, of all countries, Nigeria, claiming to stand for civilian government and against the illegitimate assumption of power. It was, after all, this same General Dogonyaro who in 1985 had announced on Nigerian radio the military coup which had brought his friend General Ibrahim Babangida to power.[38]

Soon Johnson did not even have control of the presidential motorcade, as most of the limousines were commandeered by Nigerian soldiers and shipped abroad. Taylor, meanwhile, remained in a strong position as he controlled most of Liberia and had the backing of the governments of Libya, Burkina Faso and, most importantly, Côte d'Ivoire, France's leading ally in West Africa. The Liberian war had opened up a serious division between English- and French-speaking countries in the region. Johnson himself was soon to be knocked out of the contest, and went to live in Nigeria, whose ally he had become, but it transpired that his intervention and the murder of President Doe, rather than bringing the struggle to a climax, had fractured the brittle coherence of various armed forces, while the Ecomog expedition was to lead to the further implication of other countries in Liberia's

[37] Quoted in 'Nigeria Considers Military Intervention in Liberia', *Financial Times* (London), 4 August 1990.

[38] Agetua, *Operation Liberty*, p.3.

affairs. 'It's finished, the war ends today,' one Ecomog soldier had observed, as he watched Doe's abduction on that bloody Sunday afternoon.[39] This was to prove sadly over-optimistic. The emergence of new warlords, the massive flight of Liberians as refugees abroad, and the general indifference of the industrialised world to events in Liberia were to lead to a prolonged war. The fighting was to spill into a neighouring country, Sierra Leone, which followed Liberia into civil strife in 1991 after a cross-border attack by Taylor's NPFL.

The common tendency of Liberians to assume that significant political events, such as the murder of Samuel Doe, are not the result of coincidence or confused decision-making, but represent deeper conspiracies or even movements in the world of spirits, is deeply rooted in Liberian thought. One of the consequences, as we shall see, is that events which may seem to Western journalists to be banal or coincidental, and conduct which may appear to them to be frankly inexplicable, are considered by many Liberians to be evidence of deeper patterns at work in the course of human life. Such apparently bizarre events as the filming of Samuel Doe's death by people who believed in the President's ability to cause part of his being to fly like a bird by the use of esoteric powers are perfectly comprehensible to the very many Liberians who assume that the invisible world exists and is a major resource in daily life. Accordingly, it is often useful for analysts of Liberian affairs – and readers of this book – to be alert to the fact that accounts of events can be read at two levels, both as descriptions of visible events and as possible evidence of more arcane forces at work. This is how Liberians themselves generally interpret what happens and what they hear.

Traditionally, many of the beliefs concerning the esoteric connection between power and the invisible world is expressed in Liberia by the use of masks. Although traditional masking societies no longer play the same role in public life as they did in the old days when such societies were the mainstays of political and social order in many rural communities, many Liberians nowadays continue to hold a residual belief that masks can serve as expressions of the elusive nature of reality and as instruments of order, and that, behind the social conventions which masks represent, there lurk deeper forces, invisible to the naked eye. Hence, some Liberians thought that the murder of Samuel Doe, grotesque as it was, had a wider meaning for society at large. Blamo Nelson, a former government official who was to become one of the main

---

[39] Quoted in 'Last Moments of Doe', p.2651.

organisers of food distribution in Monrovia during the war, commented after seeing the video of Doe's murder, 'I identified with those crazy people. We all wear masks. Behind those masks is a mad, horrified people.'[40]

War and barbarism

The general inability of Western observers to understand the importance of religion in Liberian life is clear in reports of the war by the many foreign journalists who found the behaviour of Liberians to be utterly baffling.

The world's press became aware of the Liberian tragedy in mid-1990. Many international journalists sent to cover the war chose to travel with the advancing NPFL forces or associated themselves with Prince Johnson's breakaway group, the INPFL, after it had reached Monrovia in July 1990. They were fascinated by the bizarre accoutrements of the rebels, who were generally happy to pose for photographs. Many NPFL fighters in the first months of the war dressed up in costumes which, to a foreign correspondent fitting in a visit to Liberia before flying to another of the world's trouble-spots, seemed more suited to a carnival, or possibly a lunatic asylum, than to a war. Many male fighters wore women's wigs and decorated themselves with human bones or other grotesque decorations. 'Travelling with the rebels' motley spearhead of fifty men is a terrifying, bizarre experience,' wrote a reporter for a British newspaper in August 1990 after hitching a ride in a NPFL vehicle, in a report fairly typical of many at the time. 'Some are kitted out for battle in women's wigs and dresses. One wore a flowery lavatory seat cover on his head.'[41]

The NPFL advance took place in the period between the fall of the Berlin Wall and the start of the Gulf War, when the accepted rules governing international relations were changing fast, in what direction no one knew. Liberia, previously almost unknown to the world's newspaper-readers and television-watchers, briefly represented a post-Cold War vision of an Africa rooted in primeval savagery with a touch of Hollywood futuristic. The seemingly incomprehensible slaughter, carried out by fighters who did their best to look like freaks, formed a marked contrast with the high-tech battles of the Gulf War which were to follow the Iraqi attack on

---

[40] Quoted in Berkeley, 'Between Repression and Slaughter', p.56.

[41] Matthew Campbell, 'Rebels Deal out Death on Road to Monrovia', *Sunday Times* (London), 12 August 1990.

Kuwait on the night of 1-2 August 1990. Further events in Africa in the 1990s, notably resistance to the US intervention in Somalia in 1992-3 and the Rwandan genocide of 1994, appeared to some commentators to signify that Africa had turned its back on progress, and was sinking into an anarchy marked by savagery and superstition. 'Welcome to Liberia, scene of one of the wackiest, and most ruthless, of Africa's uncivil wars,' wrote a *Washington Post* correspondent who covered Liberia:[42]

> It's a war with a general named Mosquito, a war where soldiers get high on dope and paint their fingernails bright red before heading off to battle. It's a war where combatants don women's wigs, pantyhose, even Donald Duck halloween masks before committing some of the world's most unspeakable atrocities against their enemies. It's the only war that hosts a unit of soldiers who strip off their clothes before going into battle and calls itself 'the Butt Naked Brigade'. It's a war where young child soldiers carry teddy bears and plastic baby dolls in one hand and AK-47s in the other. It's a war where fighters smear their faces with makeup and mud in the belief that 'juju', West African magic, will protect them from the enemy's bullets.

This report was written by an African-American journalist from a respected newspaper in an effort to inform other African-Americans in particular about the real nature of the Africa they so often romanticise. While descriptions like this are routinely dismissed as sensational journalism by high-minded academics, it would be foolish simply to scoff at the opinions of correspondents who glean their impressions at first hand, no matter how superficial their analyses may sometimes be. Journalists acquire detailed knowledge, and an appreciation of the flavour of events, which can escape more distant observers. Perhaps more to the point, their reports are consumed not only by the world's reading or viewing public, but also by policy makers and politicians who may take action in consequence of the information they provide. Reality and its representation thus have a dialectic effect on one another in Western policy-making just as much as in the minds of Liberian fighters or their victims, albeit couched in different idioms in the two cases.

A number of influential works are worth discussing briefly as influential purveyors of the point of view that the Liberian civil war represented some sort of chaos. The first is an article published

[42] Keith Richburg, *Out of America: a black man confronts Africa*, New York, 1997, p.134.

by the American journalist Robert Kaplan, by coincidence just
a few weeks before the Rwandan genocide of 1994. Kaplan was
already the author of a book on the Balkans which he had written
in an attempt to educate the US public on the merits of military
intervention in the Yugoslav crisis.[43] This book was known to have
been read and admired by President Clinton, a fact which brought
Kaplan great kudos in Washington. In February 1994 Kaplan published a long essay in the prestigious *Atlantic Monthly* entitled 'The
Coming Anarchy', which began with a discussion of war in Sierra
Leone and a brief mention of Liberia before going on to consider
Turkey, Pakistan and other parts of the world. Briefly, Kaplan's
argument was that in various parts of what used to be called the
third world, vast population movements from the countryside to
the city, caused partly by environmental degradation and high
birth-rates, were resulting in the appearance of large numbers
of desperate, deracinated, unemployable youths who were the driving force behind wars like those in West Africa. This was, suggested
the magazine which published Kaplan's article, the forerunner
of a global trend, 'a preview of the first decades of the twenty-first
century'.[44] This last suggestion was an editorial master-stroke, for
whereas wars in West Africa are generally regarded by mainstream
Western journalists and their public as affairs of marginal importance to the rest of humanity, Kaplan was turning the argument
on its head: on the contrary, he suggested, it could be that wars
like these would soon be breaking out in other parts of the world
too, and that West Africa was ahead of the trend.

Kaplan's article had an immediate impact in Washington. Tim
Wirth, under-secretary for Global Affairs at the US State Department, is reported to have faxed a copy to every US embassy in
the world. Kaplan was read by US and other Western officials
at every level. In 1997, when Kaplan visited Europe to launch
a book inspired by the success of his article, he was able to draw
over 100 busy diplomats from behind their desks for a lunch-time
lecture at the Dutch Ministry of Foreign Affairs.[45] It was clear
that his arguments had touched a chord with Western policy-

[43] Robert Kaplan, *Balkan Ghosts: a journey through history*, London, 1993. The motive
was explained to me by Robert Kaplan himself.

[44] Robert Kaplan, 'The Coming Anarchy: how scarcity, crime, overpopulation and
disease are rapidly destroying the social fabric of our planet', *Atlantic Monthly*,
February 1994, pp.44-76 and front cover.

[45] Lecture by Robert Kaplan, The Hague, 27 January 1997. This was to launch a
European edition of his book *The Ends of the Earth: a journey at the dawn of the 21st
century*, New York, 1996.

makers, and not only in the English-speaking world. In France, some of his points had been pre-empted by a French academic influential with his own country's ministry of defence who argued, in a reference to the decline and fall of the Roman empire, that Western civilisation was once more threatened by warlike and aggressive barbarians at its gates.[46] A further contribution to this debate came from the well-known Harvard professor Samuel Huntington, who in 1993 published an article in *Foreign Affairs,* the house journal of the Washington foreign policy establishment. Entitled 'The Clash of Civilizations?' (and forerunner of a book of similar name), it argued that all over the world, wars between ideological blocs were now giving way to wars between broadly defined cultural blocks or civilisations.[47]

Academics who specialise in African studies, as well as African intellectuals, almost all reject such views.[48] Paul Richards, author of a study of the civil war which spread to Sierra Leone from Liberia in 1991 and then gained a momentum all of its own, suggests that the work of Kaplan and Huntington amounts to a school of thought concerning wars in Africa, and perhaps some other parts of the world, which he terms the New Barbarism thesis.[49] Richards refutes this by demonstrating that the causes of the war in Sierra Leone stem more from a collapse of the patrimonial state erected in late colonial times than they do from either environmental decay or a crisis of cultural identity. He argues passionately that war is always horrible, and that this is so whether it is fought with matchets and light machine-guns, in which case killing is at close quarters, or with computer-guided bombs. 'It makes no sense to call one kind of war "barbaric",' he argues, 'when all that is meant is that it is cheap.'[50] His argument is that war is war, and that attempts to portray West African wars as unusually barbaric amount to no more than the revival of some old clichés about the Dark Continent. Richards, however, in his turn, has been criticised by a number of African authors who accuse him of overlooking empirical evidence, idealising the main rebel movement in Sierra Leone and ignoring its cultural

---

[46] Jean-Christophe Rufin, *L'empire et les nouveaux barbares,* Paris, 1991.

[47] Samuel Huntington, 'The Clash of Civilizations?', *Foreign Affairs,* 72, 3 (1993), pp.22-49; *idem., The Clash of Civilizations and the Remaking of World Order,* New York, 1996.

[48] E.g. Nuruddin Farah, 'Highway to Hell', *Transition,* 70 (1996), pp.60-71.

[49] Paul Richards, *Fighting for the Rain Forest: war, youth and resources in Sierra Leone,* London and Portsmouth, NH, 1996, pp.xiii-xxix.

[50] *Ibid.,* p.xxv.

origins, and assigning single causes to events which have complex roots.[51]

There can be no doubt that the Western press has generally represented the Liberian war as 'bizarre documentary-style coverage from the "Heart of Darkness" rather than news of a serious threat to international peace and security', as a study of media reporting on the subject has concluded.[52] Nevertheless, those who would argue simply that wars such as that in Liberia are represented by fickle journalists as being more anarchic than is really the case are missing a number of important points. The observation that wars like that in Liberia result from the breakdown of a specific political order begs questions about why such an order breaks down, and why the resulting conflict takes certain patterns. Some African academics who have themselves lived through recent civil wars in the continent have suggested that the disruption of whole societies as a result of massive failures of social engineering may be a cause of violence in the continent, and that at least some African wars have to be understood as complex social phenomena.[53]

In truth, many Liberians and other West Africans consider the Liberian war to have been peculiarly horrible. One survivor notes:[54]

In all frankness the Liberian civil and guerrilla war topped and surpassed [all other wars] in form and character, in intensity, in depravity, in savagery, in barbarism and in horror. [....]

As far as the men behind the war were concerned, one should be forewarned that the world could be breeding a new species of mankind with no contrite hearts, with no compassion, with no regard for law and order and whose ambitions in life have no bounds at the peril of others.

It has started off in Liberia, but one should beware that there are many more Charles Taylors and Prince Johnsons, the new

---

[51] *Africa Development,* XXII, 3-4 (1997), special issue on 'Lumpen Culture and Political Violence: the Sierra Leone civil war', Ibrahim Abdullah and Yusuf Bangura (eds). See also Ibrahim Abdullah, 'Bush Path to Destruction: the origin and character of the Revolutionary United Front/Sierra Leone', *Journal of Modern African Studies,* 36, 2 (1998), pp.203-35.

[52] Larry Minear, Colin Scott and Thomas Weiss, *The News Media, Civil War, and Humanitarian Action,* Boulder, CO, and London, 1996, pp.47-50.

[53] E.g. Ali El-Kenz, 'Youth and Violence' in Stephen Ellis (ed.), *Africa Now,* The Hague, London and Portsmouth, NH, 1996, pp.42-57. A more general discussion is Donal Cruise O'Brien, 'A Lost Generation? Youth identity and state decay in West Africa' in Richard Werbner and Terence Ranger (eds), *Postcolonial Identities in Africa,* London, 1996, pp.55-74.

[54] Leonard Brehun, *Liberia: the war of horror,* Accra, 1991, p.113.

species of human kind, around not only in Liberia, but in other places, especially in Africa today.

While all wars involve suffering and terror, this does not mean that all wars are equally horrible. Warfare tends to develop rules or codes of practice which are not necessarily intended to make fighting more humane, but which may arise as a result of the logic imposed by the aims of the fighters, the weapons at their disposal, the climate and terrain, or similar factors. When wars are fought according to rules, or at least within limits, which are widely understood by those affected, they may appear less barbarous to survivors than wars in which the participants have a sense that there are no rules, or that the ones previously in use are no longer being observed. Hence the perception that one war is more barbaric than another is related not only to the number of victims, but above all to the observance or otherwise of rules, or at least unwritten norms, and the element of drama which is such an important aspect of war. For example, the modern type of combat called terrorism is seen by many as barbaric precisely because it refuses to observe the rules codified in the Geneva Conventions on warfare and frequently uses a powerful new dramaturgy in its choice of targets, in the use of costumes and props such as the face-masks favoured by street-fighters in Northern Ireland and by elite troops in Algeria, the whole theatrical effect being magnified by the modern media of communication.[55]

It is reasonable to assert that the opinions of Liberians themselves, and to a lesser extent of other West Africans, are of considerable importance in assessing the nature of the Liberian civil war, since they have experienced it most fully and have the best understanding of the issues it raises, and in this regard we are fortunate in disposing of several books written by eye-witnesses,[56] as well as essays in Liberian newspapers. Their views surely have some weight.

There is no doubt that some of the acts of war in Liberia which have been considered particularly atrocious contain, at least in the view of many Liberians, references to known repertoires of spiritual symbols, as I have argued more superficially elsewhere. These symbols, while recognisable, are sufficiently distorted or abused as

[55] Cf. Martin van Creveld, *The Transformation of War*, New York, 1991.

[56] E.g. Brehun, *War of Horror;* Youboty, *Liberian Civil War;* Bill Frank Enoanyi, *Behold Uncle Sam's Step-Child*, Sacramento, CA, 1991; G. Henry Andrews, *Cry, Liberia, Cry!*, New York, 1993; Joseph Njoh, *Through the Liberian Storm*, London, 1996. The best account by a non-African is Huband, *The Liberian Civil War*.

to cause widespread disgust.[57] Most notably, these repertoires are those relating to religion. Many of the main protagonists in the war have claimed, some with obvious sincerity, to have been in direct communication with God at various stages of their bloody careers. This is not just a personal quirk, but is situated in a history in which religious belief has functioned as a mainstay of political and social order, as we shall see in due course. While there are social scientists who believe that religion is a form of false consciousness, a set of beliefs which actually express other forces at work in society, the present book will proceed on the assumption that most people who express religious beliefs actually believe these to be true, and that those who perform religious rituals really believe in their efficacy.[58] If this is so, then a study of why a given political order which is rooted in religious belief breaks down must devote at least some attention to the features of such beliefs, and how these have changed over time. The reasons for this have been well described by Paul Gifford:[59]

A religion provides definitions, principles of judgement and criteria of perception. It offers a reading of the world, of history, of society, of time, of space, of power, of authority, of justice and of ultimate truth. Religion limits or increases the conceptual tools available, restricts or enlarges emotional responses, or channels them, and withdraws certain issues from inquiry. It inculcates a particular way of perceiving, experiencing and responding to reality. Religion can legitimise new aspirations, new forms of organisation, new relations and a new social order. Every religion involves struggles to conquer, monopolise or transform the symbolic structures which order reality. All these are issues for political analysis.

To take religious beliefs seriously, in the sense of assuming that those who hold them trust them to be true, does not imply that an analyst must share those beliefs. It is possible to study the evolution of religious beliefs and their effects on society and politics while remaining personally detached. There are excellent precedents for approaching religion and its effect on politics and society in this way, most obviously the seminal work of Max Weber.[60]

---

57 Stephen Ellis, 'Liberia 1989-1994: a study of ethnic and spiritual violence', *African Affairs*, 94, 375 (1995), pp.165-97.

58 Cf. Robin Horton, *Patterns of Thought in Africa and the West: essays in magic, religion and science*, Cambridge, 1997, pp.1-49.

59 Paul Gifford, *African Christianity: its public role*, London, 1998, p.26.

60 Max Weber, *The Protestant Ethic and the Spirit of Capitalism*, London, 1992 (German

Accordingly, the present book will devote perhaps more attention than is customary in the analysis of African politics to the religious ideas which have been so important in forming Liberians' views about the events which they have witnessed or in which they have participated, convinced that their actions were governed by some sort of divine will. 'Halleluyah!' Prince Johnson declared as he harangued a group of frightened civilians shortly after Doe's murder. 'Yes! I killed Doe through the power of God.[...]I killed plenty people that day right here at this Freeport here. Praise the Lord.'[61]

Of course, human beings have often claimed the support of God when they have gone to war. But we need to ask more precise questions about how this happens. A work of history should aim to discover why events occur at a particular time and in a specific sequence, in a given form, and that generally involves an attempt to penetrate the thinking of the historical actors involved. As we shall see, Liberians, like other nations, have in the past believed that it was morally acceptable to kill human beings in the pursuit of power and wealth in certain circumstances, but that does not mean that they have generally believed, as Prince Johnson appears to have done, that anyone is justified in enlisting the support of God in killing whomever they choose. The Liberian spiritual world in the past was governed by rules and procedures which had the effect of imposing moral and political limits on individual entrepreneurs of violence, people like Prince Johnson, Charles Taylor and Samuel Doe. How and why these rules of moral behaviour have changed, so closely related to human access to the perceived resources of the spiritual world, is a central concern of this book. While it is certainly not our intention to argue that economic developments or changes in international relations are unimportant, it is the case that these have been more adequately treated in other works than the developments in the realm of the imagination, particularly the religious imagination, which have been so important in determining how Liberians have behaved. This point will be further elaborated in due course, especially in chapters six and seven.

Many of the rank and file participants in the war, whether fighters or victims, have sought spiritual guidance or protection from harm during the conflict. Most have interpreted what they have seen happening around them, and identified the springs of their own action, in movements in the invisible world which

---

original 1904-5, rev. edn 1920-1). This point is also made by Gifford, *loc. cit.*

[61] Quoted in Youboty, *Liberian Civil War*, p.449.

they believe may be discerned in revelations, signs and portents, often conveyed from person to person in the form of rumour, which they take to be indicative of communication with or from that invisible world. Samuel Doe himself, for example, believed strongly that some thing or some force he identified as God – whether it existed only inside or outside his own head should become a little clearer in the course of reading – was directing his fate, like the voices heard by Joan of Arc and many another heroine or hero of old. Doe believed that he was invulnerable for as long as he had this protection. He claimed, during one of his last public speeches, that he first 'came to know God', as he put it, in 1981 when, as a leading member of the military junta which had taken power the previous year, he prayed before signing a death warrant for five of his colleagues, some of them acquaintances of long standing. He also claimed to have had a direct warning from God on 10 November 1985 while he was hunting in the forest near his home town in Grand Gedeh County. A mysterious voice, which he believed to be that of God, insistently told him to return to Monrovia. He immediately obeyed this advice and was in the city to repel a coup attempt by his arch-rival Thomas Quiwonkpa two days later. Doe was convinced that it was this divine warning which had saved him.[62] Nor is this considered by most Liberians to be an eccentric or unlikely belief. A leading Liberian writer recalls:[63]

> Samuel Doe was widely credited with the power not only to be impervious to bullets, but also of disappearing in the face of danger, including plane crashes. He had a coterie of juju men from all over Africa, notably Togo. And some of the rituals he was rumored to be practising in order to maintain the potency of his powers included drinking the blood and/or eating the fetuses of pregnant young girls. Once in a while he himself would boast publicly that no gun had yet been made that could kill him. And the people believed it.

The spiritual powers invoked by Doe continued to haunt others even after his demise. Almost two years after his death, when the war had lapsed into a temporary stalemate without producing a definite peace, Doe's murderer Prince Johnson (who, incidentally, had taken part in the 1985 Quiwonkpa coup attempt which Doe had suppressed with the benefit of advice from God) had a vision

[62] Report of a New Year's Eve sermon by President Doe, in James Seiltua, 'I Came to Know God in 1981', *Daily Observer* (Monrovia), 9, 215, 5 January 1990.

[63] Enoanyi, *Behold Uncle Sam's Step-Child*, p.36.

that the stomach of Doe's corpse contained a ring whose power was the cause of continuing division among Liberians. Johnson interpreted this to mean that the war was being prolonged as a result of the influence of Doe's spirit from beyond the grave. This, he believed, could be rectified only by sending Doe's ashes to Mecca, an interesting detail as Doe was not regarded as a Muslim, although he occasionally used to attend the mosque. Johnson ordered Doe's body to be exhumed and cremated 'to prevent his spirit from dividing the country'.[64] The body, like that of a medieval saint, was found to be miraculously free from decomposition. There can be no doubt that Johnson, no matter how violent, was a man constantly preoccupied by spiritual matters.[65] When in early 1993 he was forced to give up his ambition to rule Liberia, and effectively retired from the war, it was to attend a theological college in Nigeria. Later he announced himself to have been born again in Christ. Like war, religion also produces a rich dramaturgy.

The present book is organised in two sections. The first, which is presented in the form of a chronicle, or rather a series of chronicles describing the unfolding of events at different levels of society, recounts the history of the Liberian civil war which began in 1989 (although some Liberians would argue that earlier dates such as 1980 and 1985 marked the true beginning of hostilities). Chapters one and two retrace the course of these events as succinctly as possible, while at the same time attempting to convey the complexity of military and political affairs. Only after establishing the identity and motives of some of the participants, which is done in chapter three, and the nature of the international actors, described in chapter four, is it possible to analyse the origins of these events in more detail. This paves the way for the second section of the book, which aims to discover the historical roots of the violence in Liberia. It inquires why things happened the way they did. Chapter five examines certain aspects of Liberian history and Liberian society, or perhaps societies, and notably the manner in which the national government in Monrovia extended its influence into the interior of the country over a long period. Chapter six concentrates particularly on the religious history of these encounters. This is done with a view to identifying some of the psychological or cultural roots of the war, in other words the ways which Liberians have developed of thinking about the nature of power in their society and about their politics and which

---

[64] Reuters despatch, 21 April 1992; 'Doe's Body Exhumed',*West Africa*, 3894 (4 May 1992), p.768.

[65] Daniels, *Monrovia Mon Amour*, pp.87-102, and esp. 99.

have guided the actions of various participants in the war. Since the institutional and economic factors which produced this crisis in Liberian history have been documented elsewhere,[66] what is most urgently required is a deeper consideration of the ideas which Liberians had about themselves and their country, if we are to understand why Liberians and others acted as they did during these years.

It is to be hoped that this exercise not only says something about Liberia, but also provides insights which have a bearing on debates about the nature of other wars in Africa and elsewhere in the former third world. Some passages of the argument are particularly relevant in this regard. Chapter four, for example, studies how the Liberian war drew in interests from elsewhere in West Africa and, indeed, from outside the continent. For, while it is in many ways most desirable to seek the causes of individual conflicts in local histories, such an approach carries the risk of making contemporary wars appear unconnected, as though there were no relation between, say, the war in Liberia, that in Congo, and that in Somalia. All have particular histories, of course, but an exclusive concentration on a historical narrative limited to a single country carries the danger of obscuring some factors which may be common to wars in even the most apparently unconnected places. In fact, Liberia's war has wider effects and implications. Most obviously, events in Liberia have had an impact on military and political struggles in a number of nearby countries, such as Sierra Leone, Côte d'Ivoire and Gambia, and the Liberian war has drawn in outside intervention, most notably by Nigeria. The wider implications of events in Liberia, however, go beyond the observation that the Liberian war has served to remodel the manner in which West African entrepreneurs and their overseas partners have negotiated or renegotiated access to global markets in commodities including hardwood, diamonds and drugs. One of the defining features of the former third world is the experience of seeing political elites emerge, whether under formal colonial rule or under an independent constitution, as intermediaries between various local and international interests. These political elites, while closely related to foreign interests, have roots in the societies in which they are located and, indeed, one of the salient characteristics of political rule in many countries of the former third world, most particularly in Africa, is the way in which politicians use social networks to maximise and articulate their power. This is particularly

---

[66] E.g. Amos Sawyer, *The Emergence of Autocracy in Liberia: tragedy and challenge*, San Francisco, 1992.

so when the formal procedures of bureaucratic government have become weak.[67]

It is in this sense that consideration of Liberia's experience may provide food for thought for the analysis of conflicts in other countries, or even other continents. These matters are briefly discussed in the final paragraphs of chapters four and seven. Some readers will find these discussions too brief. If so, it is because the function of this book is not primarily to debate theories of international relations or the nature of historical change in general so much as to examine the experience of one country, in the belief that careful consideration will reveal more lessons for elsewhere then might at first be apparent.

[67] Cf. William Reno, *Warlord Politics and African States*, Boulder, CO, 1998.

Part I
A CHRONICLE

1

THE FIRST OF THE WARLORDS

A frontier society

Samuel Doe was born around 1951 at Tuzon in south-eastern Liberia. His father is said by some people to have spent part of his life in what was then the neighbouring French colony of Côte d'Ivoire, while his mother was from Liberia itself. The first offspring of the marriage were born in the French colony, and Samuel was the first child actually born in Liberia.[1] Doe's father served as a private in the Liberian army, and Samuel, with little formal education, himself joined the Armed Forces of Liberia in 1969.

Samuel Doe's home area is, to this day, one of the densest forests in Africa. It is thinly populated, mostly by farming and hunting communities who are nowadays considered to form a distinct ethnic group, the Krahn, one of the smallest of Liberia's sixteen official 'tribes', as Liberians usually call them. The Krahn are generally reckoned to compose only about 5 per cent of all Liberians. At the time of Doe's rise to power, they had a reputation for being a rather marginal group, having had little opportunity for higher education. What exactly constitutes a Liberian 'tribe' is no simple matter to describe, not least because the notion gives rise to so many misunderstandings. Although Liberians will agree that Samuel Doe was a Krahn, even at the time he was reaching adulthood many of the very people considered by government officials in Monrovia to be Krahn hardly used that label. In most of rural Liberia social ties – people's idea of who exactly they are and to whom they have moral obligations – are based on kinship. In the past, clusters of lineage groups formed so-called 'stateless societies', in which notions of kinship and common ancestry serve as the main glue for communities without strong centralised political institutions. Such communities were widespread in most of Liberia until recently. Only in the present century did every area

[1] On Doe's early career, see Günter Schroeder and Werner Korte, 'Samuel K. Doe, the People's Redemption Council and Power: preliminary remarks on the anatomy and social psychology of a coup d'état', *Liberia-Forum*, 2, 3 (1986), pp.3-25.

in the country come under the rule of a republican state based
in Monrovia, whose constitution is, in theory at any rate, modelled
on that of the United States, and it was in this process of interaction
between national and local politics that the vaguely-defined, kin-
ship-based communities of the past, having no permanent political
centre, became classified as distinct 'tribes', containing equally
distinct sub-tribes called 'clans'.

So-called stateless societies of this type are remarkably flexible,
since a highly elastic determination of who exactly is a relative,
by birth or by adoption, enables people to combine in larger
or smaller units according to circumstances, by choosing to invoke
or ignore broader kinship ties for specific purposes while retaining
the capacity for individual enterprise or action.[2] But while rural
Liberians are committed to the bonds which link them to members
of their family, town or region, they are at the same time rugged
individualists. Many appear to think of themselves as hardy pioneers,
whose main farming tool, the cutlass or matchet, occupies a place
similar to that of the gun in American frontier mythology.[3] The
frontier on which they live is that of the rain forest, a fertile
environment but also the home of wild animals and believed to
be the abode of dangerous spirits.[4]

As late as the 1970s, members of the sixteen or more identifiable
groups which today are generally considered by officials to constitute the Krahn people could hardly understand each others'
dialect, which says much about the inaccuracy of the use of the
word Krahn as an ethnic category.[5] A British anthropologist who
lived in the home village of Samuel Doe's mother in the mid-1970s
recalls that 'in all the period I lived there, I heard the word "Krahn"
used only two or three times (except when I initiated discussion
of its meaning myself). At that time, the term implied almost
nothing at all, except a vague geographical identity.'[6] It was, say,
roughly equivalent to referring to a white person from America
or northern Europe today as an Anglo-Saxon – a known expression,

[2] Robin Horton, 'Stateless Societies in the History of West Africa' in J.F. Ade Ajayi
and Michael Crowder (eds), *History of West Africa*, 2 vols, Harlow, 1985, I, pp.98-9.

[3] Cf. Richards, *Fighting for the Rain Forest*, pp.61-86.

[4] Cf. Jan Vansina, *Paths in the Rainforests*, Madison, WI, 1990, pp.39-46, which
cautions against the propensity of Europeans since the nineteenth century to consider the rain forest a sinister place.

[5] One of the few published ethnographies of the area is Günter Schröder and
Dieter Seibel, *Ethnographic Survey of Southeastern Liberia: the Liberian Kran and the
Sapo*, Newark, Delaware, 1974.

[6] Letter from David Brown to the author, 1 December 1996.

but hardly one which can be used as a basis for any sort of systematic social or political transaction. Even now there are few political or cultural institutions which unite the various Krahn lineages, like many of the clusters described by ethnographers of Liberia as ethnic groups, other than the tendency of successive governments to lump them together for administrative convenience. In the case of the Krahn, the existence of age-sets has been a vital internal mechanism of social control in the past, and in other parts of Liberia religious institutions, particularly oracles, initiation schools and secret societies, have played a similar role. The Krahn are notable for having had little tradition of chieftaincy before this was imposed on them by a national government. The various Krahn dialects are related to the language cluster of the neighbouring Sapo people, whose emergence as a distinct ethnic group is equally recent, and both are regional variations of one language family, sometimes called Ngere.[7] Another ethnic group today classed as an autonomous 'tribe', the Grebo, are actually said to have originated from the Gbobo clan of the Krahn.[8]

As in many other parts of Africa, the units of political ethnicity which are so generally used in national politics – such as the label Krahn – do not describe the modern descendants of ancient micro-nations but are recent formations, whose history is inseparable from the politics of the modern state. Generally speaking, only when people migrate to Monrovia and congregate in neighbour-hoods based on their region of origin do some of the local differences between lineages erode, and the 'tribal' labels become more important. The great flexibility of stateless societies means that small groups which normally guard their autonomy quite jealously tend to combine when faced with some overwhelming threat from outside.

Although none of the various Liberian 'tribes' has a history of continuous centralised organisation of the sort Europeans or North Americans would call states, all have traditions of social organisation which have at least some elements in common. In the coastal area of south-eastern Liberia, which is probably where some of the various population groups today classified as distinct 'tribes' have been in the longest occupation of the land, there is a strong tradition of lineage societies being organised by age-sets.

[7] Svend E. Holsoe and J.J. Lauer, 'Who are the Kran/Guéré and the Gio/Yacouba? Ethnic identifications along the Liberia-Ivory Coast border', *African Studies Review*, 19, 1 (1976), p.139.

[8] Republic of Liberia, *Traditional History and Folklore of the Glebo Tribe*, Monrovia, 1957, p.2.

The most important social bonds arise from the belief that the ultimate source of power lies in the invisible world of gods and spirits, which leads to a variety of arrangements to control or communicate with these spiritual forces. The resulting religious institutions also function as mechanisms of social and political control. In central Liberia, symbols of religious communication, especially masks, are reflected in political and social organisation more directly than in the south-east of the country. In north-western Liberia, there are complexes of religious corporations which all follow a similar model of initiation, known as Poro. 'In all of these cultures', comments one ethnographer, 'man sees himself as inhabiting a world peopled and controlled by an invisible order of personalized spiritual beings which interact with humans in a variety of ways and which must be taken into account at every juncture.'[9] Various religious sodalities, often called 'secret societies' by ethnographers, have intertwined with kin groups and chief-taincies to produce characteristic patterns of political and social authority. All of these have interacted with the modern politics of the Liberian state to form the entities recognised by modern Liberians as 'tribes'. Later chapters[10] will consider these develop-ments in more detail, as well as the important role played by world religions such as Christianity and Islam in the constitution of Liberia's spiritual order.

A really thorough political ethnography of modern Liberia would require a detailed study of the component parts of each of the sixteen generally recognised Liberian 'tribes', all of which contain numerous clans and other sub-groupings and have a complex in-ternal politics of their own which has changed markedly during the twentieth century. The designation Kpelle, for example, nowadays conventionally regarded as the name of the largest Liberian tribe, was said in the 1920s to be 'used to designate a group of tribes more or less related', but not to represent any political unit. There was no central locus of political authority beyond some 50-60 Kpelle paramount chieftaincies.[11] Broadly similar observations may be made of the Kru, the Grebo and others which are nowadays regarded as political units but which until recent decades were primarily congeries of clans or towns.[12] Many

9 William C. Siegmann, 'Spirit Manifestation and the Poro Society', *Ethnologische Zeitschrift Zürich,* I (1980), pp.89-95.

10 See below, Chapters 5 and 6.

11 J. Sibley and D. Westermann, *Liberia – Old and New,* London, no date, p.140.

12 On the Kru see Ronald Davis, *Ethnohistorical Studies on the Kru Coast,* Newark,

Liberians are multilingual and are thus very familiar with the customs and histories of 'tribes' other than their own. Some tribes, or sections of them, have close relations with one another, such as through religious fraternities of the Poro type, or with other groups whom they may consider to be distant relatives even when they speak a different language. More recent religious allegiance, such as to a Christian church, also creates new fora for individuals and their families to associate with others.

Since the compiling of a complete ethnography would take excessive space, for present purposes we will go into more detail in regard to just a few Liberian 'tribes', beginning with the Krahn, since this helps to illuminate Samuel Doe's career and its effect on Liberian politics generally. Those Liberians today generally classified as Krahn consider their home area to be Grand Gedeh County, an administrative division which was created only in 1963 but which has had a significant impact on the way the people of the region think of themselves and form various local alliances. Other Krahn live on the other side of the Ivorian border, where they are known as Guéré. Samuel Doe's father was from the Gborbo clan and his mother was from the Konobo clan, two of the many clans of the Krahn.[13] Samuel Doe married a woman from the Niabo clan, which gave him a family connection to a third clan of the various sub-divisions of the Krahn. While each clan of the Krahn normally considers itself to be a separate group, some clans consider themselves linked by particular ties to other groups in a relationship called *dodi*. Such allies are expected to show particular regard for one another. They are forbidden to shed each other's blood, for example, and the men of such clans are traditionally allowed free sexual access even to the married women of related clans. Within each clan people are grouped according to their age-set, whose solidarity may be demonstrated by a distinctive mask.

The delineation of Grand Gedeh County in 1963 has affected the way in which the Krahn in general consider neighbouring 'tribes', which themselves have equally complex sub-divisions. For example, the administrative creation of Grand Gedeh County was performed in such a way as to incorporate two districts occupied

---

Delaware, 1976; Jo Mary Sullivan, 'Settlers in Sinoe County, Liberia, and their relations with the Kru, c.1835-1920' (Ph.D. thesis, Boston University, 1978); on the Grebo see Jane Martin, 'The Dual Legacy: government authority and mission influence among the Glebo of Eastern Liberia, 1834-1910' (Ph.D. thesis, Boston University, 1968).

[13] The notion of Liberian 'clans' is as much in need of deconstruction as that of 'tribes', a task beyond the scope of this chapter.

mostly by Grebo people, whose main centre is in Maryland County. This sometimes causes Grebo and Krahn to take opposite sides on particular issues in the minutiae of Grand Gedeh politics. To complicate matters further, one clan generally considered to be Krahn, called Putu, is also sometimes considered a sub-section of the Sapo, speakers of a related tongue of the Ngere language family who live in a different county.[14] One author, himself a Krahn, considers that the Sapo are actually speakers of Krahn who nevertheless consider themselves a separate 'tribe' mainly because they are not from Grand Gedeh County.[15] Some commentators would object that there is no such thing as a single Krahn language. In other words, Krahn, Grebo and Sapo could all be accounted related ethnic groups if ethnicity were defined only by reference to language, but in fact members of these groups have responded to various political events and administrative divisions to the point of being widely considered three different 'tribes'. Modern ethnicity has been formed largely in response to political and administrative incentives and opportunities, even when this was no part of the central government's intention.

Examining the notion of 'Krahn-ness' in such detail enables us to make a number of points which are important for understanding what ethnicity means in modern Liberia, at least in the political field. An obvious comment is that there are cases in which people on both sides of an international border – such as the Guéré of Côte d'Ivoire and the Krahn of Liberia – in spite of the different names used by ethnographers, acknowledge that they are related to one another. Marriages and other practical arrangements may be made between Ivorian Guéré and Liberian Krahn. In practice, most rural people of Liberia's Grand Gedeh County are far more likely to identify themselves as residents of a particular town or district, or by the name of their lineage, than as members of the Krahn 'tribe', and indeed local politics is often dominated by rivalry between individual lineages. The notion of 'Krahn-ness' only gains much meaning in matters of national politics, where politicians compete with each other to build constituencies and to demonstrate that, while living in Monrovia, they have not lost touch with their rural roots. It is particularly important for city-dwellers to stay in touch with their ancestral village as this is considered a central point of public morality. People would think it highly immoral if a country man or woman were to get a good job in

[14] 'Case Study of Grand Gedeh County', notes by a Liberian informant communicated by Bart Witteveen, 14 September 1997.

[15] Youboty, *Liberian Civil War,* p.228.

Monrovia and then forget the relatives back in the village, so that even the most impoverished rural area can sometimes exert a considerable moral hold on even the most cynical national politician. At the same time, even passionately-held tribal identities may be forgotten with remarkable haste when the logic of administrative and political events requires it, as the Sapo and Krahn have shown in drifting apart since the creation of Grand Gedeh County less than four decades ago.

Although it is possible to trace the broad history of Liberia's various tribal populations some centuries back, many of the fundamental concepts operative today, and indeed the name Liberia itself, date from the arrival of the first American colonists in the territory in 1822. It was a gradual process by which the descendants of the first settlers spread their influence over the whole of the area today inscribed on the map as the Republic of Liberia. These settlers, the descendants of American slaves, drew much of their prestige from their association with the United States. They christened their West African home Monrovia, in honour of the fifth US president, James Monroe, and they called the country whose capital it became Liberia, the land of the free. For much of the nineteenth century the American settlers and their offspring on the coast rarely ventured more than a few miles inland. The hinterland was brought under the control of the government in Monrovia only during the late nineteenth and early twentieth century, by conquest and by co-opting local elites in a form of indirect rule.

The history of the coastal settlements is by far the best documented aspect of Liberia's history due to the fact that the nineteenth-century settlers established an American style of government which kept written records and they included some outstanding intellectuals, such as the great pan-Africanist Edward Blyden.[16] But this is the history only of a few thousand settlers and their descendants in a country which, before the war of 1989, counted some 2,600,000 inhabitants. The older history of the forest communities of the hinterland is harder to ascertain since these generated few documentary records, even indirectly, until the twentieth century.

The main source used by modern authors to reconstruct the earlier history of the forest peoples has been oral traditions, occasionally compared with contemporary accounts written by the few hardy settlers who ventured from Monrovia into the dense forests of the interior or by European and American traders and

---

[16] Among many other settler histories, see Ernest Jerome Yancy, *Historical Lights of Liberia's Yesterday and Today,* 3rd edn, Tel Aviv, 1967.

missionaries living on the coast. Oral traditions collected in various
locations not only differ on points of detail but even contradict
each other on basic data, which is not surprising since people
all over the world tend to remember only those parts of their
history which reflect them in the best light or which they find
it most useful to recall. A good example concerns the Mandingo
inhabitants of present-day Liberia, the name used by a predominantly Muslim group, generally traders rather than farmers, who have
settled widely throughout the country. Most histories written by
Mandingo themselves, or told by them to others, describe the
Mandingo as a section of the Malinke people, descendants of
the ruling dynasty of medieval Mali,[17] the great empire of the
savannah whose existence had such an influence on the history
of West Africa until its decline in the sixteenth century.[18] Mandingo
today generally see themselves as descendants from an ancient
aristocracy of traders and warriors who migrated from the savannah
to the forest area, for whom their profession of Islam is a badge
of high status. But other Liberians sometimes give a different account of who the Mandingo are and where they come from. While
there were certainly some powerful Mandingo chieftaincies in northern Liberia in the early nineteenth century, some people from
Lofa County today suggest that part of the Mandingo who live
in Liberia are in fact the descendants of forest-dwellers who were
enslaved by the Malinke, the true aristocrats of the savannah, and
who have, as a result of renouncing their original birthright, lost
their rights to regard the forest as their homeland.[19] Any reader
who considers it quaint to regard such obscure debates on origins
as being of much importance has only to consider the position
of Protestants in Northern Ireland or of African-Americans today
to realise how widespread is the human propensity to equate origins
with social status or claims to political power. The attitude in
this matter of the core group of Malinke, whose heartland is in
the modern republic of Guinea, is telling. The Malinke of Guinea
enjoy considerable prestige throughout West Africa due to their
descent from the ruling group of the medieval kingdom of Mali,

[17] Medieval Mali was situated in the upper reaches of the Niger valley, and is not
to be confused with the modern republic of that name.

[18] Warren L. d'Azevedo, 'Phantoms of the Hinterland: the Mandingo "presence"
in early Liberian accounts', *Liberian Studies Journal*, XIX, 2 (1994), pp.197-242. An
article which summarises how Liberians think of Mandingo today is Augustine
Konneh, 'Citizenship at the Margins: status, ambiguity and the Mandingo of Liberia',
African Studies Review, 39, 2 (1996), pp.141-54.

[19] Author's interviews, Monrovia, 6 April 1997.

but they themselves generally regard their Liberian offshoot with
some disdain, referring to some of them as Konyanké, or 'people
of the forest', who have a long history of interaction with the
forest peoples.[20]

One of the few conclusions which may be drawn with confidence
from these conflicting accounts is that the name, status and history
of various groups are all related and have an important effect
on their current claims to own land. It is equally clear that today
many Liberians persist in regarding Mandingo as outsiders, people
who do not belong in Liberia even when they have lived there
for generations, and this is related to a not-so-distant memory
of Mandingo in their role as slave-traders. The widespread Liberian
prejudice against Mandingo is not to be confused with a jaundiced
view of Islam, despite the fact that Mandingo have served as historical transmitters of the Muslim religion in Liberia. Quite a few
Liberians have adopted Islam without ever being assimilated with
the Mandingo (there are substantial numbers of people from the
Vai, Gola and Gbandi groups of western Liberia, for example,
who follow the central tenets of Islam, often while retaining elements of other religious beliefs). Of all these Muslim populations,
only the Mandingo are considered outsiders, people whose real
home is elsewhere.[21]

A second major source for early Liberian history, namely linguistic analysis, is just as ambiguous as oral tradition when it comes
to determining the precise history of modern ethnic groups, but
equally revealing of the social mechanics by which Liberians make
their own history. Liberian languages can be divided into distinct
categories by reference to their grammatical structures, most people
in western Liberia speaking languages of the Mande group, and
those in the south-east speaking languages from the Niger-Congo
group, with a few isolated pockets of other language groups, including West Atlantic languages, in between. This raises a problem
only when we try to deduce historical migration patterns from
this distribution since, as others have pointed out,[22] there can
be several explanations for how two or more geographically
separated clusters of people have come to speak related languages.
For example, an original group may split in two through migration
from a point of departure, but people who have lived in one

---

[20] Yves Person, *Samori: une révolution dyula*, 3 vols, Dakar, 1968, 1975, I, p.45,
describes the Konyanké as 'lost children of the Malinke'.

[21] Mohammad Alpha Bah, 'The Status of Muslims in Sierra Leone and Liberia',
Journal: Institute of Muslim Minority Affairs, 12, 2 (1991), pp.464-81.

[22] Richards, *Fighting for the Rain Forest*, pp.74-8.

area for centuries may also adopt the language of newcomers. As we have just seen, some Liberians believe that the latter is the case with some Liberian Mandingo, particularly those of Upper Lofa County: that they are not immigrants from the savannah, as they claim, but the descendants of indigenous inhabitants of the forest who have adopted the language and identity of outsiders and who are thus considered by some to have declined in status. There can be little doubt that the ancestors of the Mandingo of today include both offshoots of the Malinke of the savannah who have migrated southwards over the last two centuries, and people from the forest who were forcibly converted to Islam by Almamy Samory Touré, the mighty Malinke warlord who imposed his authority over a large swathe of modern Guinea and neighbouring areas at the end of the nineteenth century.[23]

On the whole, it seems that the ancestors of most modern Liberian peoples originally migrated from points to the north and east, probably within the last millennium. This includes many of those groups which live in the Liberian forest and regard themselves as archetypal forest-peoples. Some groups may have come early to the forest, like the Kru, probably the group longest established on Liberian soil, where they have absorbed many other migrants. Others came particularly during the sixteenth century, when the whole of the savannah region of West Africa was disturbed by instability and war associated with the decline of Mali. The Mano of modern Nimba County were themselves subjects of the kings of Mali who never converted to Islam, and who migrated to the forest some four centuries ago.[24] Others migrated originally from the east, the direction of modern Ghana. Older forest-dwellers may have absorbed fugitives from political disturbances in Mali or elsewhere.[25] Religious corporations, most notably the Poro society (for men) and Sande society (for women), have acted as channels for inter-ethnic communication and the building of alliances. It is likely that in some cases, groups of people today regarded as ethnically and linguistically distinct do not represent immigrants who have settled alongside older populations, but groups who have lived together for very many centuries and have developed distinct identities in the course of time. When rivalries

[23] Person, *Samori*.

[24] James C. Riddell, 'The Gbannah Ma (Mano) in Two Economies: dynamics of finite-labour economics' in Vernon R. Dorjahn and Barry L. Isaac (eds), *Essays on the Economic Anthropology of Liberia and Sierra Leone*, Philadelphia, PA, 1979, p.123.

[25] J.D. Fage, *A History of West Africa*, 4th edn, Cambridge, 1969, p.38.

exist, they usually stem from competing claims to land or problems stemming from national politics rather than from ancient enmities rooted in the history of medieval Africa. Whether it is in the Balkans, the Great Lakes of Africa, or elsewhere, it is wise to be wary of stories of ancient ethnic hatreds. Like all social creations, quarrels have histories; antagonists will easily recall past acts of treachery, rather than old bonds of friendship, when it suits them to do so. Not even old rivals are fated forever to fight each other, like cats and dogs.[26]

The newest of all modern Liberians[27] to arrive in the country are those who came on ships from America in the nineteenth century, convinced of their superior civilisation, possessors of powerful techniques of war, trade, religion and government. In 1847 the settlers in Monrovia declared the foundation of the Republic of Liberia. The fledgling republic laid serious claim to the hinterland only in the later nineteenth century, when Britain and France were expanding their own formal spheres of influence in West Africa. The descendants of the American settlers, forming a new ethnic group nowadays often referred to by Liberians as Congos,[28] were obliged to declare where the boundaries of their state lay in order to prevent the little republic from being partitioned by governments in Paris and London under pressure from their own traders and various other interest-groups. Liberia could easily have been swallowed up as a European colony at any time until the late 1930s. Having laid claim to what it perceived as its natural hinterland, the Liberian government, just like neighbouring European ·colonial administrations, then found itself obliged to exercise real control over the area it claimed. The writer Edward Blyden, himself an immigrant from the West Indies via the United States, noted accurately: 'The new government of Liberia was not the result of popular feeling. It was not the growth of the soil. It was forced upon the people as a protective measure in con-sequence of the impositions practised upon their revenue by foreign

---

[26] An analogy borrowed from Gérard Prunier, *The Rwanda Crisis, 1959-1994: history of a genocide*, London, 1995, p.xii.

[27] Certain other groups, most notably the Lebanese, came even later, but people of non-African ancestry are prevented by Liberia's racially-based constitution from becoming citizens.

[28] The designation 'Congos' was earlier applied to the descendants of slaves landed in Liberia after being intercepted by the British or US navies during the Atlantic crossing, but has now become more generally applied to English-speaking descen-dants of black settlers.

[i.e. European] adventurers, who had no respect for a community which neither was a nation nor a colony of a nation.'[29]

From the late nineteenth century, the period of the European scramble for colonies in Africa, successive governments in Liberia extended their claims over the hinterland through a colonial-style form of indirect rule, appointing commissioners who were required to uphold the authority of Monrovia over the various peoples living in the interior, supervising native collaborators who were designated as paramount chiefs. The creation of paramount chieftaincies was often a brutal business, with petty chiefs who refused to accept their authority being imprisoned and even hanged. The government's district commissioners had considerable power since they had armed force at their disposal and, as the years went by, were able to dispose of progressively greater resources of political patronage. Indirect rule became a source of revenue, and the interior a reserve of wealth for Liberian officialdom, from which the great majority of the indigenous population gained little.[30] Hinterland Liberia, consisting of those areas claimed by the government but over which it had had little control before the late nineteenth century, was administered through a system of indirect rule until 1963, when the government abolished the former hinterland jurisdiction and formed from it four new counties including Grand Gedeh, which incorporated Samuel Doe's birthplace of Tuzon. It was only then that Liberia had for the first time a uniform system of administration extending throughout the Republic.

In short, Samuel Doe, like other people born to a non-settler family in the hinterland before the 1960s, was brought up under a colonial-style system of government in which national power and prestige lay with an oligarchy of people, most of them with some American ancestry, who professed Christianity, were literate in English, and made a public display of what they themselves called 'civilisation'. People whose ancestors had never lived outside Africa were regarded as uncivilised, and unworthy of full civic rights, until they had assimilated the values which the first settlers had brought from America. Those people from the hinterland who did acquire the hallmarks of settler culture still had a lower status due to their lack of an American pedigree, certainly until the 1980s. It was only after the military coup of 1980 that it became advantageous for aspirant national politicians to claim 'country'

---

[29] Quoted in Robert A. Smith, *The Emancipation of the Hinterland*, Monrovia, 1964, p.5.

[30] Martin Ford, *Indirect Rule and the Emergence of the 'Big Chief' in Liberia's Central Province, 1918-1944*, Bremen, 1992, p.2.

roots, and to emphasise their African-ness rather than their American connections.

During the heyday of the rule of the settler-dominated True Whig Party, which governed Liberia for all but six years between 1870 and 1980, elite families were intensely proud of their Christian heritage and the American-style institutions of government and culture which marked them out from the despised 'country people' or 'tribal people', the name generally applied to Liberians of non-American origin.[31] As late as the 1960s, Liberian politicians dressed for formal occasions in top hats and tail-coats. Elite Liberians did not speak African languages. Office workers sweltered in three-piece suits, collars and ties. Young Liberian sophisticates danced to Tamla Motown at discos and parties and despised African music. The sons and daughters of the wealthy, educated in the United States and Britain, referred to other West Africans disdainfully as 'coasters'. Nevertheless, this great show of being American by taste and culture, after six generations or more in Africa, hardly disguised the fact that there had been a large amount of in-breeding between Liberians with proud settler surnames and those of country origin, while others with no foreign ancestry managed to get themselves accepted at least on the outer fringes of the national elite. Americo-Liberians, in fact, were as much a social and political class, a type of aristocracy, as they were a true ethnic group.[32]

Government, trade and politics

The extension of political and administrative institutions of American origin into the hinterland was carried out in the first instance so that the Liberian government could uphold the sovereign status which leading world powers grudgingly accorded to it after 1847, giving Liberia the status of Africa's oldest republic. That it was able to survive the colonial partition of Africa was largely due to the ability of successive governments to claim diplomatic protection from the United States. The US government had no wish to acquire a formal colony in Africa, but during the Second World War and during the Cold War which followed, it grew to find its special relationship with Liberia a useful asset.

For most of its first 100 years the Liberian republic hardly had the financial means to run the American-style administration to

[31] David Brown, 'On the Category "Civilised" in Liberia and Elsewhere', *Journal of Modern African Studies*, 20, 2 (1982), pp.287-303.

[32] Eghosa Osaghae, *Ethnicity, Class and the Struggle for State Power in Liberia*, Dakar, 1996.

which it pretended. Its earliest source of revenue was taxes on commerce which traders, whether African, European or American, were reluctant to pay to a government whose legitimacy they barely recognised. In 1870 the government contracted its first foreign loan, £500,000 secured from a London bank under extortionate conditions. Further loans raised in London in 1906 and in the United States in 1912 eased the government's cash crisis but created a burden of debt, bringing the republic's sovereignty into doubt as creditors were granted rights to customs revenue as security and European and American personnel were appointed to posts in the customs, treasury and army.[33] A major new source of government revenue emerged in 1926 when the Liberian government headed by President Charles King agreed a series of contracts with the Firestone Rubber and Tire Company of Akron, Ohio, and its associated companies. British companies, which at that time controlled some eighty per cent of world rubber production thanks to Britain's tropical colonies, were driving up the price of rubber, of which seventy per cent was consumed in the US.[34] The American rubber tycoon Harvey S. Firestone Sr., with the support of the US State Department, engineered a major business coup by signing a 99-year lease on a million acres of land in Liberia, soon to become the world's largest rubber plantation. To secure the deal Firestone established a subsidiary finance company which loaned the Liberian government five million dollars. The precariousness of Liberia's government enabled Firestone to drive a hard bargain since, as a Firestone employee observed, 'a mob of creditors and invading French troops were threatening to tear down President King's whole house of cards'.[35]

Liberia's drive to acquire the income necessary to function as a sovereign state was thus achieved only by placing itself under the diplomatic protection of the United States and by leasing a vast area of land to the Firestone Company. US dollars increasingly drove out sterling or locally-made iron bars as the main currency in use. These developments had a massive effect on Liberian politics and government. The 1926 loan and the royalties paid by Firestone enhanced the power of the executive branch of government relative to the judiciary and legislature, since the president became less dependent on taxes voted by the House of Representatives and

[33] Yancy, *Historical Lights*, pp.85-94; R.F.C. Maugham, *The Republic of Liberia*, London, 1920, p.69.

[34] Arthur Knoll, 'Harvey S. Firestone's Liberian Investment (1922-1932)', *Liberian Studies Journal*, XIV, 1 (1989), pp.13-33.

[35] Arthur Hayman and Harold Preece, *Lighting Up Liberia*, New York, 1943, p.68.

the Senate. The sharp increase in the state budget encouraged an existing tendency, already apparent since the 1860s, for government and the law to become the professions of choice of Liberians of settler descent, now firmly established as a ruling oligarchy.[36] Whereas the first president of the Republic, J.J. Roberts, had himself been 'a trader of great reputation',[37] and the first two generations of Americo-Liberian settlers had generally made their careers in business, by the 1920s elite Liberians had come to regard commerce as an ungentlemanly occupation, and the pursuit of a mannered leisure as the hallmark of a civilised person. The executive branch of government, presided over by the head of state, actually preferred to grant trade concessions and licences to foreigners, whether Europeans, Americans, Lebanese, or Mandingo traders, since non-nationals were less likely than Liberian citizens to use their commercial positions to build political constituencies.

The True Whig Party, founded in 1869, became the sole avenue to political success, while the settlers' leading cultural and religious institutions, the Freemasons' lodge and the Christian churches, became sources of social advancement. The provinces of the hinterland were sub-divided into paramount chiefdoms, even in areas without any tradition of strong chiefdoms, each province being under the control of a provincial commissioner assisted by district and assistant commissioners responsible for law enforcement and supervision of the tribal administration. Each district headquarters was supported by a squad of the Liberian Frontier Force to serve as a mobile police unit. Paramount chiefs were elected by a council of clan chiefs, subject to appointment by the President, and the appointees served for life. Paramount chiefs collected taxes, of which they were allowed to keep a ten per cent commission, and organised public works. All male citizens were liable for forced labour for public works and to carry goods for passing travellers or central officials,[38] although in practice a chief could exempt his favourites. Since Firestone required large numbers of workers which it was unable to recruit freely, in the absence of a national labour market, the government arranged for chiefs to draft forced labourers for the rubber plantations according to a quota system.[39]

---

[36] S. Byron Tarr, 'The Ecomog Initiative in Liberia: a Liberian perspective', *Issue: a Journal of Opinion*, XXI, 1-2 (1993), p.74.

[37] Yancy, *Historical Lights*, p.38.

[38] 'Revised Laws and Administrative Regulations Governing the Hinterland', Department of the Interior, 1949. National Documentation Center, Monrovia.

[39] Dorjahn and Isaac (eds), *Essays on the Economic Anthropology of Liberia and Sierra Leone*, p.17.

In 1929 the use of forced labour and a system of indentured labour tantamount to slavery was the occasion for an attempt by European powers, acting through the League of Nations, to abolish Liberian sovereignty and have the country proclaimed a colony of one or other European country. Real though the abuses were, the European campaign against them was something of a pretext, since some European colonies in Africa employed labour recruitment methods every bit as harsh.

The rule of provincial officials and paramount chiefs was supported by the Liberian Frontier Force, created in 1908. This armed force lived to a large extent off the land, commandeering labour, food and other requirements at will. The brutality of the Liberian Frontier Force (whose name was changed to the Armed Forces of Liberia in 1962) is well attested.[40] The army was dominated by an American-Liberian officer corps and in its early years supported by a number of African-Americans on secondment from the US armed forces. Rank and file soldiers were the 'personal servants of senior government officials' and army officers.[41] The heavy hand with which the Liberian army originally forced the hinterland peoples to submit to the rule of Monrovia provoked a series of armed rebellions, particularly in the south-east, the last of them as late as the 1930s.[42] Citizens of the hinterland had to pay hut tax and a host of other charges far heavier than the citizens of the county jurisdictions. According to one modern study, 'In 1925, for example, the hut tax on the tribal population stood at $300,000, whereas the property tax (the main tax on the Americo-Liberians) realised only $4,668 for the country as a whole.'[43]

The hut tax was intended not only to provide the government with revenue, but also to force rural Liberians to offer their labour for hire, as workers for Firestone or the other companies which began to establish themselves in the country. Successive governments after 1926 used the Firestone agreement as a model for further concessions to foreign investors, particularly in regard to mining rights, in return for royalties which provided the government with the funds with which to build a centralised administration. William Tubman, a lawyer who came not from one of the major

[40] Harrison Oladunjoye Akingbade, 'The Role of the Military in the History of Liberia, 1822-1947' (Ph.D. thesis, Howard University, 1977).

[41] Tarr, 'The Ecomog Initiative', p.74.

[42] Robert Kappel, 'Resistance of the Liberian People: problems of the ignored facts' in Eckhard Hinzen and Robert Kappel (eds), *Dependence, Underdevelopment and Persistent Conflict: on the political economy of Liberia*, Bremen, 1980, pp.169-96.

[43] Brown, 'Recollections of Early Liberia', *West Africa*, 3328 (11 May 1981), p.1021.

families of Monrovia but from a settler family in the small coastal
town of Harper, became president in 1944 and developed what
was officially labelled an Open Door economic policy, welcoming
foreign investors on favourable terms. Enjoying the protection
of the United States and taking the US side in Cold War diplomacy,
in the three decades of his presidency (1944 to 1971) Tubman
used the income generated by foreign concessions to build Africa's
first party-state at a period when other West African countries
had not yet achieved independence from colonial rule. The whole
country was incorporated in the vast True Whig Party patronage
machine dominated by the President. A former newspaper editor
of the time recalled:[44]

> The birth of the Tubman era saw political bossism at its zenith.
> Tubman packed the Legislature with his servants, cronies and
> favorites, many of them illiterate. One had functioned as his
> social secretary, another as his official chauffeur, and another
> as his valet, another was his ward, a fifth was his business agent,
> and a sixth served as his press secretary. Chiefs elected on the
> basis of Tubman's selection were largely illiterate. [...] Dominat-
> ing the True Whig Party as standard bearer, he handpicked
> all its officers in much the same way as he selected members
> of the Legislature. Judges, magistrates, justices of the peace
> and tribal chiefs – all owed their appointments to him, and many
> were summarily removed from office when they incurred his
> displeasure.

The presidency became the subject of a personality cult in which
Tubman was represented as the father of the nation. As a later
head of state, Amos Sawyer, said, 'all incomes were perceived to
be derived from President Tubman. Accordingly, all praises went
to him'.[45] Tubman became the first president of Liberia to travel
frequently into the interior with an entourage of ministers and
aides, inspecting provincial officials and chiefs and holding councils
in which he would publicly mediate in chieftaincy matters and
hear complaints against district commissioners. No government
payment in excess of $250 could be made without the President's
personal approval.[46] He even mediated in family quarrels and mari-
tal disputes, as many West African heads of state still do in fulfilment
of their role as paterfamilias of the nation.

[44] Tuan Wreh, *The Love of Liberty... The Rule of President William V.S. Tubman in Liberia, 1944-1971,* London, 1976, p.3.

[45] Amos Sawyer, *The Emergence of Autocracy in Liberia,* p.285.

[46] John Gunther, *Inside Africa,* New York, 1953, p.853.

Tubman proclaimed himself a champion of national unification. The crowning event of his nation-building programme was the abolition of separate jurisdictions for the coast and the hinterland and the creation of a united republic with nine counties.[47] But, as with so many personality-cults, the image of Tubman's omnipotence disguised a more complex reality, in which the president had to manage a patronage system consisting of myriad factional interests often based on complex local rivalries like those between the various clans of the Krahn, the latter only one of sixteen officially recognised tribes, each of which in fact was less a united group than a cluster of smaller and often competing clans, towns or other groups. Presidents mediated in chieftaincy disputes and family quarrels in their own interest, cultivating local notables and recruiting young talents while penalising opponents, in a permanent exercise of negotiation, reward and punishment.[48]

At its height in the 1950s, the Open Door economy provided abundant resources for the maintenance of a patronage machine which enabled the country's leading families to extend their influence into the interior and to forge alliances with local notables in the hinterland. The military resistance to government from Monrovia which occurred in the early twentieth century had by this time given way to politics through the dispensation of patronage, which in rural areas hinged especially on chieftaincy affairs. The key aim for individuals was to acquire a connection with a more powerful person or family, and then to use this so as to secure an appointment either in the central bureaucracy or as a tribal official. Hinterland families who wanted to establish links with the elite sought to attach their children as wards to families of the Americo-Liberian oligarchy. Country people found that membership of a masonic lodge and a mainline church was one of the best means of developing the connections with elite families necessary for participation in the True Whig patronage system. While Liberians of 'tribal' origin were excluded from full membership of a hereditary elite, this did not exclude them from using the patronage system to their advantage. The True Whig Party at its height was able to achieve an almost totalitarian dominance of society, even in the absence of an efficient bureaucratic administration, due to its success in managing social relationships.

During the Tubman era, the growth of political patronage and the creation of a national labour market to provide workers for

---

[47] Smith, *The Emancipation of the Hinterland,* pp.54-68.

[48] Wreh, *The Love of Liberty,* remains the outstanding description of the Tubman system.

the Firestone plantation or some other foreign concession or for the plantations owned by the wealthier members of the Americo-Liberian elite, meant that the recruitment of forced labourers became less harsh. People began to work for salaries voluntarily. The resulting transfer of labour from the subsistence sector to the concessions[49] tended to undermine the traditional social mechanisms of rural areas, where male elders exercised authority through their monopoly control of land, trade and women. Increasingly, young people were able to circumvent the authority of elders by joining the army or finding salaried work, perhaps as a migrant worker on a plantation. With the capital they saved, young men could return to their villages, marry and establish a family, or they could migrate to Monrovia and try to find a salaried job there.

The development of a labour market in the hinterland was accompanied by the rhetoric of economic development. Economic activity boomed, so that between 1952 and 1957 Liberia actually achieved an economic growth rate of an average fifteen per cent per year, higher than any country other than Japan. But by the 1960s pertinent public criticism of this system was emerging, particularly in the United States,[50] where many of the Liberian elite received their higher education. An influential study carried out by a team from Northwestern University for the US government, published in 1966, criticised an economic system which it described as 'growth without development', pointing out that the substantial amount of revenue earned by the government from royalties paid by foreign mining companies and concessions was not being invested in rural infrastructure, education, or other aids to economic development.[51] Rural education, for example, was largely left to the mission-schools. Foreign exchange was instead being spent largely on imported goods which enabled the elite to aspire to an American life-style. Partly under the influence of American colleges and universities, a new counter-elite was emerging, consisting of young men and women from country families who had achieved a high degree of education, had moved outside the ambit of the politics of tribes and chiefdoms, and who sought employment in the public administration, the key to wealth and high status. People completing their higher education in the 1960s or 1970s, whether of 'country' origin or from settler families, were influenced

---

[49] Robert W. Clower, George Dalton, Mitchell Harwitz and A.A. Walters, *Growth without Development: an economic survey of Liberia*, Evanston, IL, 1966, pp.259-335.

[50] E.g. J. Gus Liebenow, *Liberia: the evolution of privilege*, Ithaca, NY, 1969.

[51] Clower *et al.*, *Growth without Development*.

by the fashion for student radicalism and attracted by the ideologies of radical nationalism in vogue throughout Africa. Some contested the power wielded by families whose ultimate claim to govern rested on no more than the fact that some at least of their ancestors had emigrated from across the Atlantic.

These pressures for change were not fully apparent until the latter part of Tubman's long reign, by which time almost the whole of West Africa had secured independence from colonial rule and a range of new influences was at work. Liberia could no longer be convincingly described as the beacon of hope to black people the world over, the only independent negro republic, but was looking more like a corrupt and ramshackle neo-colony managed on behalf of the US government and the Firestone rubber company. Tubman's successor, President William Tolbert (1971-80), saw the need for reform of a political system which was finding it difficult to accommodate young people who had received an elite education, including increasing numbers of country origin, and who were calling for access to top positions, or to satisfy young intellectuals from settler families who had embraced fashionably radical ideas. Tolbert was faced with public criticism from intellectual and student opposition groups such as the Movement for Justice in Africa (MOJA), founded in 1973 at the University of Liberia, in which Amos Sawyer was a leading figure, and the Progressive Alliance of Liberia (PAL) of Baccus Matthews, who espoused a quasi-Marxist political ideology of militant African nationalism. MOJA especially was staunchly pan-Africanist and had branches in Gambia and Ghana. The more concessions Tolbert made to those who called for political reform, the more he became estranged from the conservatives in his own party. Under pressure from radical critics, Tolbert took a less pro-American line in foreign affairs than his predecessors, which eventually earned him the hostility of the Pentagon and the CIA, which had its West African headquarters in Monrovia.

After the government had raised the price of rice, the staple food, in an effort to discourage costly imports and to stimulate domestic production, there was serious rioting in Monrovia on 14 April 1979 which severely damaged an already feeble government. The rice riots were followed by widespread looting in Monrovia which even some soldiers joined in. MOJA, PAL and other radical networks were able to tap a rich vein of grievances and to acquire genuine popular support. Throughout the rest of the year the Tolbert government was widely considered by observers to be on its last legs. Tolbert found himself squeezed as his efforts at reform produced only more strident demands for equality. He

had to manage change through a political system in which everything revolved around the head of state, surrounded by officials
who manoeuvred ceaselessly for factional advantage, 'as if in an
oriental court, as attendants jestering for positions'.[52]

The factionalism and flattery of Tolbert's court was characteristic
of the Liberian political style. Becoming part of a clique, faction
or network, or even of as many such groups as possible, was the
best way for those with ambition to secure preferment, including
the generation of young, self-proclaimed 'progressive' politicians
who led the opposition to Tolbert. One young opposition politician
later recalled how 'status was bestowed by coterminous leadership
or membership in associations together with senior positions in
government. The value of membership in an association derived
from how many members of such associations were in senior government positions. Social, political and religious and professional
groups became indistinct; no arm's length transactions were possible
among them, for memberships were interlocking.' The atmosphere
was one in which 'hard work, intellectual pursuit and professional
training' were despised.[53] This was, and largely remains, the authentic atmosphere of Liberia's elite politics. Meanwhile, those country
people who aspired to wealth and position, but who could not
flaunt a college diploma or other marks of high culture sufficient
to gain acceptance to the ranks of the Monrovian elite, busied
themselves with the politics of chiefdoms, often equally deadly.
To this day, Liberians are expected to visit regularly whichever
rural area their family originally came from, and to provide benefits
and to dispense largesse to the kinfolk who still live in their rural
area. Leaders of rural communities – generally men of middle age
or beyond, who hold positions as chiefs or leaders of local religious
sodalities – apply pressure to the sons and daughters of the village
to help them financially, even when these absentees are living
in Monrovia or even the United States. This results in a curious
paradox whereby the moral system of the village continues to
exert an influence over Monrovians, and even over national politics,
in spite of the high degree of centralisation which was the legacy
of Tubman's party-state.

Although the Liberian armed forces played a prominent role
in the submission of the provinces to the power of Monrovia in
the earlier twentieth century, the wily President Tubman took great
care to keep them out of national politics. Nevertheless, as the

---

[52] S. Byron Tarr, 'Founding the Liberia Action Party', *Liberian Studies Journal*, XV,
1 (1990), p.43.

[53] *Ibid.*

political system became more difficult to manage through a combination of the economic difficulties which affected all of Africa
in the 1970s and growing militancy among young political activists,
the role of the armed forces became more important. In an effort
to manage political change, President Tolbert used the army as
part of his general strategy of distributing jobs and largesse to
various constituencies which had previously been excluded from
power, recruiting soldiers from the urban unemployed in an effort
to reduce one of the sources of pressure. The change in recruitment
policy for political reasons not only upset the ethnic balance within
the armed forces but also introduced into the soldiery some people
from the least stable sector of society, the urban unemployed,[54]
yet men from country families who had joined the army, like
the young Samuel Doe, still found their chances of promotion
blocked by officers from Americo-Liberian elite families.

In the tense atmosphere after April 1979 there were widespread
rumours of an impending coup. The CIA and the Pentagon, an-
noyed by President Tolbert's tilt to the left in his foreign policy
and especially by his refusal to allow bunkering facilities at Roberts
Airfield for a US Rapid Deployment Force, withdrew their support.
American security and defence officials began actively to search
for a possible replacement in the event that Tolbert should fall,
as seemed increasingly inevitable after the rice riots of April 1979.[55]
The political activists of MOJA and PAL continued to apply pressure
on the government, with PAL formally launching itself as an opposition party, the Progressive People's Party (PPP), while MOJA,
seeking to politicise the army, established a night school known
as the Barracks Union, of which Amos Sawyer was the principal.[56]
Tolbert responded by banning the PPP and detaining a number
of militants whom he threatened to execute. So pervasive was
the sense of impending change that one man intent on making
a political career, a leader of the Liberian student movement in
the United States, headed back to Monrovia to be at the heart
of things. His name was Charles Taylor.

Foreign diplomats and Liberian politicians alike could see that
the Tolbert government was running out of time. But by what
precise means was it to be replaced? The young politicians of

[54] Amos Sawyer, *Effective Immediately: dictatorship in Liberia 1980-6: a personal perspective,*
Bremen, 1987, p.5.

[55] D. Elwood Dunn and S. Byron Tarr, *Liberia: a national polity in transition,* Metuchen,
NJ, and London, 1988, p.91.

[56] Emmanuel Dolo, *Democracy Versus Dictatorship: the quest for freedom and justice in
Africa's oldest republic, Liberia,* Lanham, MD, and London, 1996, p.50.

MOJA and PAL, hungry for power and full of radical talk, had a genuine popular following but lacked the means to force their way into power. Rumours of an impending military coup were most often associated with the name of Major William Jarbo, who had trained as a ranger in the United States and was said to have excellent connections to American security officials. Jarbo was not the only soldier with political ambitions. Although the exact sequence of events remains unclear, it seems that militants of MOJA and PAL had established connections with a group of lower-ranking soldiers, including notably a certain Sergeant Thomas Weh Syen. Radical political militants and intellectuals urged their new friends in the armed forces to act, hoping that a coup d'état would be the means for a new generation of politicians to come to power.[57] Another soldier, Sergeant Thomas Quiwonkpa, also led a group intent on taking some sort of action against the government. Urged on by the political activists, the soldiers believed that the government was planning to execute a batch of political prisoners on the first anniversary of the 1979 rice riots. To forestall this, seventeen soldiers, led by Quiwonkpa, and including Weh Syen and others, launched a coup on the night of 12 April 1980. They had expected Tolbert to be staying at his private residence, but instead the group which invaded the Executive Mansion, led by Master Sergeant Doe, found the President sleeping at his office. There they killed him. It was Doe, the most senior in rank of the plotters, who went on the radio the next morning to announce the successful overthrow of the True Whig Party government. In the popular quarters of Monrovia, people celebrated in carnival mood, some dressing in masks and extravagant costumes. Looting, celebrating and politics combined in one wild street party.

Thirteen leading members of the Tolbert government were passed before a tribunal, convicted of corruption, and executed on the beach in Monrovia on 22 April 1980, amid unprecedented international publicity. Major Jarbo, who had been on the verge of launching his own coup, and who surely would have been most acceptable to the CIA, headed for sanctuary abroad but was hunted down and killed by the new junta.[58] Another late casualty of the coup was Adolphus Tolbert, the son of Liberia's murdered president. Adolphus Tolbert's wife, Désirée Delafosse, known in Liberia as Daisy, was a god-daughter of the Ivorian President Félix Houphouët-

---

[57] Cf. Andrews, *Cry, Liberia*, p.xvi.

[58] J. Pal Chaudhuri, 'Liberia Under Military Rule (1980-85)' in R. Kappel, W. Korte and R. Friedegund Mascher (eds.), *Liberia: underdevelopment and political rule in a peripheral society*, Hamburg, 1986, p.49.

Boigny. She hurried to Abidjan and appealed in tears to her god-
father, the grand old man of West African politics, to spare the
life of her husband, who had taken refuge in the French embassy
in Monrovia. Houphouët-Boigny immediately contacted Samuel
Doe and extracted from him a promise that Adolphus Tolbert's
life would be spared. Nevertheless, Adolphus Tolbert was abducted
from his sanctuary at the French embassy in June 1980 and murdered, a slight which Houphouët-Boigny never forgave.[59]

Chairman Doe

Thomas Quiwonkpa was the acknowledged leader of the seventeen
soldiers who murdered President Tolbert on the night of 12 April
1980 and declared that power was now in the hands of a junta
known as the People's Redemption Council (PRC). Quiwonkpa,
promoted to the rank of brigadier-general, became commanding
general of the army and used his influence to get his friend Samuel
Doe accepted as nominal head of state and co-chairman of the
PRC. The two sergeants, neither of them yet thirty years old, had
been friends since their school days.[60]

West Africa was used to coups, but the events of April 1980
caused considerable consternation among other governments in
the region because of the bloody and highly public manner in
which leading members of the previous government were killed.
The new administration purported to be acting on behalf of
Liberians of indigenous origin, the country people whom they
claimed to have liberated from 133 years of oligarchical rule, and
indeed the new junta was popular at first. It increased civil servants'
and soldiers' salaries and abolished the hated hut tax. Some
prominent Americo-Liberians, unnerved by the public executions,
went into exile.

Neither individual members of the junta, nor the PRC collectively, had control of a real patronage machine, but they were
under huge pressure to satisfy the expectations of all those Liberians
who had previously been excluded from the benefits of the most
senior public offices. Doe and his fellow-putchists, having no experience of public administration, co-opted to their service former
members of the Americo-Liberian elite and members of the generation of progressive politicians, many of whom believed that, since
the soldiers were uneducated men inexperienced in the ways of

---

[59] Youboty, *Liberian Civil War,* pp.59-61.

[60] Interview with Samuel Doe in *New Shaft* (Freetown), 7 January 1990.

politics, policy would actually be made by their advisors who would be able to carry out their revolution from behind the scenes. The new junta presided over a government which included an unstable mixture of radicals, some of them advocating an alliance with Libya, Ethiopia and other socialist governments, and former True Whig Party stalwarts who had ingratiated themselves with the new dispensation. The left-leaning inclinations of this new government did not last long, chiefly due to the weight of Liberia's dependence on the United States. PRC Chairman Samuel Doe, although almost illiterate, was quick to master the rudiments of international affairs and gained ascendancy within the PRC largely through the alacrity with which he realised that he could get American support in the factional politics of the junta by arguing a pro-Western line in foreign affairs. Within a short time the more radical elements in the new administration were tending to gather around Thomas Weh Syen, one of the three sergeants who led the PRC. Divisions came to a head over the question of relations with Libya, and having won this argument, in August 1981 Doe's faction executed Weh Syen and four other members of the PRC whom Doe had marked down as enemies. This was the occasion, Doe later claimed, that he first came to know God.[61]

There were constant rumours of other executions and plots within the barracks as rival factions within the armed forces competed. The 1980 coup itself, and the instability which followed, frightened some investors into moving their money overseas. Since the currency of Liberia was the US dollar, this caused a shortage of cash which the PRC rectified by minting its own coins, the so-called 'Doe dollars'. These were rapidly discounted on the black market, creating a two-tier currency which was to the advantage of government officials who could manipulate the two currencies by accounting in US dollars and paying in Doe dollars. As members of the junta vied with one another for power, the most prominent of them also competed to build political bases for themselves by any means possible, but particularly by managing the systems of patronage which linked tenure of senior positions in Monrovia to provincial officials and chiefs. Quiwonkpa, initially regarded by foreign diplomats as the real strong man of the government because of his command of the army, could rely on solid support in the armed forces, especially from soldiers from his home county of Nimba. Quiwonkpa's continued residence in the barracks permitted him to remain close to the soldiers and, as Doe manoeuvred to impose his authority as head of state, Quiwonkpa was sometimes

[61] Above, p.25.

seen as a straightforward military man in contrast to Doe, the aspiring politician.

Country people expected their representatives at the centre, which Doe, Quiwonkpa, Weh Syen and the other young men of the PRC purported to be, to bring money, jobs and other resources to their home areas. By the same token, this meant that when there were divisions within the junta, these rapidly had repercussions in the rural areas where its individual members had their family origins. Thus, when in 1981 Doe ordered the execution of rival members of the PRC including Thomas Weh Syen and Nelson Toe, the price he paid was to lose the support of those areas of the south-east where the two men originated. Nelson Toe's father, an influential elder in the Gbarzohn division of Grand Gedeh, became an implacable enemy of Doe.[62] Both men were Krahn, but thereafter Doe is said to have 'totally neglected' the Gbarzohn, Webbo and Gbeapo districts of his own native county, Grand Gedeh. 'Doe', it is reported, 'did not consider himself as a proud emissary of Grand Gedeh County, but only for [Gborbo] and Konobo [clans].'[63] Members of these two favoured clans, those of Doe's parents, enjoyed effective immunity from prosecution and full access to the resources of government during Doe's tenure of power, but these were only two out of the sixteen or more Krahn clans. Many other Krahn felt just as excluded from power as other Liberians.

In the scramble for government jobs by the 'progressives', the young, radical politicians who worked as officials and ministers of the junta, ethnicity was an important instrument, just as it could be used in a rather different way by associates of the former True Whig government, now trying to reposition themselves. Both 'progressives' and recycled True Whig politicians used the same courtiers' arts of flattery and intrigue to advance their cause. On the very day of the 1980 coup, Doe appointed a young progressive activist called George Boley to be Minister of State, responsible for political affairs and in effect his political business manager. Boley, whose father was from the Putu clan of the Krahn, was one of the very few people from Grand Gedeh County to have completed a doctorate in the United States. Doe systematically promoted Krahn from selected clans to sensitive posts in the government and the army, fuelling an ethnic rivalry at the heart of the armed forces. Quiwonkpa, a Gio, also appointed his own placemen.

---

[62] Youboty, *Liberian Civil War,* p.67.

[63] 'Case Study of Grand Gedeh County', September 1997.

One of these was Charles Taylor, a graduate from a US college who was married to a close relative of Quiwonkpa's. It was through this connection that Taylor began work at the General Services Agency, a government procurement office. As *de facto* director of the GSA, Taylor is then said to have caught the eye of PRC Chairman Samuel Doe by using the agency to procure a new Honda car for each member of the junta. He refurbished Tubman's old Mercedes stretch limousine, and rapidly became a favourite with Doe while retaining his connection with Quiwonkpa.[64] Taylor, although little known to the general public, wielded considerable influence behind the scenes. He had cabinet rank and attended both ministerial meetings and sessions of the National Security Council. Taylor claims to have drafted the government's first national security plan. 'I consolidated the revolution in Monrovia', he later told an interviewer. 'I did all the posting of the army at the radio station and Roberts International Airport.'[65]

Virtually all of the leading 'progressive' politicians of MOJA and PAL accepted Cabinet posts or other senior jobs under the PRC, and even after the execution of Weh Syen, the leading advocate of ties with Libya, many continued to serve the junta. Few politicians demurred when the PRC insisted that senior civilian officials accept commissions in the armed forces as a way of imposing a military command structure on the government, and they began to appear in public wearing military uniform. At the same time, some civilian politicians were working hard at dividing Doe and Quiwonkpa, now the two key members of the junta, in order to strengthen their own position. The PRC was under pressure to announce a return to civilian rule, and in early 1983 Doe began to hint that he had ambitions to become civilian president under a new constitution, a path often taken by soldiers who have assumed power. This disturbed Quiwonkpa, who feared that a move to constitutional rule would hand Doe further control of the government while his own influence remained limited to the armed forces. Doe pushed the draft of a new constitution through the PRC in 1983 and this was approved by referendum for implementation in 1985. On the suggestion of one of his inner circle of Krahn advisors, Doe informed Quiwonkpa that he was intending to remove him as commanding general of the army and transfer him to the weaker position of secretary-general of the PRC. Quiwonkpa

[64] J.N. Elliott, 'Story of the Animal Farm and the Progressives are All Out', *Monrovia Daily News*, 25 May 1995, pp.4-5.

[65] Charles Taylor interview with Baffour Ankomah, *Ghanaian Chronicle* (Accra), 12-18 Oct. 1992.

refused, and in late 1983, fearing that his power was slipping away and that his life was in danger, he fled into exile. Among those who followed Quiwonkpa into exile was his military aide-de-camp, Prince Johnson, a Gio like himself, who was to murder Doe in 1990. Some of Quiwonkpa's other protégés and allies also fled the increasingly menacing atmosphere in Monrovia. One of the former 'progressive' politicians and bureaucrats who decided to leave the country was Charles Taylor, who fled to the United States shortly before Quiwonkpa's own escape. Doe promptly requested his extradition, accusing Taylor of having embezzled $900,000 from the General Services Agency where he had been working. Taylor was arrested in Somerville, Massachusetts, in May 1984 and spent the next fifteen months detained at the Plymouth House of Correction, in the same state.[66]

Several of Quiwonkpa's military supporters fled to Côte d'Ivoire and from there launched a raid into Nimba County, attacking government offices and the premises of the iron-ore mine at Yekepa and killing a number of people. Since the insurgents had family connections in Nimba they probably hoped to spark off a full-scale insurrection.[67] The Nimba County raid of 1983 was the first open sign that the Krahn-Gio ethnic rivalry created within the armed forces by Doe's and Quiwonkpa's competition for supreme power had spilled over from the barracks into the country itself. It was to be a prominent feature of struggles over the next decade. The man who commanded the security force at the Yekepa mine complex at the time of the 1983 Nimba raid, Charles Julu, was later to become the most implacable of all Doe's generals, leading campaigns of terror in Nimba County in 1985 and 1990.

Quiwonkpa's flight cleared the way for Doe to organise the return to civilian rule urged on him by his US allies and others. This would enable him to perpetuate his rule by transforming himself into a civilian politician like other US allies had done, such as Marshal Mobutu in Zaïre or General Pinochet in Chile. He formed his own political party and used his control of government resources to recruit supporters prepared to stand against politicians from other parties. But even with abundant campaign finance and expert advice, plus all the advantages of incumbency, Doe's political base remained largely limited to the administrative machine which he was now running. Even though the presidential election held in October 1985 was blatantly rigged, Doe could

---

[66] Edward L. Wonkeryor, *Liberia Military Dictatorship: a fiasco 'revolution'*, Chicago, 1985, pp.166-8.
[67] Tarr, 'Founding the Liberia Action Party', p.31.

do no better than claim to have won with an unimpressive 50.9 per cent of the vote. The election did, however, succeed in its main aim, which was to be hailed as legitimate by the US government.

The rightful winner of the 1985 presidential election was generally reckoned to be Jackson F. Doe of the Liberia Action Party, a former education minister under Tolbert. Despite his similar name, Jackson Doe was not related to Samuel Doe but, like Quiwonkpa, hailed from Nimba County. Jackson Doe was a good example of how in its last years the True Whig Party had become more open to people from country families. The son of a Gio chief who had worked with the government, Jackson Doe had, as a youth, become a ward of a powerful settler family. He was educated at a leading school in Monrovia and at the University of Liberia, and after graduating he became a school principal in his home county of Nimba. Admitted to the Bar, he became an officer in the militia and an official of the True Whig Party, eventually holding the position of first national vice-president. President Tolbert appointed him minister of education and, later, gave him a seat in the senate. After the 1980 coup, Jackson Doe was recruited by his fellow-Gio Thomas Quiwonkpa to work as an advisor to the government. Considered by US diplomats as presidential material, Jackson Doe ran as the candidate of the Liberia Action Party in the 1985 election which Samuel Doe stole.[68]

While Samuel Doe was rigging his election as president of Liberia at the expense of Jackson Doe, his former schoolmate Thomas Quiwonkpa was actively preparing his own return from his place of exile in the United States. Quiwonkpa's support in his home region of Nimba County was all the more solid after the brutalities committed by Doe's troops in the aftermath of the 1983 Nimba Raid and due to the widespread belief that Jackson Doe, also a son of Nimba County, had been the real winner of the 1985 presidential election. In November 1985, Quiwonkpa infiltrated the country from Sierra Leone at the head of a group of dissident soldiers. On 12 November 1985 he entered Monrovia with an armed force and took over the national radio station, announcing that what he called the National Patriotic Forces of Liberia had taken power. There was widespread jubilation in Monrovia. Doe, however, had been tipped off about the invasion by US embassy officials.[69] He summoned reinforcements from an army base some miles down the coast and re-established control of the capital. The good fortune which enabled Doe to vanquish his enemies was, the President claimed, due to the direct intervention of God for the second time in his life.[70]

The coup attempt sparked a shocking display of public brutality. Doe's soldiers triumphantly paraded Quiwonkpa's mutilated corpse around the city. Eye witnesses recorded seeing some of Doe's troops hacking off bits to keep as souvenirs and even eating pieces of the body.[71] One Nigerian journalist, for example, who saw Quiwonkpa's body being used in this way, called it 'a macabre cannibalistic ritual by some of Doe's soldiers who, astonishingly in these modern times, still believe that by eating bits of a great warrior's body, some of that greatness would come to them. The heart, of course, was the prize delicacy and it is traditionally shared on a hierarchical basis.'[72] Doe proceeded to take revenge on people accused of supporting the Quiwonkpa coup and anybody considered to have celebrated Quiwonkpa's short-lived success during the hours when he appeared to have succeeded in taking power. Charles Julu, former security chief at the Yekepa iron mine during the raid two years earlier, was now despatched by Doe to carry out a purge of Nimba County, which he did with great brutality. The coup and its aftermath resulted in an official figure of 600 dead and a probable number of closer to 1,500 people killed.[73]

With the rigged election and the death of Quiwonkpa, both within a few weeks of each other in late 1985, Doe had effectively eliminated all serious internal opposition. Despite his evident unpopularity, his tenure of the presidency gave him the resources to build his own patronage network. This he constructed especially on an ethnic basis, filling senior military positions with Krahn promoted from the ranks, cultivating the few Krahn 'book men' and politicians as advisors, and isolating Gio soldiers from Nimba County. The same strategy of building support through the extension of patronage to specific ethnic networks led Doe to woo prominent members of Liberia's Mandingo community. This he seems to have done primarily because of his suspicion of the Gio of Nimba County, guilty by association with the ethnic patronage network which Quiwonkpa had himself built in the army, for

---

[70] Above, p.25.

[71] Robert Kappel and Werner Korte (eds), *Human Rights Violations in Liberia, 1980-1990: a documentation*, Bremen, 1990, p.292.

[72] Quoted in Lawyers' Committee for Human Rights, *Liberia: a promise betrayed*, New York, 1986, p.58.

[73] Kappel *et al.*, *Underdevelopment and Political Rule*, p.10.

although Nimba County is regarded as the homeland of the Gio
and Mano peoples, there were also considerable numbers of Mandingo
living there, as indeed throughout much of the north and west
of the country, generally as shopkeepers and small traders. From
the early 1980s, Doe appointed Mandingo officials to positions
in Nimba County and encouraged them to purchase land. At the
national level, he appointed Alhaji G.V. Kromah, a Mandingo,
as head of the Liberian Broadcasting Service and, later, minister
of information. In 1986, in the aftermath of the Quiwonkpa coup
attempt, Doe explicitly recognised the Mandingo as a Liberian
ethnic group, to the outrage of the many Liberians who generally
regarded them as foreigners.[74] This caused resentment in many
parts of the country, leading to street fights between Mandingo
and others in Gbarnga, the capital of Bong County, in January
1988.[75]

Samuel Doe was by no means the first president of Liberia
to cultivate an alliance with the Mandingo community, giving them
commercial privileges in return for their support, precisely because
they were not considered Liberian and could not therefore form
an independent political bloc of national importance. Already by
the 1920s, 'local Liberian commerce through Liberian and tribal
traders had been slowly supplanted by networks of foreign merchants who virtually controlled the entire economy of the country
and were able to alienate a large portion of profits through speculation and manipulation of goods', one researcher has noted.[76] These
'foreign merchants' included Mandingo. Doe's innovation was in
giving official positions in government as well as commercial
privileges to Mandingo people, which gave them a considerably
stronger position than before in those areas of the country where
they had previously lived as traders and suppliers of credit to rural
farming communities in some sort of harmony with local chiefs
and elders.

This sort of calculated use of official procedure for informal
purposes, political and commercial, in fact operated at every level
of the administration. In rural areas, district commissioners and
paramount chiefs enjoyed wide powers of coercion and possibilities
for accumulating wealth which they habitually used in the management of local social networks, which they thus turned into political

[74] Brehun, *War of Horror,* p. 31.

[75] *Daily Observer* (Monrovia), 24 February 1988, quoted in *Liberian Studies Journal,*
XIII, 1 (1988), pp.149-50.

[76] Warren L. D'Azevedo, 'A Tribal Reaction to Nationalism', pt. II, *Liberian Studies
Journal,* II, 1 (1969), p.55.

constituencies. Chieftaincy disputes could be every bit as sharp as national political divisions, and were all the more bitter for pitting kinfolk against each other in small communities. It was the very factionalism to which chieftaincy affairs were prone which gave the government its foothold in local politics, since the power of the central government to approve or reject a local chief or to play one candidate against another gave nationally appointed officials scope to cement alliances at the local level.

For half a century, until the 1970s, the True Whig Party was able to run this system with little open dissent precisely because control was exercised through social networks. The leaders of the True Whig Party were able to maintain an ideological hegemony by invoking the virtues of harmony, prosperity and Christianity, and by addressing to each section of the nation appeals to local values in the guise of traditional or tribal culture, the latter ruthlessly exploited by paramount chiefs so as to create political constituencies for themselves. Certainly until the 1970s, sufficient resources were available to keep this patronage machine oiled and running. After 1980, a new ideological justification was introduced in the form of the claim made by Doe, the PRC and the 'progressive' politicians that they were now managing an almost identical system in order to liberate the tribal people from the oppressive rule of the True Whig Party. The 1980 coup did indeed provide new opportunities at the national level for a relatively small number of people whose political scope had previously been restricted, but no leader associated with the PRC was able to assemble a combination of interests sufficient to convince a clear majority of Liberians that the government was operating to their benefit. The few people able to acquire a slice of government patronage under Doe were in such haste to acquire wealth and power that they behaved more like looters than governors, covered only by the thin veil of legality provided by the constitution. Amos Sawyer described the Doe years, accurately enough, as 'years of rape and plunder by armed marauders whose ideology is to search for cash and whose ambition is to retain power to accumulate and protect wealth'.[77]

After his defeat of Quiwonkpa in 1985, a threat to Doe seemed possible only from a coup or assassination attempt by people close to him, particularly if it were to be supported by an external force. Doe's personal security detail was largely composed of Krahn, and he had the best advice available from the United States and later from Israeli specialists who trained his bodyguard and other elite units. In addition to these assets, Doe had a fine instinct for detecting

[77] Sawyer, *Effective Immediately*, p.8.

treachery, real or imagined, and came to believe increasingly in his own invulnerability as he surrounded himself with ever more numerous religious advisors, diviners and suppliers of amulets and other spiritual protection.[78] By 1990, he claimed to have survived no fewer than thirty-eight coup or assassination attempts. He was much given to claiming that it was God who had raised him to the presidency and God alone who could depose him. Many of his soldiers clearly believed this too, and cultivated what Amos Sawyer called a 'magico-super naturalism' in their unceasing quest for spiritual power.[79]

More prosaically, the US government had the ability to unseat Samuel Doe if it really wished. But while US officials became exasperated by Doe's brutality and corruption, the government in Washington consistently supported the former master sergeant when it mattered most. Throughout the 1980s the US government actually gave the Doe government more financial help than it accorded to any other government in sub-Saharan Africa, relative to population, in spite of its appalling record on human rights and corruption.[80] The United States resorted to sending a team of accountants to oversee government finances, but to little effect, as Doe out-manoeuvred them with ease.[81] Perhaps most importantly of all, the United States endorsed Doe's victory in the thoroughly fraudulent 1985 presidential election, on the grounds that even a rigged election was better than no election at all. This effectively shut off the last possibility of evicting Doe from power by constitutional means, or at least by peaceful ones.

US Assistant Secretary of State for African Affairs Chester Crocker issued a series of statements after the rigged 1985 elections referring to what he called the 'positive aspects' of the poll, especially in relation to the standards of 'a part of the world where the norm is single-party rule'. In January 1987 Secretary of State George Shultz, passing through Monrovia, praised President Doe's government for its 'genuine progress' towards democracy.[82] Doe understood well that if his personal security remained good enough to prevent an assassination or a palace coup of the same type as had brought him to power in 1980, he could retain US support

[78] *Ibid.,* p.29.

[79] *Ibid.,* p.11.

[80] Cf. George Klay Kieh, 'Merchants of Repression: an assessment of United States military assistance to Liberia', *Liberia-Forum,* V, 9 (1989), pp.50-61.

[81] Frank Kimble, 'The United States-Liberia Operational Experts Project', *Liberian Studies Journal,* XV, 1 (1990), pp.1-12.

[82] Berkeley, 'Between Repression and Slaughter', p.60.

by vague promises of reform which meant little or nothing in reality. As long as the Cold War endured, he could be sure of US protection since Liberia was the main seat of US power in West Africa and the site of an important satellite-tracking facility and a major CIA station and was therefore too important for the United States to risk losing for the sake of a democratic crusade. The US position was well described by a correspondent for the *Washington Post*.[83]

> What the Americans ended up buying was neither stability nor democracy. They paid, instead, for Doe's legitimacy: weapons to coerce loyalty, money to rent it. The skinny backwoods sergeant was more cunning than he looked. Repeatedly, he outfoxed the State Department. He promised to return to his barracks, which he did not. He promised free and fair elections, which he rigged. He promised financial discipline, which he faked. For his every promise, the US government rewarded him with aid. For his every betrayal, the US government accepted another promise.

Doe continued to work his patronage system with impunity, like his True Whig predecessors, by granting concessions to foreign businessmen who were beholden to him for commercial opportunities and by taking bribes from them with which to buy local political support. He is said to have presided over the embezzlement of some $300 million of public funds in ten years, roughly equal to half the Gross Domestic Product for 1989.[84] In effect, the decline of the economy made little difference to the size of Doe's personal war-chest since the income which previous governments had derived from their Open Door economic policy was substituted by financial aid from the US government.

It is interesting to consider briefly the ways in which Doe differed from his predecessors of the True Whig Party, whose rule was originally built on the use of a brutal military force and was maintained by the use of social networks for political purposes. Doe used similar techniques, but advanced a novel ideological justification by asserting that his 1980 'revolution' had liberated the country people, a claim which rang increasingly hollow as Doe made ever wider use of former True Whig officials doing much the same work as they had previously done for Tolbert and Tubman. Doe's youthfulness, his military culture and his massive sense of insecurity

---

[83] Blaine Harden, *Africa: despatches from a fragile continent,* quoted in Africa Watch, *Liberia: the cycle of abuse. Human rights violations since the November ceasefire,* original publication reprinted in *Liberian Studies Journal,* XVII, 1 (1992), p.155.

[84] Berkeley, 'Between Repression and Slaughter', pp.53-64.

made him quicker and more implacable in his use of violence than his immediate predecessors. But perhaps the key distinction between Doe and previous Liberian heads of state was in the strategic effect of his manipulation of factions. Doe was the first Liberian head of state since the conquest of the hinterland who excluded certain social groups entirely from political society, most notably the Gio and Mano of Nimba County. He used the full weight of military force against groups which themselves had no military potential, such as university students. Social groups who had lost the President's favour fell outside the range of conventional political instruments, which made Doe's brand of divide and rule steadily more frenetic as the stakes rose and as entire communities lost all access to government patronage. Probably, Doe's actions were motivated by a combination of personal vindictiveness, fear, and the lack of political resources which had been available to his True Whig predecessors.

The more he had recourse to violence, and the more he excluded entire social groups from political society, the more unconvincing was Doe's claim to be president of all Liberians. In effect, the political realm was open to only a shrinking proportion of the nation. It is because of his excessive use of violence and his hostility to whole social groups that Samuel Doe could reasonably be described as the first of the modern Liberian warlords. In this perspective, Liberia's crisis began in 1980 when the old order was overthrown. A civil war began in 1989 only when Doe lost the monopoly of armed force he had hitherto enjoyed, and the opportunity to restore a new monopoly of national power was disputed between various political-military entrepreneurs often called warlords, many of whom had actually held public office under the PRC or under Doe in the 1980s. This conflict ended with the victory of one warlord, Charles Taylor, in 1997.

Quiwonkpa's legacy: the NPFL

'Before Doe', according to a leading American commentator, 'Liberia was one of the few African countries without serious tribal hostility.'[85] This was before it had experienced a coup by lower-ranking soldiers associated with a generation of new politicians avid for power. These were young men in a hurry, who turned the social distinctions in which the Liberian state had its roots

---

[85] Blaine Harden, quoted in Paul Gifford, *Christianity and Politics in Doe's Liberia*, Cambridge, 1993, p.34, n.72.

into major political cleavages at frightening speed. By 1983, the rivalry between Doe and Quiwonkpa had created rival camps of Krahn and Gio in the army. After Quiwonkpa's failed coup in 1985, Nimba County, home of the Gio, was almost excluded from Liberian society. Nimbaians found it hard to find jobs in government since they were suspected of disloyalty to President Doe, while commercial privileges and state employment in their home county were given to Mandingo, regarded as outsiders. People from the area nursed a sense of grievance for the suffering inflicted on them in 1983 and 1985 and the injustice of having their favourite son, Jackson F. Doe, cheated of an election victory in 1985. The frustration and resentment building up against anyone suspected of association with the Doe government were often directed against all Krahn, even the many who had not benefited at all from Doe's government. In 1986 one Krahn farmer told an interviewer, 'there will have to be revenge. We know that something is in the making. When it explodes, then God have mercy on all of us.'[86] A report written by a US human rights' group in the same year predicted all too accurately 'the prospect of massive reprisals against the Krahn if President Doe is violently removed from power'.[87]

If the people of Nimba County were overwhelmingly opposed to Samuel Doe, so too were the majority of Liberians living abroad, mostly in other West African countries and in the United States. The main concentration of Liberian exiles in West Africa was in Côte d'Ivoire, where Americo-Liberians who had left the country after the 1980 coup fraternised with later waves of refugees, mostly Gio from Nimba County. Côte d'Ivoire's President Félix Houphouët -Boigny, the patriarch of French-speaking West Africa who had cultivated dynastic alliances throughout the region, had harboured a grudge against Doe ever since the treacherous murder of his relative by marriage, Adolphus Tolbert, in 1980. After the death of her husband, Adolphus Tolbert's widow Désirée Delafosse moved to Burkina Faso. Many Liberians state it as a fact that her next marriage was to Captain Blaise Compaore, one of the quadrumvirate of young officers who ruled Burkina Faso after 1983, although this does not appear to be true; Compaore was in fact married to Chantal Terrasson, another protégée of the Ivorian president,[88] although it does appear that Delafosse also became part of Compaore's entourage, which is presumably the

---

[86] Quoted in Dolo, *Democracy Versus Dictatorship*, p.67.

[87] Lawyers' Committee for Human Rights, *A Promise Betrayed*, p.23.

[88] Huband, *The Liberian Civil War*, p.105.

source of rumours concerning her marriage to him. What is beyond dispute is that Compaore, commander of Burkina Faso's elite parachute regiment, was tied to Houphouët-Boigny through marriage and that he developed an interest in Liberia and the Liberian exiles who were roaming West Africa in search of support.

In the context of the Cold War, sources of international support for an anti-Doe movement were hard to find. Since the United States was Doe's ally, there was no hope of securing US backing for an invasion or coup attempt. Nor would America allow a Soviet client to take power in Liberia, and in any case after Mikhail Gorbachev's rise to power the Soviet government had no interest in supporting adventures of this type. The Liberian exiles with the best international connections, such as the professor Amos Sawyer and the banker Ellen Johnson Sirleaf, lived in the United States, where their campaigns against the Doe government met with little more than polite attention from US policy-makers. The person who made the most progress in the trawl for military and financial support was Charles Taylor. Born in 1948 near Monrovia, the third of fifteen children in an Americo-Liberian family of modest means, Taylor followed his father's footsteps to train as a school-teacher before heading for the United States in 1972, where he acquired a degree in economics and made a name in student politics. After returning to Liberia in 1980 in time to taste power as a senior official under the PRC, he left once more for America in 1983 – allegedly with $900,000 of Liberian government funds in his pocket – after the fall of his first patron, Quiwonkpa. In America he was arrested pending extradition to Liberia where he was wanted on charges of embezzlement. He escaped after fifteen months in a Massachusetts prison in circumstances which remain mysterious to this day. The former sheriff of Plymouth County, Massachusetts, told the press years later that Taylor and four other inmates, all petty criminals, sawed through their cell bars and climbed out of their cell window using knotted sheets.[89] Taylor is said to have paid $50,000 for his share in the plan.[90] According to Taylor's lawyer, Ramsey Clark, who is no less than a former US attorney-general, no charges were ever filed against Taylor as a result of his escape.[91] This oversight strengthens

---

[89] David L. Marcus, 'Liberian President has Problem in Plymouth', *Boston Globe,* 14 August 1997.

[90] H. Boima Fahnbulleh, *In Whose Interest? Disarmament and the international community in the resolution of the Liberian civil war,* Monrovia, 1994, p.8.

[91] 'Taylor's Gaolers', *Africa Confidential,* 38, 14 (4 July 1997), p.8.

suspicions that the US security services turned a blind eye to Taylor's escape, after the event, for political reasons.[92]

After his jailbreak Taylor passed through Mexico before arriving in Accra in February 1986. By his own account, he headed for Ghana at the invitation of an exiled Liberian politician, H. Boima Fahnbulleh, a former minister under Doe who was the most thorough-going Marxist among the MOJA leaders and was close to leaders of the Ghanaian government, especially the redoubtable security chief Kojo Tsikata. After just one week in Accra, during which time he met various Ghanaian officials, Taylor was again detained. 'They said they did not understand how I got out of jail in the US and that I may have been a CIA spy,' Taylor recalls. 'Later I found out that because I had not joined the MOJA opera-tions in Ghana, the very Harry Fahnbulleh who invited me to Ghana engineered my arrest.' Indeed, Fahnbulleh was creating his own opposition group, the Front for Popular Democracy in Liberia (FPDL). After three months in a Ghanaian prison Taylor was released and granted political asylum. This time he was able to befriend the ambassador of Burkina Faso in Accra who arranged an audience with Thomas Sankara, then president of Burkina Faso and a hero to young revolutionaries throughout West Africa. In early 1987 Ghanaian security again detained Taylor, he claims as a result of further intrigues by MOJA leaders including Fahnbul-leh and Sawyer.[93] Released a second time, he headed for Burkina Faso, where there was a small concentration of Liberian exiles who had received some sort of promise of military support from the Burkinabe government. Among the Liberian army deserters who had assembled in Burkina Faso were Prince Johnson and Samuel Varney, colleagues of Quiwonkpa who had taken part in his failed coup of 1985. These Liberians were now approached by Blaise Compaore who asked them for help with a coup of his own against the Burkinabe president, Thomas Sankara. Ac-cording to a former aide to Compaore, the powerful Houphouët-Boigny was aware of Compaore's ambitions.[94] On 15 October 1987 Burkinabe soldiers under Compaore's orders, supported by a squad of Liberian exiles including Prince Johnson, killed Sankara. Blaise

---

[92] Huband, *The Liberian Civil War*, pp.45-7.

[93] Charles Taylor interview with Baffour Ankomah, *Ghanaian Chronicle* (Accra), 12-18 Oct. 1992; Kwesi Yankah and Lazarus D. Maayang, 'Charles Taylor: dark days in Ghana', *Uhuru* (Accra), 3 (1990), pp.39-42; Huband, *The Liberian Civil War*, pp.47-51.

[94] Bernard Doza, *Liberté confisquée*, Paris, no date, pp.247-51.

Compaore, once Sankara's close friend, became president of Burkina Faso.[95]

Thus, by 1987 the anti-Doe movement outside Liberia had become inextricably involved in a wider pattern of West African intrigue. After October 1987 the rulers of Côte d'Ivoire and Burkina Faso were allies and had in common a dislike of Samuel Doe. Compaore was particularly beholden to the Liberian expatriates who had helped him to take power and he helped them with further introductions. It was through Compaore that Charles Taylor was able to secure a line of communication with Libya's Colonel Gadaffi and to convince the Libyan leader of his revolutionary credentials. For the first time, Taylor now had access to a foreign government which had the wherewithal to finance and arm an insurrection on a large scale. Gadaffi took an interest in these West African intrigues in pursuit of his own vast revolutionary ambitions, which extended to the whole of Africa, the Middle East and other parts of the world, from Northern Ireland to Colombia and the Philippines. The Libyan secret services had established a body known as al-Mathabh al-Thauriya al-Alamiya ('World Revolutionary Headquarters'), an institute based in Libya whose purpose was to train volunteers in revolutionary warfare from all over the world.[96]

For a decade, Gadaffi's campaign to rid Africa of European imperialism had centred on Chad, his southern neighbour, where he had clashed with French troops. Since then, a sequence of setbacks had combined to turn Gadaffi's attention away from Chad and to soften his resolve to counter French influence, while sharpening his anti-Americanism. In April 1986 Gadaffi had been shaken by a US air raid on his residence in Tripoli, which had killed one of his daughters and from which he himself escaped only narrowly. In 1987 the Libyan armed forces suffered a series of stunning defeats at the hands of the Chadian army, which benefited from US intelligence and training.

The Chadians took so many Libyan prisoners of war that the CIA was able to begin work on turning them into a contra-style army to overthrow Gadaffi.[97] Now wary of his Chadian neighbour, Gadaffi took steps to restore his good relationship with France

---

[95] Agetua, *Operation Liberty*, pp.23-4, specifically mentions Liberian involvement in Sankara's death. The involvement of Liberian exiles in the Compaore coup has been confirmed by Prince Johnson in various interviews including with the French researcher François Prkic, to whom I am grateful for sharing this information.

[96] Author's interviews. See also Abdullah, 'Bush Path to Destruction' in *Journal of Modern African Studies*.

[97] 'USA/Chad: target Gadaffi', *Africa Confidential*, 30, 1 (1989), pp.1-2.

and concentrated on ways of gaining revenge against America. The concentration of Liberian exiles in Burkina Faso, and their close relationship with his friend Blaise Compaore, inspired the idea of targeting Liberia, the main base for US intelligence in West Africa. By late 1987, Gadaffi was showing interest in proposals to host an anti-Doe movement and to put at its disposal all the training facilities of his World Revolutionary Headquarters.

Until this point, probably the most successful recruiter of Liberian military exiles was Moses Duopu, yet another former minister in Doe's government who had fled at the time of Quiwonkpa's eclipse. Duopu, a Gio from Nimba County, had been a student activist with Taylor in the 1970s, when both were studying in the United States, and he was married to Taylor's sister-in-law. Throughout 1986 and 1987, while Taylor was in and out of detention in Ghana, Duopu was contacting known opponents of the Doe government, particularly those with military experience, and inviting them to Burkina Faso for further training. Among those who responded to his call were Quiwonkpa's former aide-de-camp Prince Johnson, Samuel Varney and Elmer Johnson, the latter a Liberian who had served in the US marine corps. It was through Duopu that Prince Johnson, Varney and others found themselves in Burkina Faso in October 1987, in time to help Compaore in his coup.[98]

Although the few dozen Liberian exiles in Burkina Faso and Libya were often suspicious of Taylor, once he had secured Gadaffi's personal support he was able increasingly to impose himself as the key intermediary between the international backers and the Liberian soldiers who were to form the sinews of a revolutionary army. Responding to Gadaffi's urging to create a pan-African revolutionary force, Taylor began shuttling from one capital to another, travelling generally on a Burkinabe passport. He returned to Accra, where he met Togolese dissidents who were supported by the Ghanaian government.[99] He had less success in Freetown, where he was briefly jailed in 1988.[100] It appears to have been on a later occasion that Taylor offered to pay President Momoh for permission to allow the Liberian exiles to operate out of Sierra Leone, which has a border with Liberia. The notoriously venal Momoh promptly

[98] See profile of Samuel G. Varney in *Torchlight* (Monrovia), 1, 1 (26 October 1990), p.2.

[99] Charles Taylor interview with Baffour Ankomah, *Ghanaian Chronicle* (Accra), 12-18 Oct. 1992; the best account of Liberian exile politics in this period is Huband, *The Liberian Civil War,* pp.45-62.

[100] Ibrahim Abdullah, 'Bush Path to Destruction: the origin and character of the Revolutionary United Front (RUF/SL)', *Africa Development,* XXII, 3-4 (1997), pp.45-76.

sought from Samuel Doe a higher sum, turning the approach into an auction,[101] an action for which his country was later to pay dearly. In their training camps in Libya and Burkina Faso, the Liberians met a whole range of African revolutionaries, some of them veterans of coups and wars, others destined to play important roles in the future. By mid-1989 Taylor had managed to seal an alliance with a group of Libyan-trained Sierra Leoneans led by a former army corporal, Foday Sankoh, and calling themselves the Revolutionary United Front/Sierra Leone.[102]

The Liberian exiles also adopted a name: the National Patriotic Front of Liberia. According to Tom Woewiyu, a long-standing opponent of the Doe government and an old friend of Taylor's who was to take a senior place in the movement, Quiwonkpa himself founded the organisation, but it is doubtful that the NPFL in Quiwonkpa's time actually had much formal structure.[103] It was only when it received Libyan backing that it developed a pan-African character, although it was able to build on the pan-Africanist tradition of MOJA, the Liberian radical group founded in 1973. It was in Libya that Taylor met Kukoi Samba Sanyang, a Gambian revolutionary, close to MOJA, who had been one of the leaders of a bloody Libyan-backed coup attempt in Banjul in 1981.[104] After the failure of the Gambian coup, Samba Sanyang had gone with eleven others to Cuba where, according to one of the group, 'after 18 months studying propaganda techniques they were recruited by Libya's ambassador in Havana and sent to Libya in 1983 for three years of military training'. Samba Sanyang himself stayed in Libya while others went on to fight in Uganda with Yoweri Museveni, who fought his way to his country's presidency in 1986, and with John Garang in south Sudan.[105] Another person who visited the Libyan camps was Laurent-Désiré Kabila, later to become president of Congo.[106] The Libyan camps became the

[101] Confidential diplomatic source.

[102] Abdullah, 'Bush Path to Destruction', *Africa Development*, p.67.

[103] 'Transcript of Statement by Hon. Tom Woewiyu, Minister of Labour, Liberia National Transitional Government, Delivered in Monrovia July 19, 1994', *Liberian Studies Journal*, XIX, 2 (1994), pp.342-7.

[104] On the 1981 coup attempt see Arnold Hughes, 'The Attempted Gambian Coup d'État of 27 July 1981', in *idem* (ed.), *The Gambia: studies in society and politics*, Birmingham, 1991, pp.92-106.

[105] Interview with Ebrahima Jammah, one of the eleven, in Pap Saine, 'Gambian Describes Gaddaffi's African Network', Reuters despatch, 4 August 1992. Some details have been confirmed by the author's own interviews in Monrovia.

[106] Author's interviews, Monrovia, April 1997.

Harvard and Yale of a whole generation of African revolutionaries. But there were also Liberian exiles who disliked Taylor and were jealous of his growing influence as an intermediary with their main sources of money and guns, Gadaffi and Compaore. One group of Libyan trainees remained loyal to the FPDL, the guerrilla army formed by Fahnbulleh and the old guard of MOJA, which developed its own plans to launch an invasion of Liberia from Sierra Leone. Yet another group, led by one Cooper Teah, a former army officer, was part of the NPFL but remained independent of Taylor.[107]

So it was that Charles Taylor and other Liberian exiles, although riven by factional quarrels, were able to build international support from the unlikely trio of Libya, Burkina Faso and Côte d'Ivoire. Few people either inside or outside Liberia had heard of the NPFL before the 1989 invasion of Liberia, but it had military trainees living in Burkina Faso and supporters in Côte d'Ivoire and received sympathetic attention from the national security services of these two governments and from businessmen interested in making inroads into the Liberian economy, particularly the valuable Nimba iron ore mines and hardwood from Liberia's forests. Taylor himself, who by this time had learned to speak French, opened bank accounts in Abidjan and befriended French businessmen who had good contacts at the French embassy there, one of the most important in Africa. In Ouagadougou, President Compaore introduced him to senior French politicians and officials.[108]

Throughout 1989 the NPFL was actively preparing a military assault on Liberia from positions in Côte d'Ivoire, which has a border with Nimba County. The rival FPDL group, loyal to the old MOJA leadership, was preparing something similar from Sierra Leone. Rumours of some sort of political upheaval flew around Nimba County which, in time-honoured fashion, many people believed could only be connected with developments in the spirit world. These rumours were far more than idle gossip; they were taken by many Liberians as a sign from the invisible world that some sort of major upheaval of a political nature, quite possibly of the most ominous sort, was coming. People detected all sorts of portents which they thought were signs of a forthcoming eruption of violence. Whatever one thinks of such signs, they were taken seriously by large numbers of Liberians and did much to create

107 Author's interviews.

108 François Prkic, 'The Economy of the Liberian Conflict', unpublished paper presented at a conference on Defence, Economics and Security in Mediterranean and Sub-Saharan Countries, Lisbon, 5-6 June 1998.

an atmosphere of tension which could be exploited by some. A series of murders apparently carried out as part of religious rituals intended to secure spiritual support for worldly power and wealth reached 'epidemic proportions', in the opinion of a foreign academic, in August 1989, when an important political trial was taking place in Monrovia.[109] In the same month, a man-eating leopard nightly roamed Tappita, in Nimba County, an area where a young girl had been murdered and mutilated in a presumed ritual killing some months previously.[110] The leopard, regarded as the most dangerous of all animals, is popularly thought to have a spirit which may sometimes possess humans and induce them to commit vile murders. The epidemic of ritual killings was widely discussed by Liberians who took it as evidence that important changes were taking place in the spiritual world. So many people were convinced that some form of spiritual subversion was taking place that the government ordered an expert on occult affairs from the Interior Ministry to carry out an investigation into allegations of witchcraft in Nimba County.[111] Senior officials in Nimba County were reporting suspicious cross-border movements to the security forces.

These portents and rumours of a forthcoming attack were sufficiently serious for Doe's security services to compile a dossier outlining the NPFL's plans to invade the country. In mid-November Doe set up a committee to review all the evidence, with a mandate to report to him after Christmas.[112] It appears that some key officials may in fact have been party to the planned invasion. On 20 December 1989 Stephen Daniels, the superintendent of Nimba County, publicly assured the government that the citizens of Nimba would not 'subvert the government' and appealed to the government to exercise restraint if it heard what he called 'false alarms',[113] which in retrospect appears to have been an exercise in disinformation by a man working in league with the NPFL. The plotters probably had good intelligence from inside the government in Monrovia too. A standard technique of destabilisation in Liberia, and much of the rest of the world for that matter, is to give currency to rumours which will play on people's uncertainties,

[109] Gifford, *Christianity and Politics*, p.31, n.63.

[110] Attes Johnson, Jr., 'Leopard Fear Grips Tappita', *Daily Observer*, 9, 115 (10 August 1989).

[111] *Daily Observer*, 17 August 1989.

[112] Toyin Egunjobi, 'Doe: the complete story', *Newsbreed*, 22 October 1990, p.19.

[113] Africa Watch, *Liberia: Flight from terror: testimony of abuses in Nimba County*, New York, 1990, reprinted in the *Liberian Studies Journal*, XV, 1 (1990), p.144.

a further reason why it is important to record the strange signs which were believed to link the worlds of the visible and the invisible, and which were being so widely discussed and interpreted throughout 1989.

The NPFL, on the eve of its invasion, was more a network of armed dissidents than a political party or a guerrilla army, although it did have a small core military force. It included soldiers, civilians, former politicians, radical intellectuals and others united by little except their dislike of Samuel Doe. One NPFL leader, Tom Woewiyu, was later to maintain that Charles Taylor became the leader of the NPFL only as a result of what he called 'a series of coincidences':[114]

> The NPFL was founded by the late Thomas Quiwonkpa and after the failure of his attempt, it was continued by those of us who felt that we had to continue the struggle until things changed. It could have been led by several other prominent Liberians; it could have been led by myself, Tom Woewiyu; it could have been led by Moses Duopu; it could have been led by Harry Yuan. These are people who were actually there at the resuscitation of the NPFL. Taylor was a part of that and by a series of coincidences, we agreed for him to lead the organisation.

Taylor's key asset was the personal, high-level contacts he had been able to forge in Abidjan, Ouagadougou and Tripoli, which enabled him to secure the international backing the NPFL needed. This he had succeeded in doing where better known Liberian exiles had failed. But while Taylor was the president of the NPFL, he had only modest support among the fighters who emerged from the training camps in Libya and Burkina Faso. Most of them owed their immediate loyalty to their commanders, mainly former AFL officers like Prince Johnson, or to politicians such as Moses Duopu who, like the rank and file of the fighters, were themselves from Nimba County. As for the Liberian public, most had never heard of the NPFL, and the few people who remembered Charles Taylor recalled him for the most part as a crony of Doe and Quiwonkpa who had fled in 1983 with government money in his pocket.

---

[114] Press conference by Tom Woewiyu, Monrovia, July 1994. Reported in Lindsay Barrett, 'Turning the Tables', *West Africa*, 4009 (1 August 1994), pp.1342-4.

2

LEAN AND HUNGRY YEARS

The Nimba County campaign

On 24 December 1989 100 fighters[1] moved over the border from
Côte d'Ivoire to attack government officials and soldiers in the
town of Butuo in Nimba County. Despite the rumours which had
been filling the air, the attack took most Liberians by surprise.
News reached Monrovia during the Christmas holiday, when people
had other things on their minds. A strange story circulated, which
many Monrovians took to be yet another disturbing portent. It
was said that a woman had given birth to a baby which immediately
began to talk in English, predicting that a deadly rain would fall
on Christmas Day. The baby pronounced that it did not wish
to live in such a violent world, at which point 'the precocious
child gave up the ghost and returned to the dead', according
to one Liberian journalist. Consequently 'when the news of the
Butuo attack reached Monrovia, although many were sceptical,
a large number linked the "deadly rain" story with the Nimba
incursion'.[2]

Those who tuned their radios to the BBC World Service's Focus
on Africa, West Africa's favourite news programme, on New Year's
Day, heard Charles Taylor claim the border attack on behalf of
the NPFL and announce that insurgent forces had also penetrated
Monrovia. He said that he had no personal political ambition,
but that the people should take up arms.[3] The NPFL, he said,
was going to get 'that boy Doe off the backs of the Liberian people'.

The NPFL attack was more confused than these bare facts reveal.
Several groups of rebels had infiltrated the country and gone to
pre-arranged points, including in Monrovia, where they expected

---

[1] Charles Taylor claimed that there were 105 'trained commandos'. Justice Minister
Jenkins Scott said there were 96 people in the NPFL's attack-party: *Daily Observer*,
9, 213 (3 January 1990). Later mythology has it that 167 people were trained in
Libya as the core of the NPFL.

[2] Youboty, *Liberian Civil War*, p.5.

[3] Schuster, 'The Final Days of Dr Doe', pp.44-5.

to receive weapons from outside or from contacts in the army. Some had problems crossing from Côte d'Ivoire, and there was a degree of internal rivalry within the NPFL from the start.[4] In addition to the NPFL groups in Nimba County, a separate battle group of some sixty fighters under Cooper Teah, a former AFL officer who had taken part in the 1985 Quiwonkpa coup attempt, had been planning to attack from another point, but Teah had run into problems and was still waiting in Côte d'Ivoire when NPFL forces went into action on Christmas Eve.[5]

Government forces arrested some twenty suspected infiltrators in Monrovia and there was a firefight at a market place in the capital which went unreported on the radio.[6] Then the murders started. On 5 January 1990 the civil engineer Robert Phillips, a member of a leading family who was suspected of involvement in Quiwonkpa's 1985 coup attempt, was found dead at his Monrovia home with his throat slashed. The US Embassy thought this was the work of Doe's Israeli-trained Special Anti-Terrorist Unit.[7] Four days later one David Hukpati was found dead, also with his throat cut. He was last seen alive being escorted by two armed men who had searched his house for weapons.[8] This was the start of a steady stream of murders marked by the appearance of headless corpses in the morning; those bodies that were identifiable were often those of people visited by soldiers or other armed men the previous night. In the next two months the army rounded up hundreds of Gio and Mano civilians in Monrovia, suspecting them by reason of their ethnic origin alone of being potential collaborators with an NPFL advance on the capital,[9] since further north in their home county of Nimba people were joining the NPFL *en masse*, and the rebel group's leaders were known to include Gio and Mano politicians and soldiers. It was clearly the beginning of another ethnic purge by the army of the type already seen in 1983 and 1985. On 22 May three headless bodies were found in the Monrovia suburb of Gardnersville, shirtless, their hands

---

4 Huband, *The Liberian Civil War*, pp.59-62.

5 Author's interviews, Monrovia, 6 April 1997.

6 Schuster, 'The Final Days of Dr Doe', pp.43-4.

7 US Department of State 1990 Human Rights report, quoted in *Liberian Studies Journal*, XVI, 1 (1991), p.117.

8 *Daily Observer*, 9, 219 (11 January 1990).

9 US State Department Human Rights Report for 1990, in *Liberian Studies Journal*, XVI, 1 (1991), pp.117-18.

tied behind their backs.[10] Two weeks later a well-known sculptor and academic, R. Vahnjah Richards, the mayor of Clay-Ashland, was killed with three others by AFL soldiers.[11] Monrovians took to grim humour, greeting each other with remarks like: 'Glad to see you've still got your head'.[12]

The official broadcasting services were giving no hard news of events at the war-front in the north, but only bland assurances that the government had the situation under control. The main sources of information were rumour and the BBC, where Charles Taylor or NPFL Defence Minister Tom Woewiyu were sometimes to be heard making claims of success and imminent victory. In fact, the NPFL was badly organised and poorly armed at least until March 1990, while from as early as January, Prince Johnson's group was acting independently from those under Charles Taylor's orders, but this was not known to the public in Monrovia. By May 1990, foreign nationals were leaving the city in droves as the atmosphere grew tense. Hundreds of Mano and Gio people from Nimba County gathered for protection in the United Nations' compound in Monrovia which, at the end of May, was raided by government soldiers who took some of the displaced people away in two jeeps, killing a UN security guard. Some of those abducted managed to escape, and testified that the party had been taken outside the city where most of them were executed. President Doe subsequently visited the compound 'to sympathise with the victims', promising that he would deal drastically with the culprits.[13] By chance, this was the very same day that delegates from various West African countries were meeting in Gambia under the auspices of the Economic Community of West African States (Ecowas) to debate the Liberian crisis, now of international concern, for the first time. Nigeria was in favour of foreign intervention. Côte d'Ivoire was not, unsurprisingly, since it was backing Charles Taylor and his forces.

Many Monrovians guessed correctly that things were going badly for the AFL at the battlefront in Nimba County. Government forces in the area had responded to the first NPFL attack by detaining suspects, which in practice meant singling out young Gio men for arrest or murder while committing other brutalities in a region

---

[10] *Daily Observer*, 10, 61 (22 May 1990).

[11] *Daily Observer*, 10, 76 (12 June 1990).

[12] Andrews, *Cry, Liberia, Cry!*, p.12.

[13] 'Armed Men Attack Refugees in UNDP Grounds', *Daily Observer*, 10, 68 (31 May 1990).

which the Krahn-dominated military regarded as enemy territory. When the government imposed a curfew throughout Nimba County, thousands of local people fled into Guinea and Côte d'Ivoire, leaving AFL troops to loot the empty towns they found. AFL counter-measures were ineffective since the army was receiving no support from any part of the population in Nimba County other than its Mandingo residents, many of them traders and shopkeepers. Substantial numbers of government soldiers were deserting, some to join the NPFL. AFL soldiers, unable to distinguish NPFL guerrillas among a generally hostile population, could make no headway, even with help from US military advisors. In the first six months of the counter-insurgency campaign, Doe changed the field commander of his forces no less than five times.[14] Charles Julu, with a sinister reputation in Nimba County from 1983 and 1985, was just one of the generals who commanded the battlefront.

Gio citizens of Nimba in particular were joining the NPFL in large numbers and attacking Krahn, whom they regarded, no matter how unjustly, as collectively responsible for the brutality of Doe, and Mandingo, who had made themselves unpopular by profiting from Doe's rule and by acquiring land in Nimba, where they were not considered to have hereditary rights. Anyone considered a collaborator with the Doe government was at risk of attack. At first, many Mano people in Nimba County seem to have been more reluctant to join the rebellion, leading to clashes with the NPFL fighters before Mano elders intervened to reconcile the two. Thereafter, the NPFL began to recruit Mano in numbers as well.[15] NPFL messengers travelled through the rural areas announcing that the NPFL was coming, and that its enemies were Krahn and Mandingo and supporters of the government. The rising was clearly taking the form of an ethnic pogrom.[16] Hatred for the Doe government and those associated with it ran so deep in Nimba County that all the NPFL guerrillas had to do was distribute arms, which they were bringing in from Burkina Faso and Côte d'Ivoire. 'As the NPFL came in', Charles Taylor recalled, 'we didn't even have to act. People came to us and said: "Give me a gun. How can I kill the man who killed my mother?" '[17] 'We all came back', recalled another NPFL leader who had himself

---

[14] Yekutiel Gershoni, 'From Ecowas to Ecomog: the Liberian crisis and the struggle for political hegemony in West Africa', *Liberian Studies Journal*, XVIII, 1 (1993), p.23.

[15] Youboty, *Liberian Civil War*, p.175.

[16] US State Department Human Rights Report for 1990, pp.120-1.

[17] Quoted in Berkeley, 'Repression and Slaughter', p.54.

lost two brothers in one of General Julu's earlier campaigns in Nimba, 'with that revengeful attitude that what was done to us must be done to them to pay the Krahn people back.'[18] At the same time, many of those joining the NPFL seemed more intent on looting than on confronting the AFL soldiers or on slaughtering their supposed enemies, and many Mandingo people were probably killed at least as much because of their status as shopkeepers and traders as on account of any political errors they were deemed to have made. In the first months of the war, both the government forces and the NPFL killed hundreds of people in Nimba County. It was noted that the NPFL was particularly recruiting children as soldiers, many of them war orphans. These were soon organised in special units known as Small Boy Units, who were to prove not only intrepid fighters but also exceptionally loyal to the man they called their father or 'papay', Charles Taylor.[19]

Within a few weeks, the NPFL, consisting of two distinct forces, one under Prince Johnson and the other under Charles Taylor, was pushing out of Nimba County towards Monrovia and the coast, continuing their ethnic purge as they went. Insurgent forces who took the port of Buchanan on 19 May 1990 killed hundreds of Krahn and Mandingo who had taken refuge there.[20] When it broke into Lofa County in July 1990, the NPFL is said to have slaughtered over 500 people at the Mandingo town of Bakedu, an atrocity which was to spark off an ethnic feud within Lofa County which was to have far-reaching consequences. The imam is reported to have been beheaded and his severed head placed on a copy of the Koran.[21]

Prince Johnson's forces were advancing on Monrovia from the north-west, Taylor's from the north and east. By 2 July 1990 they were no more than five miles from the centre of Monrovia. The city's water and electricity supplies had been cut off, and now they cut the phone lines as well. The NPFL also cut the road to Sierra Leone, the last escape route. Within a couple more days, NPFL fighters were in Monrovia itself and had begun looting shops. Casual murders were taking place all over the city. A US diplomat, one of the last to leave under the protection of the 2,000 marines who arrived in warships off the coast of Monrovia while this mayhem

[18] Sam Dokie, quoted in *ibid.*

[19] Human Rights Watch – Africa, *Easy Prey: child soldiers in Liberia*, New York, 1994.

[20] Agence France-Presse despatch, 5 June 1990.

[21] *Weekend Spark* (Freetown), 26 April 1991; author's interviews, Bakedu, 3 April 1997.

went on, saw three soldiers take a fifteen-year old boy from an embassy compound and bayonet him to death in the Peaceland Car Wash.[22] Many of the NPFL fighters were evicting people from houses and painting their names on the outside as the new owners, believing that they could come and take possession of their booty once the fighting was over.

The government was now distributing weapons in its turn, enlisting into the army Krahn and Mandingo civilians who were clamouring for guns to defend themselves. These so-called '1990 soldiers' were particularly undisciplined. On the night of 29-30 July an AFL squad led by a 1990 soldier who had had no military training, a ferocious recruit from Doe's home area whom the President had personally chosen, Captain Tailey Yonbu, attacked St Peter's Lutheran Church in the Sinkor district of Monrovia where about 2,000 refugees were sheltering, mostly Gio and Mano women and children. Beginning around 9 p.m., the slaughter went on all night, continuing as the hapless victims fled into the USAID compound. Some 600 people were massacred in the worst atrocity of the war's first period. So bloodthirsty were the new recruits that an AFL colonel who tried to prevent random killings by his men was himself arrested and murdered at the Executive Mansion on 4 August.[23] Another favourite killing-ground was the waste land at the end of the runway at Spriggs Payne airfield, where journalists later found heaps of unburied corpses, this time probably victims of the NPFL.[24]

Splits in the NPFL

Despite its success in raising the country against Samuel Doe and the army which kept him in power, the NPFL showed signs of splitting from the start of the war. Its two principal military commanders, Prince Johnson and Elmer Johnson – unrelated to each other – both had considerable influence over their respective contingents and developed a tense relationship with the NPFL president, Charles Taylor.

Elmer Johnson was the commander of the NPFL's First Battalion and the organisation's leading strategist. He and Charles Taylor had been close friends in Massachusetts in the 1970s, when Johnson

22 Schuster, 'The Final Days of Dr Doe', p.76.

23 Africa Watch, *A Human Rights Disaster,* New York, 1990. Reprinted in *Liberian Studies Journal,* XVI, 1 (1991), pp.141-2.

24 *Ibid.,* pp.139-41.

was studying at Boston University and Taylor was taking a degree at Bentley College. Johnson, from a leading Americo-Liberian family, had subsequently become a professional soldier in both the Liberian army and the US marines, taking part in the 1983 US invasion of Grenada. He lost an eye in a failed coup attempt against Doe in 1984, after which he had gone to join the NPFL group training in Libya. By the middle of 1990, Taylor was alarmed by reports that Elmer Johnson, popular with the NPFL rank and file, was putting his troops through constant training in an effort to instil some discipline. 'Taylor called me up and complained that reports were being received from the frontline that Elmer was training his own men with the ambition to over-run Monrovia, and seize the seat of goverment ahead of him', NPFL Defence Minister Tom Woewiyu later claimed.[25] Elmer Johnson was killed in an ambush near Buchanan on 4 June 1990. Although government armed forces claimed responsibility, the most detailed accounts of his death gave rise to a rumour that he was in fact murdered on Taylor's orders.[26]

Taylor also had an uneasy relationship with Elmer's namesake, Prince Johnson, commander of the NPFL's elite force, known as the Special Forces or the Black Scorpions. Johnson was born in Nimba County in 1952 but had been brought up by an uncle in Monrovia and had joined the army in 1971, since when his life had been that of the barracks.[27] He had risen to be a junior officer with the AFL where he served with Quiwonkpa, a Gio like himself, and had taken part in the 1985 coup attempt. Fleeing to Côte d'Ivoire after Quiwonkpa's death, he was one of those invited to proceed to Burkina Faso and Libya for further military training, and he became the NPFL's chief military instructor. The bulk of the Libyan and Burkinabe trainees who entered Liberia at the beginning of the war were under his direct command. He and Taylor had already had differences while they were in Libya, and as early as February 1990, Prince Johnson was refusing to take orders from the NPFL president,[28] according to Johnson himself because Taylor had objected to his execution of twelve men for theft and desertion.[29] Johnson had been trained in military

[25] Interview with Tom Woewiyu in *New Democrat* (Monrovia), 1, 41 (1-7 September 1994), p.14.

[26] Obituary in *Le Monde* (Paris), 11 June 1990; Huband, *The Liberian Civil War*, pp.84-5, 111-12.

[27] Eric Schmitt, 'A Foe to be Feared', *New York Times*, 11 September 1990.

[28] Africa Watch, *A Human Rights Disaster*, p.133.

[29] Interview with Prince Johnson, Reuters despatch, 30 July 1990.

82   *Lean and Hungry Years*

police duties in South Carolina, USA, and was a stern, often
draconian, disciplinarian. A further dispute arose in April, after
Taylor had ordered the execution of some NPFL troops following
a military reverse.[30]

By May, it was clear that Taylor's and Prince Johnson's forces
were effectively under two separate chains of command. The administrator of Cuttington University College noticed this when
he got his first sight of the NPFL forces who arrived at his campus
near Gbarnga in May 1990 and established a training camp.[31]
Within a couple more weeks, there were reports of sporadic clashes
between Prince Johnson's Special Forces and Taylor's NPFL irregulars – the hundreds of civilians who had joined the NPFL in
its campaign since the start of the year – notably after Johnson
had taken the valuable Bong iron mines in June.[32] Prince Johnson
himself accused Taylor of killing his mother and other family
members in pursuit of this vendetta.[33] According to public rumour,
the reason behind this accusation was that 'Taylor feared that
Johnson was becoming more and more powerful by the spiritual
and ritualistic help of Johnson's mother and that eliminating her
was the only course open to him to demoralise Johnson'.[34]

Johnson had almost all of the trained fighters under his command. Taylor had mainly new civilian recruits. He could rely on
the fanatical support of the Small Boy Units and also had under
his direct control a force of regular troops from Burkina Faso
supplied by President Compaore, as well as the sprinkling of in-
ternationalist revolutionaries from Gambia, Ghana, Nigeria and
elsewhere whom he had recruited in the Libyan and Burkinabe
training camps. The most prominent of these foreigners was Kukoi
Samba Sanyang, a leader of the 1981 coup attempt in Gambia.
Sanyang, using the pseudonym Dr Sarjo Manneh or Dr Manning,
was described on his visiting card as vice-president of the NPFL.
He took command of the port of Buchanan after the NPFL had
overrun it in May 1990, before retiring the following year to
Ouagadougou, the capital of Burkina Faso, after losing his influence
in the NPFL. From Taylor's point of view, the advantage offered
by Sanyang and the other Gambians was not only their military

30 Youboty, *Liberian Civil War*, pp.196-7.

31 Henrique F. Tokpa, 'Cuttington University College during the Liberian Civil
War: an administrator's experience', *Liberian Studies Journal*, XVI, 1 (1991), p.87.

32 *Ibid.*, p.90.

33 Huband, *The Liberian Civil War*, p.171.

34 Brehun, *War of Horror*, p.28.

experience but also their lack of family and personal connections in Liberia, which reduced the chances of them owing allegiance to any rival leader. Taylor also enjoyed extensive financial support from some prominent Americo-Liberians who had fled abroad after the coup of 1980 or who had fallen out with Doe later on and who saw in Charles Taylor someone who could restore them to their former position.[35] He was able to project himself to the public as the leader of the NPFL thanks to his satellite-phone and his skilful use of the media, especially the BBC's Africa service. Prince Johnson admitted that Taylor had far more professionals and educated people on his side than he himself did. When Johnson captured a former vice-president of the Republic, Peter Naigow, he told his prisoner, 'you are the first bookman I have arrested. Charles Taylor has all the other book people. I am a fighter.' Johnson added, 'I want you to help me put some ideas together on the economic and political side of this thing'.[36]

Many of Liberia's professional politicians and technocrats, 'book men' in popular parlance, particularly those living in exile, welcomed the NPFL invasion, at least in the early stages, seeing it as the only means of ridding the country of Doe. Many of the generation of 'progressive' politicians who had served the PRC military junta in the early 1980s had gone into exile and had been canvassing for foreign support for his overthrow. They were all more or less aware of the role Taylor had played in building up support.[37] With the NPFL seemingly heading for victory by mid-1990, exiled Liberians of substance opened lines of communication to Taylor. Some gave him money and others sent messages of support. Ellen Johnson Sirleaf, based in the United States and later to be Africa director of the United Nations Development Programme, admitted giving 'moral support' to the NPFL but denied allegations that she also provided cash.[38] In July, a jubilant Taylor rang Ellen Johnson Sirleaf to tell her that Jackson F. Doe, probably the most popular of all Liberian politicians, had left Monrovia and crossed to NPFL territory. Jackson Doe had not

[35] George Klay Kieh, 'Combatants, Patrons, Peacemakers and the Liberian Civil Conflict', *Studies in Conflict and Terrorism*, 15 (1992), p.130.

[36] Interview with Peter Naigow in *West Africa*, 3879 (20 January 1992), pp.102-3.

[37] Charles Taylor interview with Baffour Ankomah, *Ghanaian Chronicle* (Accra), 12-18 Oct. 1992; cf. Tom Kamara, 'Charles Taylor: the true story', *New African* (London), July 1991.

[38] ' "I Never Gave Taylor One Cent" ', *The Inquirer* (Monrovia), 1, 108 (9 December 1991).

joined the NPFL as such, but his presence in territory controlled by the NPFL obviously lent great weight to the movement.

The rallying of so many political heavyweights to the NPFL was not unalloyed good news for Taylor, however. The NPFL was in the suburbs of Monrovia and was on the verge of victory and Taylor saw the presidency within his grasp. But many Liberians thought that Jackson F. Doe had been the rightful winner of the 1985 elections which Samuel Doe had rigged. In any free political competition, Jackson Doe would surely emerge as a favourite for the presidency of Liberia, the more so as he was more acceptable to the US government than was Taylor himself. A very experienced politician, Jackson Doe was a Nimba County man like a whole string of NPFL leaders and, more significantly, like the bulk of the NPFL fighters.

When Cooper Teah arrived in NPFL territory with some sixty-four Libyan-trained special forces, the group which had been left behind at the beginning of the war, Taylor became increasingly worried about the line-up of forces inside the NPFL. Some long-standing NPFL organisers who had already clashed with Taylor in Libya were openly challenging his position as president of the NPFL. The NPFL secretary general Moses Duopu publicly made known his view that the NPFL was run by an Executive Council which should meet to choose the next president, and Duopu announced that he would be a candidate for this position.[39] In previous weeks Taylor had told several foreign journalists of his personal attachment to capitalism, even describing himself to the London *Financial Times* as 'a cold-blooded capitalist', presumably as a means of ingratiating himself with the US government and business interests. Moses Duopu seized on this remark to campaign against recognition of Taylor as the president-in-waiting of Liberia.[40]

Moses Duopu was killed in June 1990. Some alleged that this was on Taylor's orders, but conclusive evidence is lacking. With Elmer Johnson already dead, this sent an alarm throughout the senior ranks of the NPFL. Prince Johnson used his first serious contacts with foreign journalists in July to announce that he was setting up a new faction called the Independent National Patriotic Front of Liberia, consisting mostly of his Special Forces who had already taken control of the port and some other parts of Monrovia. This was officially launched on 24 July 1990. Prince Johnson, himself no sort of politician, would almost certainly have supported Jackson

---

[39] Agence France-Presse despatch, 7 June 1990.

[40] Mobolade Omonijo, *Doe: the Liberian tragedy*, Ikeja, Nigeria, 1990, p.29.

F. Doe in any competition for the presidency of the country. Taylor's fear was that with the arrival of Cooper Teah's men, and Prince Johnson's declaration of independence, Jackson Doe would have the military as well as the political backing to have himself installed as president.

The NPFL Defence Minister, Tom Woewiyu, later recalled Jackson Doe's fate:[41]

> Jackson Doe was not captured in combat, he walked over to our side, led by some of our fighters joyously to Kakata where there was a very very big festival in the middle of the war to celebrate that a leader of our people had been saved; a leader who [President Samuel] Doe wanted dead was saved. He was escorted to Harbel to Mr. Taylor. He was received. At the time I was in Sierra Leone. Taylor informed me that Jackson Doe was with him and that I should inform Amos Sawyer, Ellen Johnson-Sirleaf and all the politicians that Jackson Doe was safe, only for me to arrive in Harbel one week later and he could not tell me where Jackson Doe was.

Woewiyu and others have made detailed allegations that Jackson Doe was assassinated, 'slaughtered with a bayonet and his blood taken to Taylor'. Woewiyu also claimed that Taylor personally drank the blood of his murdered rival.[42] An eye-witness later confirmed that Jackson Doe was actually beheaded.[43] Others whom Woewiyu says were murdered on Taylor's orders were Cooper Teah and his group, Gabriel Kpolleh, also a leading politician, and a string of others.[44] All of those named by Woewiyu were people who could have mounted or supported a challenge to Taylor. In short, it is clear that, between June and August 1990, there was a series of assassinations of key figures behind NPFL lines, perhaps of eighty people in all, including Cooper Teah's group. This purge removed all of Taylor's most dangerous rivals except Prince Johnson, who had set up on his own.

While these deaths were instrumental in strengthening Taylor's grip on the NPFL, they were not widely known at the time. International attention was focussed on the thousands of other killings

[41] 'Transcript of Statement by Hon. Tom Woewiyu, Minister of Labor, Liberia National Transitional Government, Delivered in Monrovia July 19, 1994', *Liberian Studies Journal*, XIX, 2 (1994), pp.342-7.

[42] Interview with anonymous source [later revealed as Tom Woewiyu], 'Jackson Doe's Death', *New Democrat*, 1, 30 (23-29 June 1994).

[43] Donald Johnson, quoted in *West Africa*, 3841 (15 April 1991), p.560.

[44] 'Jackson Doe's Death', *New Democrat*, 1, 30 (23-9 June 1994).

which had taken place in public, sometimes before the world's
news cameras, during the NPFL's advance on Monrovia. This
mayhem was causing alarm all over West Africa, as was the exodus
of some 700,000 refugees from Liberia during the year. The NPFL's
international connections were well known to West African intelligence
agencies and some governments were particularly concerned by
the presence in its ranks of Libyan-trained revolutionaries like
Samba Sanyang. The governments of Nigeria, Gambia, Ghana and
Sierra Leone were worried that a victory for Charles Taylor would
lead to Liberia becoming a new base for Libyan-backed destabilisation. Nigeria's General Babangida, one of Doe's last friends in
the world, was particularly concerned. In April 1990, while the
NPFL was advancing on Monrovia, he was himself the victim of
a domestic coup attempt which came close to success.[45] Babangida
argued the case for foreign intervention in Liberia, using Ecowas,
in principle an economic forum, to gather diplomatic support,
and it is likely that Nigeria actually supplied weapons to Doe even
as he was being encircled.[46] In retaliation, Taylor ordered the
NPFL to detain all Nigerian citizens as hostages on the grounds
that 'President Babangida of Nigeria was not only suspected but
also accused of backing and supporting President Doe's side of
the conflict'.[47]

At this point, in mid-1990, all the English-speaking governments
in the region, and almost certainly most Liberians, would have
accepted a US intervention to halt the war, and probably France
would have persuaded the Ivorian government to swallow it too.
In the event, the US marine force anchored off Monrovia in the
middle of the year evacuated US and some other foreign nationals
but did not intervene in the war. At a crucial point, on 1-2 August
1990, something happened elsewhere in the world which took
up all America's attention and definitely ruled out any possibility
of US intervention in Liberia: Iraq invaded Kuwait.

After this it was the Nigerian military government which took
up the challenge to find a regional solution to the Liberian conflict
with a green light from Washington. On 7 August an Ecowas committee meeting, under Nigerian pressure, voted for intervention.
An expeditionary force was rapidly assembled at Freetown in Sierra
Leone. The Ecomog force which landed in Monrovia on 24 August
1990 was largely composed of Nigerian soldiers and was perceived

---

[45] 'Nigeria: more questions than answers', *Africa Confidential*, 31, 10 (18 May 1990),
pp.2-4.

[46] Vogt and Ekoko, *Nigeria in International Peace-Keeping*, pp.200-1.

[47] Brehun, *War of Horror*, p.48.

to be acting largely in Nigerian interests. There was a notable absence of French-speaking support, and the government of Burkina Faso even went to the extent of trying to block Ecomog's deployment by diplomatic means. Charles Taylor, himself reliant on Burkinabe and Ivorian support and believing that it was only a matter of time before power fell into his hands, was furious at Ecomog's intervention, which placed a new obstacle between himself and the presidency. He vowed to fight Ecomog. He had been treating all Nigerian nationals as enemies for months already, and he now began a systematic campaign of taking nationals of other Ecomog countries as hostages, threatening that for each NPFL fighter killed by Ecomog, he would kill ten Ecomog nationals.[48] He issued a stream of vile radio propaganda against the Nigerian government, accusing President Babangida of being 'a black Hitler'.

In July 1990 Taylor had seemed on the verge of success. His forces were in Monrovia, and the United States was doing nothing to stop his advance. Jackson F. Doe and anyone else who could possibly pre-empt his elevation to the presidency were disappearing from view. Just seven weeks later his hopes were to be dashed by the emergence of Prince Johnson as an independent candidate, the arrival of Ecomog, and the murder of Samuel Doe. Taylor was left in control of Liberia but excluded from the capital city.

Greater and Lesser Liberia

After Doe's murder in the early hours of 10 September 1990, the Ecomog Force Commander General Quainoo retired, to be replaced at the head of the international force by a Nigerian, Major-General Joshua Dogonyaro.[49] The new commander acted with exemplary decisiveness. He secured control of Monrovia and, having been attacked by the NPFL, he used aircraft and artillery to force Taylor's forces out of the city. For the first time, Taylor began to favour diplomatic activity in preference to military action, in an attempt to freeze the situation on the ground. Within Monrovia, Dogonyaro presided over the installation of the Interim Government of National Unity, a puppet government of Liberian politicians under Professor Amos Sawyer, and succeeded in disarming Prince Johnson's INPFL and getting the remnants of Doe's Armed Forces of Liberia back to barracks. The Nigerian general

---

[48] E. John Inegbedion, 'Ecomog in Comparative Perspective' in Timothy G. Shaw and Julius Emeka Okolo (eds), *The Political Economy of Foreign Policy in Ecowas*, London, 1994, pp.218-44.

[49] Above, p.15.

encouraged international aid organisations to return to Monrovia
and feed its population, repaired the essential infrastructure and
cleaned up the corpses littering the streets. Appreciating the value
of the media, for the first time he was able to contest Taylor's
dominance of the air-waves. But the Nigerian government recalled
Dogonyaro on 27 February 1991.[50]

Why the Nigerian government withdrew Dogonyaro when he
was making such clear military progress remains unclear. Possibly
it believed that a more conciliatory field commander could
negotiate peace with Taylor. More probably, President Babangida,
strongly opposed to Taylor, realised that a negotiated peace was
most likely to result in confirmation of his enemy as president
of Liberia, but at the same time Babangida was unwilling to launch
Nigerian and Ecomog forces on a full-scale military campaign to
defeat the NPFL. Moreover, Babangida was not immune from
the tendency of so many West African presidents who, having
taken power by force, can hardly afford any of their subordinates
to build potential power-bases of their own, such as Dogonyaro
might have done had he been allowed to proceed with a successful
campaign in Liberia. Babangida's compromise solution was to hold
Monrovia and support the puppet IGNU government while
negotiating a ceasefire with the NPFL in an attempt to calm the
situation, from which position Ecomog could work at weakening
the NPFL over the longer term. There were already signs that
some Nigerian officers were developing vested interests in staying
in Monrovia for a long time. Dogonyaro's successive Nigerian re-
placements as Ecomog Field Commander, both military engineers
rather than infantrymen, followed a policy of mediation, decreeing
a ceasefire, visiting Taylor in his own territory, and even trading
with the NPFL.[51] A tortuous round of international diplomacy
now replaced fighting as the chief means by which the warring
parties struggled for advantage.

Charles Taylor, enraged by Ecomog for denying him the military
victory which had been within his grasp, adapted quickly to the
situation by setting up a parallel government in the area under
his control, which he called Greater Liberia. Monrovia housed
the rump of the Liberian state, nominally under Sawyer's Interim
Government. Officials in Monrovia continued to go about their
work as best they could while the real power lay with Ecomog,
and particularly the Nigerian contingent. Only in Grand Gedeh

[50] Agetua, *Operation Liberty,* pp.59-110.

[51] 'A Tale of Seven Field Commanders', *The National* (Monrovia), 1, 24 (16 August
1996), p.8, culled from the Nigerian *National Concord.*

County, home territory of the Krahn, was there persistent fighting as the NPFL faced a locally-based resistance movement.[52] Many Krahn who had been in Monrovia until mid-1990 headed for Sierra Leone, where large numbers of Mandingo refugees had already gathered, before the NPFL cut the road. By October 1990, just a month after Doe's murder, there were already rumours that some exiled Liberian politicians and soldiers living in Freetown were recruiting among the Krahn and Mandingo refugees in Sierra Leone with a view to organising a military force which could counter-attack the NPFL from bases in Sierra Leone.[53]

While Taylor was waiting to make a final assault on Monrovia, he was building an impressive personal fief. All roads in NPFL territory, the greater part of Liberia, were sealed with numerous check-points where travellers were liable to be stopped and in-terrogated and have their goods looted by those on duty. Many Monrovians derive some of their worst memories of the war from the period in mid-to-late 1990, when the NPFL was establishing itself outside the city. All over its territory, the NPFL set up check-points known as 'gates' along the road, usually consisting of a piece of rope stretched between two poles, manned by gun-toting NPFL fighters, sometimes no more than children. Often these check-points were decorated with ghastly trophies such as human skulls. The most notorious gates acquired sinister nicknames. The US embassy estimated that at one NPFL check-point known as 'No Return', no fewer than 2,000 people were killed in the course of 1990, their bodies often remaining unburied in the surrounding bush.[54] No one would touch them for fear of being considered a government collaborator. The few travellers who could move freely were Gio and Mano people, overwhelmingly supporters of the NPFL, who soon acquired control of local trade.[55]

Taylor, although consumed more than ever by an ambition to become President of Liberia, learned rapidly that there were significant advantages in being the leader of an unofficial Greater Liberia. He had developed relations with leading Ivorian, French and Lebanese business people in Abidjan before the war, and once he had taken control of the port of Buchanan in May 1990 he discovered that these and other traders were not averse to doing business with the new Liberian strong man. For those with

[52] Africa Watch, *The Cycle of Abuse,* pp.130-9.

[53] 'Liberia: waiting in the wings', *Africa Confidential,* 31, 20 (12 October 1990).

[54] US State Department Human Rights Report for 1990, pp.120-1.

[55] Africa Watch, *The Cycle of Abuse,* p.137.

established interests in Liberia, such as the rubber company Firestone or the Liberian Minerals Company which ran the iron ore mines in Nimba County, it was imperative to restart production and export their products. Since the NPFL now controlled virtually the whole country outside Monrovia, they had every incentive to deal with Taylor. Newer arrivals, particularly in the logging business, also discovered the attractions of the NPFL. Taylor proved himself a shrewd negotiator who liked to discuss matters personally with leading foreign business people, which meant a minimum of time-wasting bureaucracy. He would grant a licence to operate in return for personal payment of tax in US dollars. With the income from these business deals, Taylor was able to procure weapons from the former Warsaw Pact countries, where arms of all sorts could be got for bargain prices, which he imported through Côte d'Ivoire and via Burkina Faso.[56] He was free to use his money for military purposes or to mediate political relationships, while he kept the balance in accounts in Abidjan, Ouagadougou and elsewhere. Sometimes, Taylor would ask his foreign business partners to write out cheques to pay various bills or to perform other services on behalf of the NPFL in lieu of taxes. Many of Taylor's business managers lived in Abidjan, where they held regular gatherings at a well known restaurant, *La Maison blanche*. One was a leading arms-purchaser, another a timber magnate exporting through the Ivorian port of San Pedro, a third was Taylor's main legal advisor, a son of the former Chief Justice of the Supreme Court of Liberia, one of those executed by Doe in April 1980.[57]

From late 1990 Taylor was able to generate a vast income by his control of Greater Liberia, despite the fact that it was a state unrecognised by the international community. US Ambassador William Twaddell, testifying to the Africa sub-committee of the US House of Representatives in 1996, reckoned that between 1990 and 1994, Liberia's diamond exports averaged $300 million per year; timber exports $53 million; rubber exports $27 million; and gold exports $1 million. Iron ore exported from 1990-1993 averaged $41 million annually. Taking these figures into account, he estimated that 'Charles Taylor, who has long controlled the most lucrative areas of the countryside, could have upwards of $75 million a year passing through his hands' as a result of taxes levied on

[56] William Reno, 'Foreign Firms and the Financing of Charles Taylor's NPFL', *Liberian Studies Journal*, XVIII, 2 (1993), p.181.

[57] 'Taylor's Cabinet in Côte d'Ivoire', *West Africa*, 3940 (29 March 1993), p.503; for a general survey, François Prkic, 'The Economy of the Liberian Conflict', unpublished.

these trades.[58] The finance and justice ministers in the Interim Government in Monrovia estimated Taylor's income at over $100 million a year.[59] It is notable that these figures did not include the income from marijuana, grown in northern Liberia and exported in containers via Buchanan and the Ivorian port of San Pedro.[60] Meanwhile, the Interim Government headed by Professor Sawyer, the only one which had some formal international recognition, was heir to debts of up to $3 billion, which it had to manage with a paltry income of little more than perhaps $20 million per year, three-quarters of which was derived from fees paid on the international fleet of Liberian-registered ships.[61]

Taylor's great wealth enabled him to pay salaries to some of his military commanders and to distribute cars and other largesse to senior officials in the area he called Greater Liberia, but most of his soldiers had to survive on bribes and plunder. Taylor was shrewd enough to seek the support of clan chiefs and other local leaders where possible, so that daily life continued with some degree of normality in much of his territory after the disruption caused by the first months of war. A senior Senegalese politician who visited Greater Liberia in October 1990 thought it well-organised.[62] Some foreign businessmen operating in Taylor's Greater Liberia in 1991 thought conditions better than they had been for a number of years. In interviews, foreign businessmen recalled almost nostalgically how they could sort out problems by going straight to the local NPFL army commander or military police commander. Some claimed that it was possible to drive right across the country with cash provided that taxes had been paid to Taylor.[63] Two banks opened in Gbarnga, Bong Bank and Grand Bank, both headed by a former governor of the National Bank of Liberia. Other businesspeople may have found circumstances less easy, especially later in the war, like the American gold and diamond-buyer Robert Hoff, killed by an anti-NPFL group in Greater Liberia. After 1994 particularly, Taylor's territory was to be subject to

[58] Testimony by Ambassador William H. Twaddell, reproduced in *The Inquirer* (Monrovia), 5, 55 (13 August 1996), pp.2-4.

[59] Philip Banks and S. Byron Tarr, 'A Negotiated Settlement: our only way out: A rejoinder', *Liberian Studies Journal,* XVIII, 2 (1993), p.275.

[60] Observatoire Géopolitique des Drogues, *Atlas mondial des drogues,* Paris, 1996, p.159.

[61] *Marchés tropicaux et méditerranéens,* 2594 (28 July 1995), pp.1603-5.

[62] Kaye Whiteman, 'The New Democracy', *West Africa,* 3819 (5 November 1990), p.2787.

[63] Author's interview with two expatriate businessmen, Monrovia, 24 July 1994.

widespread disturbances as NPFL troops in some areas took to wholesale looting of the towns they occupied.

The extent of Greater Liberia in its heyday of 1990-2, and Taylor's success in recruiting experienced managers and technocrats, including many who had previously worked for Doe, enabled him to appoint a full range of ministers and officials. Taylor established his executive mansion and government in Gbarnga, the capital of Bong County, strategically situated in the middle of Liberia. It is debatable how many of the ministers and director-generals of Taylor's provisional government actually ran much in the way of real departments, other than those responsible for security and military matters or those business managers who were answerable directly to Taylor himself. Taylor decreed a minimum wage for workers in the logging business of two US dollars a day, more than they had been getting before, although according to some sources this was paid to Taylor's Forestry Development Authority rather than to the loggers themselves. The diamond and gold trade was the preserve of a handful of close aides, including his brother Nelson Taylor.

Taylor, more than most of his rival warlords, was also adept at mass political communication of a sort which reminded some observers of the old True Whig Party style. One Liberian who crossed over from Taylor-land to Monrovia in 1991 said that NPFL fighters told the Kru fishermen on the coast 'that every fish in the ocean belonged to the CIC [Taylor]'.[64] Travellers to Taylor's capital at Gbarnga noticed growing signs of a personality cult. An American journalist visiting in 1992 saw hundreds of placards of Taylor displayed, the most recent ones showing just his face and the single word 'Ghankay' underneath.[65] This was a Gola word meaning 'strong' or 'stubborn', adopted by Taylor as a praise name designed to emphasise his indigenous roots. The man who in his youth had been proud to call himself Charles MacArthur Taylor began to claim that his mother was in fact a Gola woman, and he made efforts to learn an African language for the first time in his life, although by all accounts he has never really succeeded.

Many of Taylor's closest aides were foreigners, including the Gambian revolutionaries, or they were Americo-Liberians. Many of his bodyguards were Burkinabe. Beyond this commercial and military core, he distributed jobs and largesse to maintain an ethnic

---

[64] Quoted in Africa Watch, *The Cycle of Abuse,* p.136.

[65] Report by Kenneth Noble, *New York Times,* 14 April 1992.

and regional balance of support, in the usual fashion of West African politicians. The crucial Liberian-Ivorian border crossing was under the command of a Gambian, Mustapha Jalloh, a fluent speaker of French and Spanish, the latter acquired during a stay in Cuba. Jalloh, known in Liberia by the pseudonym General Kolleh, sometimes claimed that, as a revolutionary rather than a soldier, he was personally uncomfortable with the title of general. One of Taylor's main connections in Abidjan was a French businessman, Robert Saint-Pai, who had lived in Monrovia before the war and was friendly with leading Ivorian businessmen and politicians. Saint-Pai also enjoyed access to the French ambassador in Abidjan, Michel Dupuch, who visited both Gbarnga and Buchanan and developed close links to Taylor. Dupuch was later promoted to become the principal advisor on African affairs to the President of France.[66] The German ambassador to Sierra Leone and a South Korean ambassador also visited the capital of Taylor-land at Gbarnga.

The conquest of Greater Liberia, combined with his drive to dominate trade, soon brought Taylor into contact with social networks and informal trade routes which traversed Liberia's borders and brought opportunities for extending his influence on foreign territory. Taylor went on the offensive outside the country. He had long sought revenge against President Momoh of Sierra Leone, who had slighted Taylor personally when he was seeking support for the launch of the war and had provided a base for the Ecomog expeditionary force in 1990. Renewing his acquaintance with the Sierra Leonean rebels of the Revolutionary United Front (RUF) whom he had met in Libya and Burkina Faso, Taylor threatened Sierra Leoneans in a radio broadcast that they too would 'taste the bitterness of war'. In March 1991 he sent some of the toughest units of his armed forces to accompany a group from the RUF over the border to Sierra Leone, where they attacked villages in the diamond-rich districts around Koindu, a major centre of international trade visited by trucks from as far afield as Côte d'Ivoire, Mali and Senegal.[67] The RUF was soon able to establish permanent headquarters inside Sierra Leone under the leadership of Foday Sankoh, the Sierra Leonean ex-army corporal whom Taylor had known for some years. This war was soon to develop a logic of its own, although it remained connected to the conflict in Liberia.[68]

Even though Ecomog had prevented the NPFL from capturing

---

[66] Agir Ici-Survie, *Jacques Chirac et la Françafrique. Retour à la case Foccart?*, Paris, 1995, p.24.

[67] William Reno, *Corruption and State Politics in Sierra Leone,* Cambridge, 1995, p.147.

[68] Abdallah, 'Bush Path to Destruction', *Journal of Modern African Studies.*

Monrovia, Liberia's war had been exported to another West African
state. The Nigerian government's great fear had now been realised.

New factions

Throughout 1990, Mandingo refugees were fleeing from Liberia
to Guinea, which many regarded as their historic homeland since
it was the home of the Malinke people, and to Sierra Leone,
where many Krahn refugees had also gathered. Leading Liberian
politicians, soldiers and businessmen in exile immediately began
discussing how to organise themselves to get back home. In Conakry,
Alhaji Kromah, a professional journalist and one-time information
minister, founded an association grandiloquently titled the Movement for the Redemption of Muslims (MRM), on 21 February
1991. Although Kromah was himself married to a Christian woman
from a prominent Americo-Liberian family, and had been educated
at a Catholic school,[69] he hoped that by emphasising his Muslim
religion he could rally support from Guinea and, perhaps, finance
from the Middle East. His organisation's executive committee of
thirteen consisted of eight Mandingo and five others. He called
on Muslims to launch a *jihad* against the NPFL, which he accused
of being anti-Muslim, by reference to its recent persecution of
Mandingo.[70]

The MRM issued a stream of inflammatory propaganda, claiming
that Muslims were the 'single most victimised group in the whole
conflict'[71] and that the NPFL had burned more than 1,000 mosques.
and Islamic schools,[72] although Taylor had recently announced
full liberty of worship in Greater Liberia. Kromah could in fact
count only a few fighters in his organisation. Most Liberian exiles
who were disposed to fight the NPFL, including many Mandingo,
preferred to join a rival group which was being set up by former
AFL personnel, some of whom had had US and Israeli training.
The main organiser of this second, more formidable, exile group
was General Albert Karpeh, a US-trained special forces officer and
former minister of defence in Liberia, who had been Doe's last
ambassador to Sierra Leone. On hearing of the RUF/NPFL attack

[69] Interview with Alhaji Kromah in *West Africa*, 4082 (15 January 1996), pp.65-7.

[70] Augustine Konneh, 'Indigenous Entrepreneurs and Capitalists: the role of the
Mandingo in the economic development of modern-day Liberia' (Ph.D. thesis,
Indiana University, 1992), pp.476-7.

[71] Quoted in *Weekend Spark* (Freetown), 26 April 1991.

[72] Associated Press despatch, 8 April 1991.

on Sierra Leone on 23 March 1991, General Karpeh, a Krahn, offered his support immediately to the Sierra Leonean government, promising the services of the many AFL veterans and other Liberians now living as refugees in Sierra Leone, many of them Krahn and Mandingo. He called his group the Liberian United Defense Force (LUDF).

Kromah, seeing that Karpeh was attracting significant support including weapons from the Sierra Leonean government, proposed to join forces with Karpeh and with an organisation called the Liberia Peace Council, headed by George Boley, another ex-minister under Doe. Kromah claimed to have far more Mandingo fighters under his command in Guinea than was actually the case, hoping to get himself a leadership position in the new organisation, whereas many Mandingo refugees had actually joined Karpeh's new force already.[73] Karpeh and the other Krahn warlords gave Kromah only the post of spokesman, in deference to his journalistic skills. Encouraged by the governments in Freetown and Conakry, these elements combined to form the United Liberation Movement for Democracy in Liberia (Ulimo). The new organisation, officially launched in Conakry on 29 May 1991, was a direct result of Karpeh's offer of assistance to the Freetown government some two months earlier.[74]

While Ecowas and the NPFL engaged in an endless round of peace negotations, and Charles Taylor set up his state of Greater Liberia, on the ground in Sierra Leone and Liberia both sides were developing a war by proxy. The NPFL was acting through the RUF in Sierra Leone, while Ulimo, with support from the Freetown government and the Nigerian army, mounted a sustained offensive against the RUF/NPFL forces in company with Sierra Leonean army units. By September 1991, the LUDF wing of Ulimo had re-entered Liberia in some numbers and was getting support from the Nigerian, Sierra Leonean and Guinean contingents of Ecomog.[75] Alhaji Kromah, proclaiming himself to be the leader of the Mandingo element in Ulimo, began using his access to the media to represent himself as the real force behind the organisation, much as Taylor had done so successfully when acquiring full control of the NPFL in 1990, and to work at creating an

[73] Author's interview with chief imam Sheikh Kafumba Konneh, Monrovia, 21 March 1997.

[74] James Butty, 'What Does Ulimo Want?', *West Africa*, 3912 (7 September 1992), p.1519.

[75] Reuters despatch, 7 September 1991.

ethnic split within Ulimo calculated to win over to his faction, which was otherwise short of manpower, the considerable number of Mandingo fighters who had hitherto been loyal to a Krahn, General Karpeh. Ulimo's Krahn warlords became irritated by Kromah's self-serving statements. After General Karpeh had complained, some associates of Kromah arranged for Karpeh's murder at his house in Kenema, Sierra Leone, on 1 June 1992, failing narrowly to kill Ulimo's deputy field commander, Roosevelt Johnson, on the same day.[76] Karpeh's murder set off an intense and increasingly violent rivalry between Kromah's faction and the Krahn-led group within Ulimo, each cultivating its own allies in the Sierra Leonean armed forces. In September 1992 a senior Mandingo commander, Major Solomon Kamara, a former tailor and noted soccer player from Nimba County, was killed by the Krahn faction, it is said after refusing a $3,000 bribe to desert Kromah and join the former Karpeh group, in which Roosevelt Johnson was now a rising star.[77] Once more, rival warlords were using ethnic appeals as a means of building support.

At stake in this in-fighting was not only control of a potent military force, since Ulimo had inherited hundreds of trained veterans of Doe's army, but also access to the valuable diamond and hardwood trades which could be exploited by whomever occupied lands along the Sierra Leone-Liberia border. Roosevelt Johnson, a former Liberian Ministry of Finance official, and some of his Krahn associates had successfully negotiated some diamond deals with French and Lebanese merchants, breaking into a traditional Mandingo trade, and they were paying off the top Sierra Leonean army commanders who were arming them.[78] At the same time, in 1991 the Guinean army began secretly training Ulimo personnel from the Kromah faction at Kankan in Guinea. A key intermediary was the Mandingo Alhaji Nonko Cheriff, once a diamond-dealer in Monrovia, now established at Kissidougou in Guinea.[79] The political, commercial and military rivalry within Ulimo grew increasingly acrimonious until it produced a public split into two factions in April 1994, one controlled by Kromah and his Mandingo colleagues and generally called Ulimo-K, which had good connections

[76] *The Inquirer,* 3 June 1992.

[77] *The Inquirer,* 7 October 1992; Roosevelt Johnson's own account is published in a two-part interview in *West Africa,* 4147 and 4148 (28 April, 5 May 1997), pp.681-2, 715-7.

[78] Bai M. Gbala, 'Gbala on Ulimo's Ethnic Feud', *New Democrat,* 1, 30 (23-9 April 1994); *The Inquirer,* 28 July, 28 September, 30 September, and 7 October 1992.

[79] 'The Guinea Connection', *West Africa,* 3919 (26 October 1992), p.1823.

to Guinea, the other Krahn-dominated and known as Ulimo-J from the name of its military commander, Roosevelt Johnson. Mohammed Doumbuya, field commander of Ulimo-K, boasted in a radio interview that he had replaced all the Krahn in his force and had sent them to work on his farm, 'where they are now my slaves'.[80]

The governments of both Sierra Leone and Guinea, while being so closely involved with the factional struggle for control of Ulimo and the diamonds which it was acquiring in its operations along the Sierra Leone-Liberia border, were both also contributing to Ecomog, which ostensibly was in Liberia not to wage an offensive war but to keep the peace. Sierra Leonean troops were also deployed against the RUF in the east of their own country as allies of Ulimo. The growing military prowess of Ulimo served Ecomog's overall anti-Taylor strategy. Eighteen months of international peace talks and relative peace in Liberia itself had not resolved the fundamental hostility between the Nigerian government, which dominated Ecomog, and Taylor, who was continuing from time to time to emit poisonous anti-Nigerian propaganda and who had maltreated or murdered hundreds of Nigerian hostages after the initial Ecomog intervention. Ecowas, under Nigerian pressure, now turned to applying economic sanctions against Taylor. In July 1992 the IGNU government introduced a new Liberian currency in an effort to destabilise Taylor's finances. Taylor promptly introduced severe punishments for anyone found in possession of the new currency, known as Liberty dollars, in his territory. Liberia now had three currencies: in Taylor's zone old Liberian dollars known as Jay-Jays were in use, so named from the portrait of Liberia's first president, J.J. Roberts, on one face; in Monrovia, the new Liberty dollars were in circulation; while US dollars continued to be traded over the whole country, and in fact remained Liberia's official currency. As an effort to subvert the economy of Greater Liberia, the launch of the new Liberty dollar was unsuccessful. Liberty dollars in fact generally changed hands on the black market at less than the value of the old Jay-Jay dollars, since Taylor was not printing his own currency but using a stable money supply, underpinned with the influx of hard US dollars he was earning through his businesses, while Liberty dollars were subject to rapid inflation.

The most potent new factor in the war was undoubtedly Ulimo which, despite the feuding between Kromah's faction and the Krahn warlords throughout 1992, was pushing into the diamond-fields

[80] Quoted in Gbala, 'Gbala on Ulimo's Ethnic Feud', *New Democrat*, 1, 30 (23-9 April 1994).

of Sierra Leone and western Liberia, now attracting the support
of at least some Nigerian Ecomog officers who were selling weapons
to Ulimo and providing it with intelligence and military support
while taking a percentage of the diamond profits. Although no
documentary proof has been made public, it is evident that support
for Ulimo was part of a more sophisticated strategy on the part
of at least some elements in Ecomog.[81] Not only were Ulimo recruits
undergoing secret military training at Kankan, Guinea, from 1991,
but so too was the core of a new security force known as the
Black Berets, former AFL soldiers who were to be put at the disposal
of Professor Sawyer's puppet government in Monrovia as a
paramilitary force. By supporting surrogate forces such as these,
certain of the governments which contributed to Ecomog – Sierra
Leone, Guinea and above all Nigeria – were able to put military
pressure on the NPFL while ostensibly adhering to a ceasefire
and deploying in positions all over the country as agreed in various
peace negotiations.

Military pressure from Ulimo, first in Sierra Leone and then
in western Liberia, and the loss to Taylor of diamond production
in these areas, was hampering still further the endless series of
peace-talks taking place in one West African capital after another.
In August 1992 Alhaji Kromah's wing of Ulimo broke into Upper
Lofa County in north-western Liberia and began to overrun valuable
agricultural and timber country previously under Taylor's control.
There is no doubt that Ulimo commanders were assisted by some
Ecomog officers in entering Liberia from Sierra Leone. Nigerian
Ecomog officers were even reported to have bribed some of Taylor's
commanders to allow Ulimo through their lines, which caused
Taylor to purge a number of his own officers in a wave of executions.
The Ulimo advance into Lofa County also drove a wedge between
Foday Sankoh's RUF, now isolated inside Sierra Leone, and Taylor's
Gbarnga headquarters. Ecomog and Taylor, each accusing the
other of bad faith, began building up their military forces on
the northern outskirts of Monrovia, where they faced each other.
This pressure led to a second battle for Monrovia, the first fighting
in the capital city since 1990.

This second battle for Monrovia, known to the NPFL as Operation Octopus, erupted on 15 October 1992. NPFL negotiators had
made secret contact with Prince Johnson, who had broken away
from Taylor at the beginning of the war and was still occupying

---

[81] François Prkic, 'Le Ghana dans la gestion de la crise libérienne', unpublished
paper presented at a conference on Ghana, Centre d'étude d'Afrique noire, Bordeaux, 29-30 May 1998.

a part of Monrovia, but who had otherwise become largely irrelevant. Reviving old acquaintances, the NPFL secured Prince Johnson's collaboration and began infiltrating fighters into the Monrovia suburbs, from which they could get access to back-paths through the swamps which penetrate to the heart of the city. At the last moment, Johnson renounced his deal with Taylor, fearing treachery. The INPFL split into two amid heavy fighting which crucially held up the NPFL assault on Monrovia and blunted the thrust of Operation Octopus. One faction of former INPFL members, led by Samuel Varney, rejoined the NPFL. When Ecomog forces realised the extent of the infiltration, they responded by mobilising their own forces and activating all possible auxiliary help, rearming the AFL which had been confined to barracks since 1990, and openly aiding Ulimo, the Black Berets, and Prince Johnson. There was widespread murder, rape and looting by NPFL forces as they pushed towards the heart of the city before their advance was eventually halted by Ecomog and its various Liberian allies. When the NPFL eventually retreated it took with it thousands of people whom it herded back behind its own lines in the direction of Gbarnga.

Accusing Taylor of treachery in launching Operation Octopus while peace talks were still in progress, Ecomog passed onto the offensive, using aircraft, naval guns and heavy artillery to bomb and shell NPFL positions in the northern suburbs of Monrovia, leading to extensive civilian deaths.[82] The INPFL of Prince Johnson now collapsed. Johnson himself, devoid of political and military support, went to live in Nigeria, to whose government he had become steadily more beholden since his moment of greatest triumph or notoriety: the murder of Samuel Doe. Ecomog, continuing to use aircraft and artillery, not only repulsed the NPFL attack on Monrovia but advanced to take the port of Buchanan, Taylor's key export terminal. Of the thousands of casualties in Monrovia during Operation Octopus, probably the bulk may be attributed to Ecomog shelling and the use of napalm and cluster-bombs. The NPFL claimed the total number of deaths through Ecomog bombardment to be over 6,500, occurring mostly in the suburbs of Monrovia in October and November 1992 and in Buchanan in April 1993.[83] Ecomog also sustained hundreds of casualties of its own.[84]

[82] Africa Watch, *Liberia: waging war to keep the peace. The ECOMOG intervention and human rights*, New York, 1993. Reprinted in *Liberian Studies Journal*, XVIII, 2 (1993), pp.278-318.

[83] 'Statistics of Ecomog Bombing Raids in Liberia', *Liberian Diaspora*, II, 12 (April 1993), pp.22-3.

[84] Prkic, 'Le Ghana dans la gestion de la crise libérienne'.

Ecomog was now on the offensive, applying economic sanctions to Taylor's Greater Liberia and strictly forbidding trade and humanitarian aid. Nigerian planes even attacked vehicles of Médecins sans Frontières, the only major aid organisation which insisted on working in Greater Liberia in the face of the Ecomog embargo.[85] The Ecomog chief of staff, the Nigerian Victor Malu, was particularly severe, warning aid personnel that economic embargoes had succeeded in the Biafra war and that similar methods would be applied in Liberia.[86] With Ecomog now in control of Taylor's leading port of Buchanan, and with Ulimo occupying much of western and north-western Liberia, yet another faction now appeared: George Boley's Liberia Peace Council, originally formed in 1991 and relaunched in May 1993 as an armed faction drawing support from veterans of Doe's old Special Anti-Terrorist Unit.[87] Ecomog was putting a powerful squeeze on the NPFL through a number of auxiliary or surrogate units, taking more of its most productive territory.

Under pressure of this sort, Taylor was now for the first time seriously interested in a negotiated settlement. But the world had largely forgotten about the protracted war in Liberia. He needed to carry out an operation spectacular enough to capture international attention and to enable him to secure international support for a ceasefire of which he was now in great need. On 6 June 1993, as negotiations were in progress towards a peace plan and a ceasefire, the attention of the world's media was drawn to a massacre of some 600 displaced people, mostly women and children, at a camp in the Firestone Plantation, an area disputed between the NPFL and the AFL, the latter still legally the armed forces of the government. An inquiry instituted by the Secretary-General of the United Nations and conducted by Amos Wako, the Attorney General of Kenya, concluded that the Harbel massacre had been carried out by the AFL, although other reports concluded that it was at least partly the work of the NPFL, which appeared to many observers to be more likely.[88] Some of the NPFL Marines,

---

[85] A pro-Ecomog report is Lindsay Barrett, 'The Relief Game in Liberia' in Lindsay Barrett, *Report on Liberia*, Monrovia, 1993, pp.32-6

[86] Author's interview with Bart Witteveen, Monrovia, 26 March 1997. Bart Witteveen, formerly an official with various aid agencies, was interviewed in his personal capacity only.

[87] Reuters despatch, 6 October 1994.

[88] This is based on the author's investigations in Monrovia in July 1994 and subsequently. The official UN report has never been published, but a summary is 'The Carter Camp Massacre: Results of an Investigation by the Panel of Inquiry...',

the unit commanded by the fearsome Nixon 'Striker' Gaye, admitted carrying out killings at Harbel.[89] The most plausible explanation for the massacre is that it was carried out by elements in the NPFL, as a means of gaining world attention and increasing the pressure for a ceasefire, which was now in the NPFL's interest. By blaming the massacre on the AFL, an Ecomog protégé, Taylor attracted a degree of sympathy for his pleas for peace.

On 25 July 1993 the three main Liberian armed factions signed a ceasefire in Cotonou, Benin. The NPFL, the AFL and Ulimo agreed to cease hostilities and to maintain the positions which they then occupied. In the meantime, provision was made for the establishment of a transitional government, which was to contain representatives of Ulimo and the NPFL as well as others nominated by the outgoing Government of National Unity. This was accompanied by a timetable for elections and a return to constitutional government. Ecomog was to remain in place as a monitoring force. Shortly afterwards, the Secretary-General of the UN established a United Nations Observer Mission (Unomil) after complaints by the NPFL that Ecomog was not an impartial force, since it had taken such an active role in fighting against the NPFL in the past. Unomil's task was to observe and report to the UN Secretary-General on the peace process. The Cotonou accord provided for the three factions which were its signatories to give up their arms to Ecomog, concomitant with the establishment of the transitional government.

Although the Cotonou accord failed to bring lasting peace, collapsing within a few months, it did mark a significant development in the war in two respects. In the first place, by providing for the dissolution of Sawyer's Interim Government of National Unity and the installation of the Liberian National Transitional Government, in which the NPFL and Ulimo were both represented, it gave the NPFL for the first time a stake in the official government of Liberia. This had the effect of gradually drawing the NPFL into Monrovian politics. Second, the Cotonou agreement indirectly spawned new armed factions as the signatories to the accord, publicly committed to peace but privately still intent on war, supported

---

unpublished, United Nations, New York, 10 September 1993. Documents giving the AFL point of view include *The Harbel Area Massacres (at Carter Camp and Camp A). White Paper of the Interim Government of National Unity on the Matter*, Monrovia, 1993; 'Report of the Armed Forces of Liberia (AFL) on the June 6, 1993, Carter Camp Massacre in Harbel', unpublished document, Ministry of Defense, Monrovia; 'AFL Reaction to the Wako Commission Report', submitted to the UN Secretary-General by Lieut.-Gen. J. Hezekiah Bowen, AFL chief of staff, unpublished.

[89] Author's interview with Bart Witteveen, Monrovia, 26 March 1997.

the creation of surrogate groups, non-signatories who could continue hostilities. The most significant new faction, the Sapo-dominated LPC, began to spread out towards the south-east from its base in Buchanan to torture and rob civilians, depopulating the area in a swathe around the port-city and depriving the NPFL of its civilian support base there. The strategy of the LPC's commanders was to force civilians into the key points held by Ecomog and to empty the countryside. In little more than a year the LPC, with clandestine support from Ecomog and the AFL command in Monrovia, took over most of the remaining ports in the south-east and gained access to trades in logs, diamonds, gold and rubber.[90] In May 1994 the AFL's own Provost Marshal, Lieutenant-Colonel Amos Garlo, was killed while fighting for the LPC.[91] Ecomog defended its failure to restrain the LPC by arguing the need for legality, maintaining that it could not take any action in regard to the LPC since the latter was not a signatory to the Cotonou Accord, and that it therefore fell outside the Ecomog mandate. Ecomog, or at least certain elements within it, far from remaining neutral, was in fact using various groups, including the AFL, the LPC and Ulimo, as foot-soldiers in the fight against the NPFL.[92] The Deputy Field Commander of Ecomog, the Ghanaian Brigadier-General John Adda, admitted 'that Ulimo is posing more problems than the NPFL by creating mass graves of both fighters and the civilian population'.[93] In his turn, Taylor began to cultivate an auxiliary organisation of his own by arming another faction which had sprung up, the Lofa Defense Force, which was fighting a local war against Ulimo-K in Lofa County.

The group which gained most from the events of 1993-4 was a clique of warlords, the remnants of Doe's supporters, who by July 1994 controlled the general staff of the AFL, LPC and Ulimo-J. It did not escape attention that these factions enjoyed the sympathy of some of the leading officers of Ecomog, particularly from the dominant Nigerian contingent. Ecomog already controlled the

---

[90] Human Rights Watch – Africa, 'Human Rights Abuses by the Liberian Peace Council and the Need for International Oversight', *Liberian Studies Journal,* XX, 1 (1995), pp.162-71; report of 6 February 1995 trip to Buchanan by Justice and Peace Commission, National Catholic Secretariat, Monrovia; author's interviews, Buchanan, 29 July 1994.

[91] 'Top AFL Man Killed in LPC Area', *The Inquirer,* 4, 89 (25 May 1994).

[92] The present author concluded on the basis of evidence available that the LPC was in fact a proxy force under the control of certain senior officers of the AFL. cf. Janet Fleischman, 'An Uncivil War,' *Africa Report,* 38, 3 (May-June 1993), pp.56-9.

[93] Quoted in *New Democrat,* 1, 36 (28 July-3 August 1994).

ports of Monrovia and Buchanan. In under a year of fighting following the Cotonou peace accord, largely through the medium of the LPC and the Johnson faction of Ulimo, these warlords, many of them from the south-east, had taken control of Liberia's remaining ports with the exception of Harper, thus occupying a strategic position. A year of peace had cost Taylor dearly, since he had lost control of a large swathe of territory. He had been unable to make the transition he sought from warlord to politician.

Under sustained military pressure from the new factions, Taylor signed yet another peace treaty at Akosombo in Ghana in August 1994. This was opposed by many civilians in Monrovia and by some warlords who were excluded from it. But most important of all, the Nigerian government was opposed to the Akosombo accord, since it was negotiated under the aegis of the government of Ghana and made significant concessions to Nigeria's arch-enemy, Charles Taylor. While negotiations proceeded, senior Nigerian officers were preparing military action on the ground which would sabotage the peace treaty, brokering an alliance between some Liberian factions which had been excluded from the negotiations.[94] In September 1994, just a few days after signature of the new agreement, Nigerian Ecomog officers coordinated the most serious challenge yet to Taylor. Having persuaded some of Taylor's key generals to change sides, the anti-NPFL coalition forces, with staff support from Nigerian Ecomog officers, combined to attack and overrun Taylor's capital at Gbarnga in September 1994. Although the coalition forces soon turned on each other, enabling Taylor to regain his capital, the political message was plain: Nigeria would not allow Charles Taylor to become president of Liberia without its assent, and the Nigerian government had the military means to destabilise his position for as long as it judged necessary.

Ecomog had supported the formation of new militias including Ulimo and the LPC, which it had helped to take a considerable area from Taylor, making him amenable to serious negotiation. However, the stronger these factions grew, the more independent they threatened to become, escaping the control of their original patrons in Ecomog. The US government, alarmed by what it considered Nigerian duplicity in fuelling the civil war while leading what purported to be a peacekeeping force, succeeded in persuading Ecowas to accept the services of an American private security company with close links to the Pentagon, Pacific Architects and Engineers (PAE), which at US expense would take charge

---

[94] On the coalition, see the interview with Kwame Amoa-Amwa in *West Africa*, 4033 (23 January 1995), pp.105-6.

of many aspects of Ecomog logistics. American managers took control of trucks which had been donated to Ecomog by the Dutch government and of other transport. This notably increased the military effectiveness of Ecomog while at the same time giving the US government some influence over Ecomog's activities on the ground.

Monrovia, 1996: the final battle

The longer the war lasted, the more factions appeared, as older groupings reformed and as existing ones developed splits. This spirit of factionalism, deeply embedded in Liberia's political history, was aggravated by Ecomog's tendency to engineer or manipulate such factions for its own purposes.

None of the more than seven factions which fielded an armed force in 1993-5 was very solid. In effect, small groups of fighters in occupation of territory used adherence to various nationally-known factions like a marketing franchise. 'Use of the Ulimo or NPFL "brand name", in effect, helps them to stake a claim to a particular territory, in the same way as small time gangsters often seek to be associated with a "Crime Kingpin" who they might never in fact meet', one Liberian author perceptively noted.[95] The object of factional activity was to wrest control of territory and economic resources, and individual war-bands often threatened to split from their patrons or fought each other for turf even within factions. Each faction occupied territory which it exploited economically, sometimes paying a rent to Ecomog, which controlled the main ports, for the right to trade and export. Ecomog did business with every faction at one time or another, trading rubber with Ulimo-J, looted goods and wood with the LPC and palm-oil with the NPFL, while Ulimo-K was trading directly across the northern border with Guinean officers from an army which was a component of Ecomog. Alliances were constantly forming, dissolving and re-forming.

The leading warlords, all of whom after 1994 also had some stake in the national government, attempted to turn this factional strife into party political gains. As part of this process each faction claimed to represent some sort of ethnic interest, with the notable exception of the NPFL which could make a better claim than others to stand for all Liberians, not least because Taylor's Americo-Liberian ancestry made it difficult for him to play the ethnic card.

---

[95] Max Bankole Jarrett, 'Civil War in Liberia: a manipulation of chaos?', (M.A. thesis, School of Oriental and African Studies, London, 1996), p.47.

In fact, in most circumstances this mobilisation of ethnic identity was more rhetoric than reality, as every faction included substantial numbers of fighters of diverse ethnic origin, and ethnic allegiance became really important only when a local grievance, rooted in local history and land disputes, became caught up with national factional activity. This happened for example in Upper Lofa County, where older differences between the local Kpelle and Loma farmers and the Mandingo whom they perceived as interlopers on their territory became institutionalised in the contest between the Mandingo-run Ulimo-K and the Lofa Defense Force, the latter drawing its support largely from Loma and Kpelle refugees in Guinea. In general, ethnic appeals by faction leaders were most successful where circumstances were obliging ordinary civilians to seek military protection.

The richest, most powerful and best-connected of all the warlords was Charles Taylor. But by 1994 at the latest, after the Ecomog-supported coalition offensive had briefly taken his capital at Gbarnga, he had come to realise that he would never be president of Liberia, the position which he craved, unless he could reach an accommodation with Nigeria, the most important of all the external actors in the war. Moreover in 1993 Taylor's arch-enemy, General Babangida, was replaced as President of Nigeria by General Sani Abacha, who was less personally hostile to the NPFL leader than his predecessor had been. At this point the stage was set for an understanding between Charles Taylor and the Nigerian government which could make it easier to achieve an end to the war.

In August 1995, these two key players – Charles Taylor and Nigeria's President Abacha – together with other leading participants reached an agreement in Abuja, the thirteenth peace accord of the Liberian war. The Abuja agreement provided for the formation of a new Council of State, in effect a collective presidency in which the principal factions were represented, with ministerial posts also being distributed among the different armed factions. There was to be a process of disarmament and of preparation for national elections. The way was now clear for Taylor to take part personally in Monrovian politics, and on 31 August 1995 he arrived back in the city for the first time since he had fled in 1983. He was greeted by cheering crowds who believed that his entry into the city meant peace at last. Dressed all in white and driving his own car, he made every effort to appear as a Messiah, like Christ arriving in Jerusalem on Palm Sunday.

The Abuja accord fundamentally changed the political and military mechanisms for securing the control of resources which was the key to peace or war. From 1990 until 1995, there had

been two main protagonists, Ecomog on one side, Taylor's NPFL
on the other, one with its fief in Monrovia, the other in the hinterland. The mastery of Greater Liberia which Taylor had had in
1990, and had since lost, had proved insufficient to secure the
presidency. Twice, in 1990 and 1992, Taylor's forces had failed
to take Monrovia with frontal assaults. Now Taylor was at last in
Monrovia, but only with Ecomog's acquiescence. This gave Taylor
the chance to dominate the national government and brought
him into contact with the generation of pre-war politicians who
lived in Monrovia, all of whom loathed him. Taylor's great wealth
gave him a massive political advantage, not least as he was able
to place some key Ecomog officers on his payroll and to propose
commercial partnerships to whomever he wished to recruit as a
political ally. The logic of the Abuja accord was to give to the
armed factions joint control of the government of Liberia, encouraging them to pursue by political means the interests which
they had previously contested in battle. This soon led to antagonisms, as when bodyguards loyal to Alhaji Kromah (Ulimo-K)
and Charles Taylor (NPFL) engaged in a fistfight at the Executive
Mansion when both their leaders tried to use the presidential
lift at the same time.[96] It also meant that Taylor could no longer
afford to antagonise Ecomog or its most dominant element, Nigeria,
since he was dependent on Ecomog for his personal security. When,
for example, on 31 October 1996, there was an attempt on Taylor's
life, he was rescued by an Ecomog force which found him hiding
in one of the bathrooms of the Executive Mansion.

While participation in Monrovia politics as a result of the Abuja
accord brought Taylor into the politics of the capital on Ecomog's
terms, it also offered all the factions a chance to occupy government
positions. The resources at their disposal were limited, being the
risibly small income of the Liberian government and the profits
of business deals they were able to broker with Ecomog or others.
Despite the government's impoverishment, there were various ways
for individual ministers and directors of agencies to make money.
For example, looted metal goods could be sold as scrap metal,
especially via the Ministry of Public Works. Airport tax, paid in
US dollars, was a useful income, as were charges on foreign nationals
for work permits. Government officials often travelled unnecessarily
outside the country in order to receive the daily allowance of
US$275, excluding transport, which could be changed on the black

---

[96] Agence France-Presse despatch, 3 November 1995.

market into Liberian dollars.[97] It was illuminating to see what the various warlords chose when parcelling out government jobs between themselves. Taylor put his placemen in strategic positions, including as director of the oil refinery and in charge of the police. Ulimo-K, a faction dominated by business-conscious Mandingo, chose the key financial portfolios. The various factions could now combine control of the resources of the hinterland with opportunities offered by access to the facilities of a sovereign state. The result was that factional disputes in Monrovia risked spilling onto the streets, as for example when Ulimo-J fighters loyal to Roosevelt Johnson attacked the central bank to demand the reinstatement of one of their faction leaders as its governor.[98] While the Abuja accord helped to resolve a fundamental dispute at the heart of the war – that between Charles Taylor and the Nigerian government – it also made Monrovia a potentially more dangerous place, since it was now occupied by fighters loyal to competing factions.

The balance of the conflict had changed to one in which political manoeuvre, backed by force, was replacing war alone as the key instrument. This put at a disadvantage those warlords who lacked political experience, like Roosevelt Johnson, or those who could not aspire to a broad national appeal, notably Alhaji Kromah whose Mandingo power-base was now a handicap. On the other hand the most successful warlord-cum-politicians, Taylor and Boley, now had to compete with a field of experienced politicians and an array of six or more established political parties which could claim never to have been involved in violence.

Taylor made one last effort to stage a major armed offensive. In December 1995, at a time when the latest peace timetable required all the factions to disarm to Ecomog, he entered into an agreement with Roosevelt Johnson, undertaking to aid Ulimo-J 'militarily and financially', as Taylor later admitted.[99] He encouraged Johnson to hold on to the western diamond fields which Ulimo-J was supposed to evacuate under the disarmament programme, and to attack Ecomog. This duly happened, with the result that Ecomog commanders were outraged by Ulimo-J's attack and by the capture of some heavy weapons from the Nigerian contingent. Taylor's ruse had worked perfectly: he had created enmity between Ulimo-J and the Nigerian officers in Ecomog. Now invoking his status as a member of the governing council

---

[97] *New Patriot Journal* (Monrovia), 2, 21 (25 March 1995), pp.6-7.

[98] Reuters despatch, 11 January 1996.

[99] *The Inquirer*, 6, 46 (27 March 1996).

and using the rhetoric of respect for law and order, Taylor seized
on a murder which appeared to have been committed by forces
loyal to Johnson to move against Ulimo-J and its leader. Claiming
that it was the duty of the government to uphold the law, Taylor's
NPFL and Kromah's Ulimo-K, with Ecomog supporting and even
selling weapons to them, moved to arrest Roosevelt Johnson.[100]
This led to the third battle of Monrovia, which began on 6 April
1996. Johnson's fighters, penned into a small area of central Monrovia, were surrounded by superior numbers of NPFL and Ulimo-K
fighters armed by Ecomog. But Johnson's group, including many
Krahn, were able to rally the support of some other militias, since
other warlords too felt threatened by the prospect of a complete
military takeover by Taylor. As the incident turned into a full-scale
battle throughout central Monrovia, bystanders including Ecomog
and the US embassy realised that if the NPFL took the Barclay
Training Center, the barracks where Johnson's Ulimo-J and its
allies were making their last stand, then there would be nothing
to stop Taylor from taking over the whole of Liberia by military
means. The US government, appalled by Ecomog's partiality, began
using the PAE security company to helicopter weapons to the
beleaguered fighters of Ulimo-J in an attempt to level the balance
of forces. Even some of the Nigerian soldiers began supplying
guns to Ulimo-J in an effort to prevent an outright NPFL victory,
which meant that Nigeria was arming both sides in the battle.

Crucially, Taylor's forces were more interested in looting than
fighting. The NPFL fighters called the offensive Operation Pay
Yourself, the last great attempt to loot 'as a form of compensation
for the combatants who have fought for several years without any
benefit from their leaders'.[101] At least 2,000 people were killed
in a few days of fighting. According to a UN assessment, the UN
and its agencies lost a total of 322 vehicles worth some $4.9 million,
while international NGOs lost a further 167 vehicles worth $3.2
million, stolen by the various factions and often sold by the fighters
to Ecomog for export.[102] While international attention was focussed
on the battle for Monrovia and the orgy of looting which it inspired,
Taylor was able quietly to take over the gold fields and forests
of the south-east and the rich agricultural areas around Kakata.

In retrospect, the third battle of Monrovia was the climactic

---

[100] Max Ahmadu Sesay, 'Politics and Society in Post-War Liberia', *Journal of Modern African Studies*, 34, 3 (1996), pp.402-4.

[101] Justice and Peace Commission, 'Human Rights Report, January-December 1996', National Catholic Secretariat, Monrovia, p.10.

[102] *Ibid.*, p.11.

engagement of the war. The Nigerian government, which had used its peacekeeping role in Liberia as a gauge of international respectability, was embarrassed by the degree to which its own forces were implicated in the battle. The Field Commander was replaced, some of his senior officers were court-martialled, and Nigeria sought to restore the peace timetable negotiated in Abuja. For the first time since the departure of General Dogonyaro in 1991, Nigeria sent a real fighting general to command Ecomog, Brigadier-General Victor Malu, who was able to spread Ecomog's control throughout the country now that Charles Taylor was dependent on the international force for his personal security. Taylor, for his part, once more learned that he could not wrest the presidency or eliminate his rivals by force alone, and above all not in the face of Nigerian opposition. Both he and the Nigerian government accepted that it was in their mutual interest to work for a solution in which Nigeria could officially proclaim that it had succeeded in its mission of pacifying Liberia, and Taylor could become president of Liberia with some show of legitimacy.

As Ecomog forces were deployed throughout Liberia for the first time since 1992, and a fragile peace enabled refugees to return, an election campaign began in which Taylor's only serious rival was Ellen Johnson Sirleaf, who had returned from exile and campaigned on the platform that she was an administrator of proven quality who had international support and whose hands were not bloodied by participation in the war. On 19 July 1997, Liberia held the fairest elections in its history, in which some 80 per cent of the eligible population voted. Three-quarters of those who went to the polls voted for Charles Taylor. In some cases people may have reasoned that a vote for Taylor was the best hope for peace, since they knew that if Taylor did not win the election, he was likely to re-start the war. But many may also have voted for Taylor because his very determination made him appear strong; when he argued that he was destined by God to be president of Liberia, it carried the ring of conviction. Some older Monrovians were shocked by the song sung by young NPFL supporters:[103]

> *He killed my Pa*
> *He killed my Ma*
> *I'll vote for him.*

After seven years of Ecomog presence, the result was exactly the one which the Ecowas countries had set out to prevent in August 1990: Charles Taylor was president of Liberia.

[103] Elizabeth Ohene, 'Chosen by God?', *Focus on Africa*, 8, 4 (1997), p.24.

3

THE MECHANICS OF WAR

Up to this point we have described how Liberia, a country with a history of political clientelism, slid into war in the 1980s as rival political–military entrepreneurs came to contest the political field using all the means at their disposal. In time, these entrepreneurs associated themselves with foreign sponsors or allies who had interests of their own. Our account has concerned elites almost entirely, simply because that is the best way of acquiring an overview of political and military events. Of course, hundreds of thousands of ordinary people were also involved. While the faction leaders of the 1990s relied greatly on armed force to advance their cause, they also tried to develop popular support by using whatever resources of patronage and pressure they could, and by appealing to various cultural values including ethnicity, religion and patriotism. Deeper study of the social bases of the rival warlord armies is required to throw further light on these patron–client relations and help us understand why at least some Liberians fought.

When the war started in the last week of 1989, it was a contest between two armed camps, both quite limited in size. On the one hand was the government army, the Armed Forces of Liberia, consisting in total of perhaps 7,000 men and women. Many senior AFL officers, and a significant proportion of the lower ranks, were people with family links to Samuel Doe's home county of Grand Gedeh. The AFL was formidably well-equipped. Throughout the 1980s the force had received massive supplies of weapons and extensive training from US personnel, while its Special Anti-Terrorist Unit was Israeli-trained. The elite units particularly had a well-deserved reputation for being hardened, cold-blooded killers. On the opposing side was the core unit of the National Patriotic Front of Liberia (NPFL), consisting of some 100 people trained in Burkina Faso and Libya, perhaps a few dozen of them professional soldiers of the AFL who, like Prince Johnson, had deserted from the AFL to join Quiwonkpa in exile, or had left Liberia after the defeat of Quiwonkpa's 1985 coup attempt, and had found their way abroad. With them was a scattering of West African revolutionaries whom the Liberians had met in Libya and Burkina Faso.

Within days of the outbreak of war, the composition of these
forces was to change as civilians acquired weapons and joined
the NPFL. In mid-1990, the AFL in turn was to arm many Krahn
and Mandingo civilians in Monrovia, the so-called '1990 soldiers',
and by early 1991 some refugees in Sierra Leone were joining
the newly-formed Ulimo. Prince Johnson's break from the NPFL,
formalised in July 1990, and the creation of Ulimo in Sierra Leone
in 1991 began the process of forming new armed factions. All
these factions had at their core former officers of the AFL, like
Prince Johnson of the INPFL, and Albert Karpeh in the case of
Ulimo. All the factions also resembled each other to some degree
in their mode of operation, not least because they all contained
at least some former professional soldiers who brought with them
a range of technical skills. Although the NPFL at the beginning
of the war recruited large numbers of civilians who were given
almost no training and were subject to little effective command,
as the war developed and new factions emerged and gained experience, each armed force was in time to adopt a basic structure
derived from the American military model, with a general staff
divided into different offices, and line units, brigades and battalions.
Each unit had a system of ranks extending down to the most
casual part-time fighters, with porters, labourers and camp followers
at the bottom of the chain of command.[1] Young men and women
who joined such groups, the great majority of whom had no prior
military experience, learned the rudiments of military command
and techniques, attributing to themselves military ranks and grandiose war names, the latter often inspired by the Hollywood action
videos which became so popular during the war-years. Although
the factions were better-organised than is sometimes apparent from
journalists' accounts of the period, it is also the case that a military
culture was formed from the bottom upwards, as it were, by
teenagers enthralled by Sylvester Stallone, motivated by dreams
of glory or nightmares of revenge.

While Prince Johnson's INPFL was eventually to dissolve, most
factions eventually gave birth to still more factions. The original
Ulimo spawned Ulimo-J, Ulimo-K and the LPC, while others trailed
smaller factions in their wake, as the NPFL allied itself with the
smaller Lofa Defense Force (LDF). These and similar new creations
greatly increased the number of people under arms throughout

[1] These remarks are based on numerous interviews conducted in Liberia, most
notably with NPFL official John T. Richardson, in Monrovia on 8 April 1997, and
discussions with Colonel Thebe, head of the UN Observer Mission in Voinjama,
3-4 April 1997.

the 1990s. The few thousand AFL veterans who formed the back-
bone of the various factions were joined by far larger numbers
of civilians. It remains to be seen what precisely induced so many
people to take up arms and, on occasion, to commit atrocities
against fellow-Liberians.

Punishing Monrovia

In the first days of 1990 many ordinary citizens of Nimba County,
especially Gio, joined the NPFL and were given a rapid training
in weaponry by its core force. These early recruits to the NPFL
were not generally deviants or misfits from the towns and villages
of Nimba County – although no doubt the war attracted such
people, where they existed – but were mostly ordinary men and
women who often joined the rebellion with the full encouragement
of their elders, the people regarded in rural Liberia as the arbiters
of correct behaviour. Indeed, old men sometimes constituted the
NPFL's home guard, guarding the rear areas, in the early stage
of the war.[2]

Anyone who saw the NPFL forces could immediately recognise
the difference between the core group, the Libyan-trained Special
Forces commanded by Prince Johnson, and the NPFL's civilian
irregulars, the new recruits, by their dress alone. The administrator
of Cuttington University College, situated a few miles outside
Gbarnga, got his first sight of the NPFL when it took over the
campus in May 1990. The hundreds of fighters were quite well-
disposed to the university staff as they requisitioned the College
and its grounds to use as a training camp. The administrator reckoned that most fighters were between the ages of ten and forty
and noted that they included both men and women. Johnson's
commandos wore green fatigues and looked like real soldiers.
The NPFL irregulars, on the other hand, were kitted out in what
the university man called 'odd clothing':[3]

> Many of the men wore wedding gowns, wigs, dresses, commen-
> cement gowns from high schools, and several forms of 'voodoo'
> regalia. All rebels wore cotton strings around the wrist and
> around the neck and shoulder. They all displayed black tattoos
> on the arm, slightly below the shoulder. They believed that
> any person who wore these talismans and tattoos, and strictly
> adhered to the laws of not eating pumpkin, having sex, touching

[2] Huband, *The Liberian Civil War,* p.79.

[3] Tokpa, 'Cuttington University College', p.87.

lime and taking a bath, could not be killed in battle by enemy fire. Because of the importance of this 'bullet proof' protection, there was a medicine man in residence at the Cuttington training base to administer these medicines at the end of their military training.

In talking to some of the fighters, the administrator was struck that most of the irregulars said they were fighting to avenge dead relatives, while some of the younger ones said that the NPFL had promised them school or college scholarships after the fighting was over. Many of Johnson's Special Forces, on the other hand, generally older men with extensive military experience, said they had been promised huge sums of money if they took Monrovia. A foreign journalist who met some NPFL irregulars in July 1990 made a roughly similar report, estimating that 10 per cent of NPFL fighters were women or girls and that most gave every indication of having received only the most cursory training. Some wore a white clay which they called *leh* smeared on their face. No command structure seemed to be much in evidence at this early stage of the war, with the exception of the NPFL military intelligence organ, known as G-2, which was clearly a key institution.[4] A man living in a suburb of Monrovia, whose house was attacked by the NPFL in July 1990, said that 'about 70 per cent of the rebels were all teenagers ranging from, say, twelve to seventeen years'.[5]

Nimba County was the place from which the NPFL chose to launch its attack, and for good reason, since it had been the epicentre of opposition to the Doe government since the early 1980s, originally because Doe's main rival in those days, Thomas Quiwonkpa, was a son of Nimba. From the outset there was no doubt that the NPFL was intent on pursuing anyone seen as a collaborator with Doe and his henchmen, including all Krahn and Mandingo, considered to be collaborators *en masse*. Needless to say, among the hundreds of Mandingo and Krahn who were regarded as guilty simply by association with Doe were many who had derived no benefit at all from his government. People from other ethnic groups too risked being slaughtered simply as a result of mistaken identity. 'If you come across rebel fighters who don't know the difference between Krahn and Grebo, you're in trouble', said a Grebo refugee, speaking from experience.[6] Confusion arose from the fact that

[4] *Africa Confidential*, 31, 15 (27 July 1990).

[5] Brehun, *War of Horror*, p.45.

[6] Africa Watch, *Cycle of Abuse*, p.149.

many peoples of south-eastern Liberia, including Grebo, Sapo and Krahn, speak related languages, and many people other than Krahn live in Grand Gedeh County, regarded by the NPFL as enemy territory because of its connection with Samuel Doe. When Prince Johnson's group captured the Bong iron mines in June 1990, they set up a kangaroo tribunal, advised by a local schoolteacher, to try people suspected of being Krahn or Mandingo or of being government collaborators. Many of those sentenced to death were actually Sapo, guilty only of speaking a language similar to a Krahn dialect. In fact, many Sapo people had had little sympathy for the Doe government ever since Doe had executed their countryman Thomas Weh Syen, a leading figure in the PRC, in 1981.[7] A similar risk attended any Vai and Mende people, whose homeland is in the far west of Liberia, who happened to be living in Nimba County, since many of them were Muslims and they therefore risked being mistaken for Mandingo. One woman said her Vai uncle was murdered because he was seen kneeling on a prayer-mat. Muslims caught up in the offensive said NPFL fighters 'told us that we are not allowed to pray in mosques.[...] We began to pray in our rooms – secretly.'[8] The NPFL zealots' knowledge of Liberian ethnography did not always match their ferocity.

The Mandingo who lived in Nimba County at the start of the war were very often traders and shopkeepers by profession, and this meant they generally had goods to loot. Their attackers acquired so much booty from these victims that some people thought it obvious that 'their motive was not liberating the people but looting their properties by use of the gun'.[9] Since the NPFL irregulars were unpaid, any fighter who was to spend more than a few days in the field would need to live off the land anyway, but the scale of looting soon resulted in clear patterns of commerce. By July 1990 there was a booming trade in looted goods exported overland by NPFL fighters for sale in the markets of Côte d'Ivoire, especially in the town of Danane. One French-speaking reporter noted the number of people from all parts of West Africa who had flocked to join the NPFL. She noted a sprinkling of Ghanaians, Nigerians, Burkinabe, Senegalese, and in particular Ivorians from the areas which adjoin Nimba County and whose people speak related African languages. For them, the war was a business opportunity. The same reporter met a Gambian, one of the core

7 Youboty, *Liberian Civil War*, pp.227-9.

8 Africa Watch, *Cycle of Abuse*, p.145.

9 W. Nah Dixon, *In Search of a Leader*, Monrovia, 1993, p.30.

group of Libyan trainees, who said his ambition was to fight in revolutionary wars. This man said he was a great admirer of the late Thomas Sankara, and claimed to have fought alongside Amilcar Cabral in Guinea-Bissau.[10] Whether or not such self-proclaimed revolutionaries were as motivated by the desire for loot as were their rank-and-file colleagues is a moot point.

When the NPFL first reached Monrovia in July 1990, fighters flocked to the battlefront to be in at the climax. This was the chance of a lifetime to acquire something valuable from Monrovia, home of the wealthy and source of imported goods. Many of the young country boys and girls who joined up to take part in the battle of Monrovia had never been to the city before. The fighters were in carnival mood, especially those lucky enough to catch a ride down to the battlefront. 'Their few vehicles resemble New York subway carriages, adorned with spray-painted graffiti such as "Here comes dead body trouble" and "No surrender, no retreat"', a British reporter wrote.[11] They called themselves by grandiose war-names, half-serious, half-playful, sometimes inspired by Hollywood movies and videos they had seen, such as 'Rambo', 'Terminator', and 'Jungle Killer'. Looking frightening is something people all over the world do when they are about to enter a fight, and in Liberia wearing the most outlandish possible clothing is an accepted way of doing this. This was a technique used by Liberians preparing for traditional forms of war rather than attempting to imitate the US-trained and olive drab-clad soldiers of Doe's army.[12] As the fighters came into Monrovia's suburbs they often painted their names on individual houses, believing that when the fighting was over they could come and reclaim the property as a prize of war. Everything they could carry, they took away.

Meanwhile, displaced people were fleeing the city in the opposite direction. It was largely for this reason that the NPFL's military intelligence staff set up check-points on the roads around Monrovia. The aim was not only to screen the refugees fleeing Monrovia to root out Krahn, Mandingo, policemen or soldiers in mufti and other perceived enemies including Nigerians and, after August

[10] Mariam Diallo, 'Voyage au bout de l'horreur', *Jeune Afrique*, 1544 (1 August 1990), pp.24-5, which also includes some fine photos.

[11] Matthew Campbell, 'Rebels Deal Out Death on Road to Monrovia', *Sunday Times* (London), 12 August 1990.

[12] Mary Moran, 'Warriors or Soldiers? Masculinity and ritual transvestism in the Liberian Civil War' in Constance R. Sutton (ed.), *Feminism, Nationalism and Militarism*, Arlington, VA, 1995, pp.73-88.

1990, citizens of other Ecomog-supporting countries. The check-
points also served to keep the NPFL fighters at the battlefront.[13]
The AFL was, after all, an infinitely more experienced fighting
unit than the NPFL. As long as Doe was holding out in the Executive
Mansion with his troops, there was a risk that the NPFL irregulars
would just drift back to their farms and towns, sated with booty,
but without having won the war.

The NPFL's check-points were a source of thousands of har-
rowing experiences, and were perhaps the single most traumatic
memory of the war for many residents of Monrovia until April
1996. Forced by hunger and fighting to leave the city in July and
August 1990, they had to pass through these controls where adolescent youths, often dressed in their bizarre costumes and wearing
traditional war regalia, wielded the power of life and of death.
At the notorious God Bless You Gate, fighters had a monkey which,
they believed, had the power to recognise Krahn, who were famed
monkey-hunters. Anybody the monkey touched would be killed
on the spot. 'The stupid rebels really believed that the animal
would touch nobody else but Krahn people because the monkey,
an endangered species, knew its predators', said one Krahn.[14] A
graphic recollection of the checkpoints was the following:[15]

> The Checkpoint. Those who have had encounters with it cannot
> forget the menace, the lingering thought of brutal death. At
> the Checkpoint, loved ones, friends are shot or maimed for
> life. There, one may live, depending on your tribe, religion
> or politics or even your looks. If one is unlucky to meet an
> old rival in command in the position 'power', well, death is
> imminent. There anything, anything can happen. You could
> be shot because of a gold ring, a pair of shoes, etc. that the
> one in 'power' wants. You may live or simply be shot. The
> Checkpoint is a place of 'power', where life is taken just like
> that. With a snap of the fingers, you are dead. 'The C.O. is
> not satisfied. You said you are Krahn when you in fact are
> Gio. You said you are Kpelle when you are Mandingo. You
> said you are Mandingo when you are Mano, etc.'

By the time the NPFL got to Monrovia in July 1990, it had
already overrun half the country, and it had attracted new recruits
from every area and from every ethnic group, but in each case

[13] Author's interview with John T. Richardson, Monrovia, 8 April 1997.

[14] Youboty, *Liberian Civil War,* p.341.

[15] 'The Trauma of the Checkpoint', *New Democrat Weekly Review,* 1, 2 (10-17 November 1995), p.2.

they were intent on revenge against collaborators with the Doe government. Thus, the checkpoints through which people displaced by fighting in Monrovia had to pass might be manned not just by Gio and Mano youths from Nimba County, but were increasingly likely to include fighters from other parts of Liberia. This made the ordeal all the more terrifying. Fighters from specific rural areas were often particularly severe on those of their fellow-countrymen whom they found living in Monrovia, Gio interrogating Gio, Kpelle interrogating Kpelle in their own language, and so on. At one check point, NPFL fighters discovered that a female police captain, one Esther Paygar, had had three children by a Krahn man. The unfortunate woman, who was herself from Nimba County, was not spared because she was from the 'right' ethnic group, but on the contrary was made to watch while her three children were beheaded.[16]

The search for national enemies became inseparable from the search for personal enemies. In a country with a relatively small population, where family and social relationships are pervasive, few Monrovians could deny a link with some rural area. If they were interrogated by someone from their home area, the questioner could soon establish a clear idea of the suspect's identity by reference to mutual acquaintances. In this guise, there was a great deal of settling of scores. 'Polemics, especially over land and domestic matters, also had their share of the widespread vengeance', recalled one survivor. 'Land disputes, family quarrels and related rifts between friends and even relatives claimed victims all over the place.'[17] A social worker later commented that, 'a poor or low status villager' could kill 'the teacher who flunked him, the man who beat him'.[18] Many fighters were actually most assiduous in killing people of their own ethnic group, either to settle a personal grudge or because they regarded anyone who had lived in Monrovia for too long as having betrayed the moral values of the village. The fighters disliked people who were obviously 'shining', as they called it, those who radiated prosperity. Evidence of this could be deduced from expensive clothes or, most telling of all, a fat belly. The NPFL fighters also made a point of killing people they thought might be cheats or fraudsters. 'In fact', said one civilian who otherwise had no sympathy for the rebels, 'I wished the rebels had focused their attention on such people

[16] Youboty, *Liberian Civil War*, pp.341-2.
[17] Brehun, *War of Horror*, p.67.
[18] Quoted in Africa Watch, *Easy Prey*, p.18.

in the society; they would have won a Gold Medal from me.'[19]
The way for a Monrovian to survive a checkpoint was to dress
poorly, look as inconspicuous as possible, and pray to God.

Adolescents under little authority, whose guns give them a sense
of power for the first time in their lives, often drunk on cane-spirit
or high on marijuana or amphetamines, are unpredictable. Some
were capable of acts of the most extreme and arbitrary violence.
One such incident was witnessed by one James Samuels while
he was fleeing towards the Sierra Leonean border. Having just
watched an NPFL fighter known as Young Killer commit a couple
of casual murders, he saw another rebel, dressed in a woman's
wig, skirt and stockings, walk along a line of refugees pleading
with them, in mock supplication, to allow him to kill them. He
would pull people out at random and shoot them. To one terrified
queue he announced 'I like the number twenty'. He began counting
from the back and killed the twentieth person in the line. Samuels
claimed to have witnessed another rebel emptying a sackful of
severed penises on the ground in front of his commander. There
were fifty-two of these trophies, and the commander, making a
joke of the episode, said the youngster with the sack should henceforth be known as Fifty-two Reporter.[20] Stories like these spread
fast among frightened people. Some were no doubt exaggerated
or even invented, but there is no doubt that many of the vast
catalogue of horror-stories from the checkpoints are substantially
true. Every Liberian has a story of violence to tell, and some still
bear the scars which bear out their words. Nevertheless, 'along
with the tales of nightmarish atrocities', recalled a person stranded
in Monrovia at the start of the war, 'I've also heard of many acts
of discipline, professional behavior, and kindness and assistance
by NPFL men to civilians'.[21]

Many of these NPFL irregulars were adolescents having an ad-
venture, at least at the start of the war. They were not professional
killers like the AFL, which was systematically slaughtering suspected
opponents throughout the first months of 1990, culminating in
the murder of 600 displaced people at St Peter's Church in Sinkor,
Monrovia, on 29-30 July. But while the AFL wore American-style
uniforms and had modern weapons, in contrast to the ancient
and poorly-maintained Beretta machine-guns which many NPFL
fighters had received from old Libyan arsenals, it was also apparent

[19] Brehun, *War of Horror*, p.69.
[20] Schuster, 'The Final Days of Dr Doe', pp.82-8.
[21] Andrews, *Cry, Liberia, Cry!*, p.37.

that the government soldiers were drawing on the same repertoire of spiritual beliefs and objects as many of the rebels. Major Tailey, who commanded the massacre at St Peter's church, was an AFL '1990 soldier', a renowned hunter from Grand Gedeh who was often seen wearing human bones and what an Ecomog press officer, a Nigerian, called 'voodoo dress'.[22] Indeed, when the Ecomog Field Commander General Dogonyaro eventually faced up to this fearsome fighter, killed by Nigerian soldiers in a firefight on 4 November 1990, this was attributed by many Liberians to Dogonyaro's use of superior spiritual powers.[23] Nevertheless, among the AFL too there were some 'good soldiers, well disciplined and patriotic', who helped civilians with small acts of kindness. The worst of them were generally 'the semi-illiterate new recruits', mostly Krahn and Mandingo civilians armed during the first battle of Monrovia.[24]

From the start, the NPFL made the organisation of appropriate spiritual protection one of the central elements of its military preparations, every bit as important as obtaining firearms and learning military drills.[25] Part of the training for the new NPFL recruits consisted of a rapid ritual, reminiscent of traditional initiation ceremonies, in which new fighters were tattooed or received small cuts on their skin said to make them immune to bullets. During the initiation a gun containing blank rounds might be fired at them to 'prove' that the medicine was effective. Clearly, for activities of this sort to be organised systematically, ritual specialists needed to be recruited and assigned to duties by the NPFL's commanders. One of the NPFL's senior officials, who claims personally to have been cynical about the whole business, has described how the NPFL 'conjured' such ritual specialists, as he put it, seeking people from abroad particularly – Côte d'Ivoire or elsewhere – and requiring them to perform any sort of ceremony, even an improvised one. Ritual experts from one part of Liberia were employed to initiate people from distant areas where they were unknown. The important thing was to impress the NPFL recruits with a sense that they were spiritually protected.[26] While the NPFL was often undiscerning in its choice of spiritual experts,

[22] Agetua, *Operation Liberty*, pp.101-3.

[23] *Ibid.*, p.104. There are some interesting passages on Tailey in Youboty, *Liberian Civil War*.

[24] Andrews, *Cry, Liberia, Cry!*, p.37.

[25] Tokpa, 'Cuttington University College', p.87.

[26] Author's interview with John T. Richardson, Monrovia, 8 April 1997.

recruiting anyone it believed could impress the young recruits, irrespective of ethnic or regional affiliation, it certainly also recruited authentic traditional priests, such as *zoes* of the Poro secret society, whenever any could be found with sufficient reputation.

All factions soon adopted similar symbols of martial prowess and ferocity and used similar spiritual techniques for their protection against danger. A British journalist who saw Ulimo fighters in 1992 noticed one wearing a woman's wig. 'Ropes, black objects, and even a dog's tail, hung from him.'[27] The AFL forces, re-armed by Ecomog during Operation Octopus, the second battle of Monrovia in October 1992, also adopted the same type of garb: 'sporting looted booty – from straggly wigs to gas masks and headphones attached to nothing – fighters with names like Captain Blood have returned to terrorize Monrovia. [...] They and other fighters steal cars at roadblocks and career around town sprawled over hoods, straddling windows and crowded into trucks bristling with gun barrels,' an American journalist wrote.[28] The AFL, which in Doe's time had been able to exploit the country's resources quite systematically thanks to its grip on state power, now showed the same propensity to indiscriminate looting as other factions. A Liberian journalist noted during the second battle of Monrovia in 1992 that the revived AFL '[have lost] direction. They become drunk with material things. They just want to loot. If someone gets in their way, they charge him with being a rebel and kill him.'[29]

The profit motive

After the NPFL had failed to take the Executive Mansion in the first phase of the war, and the conflict had begun to spawn new factions which lived by looting, it became increasingly apparent that commanders in all of the factions were encouraging their fighters to drink cane-spirit, to smoke marijuana (confusingly known in Liberia as 'opium') and to take amphetamines, known locally as 'bubble', presumably in order to keep them dependent on the commander and at the same time to make them reckless in action. An American reporter travelling with the LPC witnessed the faction's political leader, George Boley, putting eighty fighters

---

[27] Quoted in Africa Watch, *Waging War to Keep the Peace*, p.303.

[28] *Ibid.*, p.290.

[29] *Ibid.*, p.297.

through their morning exercises, jogging around a field and singing amid heavy rain. 'These are professional fighting men' Boley told his guest, while the journalist noted sourly that his generals were just lighting their first jumbo-sized joint of the day:[30]

> Colonel Action, a reed-thin killer with cane juice eyes, passes me a joint the size of a corn dog. 'Smoke it deep', he says. General War Boss III, General Rambo, General Murder and Captain Mission Impossible all nod encouragement. [...] I decline to smoke, but this is a vicious bush weed they grow here and the contact high is head-splitting. General Murder passes me a plastic bottle of cane juice.

Another foreign reporter noticed a similar complaisance while observing the elite NPFL Marines smoking marijuana in front of their leader, the notorious General Nixon 'Striker' Gaye. Two boys calling themselves MC Ram Dee, aged fifteen, and Colonel Mike Maclean, aged sixteen, entertained their comrades with a demonstration of rap singing:[31]

> Like most young Liberian fighters they can escape reality at will and pass into an imaginary world whose contours appear to be shaped by violent American films where the heroes are rapping black narcotics barons.
> Colonel Mike laid down the rap rhthym, a booming sound resonating through the bush and solely achieved with his mouth and his two hands, the left one of which is always covered in an oven glove, perhaps for improved percussion.
> Ram Dee started up.
> *I am a rebel*
> *I fought off the trouble*
> *I took in the bubble* [amphetamines]
> *I said double trouble. I'm a man who's not stable.*

Few Liberians doubt that the dress and the actions of the fighters were influenced by violent action videos they had seen, often American-made, which encouraged 'armed robbery, rape, and other related crises in the society', as the president of the National Cinematographic Association of Liberia maintained.[32] Certain acts of brutality bore all the signs of being carried out in imitation

[30] Jeffrey Goldberg, 'A War Without Purpose in a Country Without Identity', *New York Times Magazine*, 22 January 1995, p.39.

[31] Nicholas Kotch, 'Rebel Rappers Join the Cast at Liberia's War Front', Reuters despatch, 1 April 1993.

[32] Quoted in *Monrovia Daily News*, 4, 31 (2 March 1995).

of their celluloid heroes, while others, including the display of human bones and skulls, appear to have been derived from the repertoire of traditional warfare.

Like most wars, the Liberian conflict was marked by long periods, often of months, without fighting. During these lulls combatants generally wore the normal daily dress of the youthful poor throughout West Africa: jeans or shorts, flip-flop sandals and second-hand tee-shirts imported from the US. As the war continued, there were notably less cases of male fighters dressing in women's clothes or other carnival costume, and young fighters aspired to dress in the manner of youth elsewhere in the world. During the orgy of looting in Monrovia in April 1996, for example, few fighters wore the earlier warrior regalia. Most preferred sunglasses, cut-off jeans or bermuda shorts, back-to-front baseball caps, ankle-high basketball boots and bandanas, the garb of fashionable youth in American inner cities. Many fighters braided their hair in corn-row style or sported modish flat-top haircuts. So clearly did these styles become the fighters' hallmark that non-combatant youths took care to avoid them for fear of being wrongly branded as fighters. The one thing the fighters always wore, from beginning to end of the war, was objects for their spiritual protection.

While it was obvious that the war represented a major breakdown of social order, foreign journalists often saw the Liberian regalia of war as signs of a lapse into some sort of obscurantism which they found utterly baffling, and this may have caused some foreign observers especially to misunderstand the combatants' motives. 'The fighters fight to fight,' noted a correspondent from the *New York Times* despairingly. 'They destroy symbols of progress and prosperity – pumping stations, plantations – with glee, as if they're happy to wreck their country's future.' 'We don't need factories,' one fighter told him, when asked about the destruction of infrastructure caused by the war, 'it's better to come back to the bush.'[33] In truth, this observation that the war represented some sort of rejection of modernity seems wide of the mark. The fighters were less intent on destroying symbols of development than they were on acquiring what they considered to be their just deserts, the consumer goods which they prized as marks of high status and which were so hard for the poor to come by, especially in rural areas. Several authors on recent wars in Africa have pointed out how young men and women educated to believe that leaders of society have a duty to redistribute goods to their social juniors

[33] Jeffrey Goldberg, 'A War Without Purpose in a Country Without Identity', *New York Times Magazine*, 22 January 1995, p.38.

may be embittered in cases where this fails to happen, and become inclined to wreak their frustrations on the symbols of patronage.[34]

The sense of moral righteousness which characterised the NPFL in 1990, rooted in the traditional values of the village, was to diminish markedly as the war went on. On the other hand, fighters became ever more materialistic over time and as war became a way of life. Certainly some of the social workers who dealt with ex-fighters after the war reported that the youngsters were very consumer-conscious. Rather than rejecting the life of the city as immoral, they seemed most keen to live the city life themselves. Many drank and smoked. They wanted smart clothes and other expensive goods. Some adolescent ex-fighters habitually absented themselves from the post-war rehabilitation programmes run by aid organisations in Monrovia in order to visit what they called the 'ghettoes' behind Broad Street, where they could smoke marijuana and gamble.[35] By the end of the war it was hard to find any hint of the puritan moral attitude which had been detectable at an earlier stage, which some foreign observers had misinterpreted as anti-modernity. On the contrary, the war seems to have been instrumental in creating a category of young men and women who are avid consumers of imported goods which they want to keep as personal possessions. Older Liberians often interpret this as a rejection of the traditionally prized virtue of solidarity. 'Individualism,' in the view of one Liberian author, 'has also brought in a lot of sophisticated crimes that seek to place materialistic urge at the podium, emphasising individual glory over community well-being.[...] An African outwitting another African to get just one more dollar, for example, goes home with a broad smile.'[36] The youngsters' search for power and wealth went together. 'The looter mentality,' observed the same author, 'combined with witchcraft, makes them think they have special power.'[37] This was particularly shocking to older people imbued with the notion that power and prestige should properly be the attributes of age. 'They are the worst people in the world,' said one chief, speaking of the fighters, 'and they are our children.'[38] To such conservative

[34] Cf. Richards, *Fighting for the Rain Forest*, p.79 ff., which hints at this; cf. Rémy Bazenguissa-Ganga, 'The Spread of Political Violence in Congo-Brazzaville', *African Affairs*, 99, 390 (1999), pp.37-54.

[35] Author's interviews, Monrovia, March-April 1997.

[36] Nagbe, *Bulk Challenge*, p.104.

[37] Moses Nagbe, quoted in Goldberg, 'A War Without Purpose in a Country Without Identity', *New York Times Magazine*, 22 January 1995, p.38.

[38] Quoted in *ibid.*

onlookers the young fighters seemed devoid of most traditional values, including respect for elders, for life, and for group solidarity.

War always produces destruction, some of it calculated, much of it wanton. During the Liberian war there were occasional frenzies of looting when unpaid fighters at last saw the opportunity to capture the things which they thought to be their reward for taking up arms and to acquire what they would never be able to afford under normal circumstances. During the major episodes of looting, particularly the three battles of Monrovia in 1990, 1992 and 1996, people from all over Liberia and even from neighbouring countries headed for Monrovia to join in the action and to get something of value if they could, before returning home. One fifteen-year old boy, Mohammed Fofana, was from Koryama in Guinea. Although a Malinke, speaking no English, he joined the NPFL after being 'urged by his brothers to come to Gbarnga in order to acquire some cars'.[39] The lucky ones who succeeded in looting something of substantial value during an action could afford to retire from the war, at least unless they were dragged back in against their will at a later stage. A substantial number of the first generation of fighters from Nimba County may actually have succeeded in retiring with a good profit as a result of being in the first wave of looters. By the end of 1990 it was apparent that trade and transport in Nimba County were in the hands of people who had plundered something of sufficient value to set themselves up in business or build a good house, the usual symbols of prosperity in rural Liberia.[40] The same was visible in Lofa County in mid-1997, as groups of disarmed fighters continued to ply the roads, now as traders. Some sources reckon that a disproportionate number of fighters in April 1996 were from Lofa, people who had previously had little chance for serious looting.[41] While Monrovia itself was always the most valuable source of loot, there was no end to plunder, even after seven years of war, as looted goods themselves became a sort of currency, to be endlessly exchanged by sale or by force. One Liberian noted:

> [....] there is always loot, no matter how small. Most of the loot has been looted several times as territories change hands between the warring factions. Loot is also the motivation for the young fighters to take on front-line assignments. When

[39] John H.T. Stewart, 'The Influence of "Zakay"', *New Democrat*, 1, 51 (20-26 October 1994), p.8.

[40] Africa Watch, *Cycle of Abuse,* p.137.

[41] Author's interviews, Fissebu, Lofa County, 19 December 1997.

assigned to their bases in the hinterland they get little or no
pay, and may even have to beg for their food. To them any
kind of loot, be it big or small, is the only way to find any
money.[42]

To judge from the frequency with which male fighters committed
rape or abducted women as concubines and servants, women were
also included in the category of consumer items ripe for plunder.

Many ordinary people – those who cannot be regarded as part
of any pre-war political, social or military elite – often became bitter
when they discovered that the promise of financial gain was illusory,
as it was in most cases. One fighter, for example, a twenty-five-year
old Gbandi man, a high-school drop-out, joined the Ulimo faction
in Sierra Leone. He claimed that Alhaji Kromah had personally
promised him a million dollars. Several years later, holding the
Ulimo rank of brigadier-general, he was consumed with anger
after the leaders of his faction had all got top jobs in government.
'Kromah is using us for his pocket change,' he railed. 'Look at
me. I don't have anything. He is flying in an air-conditioned plane
and riding in air-conditioned cars. What about me?' The same
man also wanted compensation for his fighters, several of whom
had been maimed in the war and were destitute.[43] In similar vein,
a group of fighters from the Lofa Defense Force under one General
Spirit came to Monrovia during a ceasefire and physically assaulted
the political leader of their faction, François Massaquoi, accusing
him of not providing for them.[44] Likewise, in July 1995, forty Ulimo-J
fighters went to Monrovia and attacked the houses of their faction
leaders Roosevelt Johnson and Armah Youlo, accusing them of
having deserted their troops.[45] Yet another fighter, an NPFL veteran,
said that, when he thought about 'the five years I spent in the
bush, killing people and being shot at, I feel pretty stupid. We
were giving our lives for people who by tomorrow won't remember
how they got where they are. Most of them sent their own children
to the United States, and soon that's where they'll be keeping
all their money.'[46] Some of the more unsophisticated country

[42] Quoted in 'Selling a Rain Forest to Fuel a War', *The Pepper Bird*, 2 (1996), p.3,
Journal of the Society for the Renewal of Nature Conservation in Liberia.

[43] 'The Case of a Ulimo Fighter's US$1 m. Promise', *New Democrat Weekly*, 2, 110
(11-16 May 1995), pp.10-11.

[44] ' "Spirit" Chases Faction Leader', *The News* (Monrovia), 23 December 1996.

[45] Agence France-Presse despatch, 31 July 1995.

[46] Howard French, 'Liberia's Teen-age Soldiers Find Civil War is Over but so is
Hope', *New York Times*, 11 September 1995.

people clearly had no idea of the real value of the consumer objects they aspired to own. During the April 1996 looting of Monrovia, one fighter celebrating having stolen $2,000 in cash told his comrades that he was thinking of buying an aircraft with the money.[47] For people of humble origin to make a real fortune during the war was rare indeed, although there are known cases, such as Jungle Jim, the legendary former diamond digger who had such success in the diamond fields, and managed his relationship with the NPFL so well, that he is today a major international diamond trader, travelling regularly to Singapore and Antwerp.[48]

The chances of a lowly fighter making enough money to retire from the fray were slim, at least after the first battle of Monrovia, since a commander would soon detect any object of value being held by one of his or her combatants and would relieve the fighter in turn:[49]

Many of them, during [Operation] Octopus [in 1992], went to their early deaths hoping to acquire valuables from their misadventure in Monrovia. For those who were lucky enough to obtain anything at all, the Generals or some General took it away from them. And, as a young fighter put it, 'you go to the front, you fight, anything good you get, they take it from you. That's why you see some of those boys at the Front they don't want to come to Gbarnga because if they bring anything good, they will take it from them.'

Partly to try and get home with any loot they had taken, fighters often tried to desert during the three battles for Monrovia and other climactic combats. In a border area of Lofa County, some Ulimo-K fighters who had stolen a car, dismantled it and recruited forced labourers to carry the parts on their heads over bush paths to nearby Guinea. This was done in order for the car to be exported without being looted from them in turn by the more senior Ulimo commanders who controlled the roads. Once in Guinea, the car could be reassembled and sold.[50] During the many long months of relative calm, fighters often requested permission from their commanders to go home, to farm their land or to care for a sick relative or bury a parent. They were provided with a signed

[47] Throble Suah, 'In Pursuit of One Man', *The Inquirer*, 5, 54 (April-July 1996), pp.2-4.
[48] Author's interviews in Yekepa and Monrovia, December 1997.
[49] John H.T. Stewart, 'Taylor's Greater Liberia', *New Democrat*, 1, 30 (23-29 June 1994), pp.12-13.
[50] Author's interviews, Fissebu, Lofa County, 20 December 1997.

permit which then allowed them to travel through territory held by their faction.[51]

The discovery by the great majority of fighters that war would not provide them with permanent wealth left many deeply disillusioned. Some even went mad, like the once-feared Bush Shaker, a Gbandi man who had risen to be a general in Ulimo-K, but was said to have had a magic spell put on him by Mandingo rivals in the faction. He castrated himself, and is today a harmless and pathetic figure roaming the dusty streets of Voinjama.[52] By April 1996 many fighters seemed to have no idea why they were fighting at all, other than to acquire loot. When asked why they were killing their own people, they would often mumble something about being 'freedom fighters', but could not explain any further. One young man shot his friend in front of a UN official who asked him why he had done it. 'He pissed me off,' was the reply.[53] Fighters who stayed for long periods in the forest developed a range of problems, physical and psychological. Many suffered from venereal diseases and skin infections and abused marijuana and alcohol. Liberia's only known practising psychiatrist, Dr Edward Snoh Grant, who has treated hundreds of fighters, describes a typical adult combatant in the following terms:[54]

> He is someone usually between 16 and 35 years of age, who may have decided to become a combatant for several reasons: to get food for survival, to stop other fighters killing his family and friends, was forced to become a combatant or be killed, sheer adventurism etc. Hardly any admiration for the leader of the faction enlisting him in a fighting force. He is rag-tagged, semi-illiterate or illiterate, comes from the lowest socio-economic class of society, impoverished and disadvantaged. He is a 'native' (I have yet to examine and/or treat an America-Liberian [Congo] fighter since 1991). He is *dehumanized*. Exhibits no remorse of conscience. Has sunk so low as to be a human heart (he calls it the 'engine') eater. Rapist, plunderer and ill-tempered. Irrational, impervious to reason and has been programmed to obey and carry out orders from 'paper' Generals and COs. He is now deeply hurt because he has been told

---

[51] Author's interview with John T. Richardson, Monrovia, 8 April 1997.

[52] Author's interviews, Voinjama, 2-4 April 1997.

[53] Author's interview with UN official, Monrovia, 30 December 1997.

[54] Edward Snoh Grant, 'Something Verging on Criminality', *New Democrat*, 2, 156 (24-6 October 1995). (Emphasis in original.)

he fought for freedom and not money and is left with nothing to take home from the bushes to his family.

Dr Grant's assertion that fighters invariably came from 'tribal' families, of low income and educational status, is certainly questionable, as may shortly become apparent. There is no reason to doubt, however, his assertion that long service in a faction had a generally brutalising effect.

As the war took its course, motives became more diverse. Some people took up arms in self-defence, or individual acts of violence produced a desire for revenge, or older quarrels between towns and entire social groups which had simmered for years now boiled over into war. Hence, in some areas local civil wars developed, a sub-plot to the national conflict. In Lofa County, for example, the first incursion by the NPFL in July 1990 culminated in a major massacre of Mandingo at the town of Bakedu, an old commercial centre on a trade route from the coast to the savannah, controlled by Malinke or Mandingo traders. The memory of the Bakedu massacre was one of the chief motives for Mandingo exiles to join Ulimo-K in Sierra Leone and Guinea in 1991. When Ulimo-K invaded Upper Lofa County from its Sierra Leonean bases in 1992-3, the Mandingo fighters took cruel revenge, occupying towns where they had previously had no permanent rights of residence. To the outrage of the Loma and Kpelle inhabitants, they systematically pillaged the sacred groves of the Poro society, desecrating these holy places and stealing the masks and other religious objects. The looted masks, some of them very old, are said to have been sold on the international art market by Alhaji Kromah's right-hand man in Conakry, a Guinean dealer in African antiquities.[55] The Kpelle and Loma victims of these attacks knew precisely who these attackers were, since many were Mandingo from nearby towns, their neighbours before the war.[56] It was in retaliation for these attacks that some Loma and Kpelle refugees with military and organisational experience set up the Lofa Defense Force in 1993, established in refugee camps in Guinea with the primary aim of hitting back at the hated Ulimo-K. The faction was undoubtedly organised with the support of *zoes* of the Poro religious society from their places of exile in Guinea. Hence in many places the LDF fighters had the full support of the communities on whose behalf they were fighting, turning the war in the Upper Lofa area

[55] Author's interview with confidential source with knowledge of Ulimo-K, Monrovia, 21 March 1997.

[56] Author's interviews, Fissebu, Lofa County, December 1997.

into an ethnic contest between Mandingo on one side, and Loma and Kpelle on the other. This feud had a long history, since the area had been at the limit of the conquests of the nineteenth-century Malinke warlord, Samory, whose memory is still alive in the area.[57]

In cases such as these, young men were encouraged by their families to join one or another faction to defend their town. Quite a few Gbandi youths appear to have joined Ulimo-K in order to prevent it from committing atrocities in their own areas, and the fact that many Gbandi were Muslims helped their integration into this Mandingo-dominated force. Similarly, in Grand Gedeh County many Grebo people joined the NPFL when it first arrived in 1990 because they had long resented the fact that the government of the County was dominated by Krahn.[58] In the south-east of the country, when the LPC occupied Greenville in 1993 many young Sapo men joined this new faction enthusiastically so as to take revenge on their Kru neighbours, whom they accused of having earlier joined the NPFL to attack them and loot their property. By the end of the war, the LPC was estimated to be some seventy per cent composed of Sapo. Various battles for control of Greenville pitted nearby towns against each other.[59] It is said that in some areas the war in the south-east reopened old feuds dating back to the 1930s. Certainly, it militarised the factional disputes which had previously been the stuff of local politics, and which linked local struggles to national interests.

As the war itself gave rise to local vendettas, or as older antagonisms were settled by force at a time of war, there emerged a micro-politics of war in which certain territories suffered more than others at particular moments. The areas worst affected were those which were devastated repeatedly as local rivals launched see-saw raids and counter-attacks against one another. Many people had some reason to hate one faction more than others. The NPFL in particular was often regarded by those with experience of being occupied by various factions as one of the least destructive, and this was one of the reasons causing people to vote for Charles Taylor as president of Liberia in July 1997. One Kissi chief asserted that 'Taylor is our son,' because 'when his men came, they left us alone. We were doing our farming. They did not take our belongings. But when Ulimo [K] arrived, they

[57] Author's interview with the elders of Fissebu, Lofa County, 20 December 1997. For maps showing the extent of Samory's activity in the area, see Yves Person, *Cartes historiques de l'Afrique Manding*, Paris, 1990.

[58] Youboty, *Liberian Civil War*, pp.343-4.

[59] 'Case Study of Grand Gedeh County', September 1997.

took everything across the border.'[60] Since Ulimo-K was run by Mandingo traders, and raised many of its fighters in Guinea, it was particularly noted for its tendency to loot and export what it had stolen. Conversely, many people who fled to Monrovia as refugees from Taylor's Greater Liberia in the early 1990s, doubling the city's population,[61] have particularly bad memories of the NPFL. All Monrovians recall with horror the massive NPFL-led looting of 1996.

If some fighters felt justified in joining a faction to defend their town or village, many felt obliged to join simply for self-preservation. Every faction required large amounts of labour for porterage, and one of the worst fates was to be impressed as a slave-labourer by a faction, which resulted in heavy labour and ill-treatment, with death casually meted out to any refractories. Many people found it preferable to become a fighter. There are certainly more Liberians who took up arms for a faction, even if only under duress, than would care to recall the fact today. Precisely because many of them were ordinary Liberians, and not necessarily psychotics, fighters were capable of acts of kindness. One man whose son had been abducted by Ulimo-K near Gbarnga was terrified when a group of fighters banged on his door one night. They had returned to tell him only that his son was safe. Months later, father and son were re-united.[62]

But as the war went on and on, there did emerge core groups of fighters who, for one reason or another, were unable to leave the fighter's life other than to defect to a rival faction, which was a relatively common occurrence. Some children enlisted because their parents did, and perhaps they became separated from their parents later. Some of the longest-serving fighters were former orphans who were picked up in a commander's entourage and came to regard their patron as their father. One fifteen-year-old ex-NPFL fighter who had returned to Monrovia during a ceasefire, destitute, still regarded Charles Taylor as his 'pappy'.[63] Probably the top-ranking woman commander was the LPC's Ruth Milton, known by the war-name Attila. She had served for sixteen years in the AFL, finishing with the rank of major, before becoming the military commander of the LPC. Notwithstanding her ferocious

---

[60] 'Ethnicity and Politics', *New Democrat*, 2, 155 (19-24 October 1995), p.11.

[61] John H.T. Stewart, 'Monrovia: a swelling city', *New Democrat*, 1, 28 (9-15 June 1994), pp.12-13.

[62] Author's interview, Gbarnga, 29 March 1997.

[63] Howard French, 'Liberia's Teen-age Soldiers Find Civil War is Over but so is Hope', *New York Times*, 11 September 1995.

reputation, she claimed that she 'mothered' her captives, and in the case of the children, that is quite possible.[64] She was assiduous in negotiating an exchange of hostages, many of them children, after the war had finished. Her own children and her husband lived in Côte d'Ivoire.

Although remarkably few former child-soldiers seem to have developed clinical symptoms of psychosis, there was no doubt that their experience made them dangerous to deal with. Dr Grant noted of a typical child soldier:[65]

He is 15 years and may be as young as 9. He carries a gun that is sometimes heavier than his body weight. [...] He is very *deadly*. He has been *programmed* to carry out orders without question. He is too immature to differentiate what is good from what is evil. He has been catapulted from childhood to adulthood. He has been taught to get anything he desires forcibly. Patience, perseverance, respect for elders are not a part of the make-up of his thinking faculty. He is the one who will address you as 'papa' and at the same time order you to 'bring your ass here'. He enjoys the cracking of his gun and the sound of a gun going off, the menacing noise of a RPG [rocket-propelled grenade] while oblivious to the destruction and the taking away of life this may cause. He is 'loved' by the 'Pape' for his bravery. At 12 years he is made a General (how deceitful!).

Substantial numbers of former fighters on being demobilised feared to return to their home areas for fear of retribution. On the other hand, many social workers have been struck by the relative ease with which former child soldiers have been able to rejoin their families since the end of the war. It was rare for a family not to accept a wayward son or daughter who returned home, like the fourteen-year-old NPFL fighter who was rejected by his family because, at the age of twelve, he had disembowelled a woman.[66]

As the war went on, large numbers of fighters, adults and children, were tired of war and wanted to disarm but were simply afraid to do so, like members of the NPFL's notorious Marine Strike Force who were interviewed on the subject. 'We are aware

[64] Ruby Ofori, 'Gun-toting Mum Leads Liberians Into Battle', Reuters despatch, 29 November 1994.

[65] Edward Snoh Grant, 'Something Verging on Criminality', *New Democrat*, 2, 156 (24-6 October 1995). The emphasis is by Grant. A full study of Liberian child soldiers is Human Rights Watch – Africa, *Easy Prey*.

[66] Mark Huband, 'Ghosts of Civil War Haunt Liberia's Child Soldiers', *Guardian* (London), 13 April 1992.

that our people [the NPFL] are in Monrovia' said their commander
during one lull in the war, having heard on the radio of rehabilitation programmes for ex-fighters. 'But how can we come to town?
We are afraid of each other because of the war. We are all Liberians
but the war make[s] us to feel like that.' The commander, known
as Jungle Wolf, smoking a joint reflectively, said his men were
'tired of war' but were afraid that 'somebody will point at us'.[67]
Many former fighters, looking back, could hardly believe what
they had done, drunk with the power that comes from a gun,
fuelled by alcohol and drugs. One young Gio man who had taken
part in the 1990 massacre of Mandingo at Bakedu wrote to a
newspaper to apologise: 'We were not ourselves when these acts
were carried out; we were worked out to do them and we are
now returning to our very selves gradually as lasting peace returns
to our homeland as well.'[68]

   After the end of hostilities, in 1997, the United Nations in
coordination with various relief organisations undertook probably
the most sophisticated attempt to collect statistics on Liberia's
demobilised fighters. Of the thousands of ex-combatants who were
interviewed, twenty-one per cent were found to be children, which
is probably a misleadingly high figure due to the way in which
the demobilisation programme was designed. Many social workers
thought the true figure was closer to 15 per cent. Most fighters
were aged between fifteen and twenty-eight at war's end, with
a significant number in their thirties. Eighty-four per cent of all
fighters surveyed by the UN claimed to have attended school,
most only to a relatively low level. A surprisingly high number
claimed to have been under arms for five years or more. When
asked what they hoped to do after demobilisation, 56 per cent
of fighters said they wanted to go back to school and 28 per
cent wanted to learn a trade. Only six per cent said they would
like to go back to farming.[69]

Factions as political organisations

For several years after Ecomog had secured Monrovia in late 1990,
when it encouraged international aid organisations to establish

---

[67] Charles A. Jackson, 'An Encounter with NPFL Fighters', *New Democrat*, 2, 110
(11-16 May 1995), pp.8-9.

[68] Letter from Moses Zou, *New Democrat Weekly Review*, 1, 5 (1-8 December 1995),
pp.12-13.

[69] Letter from Shawn Messick, UN-Humanitarian Assistance Coordination Office,
with annexes, to UN-NGO Coordination Committee, 17 April 1997.

themselves, UN and other humanitarian agencies worked to disarm the factions and rehabilitate ex-fighters in society. However, the working methods of many humanitarian organisations often gave rise to a misperception about who the fighters were and about their relation to the rest of Liberian society.

Major aid organisations and UN agencies, like most Western corporations, function on the basis of statistics and budgets. Understandably, the UN, in its periodic attempts to monitor and encourage disarmament, sought first to establish how many fighters there were. By the middle of the war the figure of 60,000 combatants was in general use by aid organisations. This figure actually arose from one disarmament drive, when UN officials asked each armed faction to state the number of fighters under its control. The NPFL claimed 25,000, following which each faction provided figures roughly commensurate with the general consensus as to its relative strength, producing a total of some 60,000.[70] This figure, although too high by most calculations as an estimate of the fighting strength of all the factions combined at any one time, may nevertheless be regarded as an upper limit, the highest number of people under arms at any one time during seven and a half years of war.

Since there were estimated to be some 2,637,000 Liberians at the beginning of the the war, of whom hundreds of thousands had been forced into exile within a few months,[71] the use by relief organisations of the generally accepted figure of 60,000 fighters easily gave the impression to outside observers, including diplomats and UN officials jetting in and out, that the fighters constituted a minority of perhaps one in forty-four Liberians living either in the country itself or in neighbouring countries, and that this small minority was holding the rest of the nation to ransom. It is certainly true that nearly all Liberians were heartily sick of war long before the peace of 1997, but the use of statistics to judge the relative size of factions tends to imply a clear distinction between fighters and non-combatants. This is misleading inasmuch as there appears to have been a large number of people who took up arms at some stage during the war, but who may have been victims at other times. Moreover, even 'hard core' fighters

---

[70] A full breakdown is in *Marchés tropicaux et méditerranéens*, 2671 (17 January 1997), p.139, which also reports that John T. Richardson, head of the National Disarmament and Demobilisation Commission, reckoned the true total of NPFL forces to be 23,416.

[71] According to World Bank estimates for 1991, quoted in Human Rights Watch – Africa, *Easy Prey*, p.7, n.5.

seem to have remained attached to wider social communities to
a degree which may appear surprising. While many Liberians are
traumatised as a result of their experiences in the war, it does
not follow from this that there exists a specific class of person
who was once a full-time fighter and who, after demobilisation,
is marginal to society, as some relief workers have suggested. For
example, an official of the National Readjustment Commission
was quoted in 1992 as saying, 'most of the rebel fighters were
criminals before the war – petty thieves, pickpockets, trouble-
makers. At least 80 per cent of them were like that.'[72] It would
be more accurate to suggest that, although the war attracted some
of the worst people in society and produced maladjustment or
even madness in others, many fighters were simply ordinary people
in the sense of not being distinguished by any sort of psychological
trauma or other behaviour sufficient to cause their social mar-
ginalisation. The psychiatrist Dr Grant thought that, of the many
ex-combatants he had treated, only two per cent had mental disorders, but that 50-60 per cent had been using narcotics, of which
perhaps half had a serious drug problem.[73] One NPFL official
reckoned in 1997 that 200,000 people had fought for his faction
at one time or another, and while this figure is probably exaggerated, it illustrates the point that the official number of 25,000
NPFL fighters widely used by humanitarian and international agencies gives a false impression of the degree to which this, like other
factions, was composed of full-time fighters. In fact, all factions
retained close links with Liberian society and many people participated in an armed force at some stage of the war, acting out
of fear or self-interest, without ever becoming hard-core fighters.

As with armies all over the world, the more highly-educated
tended to have positions as staff officers, or civilian administrative
positions associated with the factions, while the foot-soldiers tended
to be less educated people from humbler backgrounds. The NPFL,
after its initial campaign in 1990, gave new recruits a basic six
weeks' training.[74] Ulimo-K had, by late 1996, some 5-6,000 fighters,
many of them Guinean Malinke in origin. Ulimo-K's general staff
supervised the command of brigades or regiments, each of which
was sub-divided into two or three battalions. The system of ranks
was highly inflated, with battalions being led by lieutenant-colonels

[72] John Nimley, quoted in Mark Huband, 'Ghosts of Civil War Haunt Liberia's
Child Soldiers', *Guardian* (London), 13 April 1992.

[73] Edward Snoh Grant, 'Please Stop the "Church Prophets"', *New Democrat*, 1, 9
(3-9 February 1994), p.21.

[74] Author's interview with John T. Richardson, Monrovia, 8 April 1997.

or full colonels. Ulimo-K, to continue the same example, maintained permanent training camps at Kolahun, Voinjama and Lofa
Bridge, where new recruits received no less than three months'
basic training. The faction had its own immigration and customs
services through which it controlled travellers' movements and
levied taxes on traders. Ulimo-K was exceptionally well provided
with arms and ammunition, probably due to its proximity to the
Guinean border and its excellent relations with the Guinean army.
During the 1996-7 disarmament exercise, it surrendered no fewer
than 800,000 rounds of ammunition, more than all the other factions put together.[75]

The biggest and most powerful faction by most standards was
the NPFL. When Charles Taylor set up his shadow government
in Greater Liberia in 1990 he appointed a full range of ministers,
directors and other bureaucrats to manage his administration.
These were not themselves combatants, but they contributed to
the war effort by running those services which the NPFL required.
Throughout the war Taylor enjoyed the support of a considerable
number of technocrats, some of them people highly respected
in Liberian society, such as Dorothy Musuleng Cooper, former
principal of Cuttington University College, or Dr Roland Massaquoi,
an agriculturalist who turned down a university lectureship in the
United States to continue working for the NPFL. In addition the
NPFL attracted the support of business people like Charles Bright,
Ben and William Cooper or Cyril Allen, to whom it was able to
offer lucrative opportunities on their own account or as business
managers for Charles Taylor. A disproportionate number of these
NPFL technocrats were of Americo-Liberian origin, that is to say
members of families, like the Coopers and the Brights, which
had formed part of the True Whig Party oligarchy before 1980.
Taylor's opponents often pointed to this fact to suggest that Taylor
was in fact an Americo-Liberian ethnic chauvinist and that the
war was no more than an attempt to restore the oligarchy overthrown in 1980. Whatever one may think of this allegation, the
number of Americo-Liberians in his entourage was a reflection
of the fact that Americo-Liberian families, like whites in South
Africa for example, have on the whole had greater access to higher
education than Liberians of indigenous origin, and have had the
chance to build family fortunes over generations. The assertion
made by the psychiatrist Dr Grant, quoted above,[76] to the effect

---

[75] Author's interviews in Voinjama, 3-4 April 1997, especially with Unomil officers.

[76] See above, p.127, n. 54.

that fighters were never from Americo-Liberian or Congo families, is certainly incorrect. To take but one example, Kuku Dennis, alias General Executioner, one of the most notorious NPFL fighters, was a former businessman from one of the most prominent of settler families. Some Lebanese also fought with various factions.

The smaller and less wealthy factions had fewer technocrats in their ranks, but each had its coterie of managers and bureaucrats nonetheless. Once the induction of the first Transitional Government in 1994 had opened the way for factions to appoint their own candidates to government posts in Monrovia, each faction strove to place its loyalists in strategic positions. This produced a logic whereby a faction which had gained ground militarily could use the extent of its territorial control as a basis for negotiating for itself a quota of top jobs in government. Office-holders who adhered to a particular faction would then be expected to use their position to generate funds for the maintenance of the faction and its fighters via a mechanism which was essentially no different from the system of political patronage which operated before the war.[77] For, even in a bankrupt state, with international debts of up to $3 billion, suspended from the United Nations and the International Monetary Fund and with an official income of only $20 million, there was money to be had from public office. In the first half of 1992, for example, the Interim Government spent some $1.3 million on travel and *per diem* allowances for its officials, including $383,564 on air tickets,[78] creating numerous opportunities for personal enrichment, especially when allowances paid in Liberia's official currency, the US dollar, were changed on the black market for Liberian dollars.

Members of armed factions could act with particular impunity in a weak coalition government. After one transitional government had decreed a ban on the export of scrap metal, since this was resulting in the stripping of Liberia's infrastructure, the chairman of the Council of State returned from a foreign trip to find that his vice-chairman, Dexter Tahyor, an appointee of the Ulimo-J faction, had unilaterally lifted the ban and exported a cargo of metal and rubber.[79] A year later a Lebanese businessman arranged

[77] Cf. Christopher Clapham, 'The Politics of Failure: clientelism, political instability and national integration in Liberia and Sierra Leone' in C. Clapham (ed.), *Private Patronage and Public Power: political clientelism in the modern state*, London, 1982, pp.76-92.

[78] *Monrovia Daily News*, 1, 121 (31 August 1992).

[79] 'Row Over Scrap Metal, Rubber, Export', *New Democrat*, 2, 95 (23-27 March 1995).

with one of the armed factions to loot material from the Bong
Mines, which he then bought from the faction and exported as
scrap metal. The transaction required licences from the Liberia
Electricity Corporation, Liberia Telecommunications Corporation,
the Ministry of Justice, the Ministry of Finance, the Liberia National
Police, the National Security Agency and an export permit from
the Ministry of Commerce, all of which could be obtained through
bribery, thus keeping civil servants and their political masters in
funds – and no doubt Ecomog too, since it controlled the port
of Monrovia, from where the cargo was shipped.[80] By 1995, the
finance ministry was being run by the brother of Alhaji Kromah,
leader of Ulimo-K, and it was witholding money from the National
Bank of Liberia, in the hands of the rival Ulimo-J. The finance
ministry on paper owed the central bank some 700 million Liberian
dollars (over US$10 million), but instead was placing its funds
with commercial banks, said to include the Banca Commerciale
Italiana in New York. The National Bank, short of liquidity, wanted
to print new notes but the security printers overseas refused until
an outstanding bill was paid in hard currency. In order to raise
the US$2.4 million necessary to settle this bill, the National Bank
of Liberia sold half the new notes in advance to major black market
operators.[81]

To investigate in more depth the role of the factions as political
organisations seeking state power, we may take the example of
Ulimo-J, one of the smaller factions and one generally regarded
as being dominated by Krahn, an ethnic group which had had
less access to higher education than some others over the years,
resulting in a relative paucity of Krahn technocrats. The leader
of the Ulimo-J faction was Roosevelt Johnson, said to be associated
with the Tchien clan from Zwedru, the Krahn heartland; Johnson
himself has testified that he was born and raised in Maryland
County, but says that his mother was Krahn.[82] A list of senior
Ulimo-J personnel from 1996 contains the names of seventeen
officials of the faction.[83] Nine of these had bachelor's degrees
from the University of Liberia, of whom the most senior in educational

---

[80] 'Lebanese Mafias Steal Millions', *National Chronicle* (Monrovia), 21-26 December
1996.

[81] *The Patriot*, 24 December 1996; Joseph T. Kleh, 'The National Bank of Liberia:
innocent victim of political and factional manipulations' [advertisement], *Daily
Observer*, 24 November 1995.

[82] Roosevelt Johnson interview with Ben Asante in *West Africa*, 4147 (28 April
1997), pp.681-2.

[83] 'Who's Who in Ulimo-J', *Monrovia Daily News*, 5, 61 (1 October 1996), pp.4-6.

138 *The Mechanics of War*

achievement was Monie Captan, a former lecturer at the University of Liberia with a master's degree in political science. Captan is part-Lebanese and is related to Charles Taylor on his mother's side. Roosevelt Johnson himself claims to have a BSc in education from the same university.[84] His leading rival in Ulimo-J, Armah Youlo, also a Krahn, had worked for the security police before the war and had obtained a BSc in criminology from a university in the USA, where he worked for a number of years. At least three of the other seventeen officials were trained accountants, of whom two had a degree in accountancy. Others had worked as senior civil servants, including Madison Wion, former chief of finance at the Ministry of Foreign Affairs, and Johnson himself, a former assistant commissioner for internal revenue. Only one member of the Ulimo-J leadership, regarded as a creature of Roosevelt Johnson, appeared not to be a high school graduate. On balance, it is clear that senior officials of this faction included a disproportionate number of university-educated people, and that they were not all from the same ethnic group, despite Ulimo-J's reputation as an essentially Krahn faction.

Other factions contained probably a higher proportion of people with professional qualifications and bureaucratic and international experience. As US Ambassador William H. Twaddell informed a House of Representatives sub-committee in 1996, 'most of the Liberian faction leaders and their associates have spent many years in the US, often as students, temporary workers, even as permanent residents. They own property, own or operate businesses, and more importantly, they know how the US system works and how to make it work for them.'[85] Although Monrovia is home to hundreds of politicians, technocrats and senior civil servants who did not belong to any military faction and who did not take up arms throughout the war, most of this same political and managerial class had served the Doe government which, in many respects, was the progenitor of all the armed factions, and some of them had even done so with unseemly enthusiasm, like the former MOJA president Togba-Nah Tipoteh, who wrote a book in praise of the PRC.[86] Moreover many of the politicians who were so viscerally opposed to Charles Taylor throughout the war had made common

[84] Roosevelt Johnson interview with Ben Asante in *West Africa*, 4147 (28 April 1997), pp.681-2.

[85] Testimony to Africa sub-committee of US House of Representatives, 26 June 1996, reproduced in *The Inquirer*, 5, 55 (13 August 1996), pp.2-4.

[86] Togba-Nah Tipoteh, *Democracy: the call of the Liberian people*, Uppsala, Sweden, 1981.

cause with him in the 1980s, canvassing support throughout West Africa for a military rising, like H. Boima Fahnbulleh, Tipoteh, and many others. Some who were with Taylor at the start of the war defected in 1994 to join the ranks of office-holders in Monrovia, notably Tom Woewiyu, Sam Dokie and Lavelli Supuwood. These three instituted their own faction, protected by Ecomog, called the Central Revolutionary council.

In short, all of the factions were run at the top level by members of the same relatively small group of politicians and technocrats who have dominated public life in Liberia since the 1970s, and who tasted power for the first time under Samuel Doe. With few exceptions, the factions' roots go back to the 'progressive' pressure groups, MOJA and PAL, which emerged under President Tolbert. From 1990 to 1994 this political elite was divided fairly precisely into those who supported the NPFL, living in Gbarnga or outside Liberia, and those who stayed in Monrovia, working for the puppet Interim Government, and thus indirectly for the government of Nigeria, the real power in Monrovia at that time. Some of them took up arms or adhered to armed factions directly, but many others supported military rule and military risings by words and deeds which fell short of taking a personal role in combat. When actual fighting has taken place, it has tended to be carried out by poorer and less educated people, often organised by professional military officers. If the managers of warring factions were in most cases almost identical to the managers of political parties and of the state itself, then the rank and file fighters were no different from the party supporters who in peace time make up voting-fodder as opposed to cannon-fodder.

The aid organisations which established themselves in Monrovia under Ecomog protection found themselves in the same unenviable position as ordinary Liberians, in the sense of being simultaneously obliged to work with various armed factions, while also at risk of being looted and exploited by them. Aid agencies provided food for Monrovia, becoming the city's second-biggest employer after government, and introduced scarce foreign exchange. As the war settled into a pattern of rival armed groups controlling territory and using it as a base to produce tradeable goods, faction-leaders became adept at persuading aid organisations to operate in their territories at the expense of rivals, if necessary by hijacking vehicles or engaging in other forms of manipulation and threats. For much of the time, aid agencies were relatively immune from workaday looting by factions. However at key moments, such as in the third battle of Monrovia in April 1996, their vehicles, computers and office equipment became targets of

strategic importance, used directly to prosecute the war or fund
the war effort. At such times, the looting of aid agencies became
a main aim of factions and was clearly carried out under the
direct orders, or at least with the approval, of faction chiefs and
even with the collusion of Ecomog officers.

Apart from making promises of loot and threats of coercion,
faction leaders also mobilised political support by appeals to ethnicity,
expecting people from particular ethnic groups or administrative
regions to support them. Exactly how ethnic mobilisation worked
may be demonstrated by reference to a minor incident, but a
telling one, involving General Isaac Musa, a former AFL officer
with a particular reputation for violence who served as the NPFL
battlefront commander and who for a time represented Charles
Taylor's interests in Monrovia in the 1994 Transitional Government.
When he arrived in Monrovia to take up his political position,
Musa, a Gio, publicly 'expressed outrage and consternation at
the ambivalent manner' with which the citizens of Nimba in Monrovia treated him when they expressed disapproval of his faction.
He made speeches in which he 'stressed that continued division
between the people of Nimba in Monrovia could only widen the
gap and make reconciliation difficult'.[87] This was a clear attempt
to use the moral codes of Nimba village life, based on the solidarity
of kinship and neighbourhood, in the service of national politics,
as has become usual in Liberian politics over many years. Hence,
once the warlords had been admitted to a share in the national
government, after a Transitional Government was instituted in
1994, people fleeing from violence in the rural areas and heading
for the city as displaced persons suffered the indignity of being
harangued by warlords like Isaac Musa, the very people who were
driving them out of their homes, who now had the gall to invoke
the traditional morality of village life and ethnic solidarity in appeals
for political support. It is small wonder that on occasion people's
frustration boiled over, such as in January 1995, when yet another
peace plan had been sabotaged by political manoeuvre, and tens
of thousands of Monrovians took to the streets and sacked the
houses of all the politicians they could find, irrespective of their
party allegiance.

In truth, the Liberian factions were no more and no less than
political parties in arms, and the ultimate aim of the main leaders
was to take state power. Rank-and-file fighters, and their habitual
victims, were also the voters in democratic elections. The most
eloquent illustration of this was that the July 1997 presidential

[87] New Democrat, 1, 30 (23-29 June 1994), p.14.

election produced a landslide victory for Charles Taylor, the greatest
warlord of them all.

Military organisations and civilian life

While factions differed in size, in wealth and in their approximate
ethnic composition, they came to resemble each other increasingly
throughout the war. Their essential attributes were a military
capacity and command structure and spokespersons or politicians
who could argue their case in the endless negotiations intended
to end the war, a continuation of the permanent factional manoeuv-
res which are the stuff of Liberia's political life. Some faction
leaders affected to be called 'Mr President' in anticipation of the
day that they would govern the whole country. Every faction had
a history of splits and many actually arose out of these splits,
making leaders nervous of powerful military commanders. Charles
Taylor was particularly adept in playing off his commanders against
each other. In the important Harbel sector, which for most of
the war faced the Ecomog front line, Taylor would appoint his
best officers to forward commands but would make sure that two
commanders who disliked each other held neighbouring districts,
minimising the risk that they would combine against him. Ecomog
itself generally avoided offensive military positions, but supported
various factions, especially the AFL, LPC and Ulimo, which it used
in effect as auxiliaries, a 'force multiplier' in military jargon.

The immediate aim of each faction was simple: it was to take
and defend a core territory from which economic resources could
be extracted, and where possible to extend this area, while the
faction's political bosses turned this strength on the ground into
political capital. A successful faction leader paid his commanders
either directly, by distributing stolen vehicles and cash, or indirectly,
by giving them access to commercial opportunities such as trades
in rubber, diamonds, hardwood and so on. Commanders in turn
had to ensure that their fighters received food at least occasionally,
although many were left to fend for themselves for long periods.
Factions which had a stake in the central government, which most
did after 1994, could also use funds pilfered from Monrovia or
generated by the opportunities presented by tenure of public office
in order to pay commanders. Any leader who could not pay his
commanders in some shape or form risked seeing them defect
or set up a dissident faction within the movement. As the war
progressed this actually became a common tactic for destabilising
a rival force. The leader of one faction would weaken a rival by
secretly approaching one of the rival's military commanders and

proposing money in return for defecting. For example, Major Solomon Kamara was killed in the internal feuding in Ulimo in 1992 after refusing a bribe.[88] Conversely, it is reported that when General Nixon Gaye mutinied against Taylor in August 1994, it was in part because he had been bribed by Ecomog or by leaders of the anti-NPFL coalition which Ecomog had helped to assemble.[89] Having bought Gaye's loyalty, a coalition of groups overran Taylor's capital at Gbarnga in September 1994 after also bribing the general defending the town, Cassius Jacobs. Jacobs, previously one of Taylor's favourites, was subsequently executed by the NPFL for treason. He was officially described as having been 'carried away by lofty promises'.[90] In similar fashion, Charles Taylor admitted aiding elements within Ulimo-J 'militarily and financially' in 1995 when he was manoeuvring for position, and this was to lead to an internal split in Ulimo-J which he then further manipulated, leading to the April 1996 battle of Monrovia.[91] During that battle, Ecomog dealt with opposing factions, including selling them weapons, for tactical and financial gain. But, just as factions easily split, they would sometimes join together against a common foe, as several factions did to form an anti-NPFL coalition in mid-1994, and as the LPC, Ulimo-J and AFL did in April 1996, when all three felt threatened by the NPFL/Ulimo-K onslaught on Roosevelt Johnson. All alliances were ones of opportunity.

Factions, and the people who lived under their yoke, were ingenious in finding new sources of livelihood or profit. A particular innovation was the collection of buried rubber waste from the Firestone plantation which, it was discovered, could be sold for reprocessing at US$50 per tonne. This led to the world's first known example of rubber being mined. It was known to the diggers as 'bouncing diamond'.[92] Fighters took food from villagers as a form of direct tribute, but they also supervised or took levies from gold and diamond-mining, rubber-tapping and palm oil manufacture, all of these processes being carried out using artisanal methods by civilians who then had to pay at least a part of the proceeds to the fighters who ruled them. Where foreign firms were operating with heavy equipment, factions would simply tax them for the right to export rubber or logs. Machinery, underground cables,

---

88 *The Inquirer*, 7 October 1992.

89 Cf. 'Taylor's NPFL in Disarray', *West Africa*, 4014 (5 September 1994), pp.1546-7.

90 Agence France-Presse despatch, Monrovia, 5 January 1995.

91 *The Inquirer*, 6, 46 (27 March 1996); Nagbe, *Bulk Challenge*, p.22.

92 'Harbel's "Bouncing Diamond"', *New Democrat*, 1, 59 (17-22 November 1994).

railway tracks, corrugated iron roofing, piping, were all stripped and sold as scrap metal. Looting was awesomely thorough: everything would be taken from a sacked town, down to electrical wiring, window-frames and corrugated iron roofs, and the buildings torched. Food aid convoys could be delayed or looted, as they frequently were by Ulimo-J in the first half of 1994.

In their core territories, most factions attempted to reach some sort of *modus vivendi* with the civilian inhabitants, if only because the fighters required them to provide food from their farms. The most successful faction in this respect was undoubtedly the NPFL, which throughout its extensive territory encouraged traditional rulers to administer justice and minor civic affairs. 'With the rebel soldiers, we don't have much problem because we are from the same group. If you know how to live among them, you'll get along,' said one woman from Nimba County at the beginning of the war.[93] Life for ordinary people in territories occupied by armed factions was hard, but was not always unbearable. For much of the war, large swathes of Liberia were occupied by the NPFL and were, until the major Ecomog-supported counter-offensive in 1994 which briefly occupied the NPFL capital at Gbarnga, relatively secure from the major looting of infrastructure since Taylor was anxious to keep economic production going. Towns and villages were obliged to host a small squad of fighters who would demand to be housed and fed and provided with women. For women, rape or forced concubinage was a constant threat. In relatively stable places like Nimba County, many men joined the dominant faction at least for a period but could otherwise live at home. In less stable areas, many men joined factions and the few who remained in their towns found travel almost impossible, since they were sure to be stopped at a checkpoint and screened as a potential enemy fighter.

In many rural areas, particularly the most hotly-contested ones, these conditions led to a radical shift in the position of women. Male civilians tended to be viewed by all factions as potential enemies and were stopped at check-points, whereas women found it easier to get through such controls. In socially conservative areas like rural Lofa County, where before the war women hardly left their towns other than to travel to the local market, they were obliged by the circumstances of war to assume various tasks traditionally done by men. Some women travelled widely to trade, and the effect has been a remarkable emancipation of women from their pre-war position. Today, there are women from this area

[93] Africa Watch, *Cycle of Abuse*, p.154.

who have moved into long-distance trade, hiring trucks to transport produce to and from Monrovia and even travelling abroad in the import-export trade. In at least one town of rural Lofa, for example, women are now expected to attend the weekly assembly whereas before the war this was for men only. Women's ability to earn cash has resulted in a notable increase in divorce in such areas, as women are economically freer to choose new partners.[94] Some women also made successful careers out of war, like Ruth 'Attila' Milton of the LPC, who later became superintendent of Grand Gedeh County, or Martina Johnson, a young Mandingo woman who became head of the NPFL's heavy artillery unit and is today head of security at Roberts International Airport.

When factions administered punishments, either to their own fighters or to civilians under their aegis, they did so brutally. In Buchanan, for example, LPC General Robert Totay, known as War Boss, got into an argument with a Ghanaian Ecomog soldier who shot him in the leg. The town was full of displaced people who had fled the LPC's vicious campaigns of depopulation in the south-east. A band of angry civilians, seeing Totay disarmed and immobilised, lynched him and one of his bodyguards, after which the LPC carried out a campaign of terror in Buchanan in reprisal.[95] The LPC later claimed to have executed four of its own fighters for committing exactions on civilians.[96] At the Ulimo-K capital of Voinjama, a former county attorney and resident judge of Lofa County, Benedict Kennedy, dared to complain to a commanding officer about his fighters' mistreatment of civilians. A week later those against whom the complaint had been lodged beheaded Kennedy in public, cut out his heart and paraded it on a stick.[97] During a ceasefire in 1996, a senior NPFL official, Cyril Allen, was outraged when his Mercedes was stopped at a road-block manned by fighters of his own faction while he was en route from Monrovia to Gbarnga. When Allen told the men to dismantle the road-block, the leader of the fighters, one Junior Logan, threatened to have him tied. Allen called for help on his radio, and a NPFL general arrived within minutes and shot Logan dead. Two others who had been manning the roadblock ran away but were hunted down and had their legs broken as punishment. The

---

[94] Author's interviews, Fissebu, Lofa County, December 1997.

[95] D. Emmanuel Nah, 'Calm Returns to Buchanan', *The Inquirer*, 5, 118 (7 July 1995).

[96] Agence France-Presse despatch, 20 November 1995.

[97] *New Democrat*, 1, 12 (17-23 February 1994), and author's interviews in Voinjama, April 1997.

commander of their brigade, General Isaac Bull, was publicly tied and flogged. Similarly, in late 1995 one of the NPFL's top fighters, the notorious Jack the Rebel, was publicly flogged in Gbarnga for maltreating civilians,[98] although he continued to serve in senior positions thereafter and is today one of President Taylor's leading security officers. But not all faction commanders were so habitually brutal. When Ulimo-J took over parts of Grand Cape Mount County in 1993-4, it was quite well received by local people who thought it preferable to the predators of Ulimo-K. This was not always by any means because of some ethnic connection. The Ulimo-J commander in Grand Cape Mount, known as General Twenty-Four Hours, a student at the University of Liberia in civilian life, was a Krahn commanding a non-Krahn territory.[99]

It was when they were invading enemy territory that the factions were at their most violent since they were generally unrestrained by any family ties or sense of moral obligation. As far as possible, factions avoided fighting other armed groups. Since the factions' economic base was the extraction of a surplus from the territory they controlled, using local civilians as concubines, labourers and porters, one of the key objectives in attacking another faction's territory was to frighten away would-be defenders. This was achieved most simply by giving advance warning of an attack on any light-ly-defended target, causing its inhabitants to run away, which made plunder much easier. Simulated attacks, designed solely to facilitate looting, were a common tactic, particularly in front line areas where tensions ran high. A group in occupation of the area would simply make a great deal of noise, shooting in the air, with the sole objective of frightening civilians into flight. After securing their plunder, the looters would then claim to have fought off the enemy and invite the townspeople to return. In Totota, for example, during 1995, this was done over and over again, with no enemy even in the vicinity.[100] Sometimes, individual informers would be recruited from a village in advance to give information on who had goods worth looting and where they were hidden. On other occasions, factions would rather seek to capture people from enemy territory for use as slave-labourers in their own core

[98] Author's interviews, Gbarnga, April 1997.

[99] Cf. Lindsay Barrett, '24 Hours with "Twenty Four Hours" in Capemount', *New Democrat*, 1, 8 (20-26 January 1994), pp.12-13. The generally favourable reaction to the Ulimo-J General Twenty-Four Hours was confirmed by the author's interviews with displaced people from the area in Monrovia in July 1994.

[100] Letter from Bart Witteveen to the author, 15 April 1998.

territory, as the LPC did extensively in 1993-4, in a manner reminiscent of the slave raids of centuries gone by.

It was factions operating in enemy areas which committed the worst atrocities, with the aim either of frightening people away or, in other circumstances, of terrifying them into dumb obedience. Stories of rape and mutilation collected from civilians, some of whom display the scars of mutilations or torture, are legion. The tortures and atrocities committed by factions on countless occasions were sometimes brutal almost beyond belief, as the reports of human rights groups testify.[101] According to a survey of 334 Monrovia high school children carried out by the World Health Organisation in February 1994, 61 per cent had seen someone tortured, killed or raped. Seventy-seven per cent had lost a friend or relative.[102] The chief of operations of the UN mission commented that 'kids get promoted in rank for committing an atrocity; they can cut off someone's head without thinking. The troops move into a village; they take everything and kill and rape. They stay a couple of weeks and then move on.'[103] Factions advertised their ferocity by putting skulls at the side of their road-blocks. Ulimo-K was even reported to have a checkpoint where the cord which blocked the road was formed by human intestines.[104]

Of all the countless atrocities carried out by the various factions, perhaps the most appalling, to many people, was the eating of human flesh. This is a practice with a long history which we shall examine in a subsequent chapter.[105] It may be recalled that Thomas Quiwonkpa's body was publicly dismembered and, it was reported, parts of it eaten, after the failure of his coup attempt in 1985.[106] Although there are few documented instances of such practices at the start of the war, after 1991 or thereabouts it became common to meet fighters who boasted of having eaten human hearts in the belief that it gave them strength, or to encounter traumatised refugees who claimed – including in front of friends and relatives who provided supporting testimony – that they had witnessed such

[101] The most accessible are publications by Human Rights Watch – Africa and annual reports published by the US Department of State. Also of great value, but more difficult to locate, are reports published by the Justice and Peace Commission of the National Catholic Secretariat in Monrovia.

[102] Human Rights Watch, *Easy Prey,* p.13.

[103] Quoted in *ibid.,* p.32.

[104] Internal memorandum, United Nations' High Commissioner for Refugees, Conakry, n.d. (January 1995).

[105] Chapter 6.

[106] See p.60.

events. There exist photos of the most appalling atrocities, sometimes taken by fighters themselves to advertise their ferocity, in much the same spirit that Prince Johnson took pride in the video-recording of the torture and murder of Samuel Doe. Wulia Zarkpa Grear, the mother of faction-leader Roosevelt Johnson, after being held hostage for some weeks by Ulimo-K in 1994 said she had been 'surprised to see human beings eating other human beings'.[107] Liberia's leading human rights group, the Justice and Peace Commission of the Catholic church, received so many authenticated reports of the eating of human flesh that it felt necessary to issue a condemnation of the practice in 1994.[108] Joe Mulbah, the NPFL information chief, confirmed to a Burkinabe journalist that cannibalism existed. 'All the factions do this,' he said. 'Even some of our own fighters eat human flesh.'[109]

Although reports of such practices relate to all factions, Ulimo-K was associated with some of the most atrocious cases during its invasion of Lofa County from its bases in Sierra Leone in 1992-3. François Massaquoi, leader of the rival LDF, accused Alhaji Kromah of having 'committed atrocities like you wouldn't imagine... I mean he's engaged in the lowest of lows – cannibalism.' Ulimo-K was said to have abducted Massaquoi's uncle, a *zo* or traditional priest of the Poro society named Paul Tarwoi, and to have consumed parts of his body.[110] A Reuters correspondent reported that Ulimo-K fighters 'admit eating the hearts of enemies, saying it gives them strength and courage'.[111] One fighter told the same reporter 'we rip the hearts from their living bodies and put them on the fire, then eat them.'[112] The Ulimo-K Field Commander took the unusual step of issuing a press release to counter the allegation that his forces had eaten human flesh. He denied the identity of those named as having carried out the murder of Paul Tarwoi, noting: 'we understand that this name [cannibalism] has become the household name in everyone's mouth in Monrovia.' He described

---

[107] 'Johnson's "Ma" Explains Ordeal in Tubmanburg', *The Inquirer*, 4, 101 (10 June 1994).

[108] 'Catholic Church Frowns on "Eating of humans"', *The Inquirer*, 4, 131 (25 July 1994).

[109] Quoted in 'Libéria', *L'Indépendant* (Ouagadougou), 108 (29 August 1995), p.11.

[110] 'Kromah Forces Engaged in Cannibalism in Lofa... Several Zoes Eaten', *Monrovia Daily News*, 3, 176 (6 September 1994).

[111] Steve Weizman, 'Killing Goes on in War-ravaged Liberia', Reuters despatch, 28 September 1994.

[112] Quoted in Steve Weizman, Reuters despatch, 27 June 1994.

it as cheap propaganda and said that, as Muslims, the Mandingo of Ulimo-K would eat only *halal* meat.[113]

Liberians, well aware of the religious meanings attached to the eating of human organs, do not doubt for one moment that many such reports are all too accurate. A Liberian journalist who visited an area fought over by rival Ulimo factions in 1995 commented matter-of-factly that 'here, the choice method of killing is to tear into a person's chest and extract the heart while the person is still alive.'[114] The LPC too was reported by displaced people to have carried out similar practices. One woman claimed that LPC fighters had murdered her husband by first breaking his ankles 'and when he was on the ground they cut his throat'. A so-called 'heartman' then arrived, known as Colonel Young Killer, who announced 'I'm taking your main machine' and cut out the man's heart, telling the victim's wife to boil water and cook it. The heart was then eaten by a group of fighters in view of several witnesses who later confirmed the truth of this account. The American journalist who collected this story heard fourteen separate accounts of similar practices from displaced people in Buchanan two days later. He observed that one or two such events could frighten a whole village into flight and concluded that 'the Liberia Peace Council uses cannibalism the same way the Bosnian Serbs use rape – as a means of ethnic cleansing.' A well-known Monrovia lawyer, Benedict Sannoh, told him, in reference to this practice, 'It is very hard to believe that it exists. But it does.'[115] During the fighting in Monrovia in April 1996, Monrovians were able to see how combatants 'shamelessly displayed human parts they had extracted from captured or killed fighters'. A leading newspaper noted 'our reporters on both sides saw fighters engaging in cannibalism and sorcery. In some instances, the fighters would kill and butcher the chest and extract the heart and later eat it. According to the fighters, "to eat the heart of a strong man at the front makes us strong too".'[116] Photos were taken of such grisly acts. Ironically, some of them show the mutilated corpse of General Doumbuya, the former Ulimo-K Field Commander who, little more than a year before, had issued the statement quoted above denying that his men engaged in such practices. He was

[113] Press statement by Field Commander Major-General Mohamed Doumuyah (sic), *The Inquirer*, 4, 171 (21 September 1994), p.3.

[114] John H.T. Stewart, 'Enter Ecomog', *New Democrat*, 20-25 April 1995, pp.12-13.

[115] Quoted in Jeffrey Goldberg, 'A War Without Purpose in a Country Without Identity', *New York Times Magazine*, 22 January 1995, p.38.

[116] Throble Suah, 'In Pursuit of One Man', *The Inquirer*, April-July 1996, pp.2-4.

slaughtered and his heart was consumed in front of dozens of witnesses in Monrovia's main barracks in April 1996.

The looting of Monrovia in April 1996 was a deep shock to Monrovians, who had previously thought themselves more or less unshockable, not least because the atrocious practices they had heard about were now happening in public before their very eyes, just as a similar shock had occurred, on a smaller scale and for shorter duration, during the Quiwonkpa coup attempt of 1985. But, in truth, for years there had been rumours and even more substantial evidence that powerful people ate human organs or drank human blood, acts regarded as means of obtaining power.

4

BUSINESS AND DIPLOMACY

Among the new intake at a school in Calabar in Nigeria in 1920 was a fifteen-year-old boy with a bright future. He was astounded by his first conversation with one of his new classmates, a Liberian. 'I first heard of a country', the Nigerian recalled fifty years later, 'whose executive and administrative officials were black men. It was unbelievable.'[1]

The young Nigerian was so impressed to learn of a country governed by black people that when he later went to America for higher study, he made a point of pursuing information about Liberia. In January 1931 he actually wrote to the Liberian government to seek employment as a Liberian diplomat, and three years later he published a book on Liberian foreign policy.[2] The Calabar schoolboy, Nnamdi Azikiwe, was later to become a leading nationalist and eventually president of Nigeria. He was only one of many young intellectuals who considered Liberia a model of African self-rule at a time when almost the whole continent was under European colonial administration.

Liberia's own elite in those days basked in the view that their country was a beacon for Africa and even a light to people of African descent in America. A visitor to Monrovia in the early 1940s noted how frequently church prayers and sermons made mention of Liberia as 'the great Negro democracy', 'the hope of the race', 'the land to which all blacks will some day return to live like the Jews to Palestine'.[3] This view of Liberia was one of the mainstays of the rule of the True Whig Party since it provided a grounding in religion and in reason for the descendants of American settlers to maintain their position of social and political superiority.

[1] Nnamdi Azikiwe, *My Odyssey: an autobiography*, London, 1970, pp.31-2.

[2] *Ibid.*, pp.164-5; his book on Liberian foreign policy is Nnamdi Azikiwe, *Liberia in World Politics*, London, 1934.

[3] Elizabeth D. Furbay, *Top Hats and Tom-Toms*, Chicago and New York, 1943, p.112.

The West African balance of power

Liberia's unique status disappeared with the gaining of independence by other West African countries, beginning with Ghana's proclamation as a sovereign state in 1957. At the time of West Africa's decolonisation, perhaps the most important single question facing diplomats and politicians was whether the old colonial frontiers would remain intact, or whether the new states would split up to form new entities, or even combine in a United States of Africa, the pan-Africanists' dream. Since Liberia still enjoyed a residual prestige as the first African republic, the wily President Tubman became a founder of the Organisation of African Unity and encouraged the organisation to develop a policy of respect for existing borders, which would help safeguard his position against radical firebrands like Ghana's Kwame Nkrumah, or his neighbour Ahmed Sékou Touré of Guinea.

The first, and to date the most searching, test of the durability of the new states of West Africa occurred in 1967, as the result of the attempt by one region to break away from the former British colony of Nigeria and to gain international recognition as the Republic of Biafra. If Biafra's attempt to leave Nigeria had succeeded, it would have broken up Nigeria, by far the largest and most powerful country in West Africa. There were some people outside Nigeria who favoured the independence of Biafra less from any great sympathy with the rights of small nations than out of calculated self-interest. Prominent among such supporters of Biafra was France's leading regional ally Félix Houphouët-Boigny, President of Côte d'Ivoire, who was instrumental in persuading France's President Charles de Gaulle to join him in helping Biafra. Both believed that Nigeria was a country too big and potentially powerful for their comfort, and that the interests of France and its West African partners were best served by keeping the anglophone countries, particularly Nigeria, as weak as possible.

Successive leaders of Nigeria have never forgotten this hostility, and continue to regard Côte d'Ivoire, which still enjoys perhaps the closest relationship with Paris of all France's former West African colonies, as their most serious long-term rival in the area. Like most long-term diplomatic rivalries, it is largely economic in nature. The massive rise in world oil prices in 1973-4 turned Nigeria, the only major oil producer in West Africa, into a regional giant, flush with petro-dollars. In 1975 the Nigerian government, hugely ambitious, was the prime mover in the establishment of a new economic community, Ecowas, intended to develop into a regional common market with Nigeria at its centre. Although this project failed to create an effective economic bloc, its continued existence is a reflection of the sheer weight of Nigeria's economy. While Nigeria was growing richer on its oil revenues, other countries were facing an economic crisis as the prices of their staple export commodities fell in the late 1970s. Côte d'Ivoire faced an alarming fall in the revenues from its main exports of cocoa and coffee.

The Ivorian government, heavily indebted to international banks, was obliged to seek help from the lenders of last resort, the International Monetary Fund and the World Bank. The bankers from Washington did not like what they found in Côte d'Ivoire, which was a government living beyond its means, over-reliant on a state-managed system of buying cocoa from individual farmers at fixed prices. As IMF and World Bank officials insisted on the liberalisation of the Ivorian economy, and as the cocoa markets in London continued to offer only low prices for the country's leading crop, President Houphouët-Boigny, drawing to the end of a long and remarkable career, grew bitter. A former head of the French secret service recalls how the octogenarian president was convinced that the difficulties faced by his country were engineered in large part by what he called 'les Anglo-Saxons', by which he meant British and American commodity dealers and bankers working in collaboration with Nigeria.[4] Houphouët-Boigny decided on a desperate gamble: he would withhold the entire Ivorian cocoa crop from the world market in the hope of forcing prices up and defeating the London commodity dealers. For eighteen months he was able to hold out, stockpiling hundreds of thousands of tonnes of cocoa and waiting for the market to buckle. But the old man had overplayed his hand. Overwhelmed by financial pressures, he was forced to admit failure and to recommence cocoa sales. In 1988 his friends in the French government helped him out by subsidising a French commodity broker to buy the huge Ivorian cocoa stockpile, 400,000 tonnes, equivalent to a quarter of the world's annual production, at a price above that of the current world market value, thanks to a subsidy from the French tax-payer arranged by Jean-Christophe Mitterrand, son of the president of France and principal advisor on African affairs at the Elysée palace.[5]

While Côte d'Ivoire had flourished since independence on its close relationship with France, its economy became dangerously

[4] Claude Silberzahn with Jean Guesnil, *Au coeur du secret : 1500 jours aux commandes de la DGSE, 1989-1993*, Paris, 1995, p.206.

[5] Jean-Louis Gombeaud, Corinne Moutet and Stephen Smith, *La guerre du cacao. Histoire secrète d'un embargo*, Paris, 1990.

uncompetitive once a general fall in commodity prices had exposed its position. Like every other French-speaking state in the region (with the exception of Guinea and, briefly, Mali), Côte d'Ivoire had remained a member of the Communauté financière africaine (CFA), a monetary union in which member states used the CFA franc which was pegged until 1994 at 50 CFA to one French franc. This made the CFA in effect a hard currency, since it had the strength of the French franc behind it. The English-speaking countries of the region, on the other hand, on becoming independent in the 1950s and 1960s had all created their own national currencies, whose international value soon declined. Potentially, the strongest of these was the Nigerian naira, in view of Nigeria's oil wealth, but the nature of the Nigerian government and its record of economic and financial mismanagement did not inspire business confidence. The one haven of monetary stability in English-speaking West Africa, at least until the 1980s, was Liberia, whose official currency was the mighty US dollar. Even when Samuel Doe began minting his own coins, with US acquiescence, the US dollar continued to be legal tender in Liberia, making it a useful location for traders wanting to switch from weak local currencies to internationally negotiable ones or for businessmen and women who, for one reason or another, wanted to 'park' dollars earned in other markets. As far back as the 1940s, Liberia had established itself as an offshore business centre where foreign businessmen could register companies which they could use for transactions in a dollar zone.

Côte d'Ivoire was not the only African country to encounter serious financial problems as profound changes in world commodity markets reduced their income and made them vulnerable to competition from new producers in Asia and Latin America. One African government after another sought help from the IMF and the World Bank. The international financial institutions insisted on similar reforms from all of their clients – budget-cutting, currency devaluation, and market liberalisation. Ghana, Nigeria and Sierra Leone were all obliged to devalue their national currencies by huge amounts and saw their market value depreciate. The French-speaking countries, confident of the firmness of their CFA franc and supported by a French government at first sceptical of the World Bank's and the IMF's zeal for free trade, were able to resist these pressures longer than their anglophone neighbours.[6] To avoid holding nairas which were not negotiable internationally,

---

[6] Nicolas van de Walle, 'The Decline of the Franc Zone: monetary politics in Francophone Africa', *African Affairs*, 90, 360 (1991), pp.383-406.

Nigerian business people operating in international markets increasingly sought to change their depreciating nairas into hard CFA francs, if necessary illegally. Major Nigerian or Nigerian-based entrepreneurs in the import-export business often deposited their CFA francs in bank accounts in London or Switzerland, where they could eventually be converted to other hard currencies such as sterling or dollars.

The depreciation of the naira hit Nigerian consumers badly, but it did have the positive effect of reducing the price of Nigerian exports and giving Nigerian manufacturers a price advantage over their French-speaking competitors. Markets throughout West Africa became flooded with goods made in Nigeria, often locally made copies of international-brand car-parts, cosmetics, pharmaceuticals, alcohol and other consumer goods, or re-exports of electrical goods from Taiwan and the Far East.[7] The tendency of Nigerian traders to convert their profits into CFA francs, and to bank these in Europe where they could be exchanged for French francs, meant that the French treasury found itself having to pay increasingly large sums of money to buy the CFA francs being offered to it. By a circuitous route the French tax-payer, as well as subsidising Ivorian cocoa, was also paying incentives to the Nigerian businessmen who were taking over traditionally French markets in Côte d'Ivoire and throughout West Africa.

Many of the low-priced Nigerian exports or re-exports which flooded West African markets were smuggled rather than going through formal trade channels. Particularly lucrative was the smuggling of petrol. The Nigerian government subsidised the sale of petroleum products on the grounds that this would allow ordinary Nigerian citizens to benefit from their country's oil reserves. However, what the subsidy also did was to enable people with the necessary connections to export petroleum products subsidised by the Nigerian government for sale at a higher price in neighbouring countries. Although this was illegal, it took place on a huge scale, and Nigeria itself sometimes suffered from periodic petrol shortages as a result. Some of the cross-border smuggling which developed so rapidly in the 1980s was no more than the continuation of age-old trade routes, such as between northern Nigeria and Niger, but rather more of it was a direct response to artificial price differentials and currency movements.[8] While

---

[7] Cf.Ousmane Samba Mamadou, 'The CFAF Devaluation, Naira Parallel Exchange Rate and Niger's Competitiveness', *Journal of African Economies*, 6, 1 (1997), pp.85-111.

[8] Abdoulaye Diagne, 'Les travaux de recherche sur l'UMOA. Un aperçu', *Africa Development*, XVI, 3-4 (1991), pp.5-26; for a specific case study, Emmanuel Grégoire,

smugglers could avoid paying official taxes and dues, they generally had to pay other charges – bribes – in order to carry out their transactions.

Over time, the growth of smuggling and informal trade throughout West Africa has created a system where traders manipulate both formal and informal markets and where officials connive at practices which they are officially supposed to prevent, creating webs of vested interests which liberalisation and privatisation have served only to make still more complex.[9] These developments have also enabled controllers of local smuggling networks to make inroads into world markets. Since the early 1980s, Nigeria has become a major importer and re-exporter of narcotics, particularly heroin from south-east Asia, a trade which involves Nigerian criminal syndicates making use of facilities in neighbouring countries for the physical transport of contraband goods as well as using hard currency zones for money-laundering.[10]

Rapid shifts in trade practices and the boom in the international narcotics trade brought Liberia to the attention of Nigerian traders especially. Liberia had an established reputation as a location for depositing and laundering funds of dubious origin, thanks to the fact that the US dollar was its official currency from 1944. As early as the 1950s, at least one major international operator, a banker to the Israeli secret services and to the US underworld boss Meyer Lansky, the pioneer of modern money-laundering,[11] was using Liberia as one of his centres of operation.[12] There is some evidence that President Tolbert was acquainted with international drug traffickers.[13] Samuel Doe continued the practice of using the facilities of a sovereign state to conduct personal deals of dubious legality with major international criminals. He cultivated a brief relationship with the notorious Italian fraudster Giancarlo Parretti, whom he made an ambassador-at-large of the Liberian government. Parretti negotiated to buy a 49 per cent share of Air Liberia and was also interested in the privatisation of Liberia's oil operations. Doe and Parretti are said to have used

---

'Les chemins de la contrebande. Étude des réseaux commerciaux en pays hausa', *Cahiers d'études africaines,* XXXI, 4 (1991), pp.509-32.

[9] Jean-François Bayart, Stephen Ellis and Béatrice Hibou, *The Criminalization of the State in Africa,* Oxford and Portsmouth, NH, 1999, pp.69-113.

[10] Observatoire géopolitique des drogues, *Atlas mondial des drogues,* pp.188-91.

[11] *Ibid.,* p.217.

[12] Robert Lacey, *Little Man: Meyer Lansky and the gangster life,* London, 1991, p.309.

[13] Nya Kwiawon Taryor (ed.), *Justice, Justice: a cry of my people,* Chicago, 1985, p.54.

the oil business as a source of revenue to buy companies abroad, and Parretti was later to use similar techniques in other parts of Africa.[14] The more the US government tried to persuade Doe to reform by putting him under financial pressure, the more he resorted to dealing informally with sleazy international business-men, bartering timber for guns[15] and encouraging all manner of money-laundering and quick-fix financial operations. In addition to a host of other dubious ventures, Doe's minister of finance, Emanuel Shaw, established relationships with an array of colourful characters trading in Nigerian oil via the Liberian National Petroleum Corporation, including with South Africa.[16]

While a few foreigners and rather fewer Liberians grew rich on rackets of this sort, the 1980s were in general an economic catastrophe for Liberia. The country's economy actually shrank during the decade when Doe was in power. Foreigners pulled their money out, creating a currency shortage which was rectified with the introduction of Liberian-issued 'Doe dollars', giving the country a two-tier currency system. Liberia's main hard currency earner was iron ore, developed in the 1950s and 1960s, which contributed some 40 per cent of the country's Gross Domestic Product in 1975. This sector too suffered in the 1980s, falling to just 15 per cent of GDP between 1981 and 1985. This decline was not entirely the result of mismanagement by the Liberian government, but was also because the country's biggest iron ore mine, at Yekepa in Nimba County, was coming close to depletion. The Yekepa mine was situated right next to Liberia's border with Guinea, and on the other side of the border there were vast reserves of ore which could be worked only with the agreement of the Guinean government. As Liberia's own iron ore reserves were depleted, international mining companies began to search for ways of developing mines on the Guinean side of the border, using Liberia's infrastructure to export the ore.

Just as the sharp movements in commodity prices in the 1980s had produced major shifts in the cocoa and oil markets, so too were there worldwide changes in patterns of iron ore production. Large new iron ore mines were opened in Brazil. Together with other producers in Canada and Australia, the Brazilians used their

14 William Reno, letter to author, 15 June 1996; on Parretti's career elsewhere in Africa, see Stephen Ellis, 'Africa and International Corruption: the strange case of South Africa and Seychelles', *African Affairs,* 95, 379 (1996), pp.186-7.

15 Jarrett, 'Civil War in Liberia', p.26.

16 Reginald B. Goodridge, 'Sovereignty on Auction', *Liberian Diaspora,* III, 2 (June 1991), pp.10-12.

market strength to push up the international price of iron ore by about forty per cent between 1988 and 1990, precisely as the Ivorian government had failed to achieve with cocoa. The European and Asian steel industries in particular, squeezed by the producers, were anxious to find a reliable new source of iron ore, and they thought they had located it on the northern side of the Nimba mountain range which straddles the border between Liberia and Guinea.[17]

Mount Nimba contains some of the world's highest-quality iron ore. From 1961 the deposit on the Liberian side, the most important source of Liberia's iron ore exports, was worked intensively by a Liberian-American-Swedish conglomerate known as Lamco, then the leading payer of tax to the Liberian government, while the reserves on the Guinean side, some three-fifths of the total, remained untouched as long as the capitalist-unfriendly President Sékou Touré was in power. After Sékou Touré's death in 1984, potential investors discussed with a new Guinean government the establishment of a consortium, Mifergui, which could exploit the ore on the Guinean side of the border. There was opposition from Western environmentalists concerned by the threat to the tropical rain forest and its flora and fauna, but a greater problem was the lack of a rail link to evacuate the iron ore from the Guinean part of the Nimba mountain range to Guinea's main port at Conakry, 640 miles away. Investors proposed bringing the Liberian government into the equation so that the existing infrastructure in Liberia could be used to export the Guinean ore via the 187-mile railway line which already ran from Yekepa, the site of the Lamco mine close to the Guinean border, to the Liberian port of Buchanan.[18] If this succeeded it would be one of the biggest mining projects ever undertaken in Africa. Experts estimated that, if the Guinean side of Mount Nimba were mined, the project could export 12 million tons of ore per year for up to fifty years before depletion. In 1989 a deal was agreed between the investors and the Liberian and Guinean governments.

Everything was set for work to begin on the Guinean side of Mount Nimba when the NPFL's Christmas 1989 offensive in Nimba County threw the scheme into doubt.

[17] Patrick de Saint-Exupéry and Sophie Roquelle, 'La "montagne de fer" que convoite l'Elysée', *Le Figaro* (Paris), 8 January 1992.

[18] Special report on Liberian iron ore in *Liberian Diaspora*, II, 7 (June 1992), pp.19-24.

The game of nations

Although European investors had developed substantial interests
in Liberian iron ore mines since the 1950s, there had never been
any doubt that the country's special relationship was less with
Europe than with the United States. Liberia had been the leading
US ally in West Africa since the nineteenth century and a source
of US raw materials since the Firestone Agreement of 1926. President Franklin Roosevelt visited Liberia in 1943, when all the other
countries in the region were still under colonial rule, to negotiate
rights to harbour and airfield facilities which made the country
also a strategic asset. By the 1980s Liberia was home to a major
CIA station, a satellite-tracking station and a Voice of America
transmitter, apart from the US economic interests represented
by Firestone and other investors. It was the American government's
concern to preserve these assets which caused Washington to
withdraw its support from President Tolbert in 1979 after he had
refused to allow Roberts International Airport to be used as a
staging-post for a US Rapid Deployment Force en route to the
Middle East.

   Perhaps the most remarkable skill developed by Samuel Doe
after he succeeded Tolbert as head of state in 1980 was his ability
to play on American fears of destabilisation. As head of state he
consistently supported the United States in international fora, even
reopening diplomatic relations with Israel at American behest.
This he traded for US financial and diplomatic support for his
government. Doe's diplomatic strategy was particularly effective
in the 1980s because of President Ronald Reagan's personal antipathy to the Libyan leader Colonel Gadaffi, whose brand of theatrical posturing seemed especially to irritate the American president.
Libya bought an estimated billion dollars' worth of arms every
year from the Soviet Union, providing an important source of
hard currency for the Soviet economy.[19] Doe used his membership
of the Organisation of African Unity and various other third world
organisations to launch a series of outspoken attacks on Gadaffi
which were greatly appreciated in Washington. As we have seen,
in 1987 the Libyan government began to host an army of Liberian
exiles with a view to driving the United States out of its main
West African base.

   It was through their shared antipathy to Samuel Doe that the
ferociously anti-American Colonel Gadaffi found himself sharing
the same set of allies as the Ivorian patriarch, the doyen of francophone

[19] Bob Woodward, *Veil: the secret wars of the CIA, 1981-1987*, New York, 1987, pp.87-8.

Africa, Félix Houphouët-Boigny. The radical young officers who
ruled Burkina Faso after 1983, revolutionary in their rhetoric and
pro-Libyan in their foreign policy, caused serious concern to
Houphouët-Boigny. The Burkinabe President Thomas Sankara,
dashing, articulate and handsome, was a hero to youth all over
West Africa, where the economic crisis of the 1980s had alienated
a generation of young people born after independence, who had
grown up expecting their governments to provide them with jobs
and education. All over West Africa there were radical students
and would-be revolutionaries seeking inspiration, some seeing it
in the Libyan system of revolutionary committees, others in the
North Korean ideology of *juche* or other alternatives.[20] It was largely
disaffected youths of this ilk who found their way to the training
camps run by Colonel Gadaffi's World Revolutionary Headquarters
in Libya.

Like other West African heads of state, Houphouët-Boigny
regarded his diplomatic friendships, business partnerships and marriage alliances as both the sinews of political relationships and
a reflection of national aspirations, like the royal marriages and
dynastic alliances of old European nobility. When Captain Compaore, married to one of Houphouët-Boigny's numerous young
female protégées, overthrew Sankara in 1987, the Ivorian president
could feel confident that the government in Burkina Faso offered
no further threat. When another ambitious young man, Charles
Taylor, in turn became friendly with President Compaore of
Burkina Faso, and when in 1989 these two used Côte d'Ivoire
for an attack on Liberia, Houphouët-Boigny did not even take
the trouble to meet Taylor. It was only later, during the numerous
peace conferences which the Liberian war inspired, that he met
him for the first time.

Where a rapprochement between the Libyan government and
the leading francophone government in West Africa might just
a few years earlier have caused serious concern in Washington,
the real threat which Libyan adventures in West Africa could pose
to the US government was rapidly diminishing in the late 1980s,
as the Cold War drew to a close and as Ronald Reagan left the
world stage. For the same reason the United States was able to
distance itself from Samuel Doe, its expensive and embarrassing
ally in Monrovia. Doe drew closer to another mentor, the Nigerian
President Ibrahim Babangida. Like Doe, Babangida was a military
man who had come to power via a military coup. He took a somewhat

<hr>

[20] Cf. special number of *Africa Development*, XXII, 3-4 (1997), especially Ishmail
Rashid, 'Subaltern Reactions: lumpen, students and the left', pp.19-44.

paternal interest in Doe and became a personal friend. The two presidents became business partners by taking joint control of the Liberian National Petroleum Company (LNPC), which acquired a monopoly for importing Nigerian oil, which it sold to the state-owned Liberian Petroleum Refinery.[21] The LNPC also exported petroleum products to Sierra Leone, Gambia, Senegal, Togo and even Nigeria itself, competing with the refinery in Côte d'Ivoire. Liberia became a main supplier of iron ore for the Nigerian steel industry.[22] President Babangida on one occasion paid Liberian government debt with Nigerian public funds, claiming this to be a gesture of pan-African solidarity.[23] The money may possibly have been deposited in Eurobank, an establishment in Monrovia in which Doe and Babangida are said to have had an interest.[24] Liberia became President Babangida's off-shore banking and business centre. The Nigerian president paid for the establishment at the University of Liberia of the Babangida School of International Diplomacy, whose staff, including at least eight Nigerian expatriates, were paid by the Nigerian government in foreign exchange.[25] A new road linking Liberia and Sierra Leone was officially named the 'IBB international highway' in Babangida's honour.[26] According to Charles Taylor, Doe was also in business with Sir Dawda Jawara, president of Gambia.[27]

Thus, by the late 1980s a new regional division of forces was emerging around Liberia as the old Cold War power-blocks unfroze. Nigeria, the aspiring hegemon of West Africa, became the Liberian government's main ally. The leader of francophone West Africa, Côte d'Ivoire, was firmly in the anti-Doe camp. So too, after the accession to power of Blaise Compaore in October 1987, was Burkina Faso, allied with both Côte d'Ivoire and Libya. Charles Taylor and other leaders of the NPFL received a consignment of weapons from Libya and, according to Prince Johnson, millions of dollars in cash to finance a campaign.[28] Taylor was shuttling between Libya, Burkina Faso, where most of the NPFL fighters

21 Toyin Egunjobi, 'Doe: the complete story', *Newbreed*, 22 October 1990, p.18.

22 Vogt and Ekoko, *Nigeria in International Peace-keeping*, p.199.

23 Omonijo, *Doe: the Liberian tragedy*, p.53.

24 Author's interviews, Monrovia, April 1997.

25 Vogt and Ekoko, *Nigeria in International Peace-keeping*, p.199.

26 Ewa Unoke, *The Untold Story of the Liberian War*, Enugu, 1993, p.98.

27 'Face to Face with Charles Taylor', interview by Baffour Ankomah, *Ghanaian Chronicle*, 12-18 Oct. 1992, pp.6-7.

28 Quoted by Gerald Bourke, *Independent on Sunday* (London), 5 August 1990.

completed their training, and Côte d'Ivoire, from which the attack was to be launched. American, French, British and Japanese businessmen and bankers were focussed on the Mifergui iron ore project, straddling the border of Guinea and Nimba County. During the first few years of the Liberian war, much of the international interest in who controlled the country was dictated by the desire of international investors to put the Mifergui scheme into full operation.

When it became clear that Côte d'Ivoire was backing the NPFL, Taylor could count on a fair degree of sympathy from the French-speaking countries of the region, and he was soon to acquire significant support in France itself. The launching of the NPFL invasion at Christmas 1989 was of particular concern to the English-speaking governments of West Africa, unnerved by the presence of exiled revolutionaries from their own countries alongside Taylor. The Nigerian government was afraid that an NPFL victory would take Liberia into the French-speaking camp and that Taylor, if he became president, would use Liberia as a base to destabilise Nigeria itself by providing arms and training to exiled opponents. The Ghanaian government was similarly disturbed by the spectre of a civilian-led uprising and by the knowledge that there were Ghanaian dissidents fighting for the NPFL.[29] According to a Ghanaian intelligence officer, '[President] Rawlings was worried that if Taylor triumphed, Liberia would be used to launch armed attacks on Ghana.'[30] The executive secretary of Ecowas later recalled: 'I think if there was one principle that united the entire West African leadership it was the one that said that West Africa, as a region, should not accept anyone who sought to shoot his way to power, especially if that person is actively aided and abetted by outside forces.'[31] In view of the number of West African heads of state who had already shot their way to power, the fact that Taylor was a civilian rather than a soldier, and that he was aided by an outside power bent on destabilisation, was presumably the most telling consideration.

By June 1990, with the Liberian insurrection six months old, thousands dead, and the international media taking a serious interest for the first time, it had become clear that this was Africa's first major crisis since the end of the Cold War, if the latter is

[29] Zaya Yerbo, *Ghana: the struggle for popular power*, London, 1991, pp.273-4.

[30] Prince Eric Acquah, quoted in Emmanuel Kwesi Aning, 'Ghana, Ecowas and the Liberian Crisis: an analysis of Ghana's role in Liberia', *Liberian Studies Journal*, XXI, 2 (1996), p.279.

[31] Interview with Abass Bundu, *West Africa*, 4036 (13 February 1995), p.224.

measured by the fall of the Berlin Wall in November 1989. All
the diplomatic players were exploring unknown territory since
the unwritten conventions governing international relations were
so clearly in flux. During the Cold War there would have been
no question of Washington allowing a protracted war in Liberia,
its main West African ally. When a US fleet with 2,000 marines
on board headed for Monrovia in June 1990, Liberians hoped
that the United States would intervene to restore order. But US
diplomats procrastinated; no vital American interest was involved
in Liberia, and the US government, reluctant to become the world's
policeman, was urging the need for regional solutions to regional
problems. For two months US intervention remained a possibility
until, as chance would have it, the Iraqi invasion of Kuwait in
August 1990 diverted American attention to another area of the
world and removed any possibility of a US military intervention
in Liberia.

The Nigerian government, on the other hand, took the situation
in Liberia very seriously. It raised the matter at an Ecowas summit
meeting in May, when Nigeria was also reported to be supplying
the embattled Doe with weapons. Washington's encouragement
of Nigeria to adopt a regional peacemaking role further disgusted
Houphouët-Boigny who, France's intelligence chief noted, complained that the Americans 'have pushed Nigeria to play the role
of the gendarme of the region, which is not acceptable either
in principle or in this specific case'.[32] Nigeria hastily secured the
backing of Ecowas, in spite of Ivorian and Burkinabe objections,
for the formation of a peacekeeping force, the Ecowas Monitoring
Group or Ecomog. Contingents were sent by the governments
of Nigeria, Ghana, Sierra Leone, Gambia and also Guinea, the
only francophone government to participate. As Liberian refugees
flooded into Sierra Leone from mid-1990 onwards, Liberia's war
inexorably sucked in its western neighbour.

The Ivorian and Burkinabe response to Nigeria's initiative was
to increase their support for the NPFL. The French national press
agency reported in September 1990 that 100 Burkinabe troops
from the elite garrison at Po, as well as Ivorian nationals, were
fighting with the NPFL. In September 1990 the correspondent
for *Le Monde* and Radio France Internationale was expelled from
Côte d'Ivoire after he reported that the Ivorian government was
supporting the NPFL. Perhaps his real fault was to have reported
a Libyan plane landing at Roberts International Airport in Liberia,

---

[32] Silberzahn, *Au coeur du secret*, p.206. The US role was confirmed by the author's
interview with a relevant State Department official, Washington, DC, 18 April 1995.

now under NPFL control, to deliver French-made weapons.[33] One of Charles Taylor's brothers, Bartus, was living at Danane in the north of Côte d'Ivoire and was in effect acting as Taylor's consul there.[34] Burkina Faso was to support Taylor consistently throughout the war, and President Compaore later publicly admitted having sent 700 troops to Liberia, while Charles Taylor enjoyed the use of a Fokker F-28 of Air Burkina.[35] He lived in Ouagadougou for much of the early part of the war, and was able to train his forces at a Burkinabe military base in Po.[36]

In this way, by late August 1990, when the United States had definitely opted for non-intervention, each of the two major armed forces then deployed in Liberia – the Nigerian-dominated Ecomog and the Ivorian-backed NPFL – was working closely with one or more regional allies whose interests were partly political and partly economic. Behind these regional powers were external backers, with France supporting Côte d'Ivoire and the NPFL while the United States, having initially encouraged the Nigerian intervention, lurched from one position to another as its diplomats railed at Nigerian corruption and blew hot and cold in their opposition to Taylor. Herman Cohen, the Assistant Secretary of State for African affairs at the State Department, when asked at the end of his term of office what was his greatest failure, said it was 'my inability to negotiate a peaceful settlement of the Liberian crisis at the beginning of the 1990s'.[37]

As the war settled into a pattern, with Ecomog controlling Monrovia and Taylor ruling the rest of the country, the Nigerian contingent in Ecomog formed alliances with various local warlords who emerged after 1990, especially Roosevelt Johnson of Ulimo-J, George Boley of the LPC, and the collective leadership of the AFL, while Guinea's interests were articulated through Ulimo-K. Liberia became a prime example of how an imploding state may lose political autonomy but extend its sphere of economic influence as an unregulated economy of plunder comes to dominate.[38] A

[33] *Le Monde,* 29 August 1990; on the explusion of Robert Minangoy, *Fraternité-matin* (Abidjan), 4 September 1990.

[34] Agence France-Presse, 1 September 1990.

[35] 'Libéria' in *L'Indépendant* (Ouagadougou), 108 (29 August 1995), p.10.

[36] 'Compaore and Regional Security', *West Africa,* 4026 (28 November 1994), p.2022; Mark Huband, 'Liberians Train Mercenaries in Burkina Faso', *The Guardian,* 19 December 1991.

[37] Quoted in Robert A. Mortimer, 'Senegal's Role in Ecomog: the francophone dimension in the Liberian crisis', *Journal of Modern African Studies,* 34, 2 (1996), pp.305-6.

[38] Cf. I. William Zartman (ed.), *Collapsed States: the disintegration and restoration of*

major realignment of alliances in 1995 brought Taylor closer to Nigeria while different factions in Côte d'Ivoire continued to support either the NPFL or the LPC, although with less conviction than previously. From beginning to end of the war, each Liberian warlord of any substance had alliances with foreign businessmen and at least one foreign government. The irony of it was that many of the governments thus implicated were also contributors to Ecomog, and were in principle supposed to be making peace in Liberia, not carving it up for plunder.

Markets and rackets

The Liberian factions which emerged during the civil war came, then, to represent the cutting edge of international business and political syndicates whose principals were in Conakry, Abidjan, Lagos and Abuja in West Africa, with associates in Paris, Washington and other centres further afield.

At the outset of the war, the greatest single economic prize was the Nimba iron ore project, promising hundreds of millions of tonnes of high-grade iron ore for the steel mills of the world's industrial nations. The most active component of the investors' consortium was the French company Bureau de recherches géologiques et minières (BRGM), which had secured funds from Japan's Sumitomo Corporation and a promise of major investment from the London-based African Mining Consortium Limited, which grouped various British, Japanese and American investors, including some US-based Liberian exiles. When Charles Taylor, a shrewd businessman and a tough negotiator, found that he had overrun most of Liberia, without yet becoming president, he immediately approached various business people, sometimes using his US lawyer Ramsey Clark. In June 1990 Taylor contacted the African Mining Consortium with a proposal to re-start iron ore exports from Buchanan and to press ahead with the Nimba scheme, since he had the port and the railway to Mount Nimba under his control. The investors agreed to continue operating the Liberian iron ore mines while major investment on the Guinean side – the real plum – would await the end of the war. Limited working of the Nimba mines began in 1991 with Taylor's accord. Seventy thousand tonnes of ore per month were exported via Buchanan, most of it shipped to the French port of Dunkerque, for which the operators paid Taylor a royalty of $80,000 per month. The director of the French company BRGM, Francis Labro, maintained regular contacts both with the French foreign ministry and with the Elysée palace, where Jean-Christophe Mitterrand handled African affairs till 1990, while the French ambassador in Abidjan, Michel Dupuch (later to become principal advisor on African affairs to President Jacques Chirac), also took a close interest.[39] Iron ore continued to be exported from the mine on the Liberian side of the border until 1993, when Ecomog took the port at Buchanan, the export outlet. This cut off one of Taylor's main sources of revenue, and the Nigerian contingent looted the town so comprehensively, exporting shiploads of industrial equipment, that the iron ore processing plant at Buchanan would require millions of dollars of new investment to become workable again.[40]

Franco-Ivorian interests benefited from other possibilities opened up by Taylor's control of Greater Liberia. Ivorian-based logging companies, having exhausted most of Côte d'Ivoire's finest hardwood, gained access to the primary forests of Nimba and the Liberian south-east. Ivorian, French, Italian, Israeli, Dutch, Thai and other logging companies all established themselves in Greater Liberia. Among the Ivorians doing business with Taylor, according to Liberian government ministers, were members of the family of President Houphouët-Boigny's political chief of staff or *chef de cabinet*.[41] The Ivorian port of San Pedro boomed on exports from eastern Liberia, and its main hotel became the base for Liberian exiles, including two ex-ministers who managed their interests in the wood and rubber businesses from this Ivorian base. In 1991-2, Taylor's Greater Liberia is estimated to have produced 343,000 cubic metres of timber which it exported to France, Germany, the United Kingdom, Italy, the Netherlands, Spain, Greece, Portugal and Turkey.[42] Liberia became France's third-biggest supplier of wood. 'The French have for centuries been great lovers of fine hardwood furniture,' noted a leading Liberian commentator. 'So, they look to the African countries, and where better than in the land of those fools in Liberia who don't have enough sense to put their act together.'[43] Among the logging businesses

[39] Patrick de Saint-Exupéry and Sophie Roquelle, 'La "montagne de fer" que convoite l'Elysée', *Le Figaro*, 8 January 1992.

[40] Stephen Ellis, 'Liberators or Looters?', *Focus on Africa*, 5, 4 (1994), p.14.

[41] Author's interview with former Interim Government minister, Monrovia, 27 July 1994.

[42] Lowenkopf, 'Liberia: putting the state back together' in Zartman, *Collapsed States*, p.98.

[43] G. Henry Andrews, 'United States and France, You Can't be Serious', *New Democrat*,

operating in Liberia was a front company which, it is alleged, had close links to the Unification Church, the Moonies.[44] Details of hardwood cargoes carried by just two ships used in the hardwood trade reveal eight shipments of logs exported from Sinoe in southeastern Liberia between December 1994 and March 1995 alone, of which four were to Bordeaux and one to Nantes, in France, and three to Leixões, Portugal.[45]

Once Ecomog had taken Buchanan from the NPFL in early 1993, and then moved on to take other ports, no faction could export from Liberian ports without paying a commission to the international force. On occasion Ecomog intervened on behalf of international merchants with whom it had reached commercial understandings. In March 1997 for example, when some citizens of Rivercess County complained to the county superintendent about the activities of three logging companies which had promised to build local infrastructure in return for rights to work in the forest, the superintendent, Jonathan Banny, had the complainants arrested by Ecomog.[46] The Liberian government institutions which had nominal authority over such matters, like the Forestry Development Authority, had fallen into the hands of warlords less concerned to manage Liberia's forest assets than to garner a rent from their exploitation. The country's unprotected coastal waters were prey to the world's long-range fishing fleets.[47] All of Liberia's natural resources were open to exploitation by international traders in league with the warring factions and Ecomog.

Similar arrangements were made in regard to the rubber trade. After the NPFL had overrun the Firestone plantation in 1990, Taylor used its buildings at Harbel as administrative offices and its workshops for military repairs. Occupation of the plantation also gave him access to a radio communications centre which he was able to convert into a broadcasting station, the forerunner of several ventures using looted transmission equipment, culminating in the music and news station KISS-FM, which were to give Charles Taylor dominance of Liberia's airwaves. He began talks

---

2, 105 (27 April-2 May 1995), p.7.

[44] Author's phone interview with Henk Dop, Amsterdam, 25 April 1997. Cf. 'Selling a Rain Forest to Fuel a War', *The Pepper Bird*, 2 (1996), p.3.

[45] 'Exploitation of Natural Resources by Liberia's Warring Factions', December 1994-March 1995, Justice and Peace Commission, National Catholic Secretariat, Monrovia, unpublished.

[46] Jarwinken Wiah, 'Mass Arrests in Rivercess', *The Inquirer*, 6, 43 (26 March 1997), p.12.

[47] *The Pepper Bird*, 3 (1995 [*sic*]), p.4.

with the American managers of the Firestone plantation, which
had been bought by the Japanese tyre company Bridgestone in
1988. On 17 January 1992 NPFL officials signed a memorandum
of understanding with the acting general manager of the Firestone
Plantations Company.[48] Although Firestone was able to export some
cargoes through Buchanan, it was never able to reach a com-
prehensive agreement with the NPFL.[49] In 1993 Firestone officially
exported only 12,000 tonnes of rubber from Liberia, compared
to 108,000 in its last year of pre-war production, 1989.[50] Liberia's
rubber plantations were now worked by large numbers of freelance
rubber-tappers, not to mention the miners of discarded rubber,
the 'bouncing diamond', both of whom sold rubber to independent
traders. As with the timber trade, Ecomog's conquest of Liberia's
seaports in 1993-4, directly and through its surrogates in the LPC,
enabled it to derive a rent from rubber exports by simply demanding
a payment for every cargo going through the ports. A survey of
shipments between September 1994 and February 1995 from
Monrovia's Freeport – the Ecomog headquarters – revealed
nineteen shipments of rubber, all but one going to Malaysia or
Singapore.[51] In response to complaints from the Firestone company,
the Liberian government imposed a ban on rubber exports, but
this had little effect because Ecomog officers and Liberian government ministers, the latter being nominees of the warring factions,
could be bribed to overlook such restrictions. The ban was effective,
though, in clearing out the private tappers and allowing the armed
factions themselves to work the Firestone rubber plantation. The
factions then trucked the rubber to Monrovia where it was sold
generally to Malaysian, Korean and Lebanese traders at some $300
a tonne. In July 1995, when a ban on rubber exports was officially
in force, a ship well-known for its activity in the rubber trade
left the Monrovia Freeport with eighty-seven containers of rubber
which had earlier been seized by the government from small-scale
rubber-tappers and traders, who were seriously hit by the official
ban.[52] One customs officer noted in February 1995 that 'there
are 200 containers waiting to move next week'. He observed that

[48] Copy in the possession of the author.

[49] Lindsay Barrett, 'The Firestone Factor in the Liberia Crisis' in Barrett, *Report on Liberia*, pp.25-9.

[50] *New Democrat*, 2, 159 (3-7 November 1995).

[51] 'Exploitation of Natural Resources by Liberia's Warring Factions', Justice and Peace Commission, National Catholic Secretariat, Monrovia, no date.

[52] Bobby Tapson, 'Government Exports Seized Rubber', *The Inquirer*, 5, 121 (12 July 1995).

'some Ecomog officers have an interest in keeping the war going'.[53]
After Ecomog had taken over ports in the south-east in 1993-4,
it was able to charge a levy on rubber exports of up to 1,700
tonnes a month, sold by factions who were said by one exporter
to 'work together with Ecomog peacekeepers hand in glove. They
all have a fixed cut.' This foreign businessman said that, since
he was paying no formal taxes, he was making a profit of up
to 60 per cent on each purchase. Another exporter pointed out
that 'there is very open bargaining power. For example, an eleven-
year-old rebel fighter came to me the other day with a sackful
of unprocessed rubber. I paid him 150 Liberian dollars [c.US$2].
My profit will be very good.'[54]

   Charles Taylor, who had become a multi-millionaire within months
of the war starting, dealt mostly with banks in Abidjan, particularly
Ecobank and the Société Générale (SGBCI), and in Ouagadougou.
He also controlled an account at Abidjan's Citibank. He is reported
to have engaged the services of a well-known public relations firm
in the United States, Swindler and Berlin.[55] The RUF/NPFL in-
vasion of Sierra Leone in March 1991 opened up a new field
of business. NPFL soldiers openly boasted that they were in Sierra
Leone 'to retrieve "properties", loot that they had sold across the
border'.[56] However, by 1992, the counter-offensive by a rival faction,
Ulimo, had gained control of diamond-rich areas in both Sierra
Leone and Liberia, enabling Ulimo leaders and their allies in
Freetown and Conakry to acquire diamonds which they sold in
Antwerp, the world's major free market for diamonds. According
to official diamond industry statistics, Liberia had become the
third-biggest supplier of diamonds to Antwerp by 1994, and in
1995 its supplies increased by 227 per cent measured by carats
and 91 per cent by value. Liberian diamonds were being exported
through Conakry, while Guinean and Sierra Leonean diamonds
could also be exported to Antwerp and represented as being from
Liberia. Even Angolan diamonds may have been traded under
cover of being Liberian goods, since the Angolan opposition movement Unita had its main business centre in Abidjan.[57] According

[53] Joshua Hammer, 'Graveyard of Failed Hopes', *Newsweek*, 6 February 1995.

[54] Quoted in Claudia McElroy, 'Liberia Traders Export War-Lost Raw Rubber to
Asia', Reuters, Monrovia, 23 January 1995.

[55] William Reno, 'The Reinvention of an African Patrimonial State: Charles Taylor's
Liberia', *Third World Quarterly*, 16, 1 (1995), pp.113.

[56] Editorial in *New Democrat*, 2, 95 (23-27 March 1995).

[57] François Misser and Olivier Vallée, *Les gemmocraties : l'économie politique du diamant
africain*, Paris, 1997, p.47.

to the president of Gambia, both diamonds and marijuana from Liberia were transiting overland through the long-distance trade networks dominated by Malinke businessmen as far as Senegal and Gambia, linking the business of the Liberian war with the marketing of war-goods from the low-level conflict in Casamance, in Senegal. Gambia became a leading diamond exporter although it has no naturally occurring diamonds.[58] As the war settled into a stalemate after Samuel Doe's death in September 1990, every Liberian faction and its external backers developed an interest in the burgeoning war economy. Diamonds, gold, drugs, rubber, wood, looted goods, scrap metal, palm oil, coffee, cocoa and, of course, weapons, were all traded. The NPFL appears to have developed connections with the Casamançais separatist movement via the sale of weapons in return for payment in marijuana grown in southern Senegal.[59]

Even more than the diamond trade, the extent of the marijuana trade was difficult to measure. Charles Taylor could have become acquainted with drug-traders during his sojourn in a Massachusetts jail in 1983-5.[60] In 1986 he was reported to have held the opinion that African governments should earn hard currency by exporting drugs. 'He further stressed that we should think of cultivating coca and marijuana,' recalled a man who shared a prison cell with him in Accra at that time. 'He was particularly peeved about the fact that African governments complain of lack of capital when they have the easy option of granting banking facilities to drug barons who have billions of dollars for laundering.'[61] During the war, marijuana is reported to have been exported from NPFL-held territory via San Pedro in Côte d'Ivoire, where well-organised Ivorian, French, Lebanese and other crime syndicates operated, including one especially prominent Corsican ring. The Corsican mafia in Abidjan had traditionally specialised in logging, cigarette-smuggling and local prostitution, but by the 1990s was increasingly involved in sending African women to work as sex slaves in brothels in Europe,[62] often also acting as couriers carrying heroin and

[58] 'Senegal: *Yamba* of the Casamance rebels', *Geopolitical Drug Despatch* (Paris), 53 (March 1996), p.8.

[59] Charles Deng, 'Casamance: ces armes qui viennent du Libéria', *Wal Fadjiri* (Dakar), 21 August 1995, quoted in Prkic, 'The Economy of the Liberian Conflict'.

[60] Huband, *The Liberian Civil War*, p.46.

[61] Kwesi Yankah and Lazarus Maayang, 'Charles Taylor: dark days in Ghana', *Uhuru*, 5 (1990), p.40.

[62] By 1997, trafficking in women was considered by European Union officials to have become more lucrative than drug smuggling. Katherine Butler, 'Shame of

cocaine. By the mid-1990s, underground crack cocaine factories were operating in Abidjan[63] but Ivorian racketeers were facing stiff competition from an influx of Nigerian drug networks, many of them operating out of Benin. These exported poor-quality Nigerian-made amphetamines, and heroin from south-east Asia, the latter often transported via Ethiopia and Nigeria itself. Before 1984 the main source of amphetamines had been Guinea; street-wise Ivorians called the Guinean-made drug 'Sékou Touré' in honour of the Guinean president of the time, since consumption caused people to talk fast and at interminable length.[64] In the face of fierce competition from Nigeria, NPFL warlords were successful in pioneering their own drug-routes. In 1997 Dutch police revealed the existence of a large-scale racket said to be operating under the protection of the NPFL. One of several people arrested by the Dutch police on suspicion of importing thousands of kilograms of hashish was the honorary consul of a West African country in Rotterdam. Also reported as wanted for questioning was one of Taylor's closest associates, a Dutchman, with interests in gambling, prostitution, hardwood and weapons-smuggling. This man had developed a business relationship with Samuel Doe in the 1980s before switching to Charles Taylor during the war. An investigation by the Dutch police is reported to have revealed that Liberia was being used as a transit-point for Pakistani hashish to be transferred to smaller boats for re-export to Rotterdam, while the distributors in the Netherlands were said to be working with Polish crime syndicates.[65]

It is likely that Ecomog at least connived in the drug trade, and it appears that this was an element in the NPFL's rivalry with Nigeria, as they competed for control of regional smuggling channels. According to a BBC reporter cited in an NPFL newspaper, marijuana was leaving Monrovia in 1993 for sale in Rotterdam.[66] Some Ecomog soldiers were rumoured to be trafficking drugs with Lebanese and Pakistani traders particularly. In March 1994 four tonnes of marijuana were seized on board a Ghanaian ship in

---

EU over 500,000 Sex Slaves', *The Independent* (London), 28 April 1997.

[63] Author's interviews with drug enforcement officials, Abidjan, 18 March 1997.

[64] *Ibid.*

[65] Bart Middelburg, 'Drugsbende Kreeg Hulp uit Liberia', *Het Parool* (Amsterdam), 12 December 1997.

[66] Quoted in *Liberian Diaspora*, III, 12 (April 1993), p.4.

Monrovia harbour.[67] In the same month, one and a half tonnes, owned by a Nigerian company, were seized at Monrovia's Spriggs Payne airport.[68] While occasional discoveries such as these were made public, it is certain that, if senior Ecomog officers indeed had interests in the trade, they would be secure from prosecution since they were in effect subject to no higher authority. A representative of the UN Drug Control Programme, Dr Kamoyo Mwale, publicly expressed concern over the increase in drug-trafficking from Liberia and called on Ecomog to cooperate with UN control efforts while he was visiting Monrovia in 1995.[69]

The import and re-export of Asian-produced heroin from Nigeria particularly began in the early 1980s, and by the time of the Liberian war major Nigerian gangs were operating out of other West African countries and were moving into the cocaine trade as well. International narcotics control officers were concerned by evidence that the Nigerian government was not serious in its attempts to halt the narcotics traffic, perhaps because of collusion between politicians or officials and the traders themselves. President Babangida's own family was widely rumoured to be involved in the narcotics trade, and this was made public during a coup attempt in Nigeria in April 1990, when putschists made damaging allegations against what they called a 'drug baronish' government in a radio broadcast.[70] A series of scandals at the Nigerian Drug Law Enforcement Agency revealed that the agency was as much interested in protecting leading traffickers as it was in prosecuting minor couriers.[71] For any Nigerian officials with interests in the narcotics trade, Liberia offered considerable attractions, not only as a potential trans-shipment facility, but also as a point of access to the Liberian diaspora in the United States, which is especially well-integrated on account of the long-standing links between Liberia and America. According to one Liberian resident in the US, Liberian drug gangs are particularly active in Staten Island, New York; Newark, New Jersey; and Philadelphia,[72] offering an ideal distribution network for any importer who is

[67] Observatoire géopolitique des drogues, *Atlas mondial des drogues,* p.159.

[68] *Ibid.*

[69] 'UN Concerned about Drug Trafficking', *The Inquirer,* 5, 36 (7 March 1995), p.10.

[70] 'The Drug Trade', *Africa Confidential,* 31, 14 (13 July 1990), p.5.

[71] US Department of State, *International Narcotics Control Strategy Report,*Washington, DC, 1995, pp.vliv, 435-7.

[72] Dolo, *Democracy Versus Dictatorship,* p.106.

able to cultivate the right Liberian connections. Researchers who have studied the records of convictions for drug trafficking by US courts report that the pattern suggests an overlap of Nigerian and Liberian dealers in the New York and Washington-Baltimore metropolitan areas.

US officials in particular sometimes suspect that Ecomog control of the Monrovia Freeport was used as a cover for shipping narcotics, but they are not known to have offered proof of this. The most that can be said with absolute certainty concerning Ecomog is that there is no doubt that Nigeria is a major importer and re-exporter of narcotics, as well as a manufacturer and exporter of amphetamines. It is relevant to note that Nigerian troops have for some years been stationed not only in Liberia but also at ports and airports in the Gambia and Sierra Leone, giving Nigeria's military government – not generally known for its respect of in-ternational conventions – a formidable transport infrastructure which has certainly been used on occasions for smuggling. Moreover in both Gambia and Sierra Leone successful military coups have been launched by officers who have served with Ecomog, suggesting a murky politics within certain of the various military forces in-volved.[73] Control of the Freeport in Monrovia gave Ecomog great scope for racketeering of all descriptions, simply by acting as a middleman to the Liberian factions. In early 1991 a German ship flying a Burkinabe flag, the MV *Renate-G*, was seized by Ecomog gunboats at sea after leaving the NPFL-held port at Buchanan. It and its cargo of rubber were impounded. It was secretly released on the orders of the Ecomog field commander, said to be in league with a Nigerian businessman who had used the ship to sell arms to the NPFL.[74]

Not only did Nigerian businessmen and officers, especially, do business with all sides in Liberia, but they were able to use the Ecomog presence to launder money and to embezzle public funds from Nigeria itself. In 1992 the Lagos correspondent of the London *Financial Times* was expelled from Nigeria after revealing that windfall oil profits from the Gulf War had been misappropriated via Ecomog through some creative accounting.[75] It was simple to inflate the quantity of oil recorded as going to the peacekeeping force while actually selling the surplus on the open market. In mid-1995 Nigeria's foreign minister stated that the government

---

[73] On Gambia, *West Africa*, 4010 (8 August 1994), p.1395; on Sierra Leone, Richards, *Fighting for the Rain Forest*, p.9.

[74] Agence France-Presse despatch, 10 May 1991.

[75] Wilson Uwujaren, 'No Retreat, No Surrender', *The News* (Nigeria), 5 June 1995.

had spent $4 billion on the Ecomog expedition over the previous five years, although there had never been more than 10,000 Nigerian soldiers in Liberia at any one time. The Nigerian government, in other words, was officially spending an average of US$80,000 every year for every soldier it had in Liberia. At the same time, there were many reports that Nigerian soldiers were receiving their basic pay of fifteen dollars per day only irregularly. In comparison, the entire UN peacekeeping budget for 1995 was only one billion dollars for operations worldwide. Moreover, by 1995 the United States had given to ECOMOG some $30.83 million. As one Nigerian academic observed, 'it is very sad to note that much of the $4 billion may have gone and may still be going into a few fat private accounts abroad.' A Nigerian journalist who investigated came to the conclusion that three-quarters of the money had been diverted. Meanwhile, wounded Nigerian veterans of Ecomog who demonstrated at the Yaba military hospital in Lagos were summarily discharged from the services and left to pay for their own medical treament.[76]

So notorious was Ecomog's role in the marketing of cars, consumer goods and scrap metal looted by itself or others that the ever-inventive rumour mill of Monrovia dubbed the peacekeeping force Every Car Or Moving Object Gone. Possibly the largest single case of industrial vandalism was in early 1994, when Nigerian troops dismantled, and exported as second-hand plant or as scrap metal, industrial equipment worth some $50 million from the port of Buchanan, which had remained intact when the port had earlier been occupied by the NPFL.[77] This was a further blow to any hopes of restarting large-scale iron ore mining. A ship seized while carrying arms for the NPFL in 1992, the MV *Sea Rose*, was sold; it was not clear exactly who pocketed the proceeds.[78] One Liberian refugee living in Nigeria noted in 1995 that 'right now, if you go to Apapa Wharf or the Tin Can Port, you will see cars, refrigerators, electronic appliances, household goods and many other things looted from my country being shipped into Nigeria. It is very painful.' Cyril Allen, a NPFL official who had himself been educated in Nigeria and knew the country well, said of Ecomog, 'most of them are involved in business. They are using

---

[76] Josh Arinze, 'They Looted my Country', *Tell* (Lagos), 3 July 1995, pp.24-7.

[77] Stephen Ellis, 'Liberators or Looters?', *Focus on Africa* (London), 5, 4 (Oct-Dec. 1994), p.14.

[78] 'Is the Sea Rose Sold?', *New Democrat*, 1, 25 (19-25 May 1994).

Ecowas facilities and Ecomog to carry out their private business.'[79]
A European missionary personally witnessed Nigerian Ecomog soldiers
bartering fuel oil in exchange for palm oil with their arch-enemies,
the NPFL, in 1995.[80] The most flagrant case was during the third
battle of Monrovia in April 1996, known to NPFL fighters as 'Operation Pay Yourself' or 'Operation Clean Sweep', when thousands
of NPFL and Ulimo-K fighters looted the city. Ecomog commanders
played a prominent role in provoking this battle. Once it had
started, Ecomog soldiers actually armed fighters on both sides
and allowed the looting to take place, except when they were
paid by wealthy Lebanese and Indian shopkeepers to defend their
premises. Some Ecomog soldiers, notably from the Guinean contingent, were widely reported to have joined in the looting directly.
Aid agency personnel reported that many of their looted vehicles
were transported from the Freeport to Conakry and Lagos with
the complicity of senior military officials. Even the Nigerian embassy was in danger of being looted, an outrage prevented only
by the intervention of Ghanaian soldiers. So flagrant was the venality
of certain senior officers that some Nigerian officials were privately
appalled. The Ecomog Field Commander, General John Inienger,
was recalled to Nigeria later in 1996, and was probably saved from
official censure only because he was a friend of the Nigerian president, General Abacha, and because he was able to transfer some
of the blame to his chief of staff, who by all accounts had actually
behaved rather creditably.

'Ecomog troops have been heavily involved since the day they
arrived in ripping off Liberians, in looting goods, in dealing in
contraband,' said a spokesperson for the US State Department
in 1996, accurately enough.[81] But Ecomog officials were able to
deflect criticism from this source with ease. Who were the Americans
to complain, when Ecomog was there largely because the US had
declined to intervene in June 1990? Throughout the war, unless
the US was prepared to see Charles Taylor take power, American
officials had little choice but to support Nigeria and Ecomog and
keep their doubts to themselves. After one round of American
criticism, Nigerian government sources let it be known that they
were thinking of pulling out of the whole peacekeeping operation.
A pro-Nigerian newspaper in Monrovia reported that the Nigerian

[79] Quoted in Arinze, '"They Looted my Country"', *Tell* , 3 July 1995, p.27.

[80] Author's interview, Amsterdam, 29 August 1996.

[81] Nicholas Burns, quoted in Jeremy Armon and Andy Carl (eds), 'The Liberian
Peace Process 1990-1996', *Accord: an International Review of Peace Initiatives,* 1 (1996),
p.21.

government had been 'particularly incensed' by what sources in Abuja called 'accusations raised by the NPFL and some American sources that they are supporting some factions in the fighting which has continued in the country'.[82] This was, to be sure, no less than the truth. But the threat of Nigerian withdrawal was sufficient to cause the US to tone down its objections. Another frustrated critic was the Ghanaian government, which was often reported to be furious with Nigeria for its conduct in Liberia but which had an interest in maintaining its own force there and was assuaged with supplies of Nigerian oil. On the whole, Ghana's Ecomog contingent is one of the few which can be said to have emerged from the Liberian war with any credit, since Ghanaian soldiers have gained less of a reputation for looting than others, and have remained generally popular with Liberian civilians, a rare achievement for a peacekeeping force anywhere in the world.

When in October 1995 a UN security officer, an American, described Ecomog in an official report as 'extremely corrupt' he was soon withdrawn,[83] not least because he had also reported UN officers for having sex with under-age Liberian girls. When a Monrovia newspaper reported that Ghanaian Ecomog soldiers had inter-cepted four truckloads of arms being sold by Nigerian Ecomog to one of the factions, the journalists responsible were hauled up before Ecomog's Nigerian chief of staff and told to apologise. He warned that Ecomog would henceforth deal 'ruthlessly' with any journalist publishing an article 'calculated to cause confusion in Ecomog'.[84] Since journalists, like everyone else in Monrovia between 1990 and 1997, owed their physical safety to Ecomog, and since they could not rely on the remnants of the Liberian legal system to defend them, there was little option but to obey.

The US government, to compound its error of persistently providing support to the brutal Samuel Doe, massively miscalculated the effect of encouraging a Nigerian-led force into Liberia in August 1990. Once the United States had lost the initiative in Liberia, it never regained it. The country remained a very low priority for politicians and officials in Washington and was generally dealt with at a relatively low level of the administration. Throughout the whole of 1990, Assistant Secretary of State Cohen never spoke to President George Bush about the Liberian crisis.[85] Former President

---

[82] 'Will Ecomog Leave?', *New Democrat*, 1, 29 (16-22 June 1994), p.1.

[83] Michael Cullier, quoted in *New Democrat*, 2, 157 (26-31 October 1995).

[84] *New Democrat*, 1, 30 (23-29 June 1994), p.3.

[85] Huband, *The Liberian Civil War*, p.114.

Jimmy Carter later tried his hand at mediation and was fairly sympathetic to Charles Taylor, which earned him the wrath of Nigerian officials. And yet by early 1995 the United States had spent no less than half a billion dollars in Liberia, mostly on humanitarian relief and much of it in the form of food aid, probably more than an intervention in 1990 would have cost.[86] Appalled by the racketeering of the Nigerian contingent, but unwilling to risk a diplomatic crisis with the Nigerian government by speaking too publicly on the matter, the US administration handed out money to ease its conscience and tried tinkering with the composition of Ecomog, at various times paying for contingents from Senegal, Uganda, Tanzania and other African countries to join, in the hope of diluting Nigerian influence, since Nigeria generally accounted for some 75 per cent of Ecomog forces with Ghana coming second. By 1994 there was a battalion of Tanzanians deployed at Kakata and several hundred Ugandans at Buchanan. The Tanzanians soon withdrew, officially because they had not received all the funding promised to them, but also, it is said, from disgust when Tanzanian troops came under attack from a coalition of Liberian anti-NPFL forces supported by Ecomog's Nigerian commanders. Eventually, the US government was able to get some sort of grip over Ecomog activities by employing a private engineering and logistics company with close links to the US armed forces, Pacific Architects and Engineers (PAE), to manage part of the Ecomog truck fleet and helicopters, and to set up a sophisticated radio communications network. This was a considerable success as it made Ecomog more efficient by strengthening its logistics. Nevertheless, the vehicles given to Ecomog for peacekeeping purposes by international donors were still often used for commercial transport, especially at night during the hours of curfew. Many Ecomog trucks stank of raw rubber. There were constant complaints of Ecomog soldiers forcing the civilian truck drivers employed by PAE to hand over the trucks to the soldiers, especially in remote areas of the country.

As so often in crises of this nature, the United States looked to the UN to provide diplomatic cover, and Taylor also approved a UN role on the grounds that this might help check Ecomog's flagrant opposition to him. This provided yet another headache for State Department officials. The first UN special representative arrived in December 1992.[87] He was treated with scant respect

[86] Letter to *Washington Post* by Gerald S. Rose, former deputy chief of mission in Liberia, reprinted in *New Democrat*, 2, 78 (24-26 January 1995), p.12.

[87] A good summary of UN policy is B.G. Ramcharan, 'Cooperation Between the UN and Regional/Sub-Regional Organizations in Internal Conflicts: the case of Liberia'

by the Nigerians especially, being made to understand that he must respect the night-time curfew which Ecomog had been operating in Monrovia since the battle of October 1992. This meant that the UN special representative and his officials were operating as watchdogs for only half the hours in the day. They did not observe what happened in Monrovia at night when illicit cargoes could be transported unhindered in Ecomog vehicles. Nor did they observe what happened at the Freeport, where Ecomog could move cargo unsupervised. When UN military observers were added to the UN mission in late 1993, the fact that they were unarmed meant that if the observers were causing complications for the Nigerian Ecomog forces, the latter had only to suggest to one or other of the factions to take Unomil observers hostage. This happened at Tubmanburg in 1994 in sight of Nigerian soldiers.[88] Rank-and-file Ecomog soldiers, badly paid and with very poor living conditions, risking their lives, were understandably resentful of UN observers who were paid UN salaries in hard currency, took few risks, and were very successful with local women.

Officers at every level of the Ecomog hierarchy developed their own business interests. The force's chief military intelligence officer, a Nigerian widely believed to be on Charles Taylor's payroll, was withdrawn in April 1997 at a time when a new Ecomog Force Commander, General Malu, was most intent on asserting his authority over Taylor and the other warlords.[89] Ecomog battalion commanders would sell weapons to all sides, and even individual soldiers were selling bullets from their ammunition clips. This sort of trafficking was probably one of the reasons why Ecomog found it difficult to deploy nationwide for most of the war. Yet Ecomog's enthusiasm for trading also facilitated its deployment at times, since it created business relationships between the international soldiers and various factions. In the opinion of some observers, the economic relationships developed between Ecomog detachments in the countryside and various groups of fighters took pressure off civilians, as it diminished the incentive to rob and harass them. When peace was gradually restored, it was at least as much due to the development of economic relationships between the international force and the various Liberian factions as through Ecomog's use or threat of force.[90]

---

in *African Yearbook of International Law*, vol. 4 (1996), The Hague, 1997, pp.3-17.

[88] Author's interview with Unomil officer, Buchanan, 29 July 1994.

[89] 'Ecomog CMIO Recalled', *Weekend Magazine*, 1, 1 (5 April 1997).

[90] Letter from Bart Witteveen to author, 15 April 1998.

Just as Ecomog took sides in the war out of a mixture of economic and political self-interest, so did neighbouring countries take a number of unilateral initiatives for similar reasons. By early 1995 the war was having a considerable impact in Côte d'Ivoire, where hundreds of thousands of Liberian refugees were living. In the north of the country, Danane had virtually become a Liberian town, and was a main staging-post for the NPFL's logistics. Ivorian gendarmes escorted NPFL convoys, leaving no doubt of the official attitude to the war. Fighting with the NPFL were 'Ivorian nationals who have been drawn into this land of activity by the lure of money and loot', alleged one Monrovian newspaper, hostile to the NPFL. 'What can I say about the thousands of tons of stolen rubber, timber, diamonds, gold, vehicles, generators and other heavy industrial equipment which have been sold across the border into that country? And of course, the ethnic rivalries between the Baoulé, the tribe of Houphouët-Boigny, and the other tribes, and what about the political opposition who have been stifled for so long?'[91]

This last reference, to the danger of ethnic clashes inside Côte d'Ivoire, became topical after Houphouët-Boigny's death in 1993. The struggle by his successor, Henri Konan Bédié, to establish himself led to dangerous ethnic divisions in Côte d'Ivoire, where many people in the western half of the country had ethnic ties to Liberia. In late 1994 President Konan Bédié received a visit from US Deputy Secretary of State Strobe Talbott, an old classmate of Bill Clinton, who seems to have warned the Ivorian president about the dangers of meddling in Liberia.[92] By the middle of 1995 both the NPFL and the LPC were launching small cross-border raids into Côte d'Ivoire, causing several deaths. LPC fighters selling looted goods to Ivorians went on the rampage after a dispute over money. The Ivorian security forces made a robust reply, killing no less than forty-six people in a counter-action in late June 1995.[93] President Konan Bédié, apparently concerned to reduce his country's role in the Liberian conflict, admitted publicly that the NPFL had imported weapons from Côte d'Ivoire.[94] Senior Ivorian officials were reported to have developed interests in the export of Liberian rubber, and some even owned plantations inside

[91] Editorial in *New Democrat*, 2, 95 (23-27 March 1995).

[92] 'Ivorians Seize Taylor's Arms', *New Democrat*, 1, 57 (10-15 November 1994).

[93] '46 Liberians Killed in Ivory Coast Identified', *The Inquirer*, 5, 117 (6 July 1995).

[94] Press conference by Alhaji G.V. Kromah reported in *La Voie* (Abidjan), 1114 (13 June 1995).

Liberia.[95] One Ivorian customs officer accused the *sous-préfet* of the town of Tai of colluding with the LPC faction. He alleged that LPC fighters were working gold deposits and had a military base, which the *sous-préfet* had visited, on Ivorian soil. Some Ivorian customs officials killed by the LPC in June 1995 were said to have been murdered, allegedly with the approval of the local *sous-préfet*, because they attempted to interrupt this traffic.[96] Ivorian officials at the town of Guiglo openly admitted buying gold, diamonds and looted goods from Liberian militiamen, provided only that they did not carry arms on Ivorian soil, and selling them rice, soap and fuel in return.[97] In July 1995 the Abidjan government appealed for help to France, which had a permanent military garrison in Abidjan, in order to seal the border.[98]

Proximity to the Liberian war also created problems for Guinea, as well as opportunities for some individual Guineans. As in Côte d'Ivoire, Guinea was home to many citizens who had kinfolk living over the border in Liberia, and Guinean officials both at local and national level developed financial interests in the war. The closer these relations were, the greater the danger that feuds between rival Liberian factions would spill over the border into Guinea and that local disputes within Guinea itself would become militarised as guns and war booty were traded freely. The forest region of Guinea was home to many Kpelle, Loma and Kissi people, the same groups as those who lived in the Liberian forest region, and they clashed on Guinean soil with the mainly Mandingo Ulimo-K.[99] The forerunner organisation of Ulimo-K was actually founded in Conakry, the Guinean capital, and later in the war another Liberian faction, the Lofa Defense Force, was also first established in Guinea. While Guinea's President Lansana Conté was an ally of the Liberian Ulimo-K, he could never be sure that Liberians would not eventually make common cause with his own domestic opponents. There were constant rumours that this was happening.[100] Even in distant Gambia, the war in Liberia had a destabilising effect. In 1996 an attack on a Gambian army barracks in which

[95] 'Trafic du latex libérien par des Barons du PDCI', *Le Nouvel horizon*, 253 (21 July 1995); Freedom Neruda, 'Un lourd tribut', *La Voie*, 1110, 8 June 1995.

[96] *La Voie*, 1148 (22-23 July 1995).

[97] Agence France-Presse despatch, 4 July 1995.

[98] Agence France-Presse despatch, 6 July 1995.

[99] Moses Tarnue Mawolo, 'To Macenta and Back', *New Democrat*, 1, 9 (3-9 February 1994), p.19; author's interviews in Guékédou and Macenta, April 1995.

[100] 'Plot to Destabilise Guinea Uncovered', *New Democrat*, 2, 91 (10-14 March 1995).

ten people were killed was said by the local press to have involved 'Gambians who fought for different warring factions in the Liberian Civil war'.[101]

Of all the countries neighbouring Liberia, there is no doubt that the war caused the greatest problems to Sierra Leone. The Freetown government committed itself to Ecomog at its inception in 1990, and was duly punished by Taylor when he lent support to the rebel RUF in 1991, giving him access to the rich diamond fields of eastern Sierra Leone. Sierra Leone fell into a complex civil war of its own, as the Sierra Leonean army itself acquired the habit of looting, sometimes in collaboration with the very rebels they were supposed to be fighting, and the RUF developed into a ruthless insurgent force.

The fact is that all of West Africa was awash with weapons. According to a US intelligence estimate, by 1997 there were some 7-8 million firearms in the region.[102] A UN investigation into the proliferation of light weapons considered that the problem dated back to the mid-1980s, when Burkina Faso's President Sankara had armed local defence committees as a revolutionary policy; many of these weapons promptly vanished, some of them to be sold on the black market. Thereafter, the outbreak of civil wars in Senegal, Mali, Liberia, Sierra Leone and Niger enormously increased the demand for weapons. Guerrilla armies occasionally received large shipments of weapons, as the NPFL did in 1990, but, according to the UN, movements of weapons from one country to another were due to trading by individuals more than to large-scale imports. Weapons had become just another tradeable product, transferred between one war zone and another. 'Many weapons are in the hands of the population and the mission heard many accounts of their easy availability in the markets of the sub-region,' the UN investigators found. 'Weapons move with bandits and insurgents back and forth along borders, others are smuggled in for sale or handed over to aligned movements. However, the mission did not find any proof of major domestic organised movement of illicit light weapons. One exception may be the movement of weapons and equipment into Liberia from other states in the sub-region.'[103]

---

[101] Quoted in *West Africa*, 4125 (18 November 1996), p.1784.

[102] Communication by Col. Moussa Diabité of the Malian Commission nationale de lutte contre la prolifération d'armes légères, 17 April 1998.

[103] Brigadier-General (ret.) Henny van der Graaf, 'The Findings of the UN Advisory Missions to the Sahara-Sahel', 25 November 1996 (draft). I am grateful to Gen. Van der Graaf for providing me with a copy of this document.

Colonies and non-colonies

'Let America come and colonize us now for twenty years so we can learn.[...]Yes, let us work for them and have peace, maybe, after twenty years' experience with colonialism we would have learned our lessons.'

This, according to a Nigerian journalist who was living in Liberia at the beginning of the war, was a prayer offered by some Liberians who thought that colonial rule in other West African countries had had 'a sobering effect on the colonized nation',[104] in contrast to Liberia, whose status as Africa's oldest republic they thought had made its people arrogant and complacent. Liberians who reasoned thus were attaching too much importance to the fact that Liberia is the only country in West Africa never to have been a European colony, for Liberia too was originally designed by colonisers. All over Africa, the actual substance of political power in modern times has been shaped by interaction between colonial governments or settler elites and the mass of the population.

To some extent confusion may arise because of two different meanings attached to the words 'colony' and 'colonialism'. The oldest use of the word 'colony' relates to the founding of settlements abroad by people of a specific origin, exactly as African-American settlers founded a colony in Monrovia in 1822. Only later did 'colonialism' come to mean the establishment of formal rule by a metropolitan power over a peripheral area to whose inhabitants it assigned subordinate rights.[105] Whereas Liberia was unique in West Africa in never having been a colony in the second sense, it has, like its neighbours, undergone the experience of having rights assigned to the majority of the population by a group of people of foreign origin who have allotted to themselves a superior status, rather like South Africa in the twentieth century.[106] Liberia also has something in common with those African countries which gained independence from colonial rule in the mid-twentieth century in that its modern statehood is juridical in origin.[107] That

---

[104] Unoke, *The Untold Story of the Liberian War,* p.40.

[105] Alan Bullock and Oliver Stallybrass (eds), *Fontana Dictionary of Modern Thought,* London, 1977, p.302.

[106] In South Africa this gave rise to a protracted debate among Marxists as to the true nature of the South African condition, which the South African Communist Party described as 'Colonialism of a Special Type'. The comparison with Liberia is specifically made by Osaghae, *Ethnicity, Class and the Struggle for State Power,* pp.2-3.

[107] Cf. Christopher Clapham, *Africa and the International System: the politics of state survival,* Cambridge, 1996.

is, Liberia did not become a state as a result of contiguous populations
evolving a system of politics and government which covered a
given territorial area, and which then gained international recognition. Rather, it was the other way round: a small group of people,
in Liberia's case not more than 12,000 in number, declared the
existence of a republic based in Monrovia in 1847 and gained
international recognition of their sovereignty. Only in the course
of time did they actually impose this state on other peoples within
the area they claimed as their national territory.

Liberia thus shares important features with other African
countries, whether they were colonised in a legal sense or simply
governed by an elite of settler origin, like Liberia itself. All underwent
during the nineteenth and twentieth centuries the experience of
indigenous societies and polities being brought more closely than
ever before within the reach of economic and political forces whose
main nodes of power were far distant. These foreign economic
and political influences were not altogether new, for the West
African coast had been within the ambit of Atlantic trading systems
for centuries before the colonial period, and even societies far
inland had been influenced by the workings of Atlantic commerce,
most notably through the medium of the slave trade. Peculiar
to the later nineteenth century was the emergence of a marked
tendency for overseas interest groups concerned with Africa to
conceive a need to reorganise the markets and political institutions
of the region. This they did by imposing colonial government
or, in the case of Liberia, by cooperation with the American settlers
who had already established a republic in Monrovia.

Colonial administrations and the independent Republic of
Liberia alike established centralised political authority on the
European or North American model; both contained many similar
features. Among the leading characteristics of all the governments
which emerged in Africa a century ago, as a result of colonial
influence, was that they were regarded as trustworthy by the leading
international powers and banks, meaning that binding legal contracts could be made and loans contracted with them,[108] an innovation
in a region with many acephalous societies and shifting loci of
political authority. Hence, the establishment of colonial government in West Africa in time created conditions which permitted
the investment of capital on a substantial scale by business elites

---

[108] For a West African view, see A. Adu Boahen, *African Perspectives on Colonialism*,
Baltimore, 1987, esp. pp.27-57; for a view in the context of British imperialism,
see Peter Cain and A.G. Hopkins, *British Imperialism: innovation and expansion, 1688-
1914*, London and New York, 1993, pp.351-96.

in the industrialised world, a necessary condition for the development of infrastructure and the exploitation of the region's natural resources, including minerals and agricultural produce, by the use of modern machinery. It also permitted the outlawing of practices judged by Europeans to be inhumane, such as human sacrifice and – by the late nineteenth century – the slave trade. In the 1950s and 1960s, the European colonial powers, under pressure from both African political elites and the superpowers at the height of the Cold War, granted independence to their former colonies with varying degrees of enthusiasm or reluctance. In each case, the hope of the former colonial powers was that the independent African states which emerged would continue to be partners with whom binding diplomatic and financial bargains could be made, not least for the pursuit of economic interest. The independence which was attained in most of Africa in the 1960s did little in itself to alter the conditions which underlay transactions between the industrialised world and Africa.

Within a couple of decades of most of Africa gaining its independence, however, it was becoming clear that the conditions which modern industrial and financial enterprises generally find most congenial were fast deteriorating in many parts of the continent. Many African states were in such deep financial difficulties that they were no longer internationally regarded as creditworthy. African governments in general were increasingly regarded by the world's leading industrial and financial concerns as unable to maintain a basic level of law and order and to uphold a system of justice sufficient to regulate commercial contracts and activities, the fundamental conditions required for long-term investment in industrial infrastructure. This growing inability of African states to ensure these conditions was partly a result of profound global shifts in economic relations, particularly following the oil price rises of the 1970s,[109] and partly the result of developments in African politics after independence.[110] These have combined to change profoundly the manner in which West Africa is inserted in the international economy.

These remarks may serve to place Liberia's civil war in a larger perspective, for the colonial period in West Africa was a chapter in the longer history of relations between three sets of people, roughly defined: first, the majority of West Africans; second, their

[109] Eric Hobsbawm, *Age of Extremes: the short twentieth century, 1914-1991*, London, 1994, p.6, is surely correct in seeing this period as more important than the later end of the Cold War.

[110] Bayart, Ellis and Hibou, *The Criminalization of the State*, pp.1-31.

political elites; and third, those external powers with which African elites maintain political relations and which, it is relevant to note, are the source of imports and investments.[111] The relations between these three sets of actors have changed periodically over the past century and a half, but the relationships which they forge and renew continue to constitute the framework in which history has unfolded, and will no doubt continue to do so.

Applying this general observation to the specific case of Liberia, it may be noted that the establishment of a sovereign state in Monrovia in 1847 created two simultaneous equations which have defined power in the country ever since. One equation is that between the government in Monrovia and its foreign partners, who historically have been located most importantly in the United States. The second equation is the arrangements made between the elite which governs the Liberian state and its subjects or citizens. The arrangements made in 1847 established certain protocols of power which have remained formally intact to this day, despite changes in the substance of the relationships between the three sets of actors we have mentioned. In the late nineteenth century, while boundaries were being fixed by imperial governments throughout West Africa, Liberia's government too was obliged to claim specified boundaries which it was able to police. It was this which led it to undertake the military occupation of the hinterland of the country. In 1980 the fall of the True Whig Party disturbed relations between Liberia's governing elite and their fellow-countrymen but did not rupture the country's relations with its outside partners. Only as Samuel Doe exasperated the State Department, as the end of the Cold War changed outside expectations of West Africa, and above all as Liberia plunged into civil war in 1989, did it become accurate to speak of a break in relations between the Liberian state and its foreign allies or partners. Some significant investors were already beginning to pull out of Liberia in the 1980s, notably those in the iron-ore sector. Others, like the Firestone company, left only a skeleton staff at the outbreak of war. While Samuel Doe never had difficulty finding other business partners, they tended to be those attracted by speculative or short-term profits, sometimes based on transactions of a questionable or frankly criminal nature, rather than people offering long-term investment in productive capacity. Even during the civil war, as we have seen, it was possible for outsiders to do business in Liberia,

---

[111] R.E. Robinson, 'Non-European Foundations of European Imperialism: sketch for a theory of collaboration' in W.R. Louis (ed.), *Imperialism: the Robinson and Gallagher controversy*, New York, 1976, pp.128-52.

but it was generally business based on the export of minerals which required little or no investment in plant, infrastructure or machinery. Typical of the short-term transactions which may actually find a war-torn country and warlord rule attractive are the export of minerals mined by hand, such as diamonds, or of scrap metal. A state without a functioning system of government, as Liberia was during the civil war, is attractive to foreign entrepreneurs interested by import-export deals, those who can manage their own economic environment in an enclave, or those who need the facade of sovereignty to conceal certain transactions, such as money-launderers or drug-traffickers. All of these can on occasion defend their interests in foreign courts by invoking some of the legal attributes of Liberian sovereignty.

The inability of the Liberian state to perform the core tasks expected of it by outsiders since 1989 means that foreign interests are unable to invest in the development of the Mifergui project, and the world's steel producers have had to forego, for the foreseeable future, the vast reserves of iron ore lying on the Guinean side of Mount Nimba. For similar reasons various international creditors, including the World Bank and the IMF, have had to forget about receiving up to $3 billion they are owed by the Liberian state. The fact that the Liberian state during the civil war ceased to be an institution with which binding agreements could be made can be illustrated with an example, that of a German ship's captain who deposited $116,500 at a Monrovia bank after delivering a cargo of petroleum in 1993. When he came to withdraw his deposit, he received only $45,000. He reported the case to the National Bank of Liberia which issued an 'unconditional and irrevocable guarantee' to repay the money by a set date, but failed to meet the deadline.[112] Cases like this indicate that the Liberian central bank has ceased to fulfil the functions expected of it by the international financial system. It is a moot point whether it will be able to restore its reputation in the foreseeable future.

Many international diplomats and officials no doubt hope that Charles Taylor will be able to restore the Liberian state to the condition required of it by international actors, as he proclaims to be his goal. However, it would be best to be prudent in considering the likelihood of this happening. President Taylor heads an apparatus which is dependent less on model bureaucrats than on sub-warlords, NPFL chieftains who do not act at all times in

---

[112] J. Nagbe Sloh, 'The Vinton, FCIB, Muller Saga', *The Inquirer*, 4, 125 (15 July 1994), pp.4-5.

the manner expected of the agents of a modern administration.[113] The record of Taylor's administration in Greater Liberia does not suggest that he is likely to emerge as a champion of what international aid donors call 'good governance'. Liberia is hardly unique in this regard. Many African states, including those which constituted the Ecomog intervention force, are headed by political-military entrepreneurs little different in style from Taylor, and many elite groups have become accustomed to using violence as a means of political advancement and economic accumulation.

Who exactly represents these international interests which governments like that of Liberia must deal with? The most important international actors in this regard are the UN, the international financial institutions, and the governments of the Group of Seven industrial nations including notably the United States. Inasmuch as these bodies have a common view of Liberia, it is that relations had in effect to be suspended between 1989 and 1997, but that the election of President Taylor in July 1997 marks the return of Liberia to some sort of international respectability. All proclaim that their strategy in regard to dysfunctional states, which Liberia has to be considered even after the end of its civil war, is to rebuild them through the imposition of financial orthodoxy and the provision of financial and other incentives towards the development of good governance. This latter term is taken to imply a government which indeed maintains an effective and legitimate monopoly of violence over a fixed territory and with which durable diplomatic, legal and financial agreements can be reached, the conditions associated with the imposition of colonial rule from the late nineteenth century onwards.

If, as we have suggested, the chances are remote in the extreme that Liberia under President Taylor will develop the qualities of governance as defined above, then decision-makers in leading industrial nations will not for ever be able to delude themselves, as they characteristically do at present, that their promotion of good governance and democracy throughout Africa is bearing fruit. Sooner or later these key international actors will be obliged, implicitly or explicitly, to ask themselves the question put by a former deputy chief of mission at the US embassy. 'The Liberian war', he wrote to the *Washington Post*, 'has potential to spread unrest throughout West Africa. Therefore, the question facing the [US] administration and the new Congressional leadership is simple: What are our interests, if any, in West Africa or elsewhere on

---

[113] Cf. Jon Lee Anderson, 'The Devil They Know', *New Yorker*, 27 July 1998, pp.34-43.

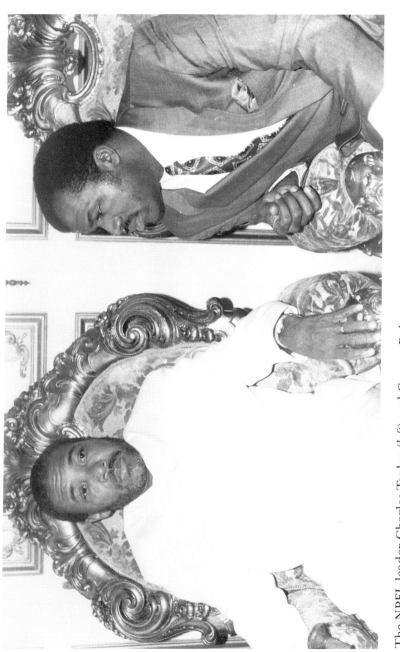

The NPFL leader Charles Taylor (*left*) and George Boley.

Leaders of the Coalition Group: (*left to right*) Roosevelt Johnson, François Masaquoi, Hezekiah Bowen, George Boley, Tom Woewiyu and Sam Dokie.

Left, former President Dr Samuel K. Doe at his last press conference in the Executive Mansion, Monrovia. *Right*, Alhaji G. V. Kromah, leader of Ulimo-K.

NPFL fighters in war attire, 1991

INPFL fighter, 1990.

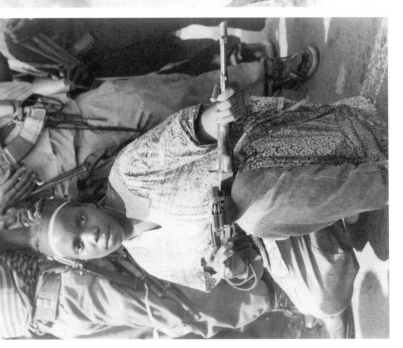

Left, a NPFL girl fighter. *Right*, an Ulimo-K boy soldier.

the continent?'[114] If the United States and other industrial powers
decide they can do without Mount Nimba's iron ore and can
write off Liberia's debt, what importance do they attach to preservation of the rain-forest, or to control of the international narcotics
trade, to say nothing of humanitarian considerations? A relationship
with a state able to make and sustain legally binding agreements
is necessary if the industrialised world wishes to implement any
policy at all on such matters.

To be sure, the deliquescence of internationally accepted
bureaucratic and legal norms in Liberia does not mean that the
country cannot be exploited economically. On the contrary,
economic activity is certainly possible even without a functioning
state, but only if such activity requires little capital investment.
This is the hallmark of the economy of plunder[115] which developed
in Liberia during the war and which also characterised the administration of Samuel Doe. An economy of plunder does not
favour capital-intensive activities such as deep mining, and it
generally discourages any form of exploitation which is sustainable,
including agriculture. These days, certain types of unregulated
exploitation are internationally regarded as reprehensible, such
as the destruction of rain forest. It would probably be a cause
for consternation if the general public in the industrialised
countries of Europe and North America was aware of what is happening to the Liberian forest, especially as some of those countries
are leading consumers of the hardwood which Liberia exports.

The juridical basis of the Liberian state is not in question. The
state of Liberia continues to exist in international law, and the
juridical recognition of sovereignty which arises from this fact constitutes a crucial element in Liberia's warlord politics. One of the
main points of interest of occupying public office, for political-
military entrepreneurs like Charles Taylor, is precisely that the
state provides a juridical base from which to deal with various
interests in local society, as well as to negotiate with international
institutions and business operators. In this respect too Liberia
is no different from its neighbours, whose states are also juridical
rather than political in origin. It is striking to note that, although
Liberia's neighbours profited from its agony to plunder its resources
and to sell weapons and ammunition to its factions, no government
showed the slightest inclination to claim even an inch of Liberian

[114] Letter from Gerald S. Rose, reprinted in *New Democrat*, 2, 78 (24-26 January
1995), p.12.
[115] A concept developed in Béatrice Hibou's essay in Bayart, Ellis and Hibou, *The
Criminalization of the State in Africa*.

territory for itself. No government, no matter how cynical or aggressive in other respects, has questioned the right of Liberia to continue as a sovereign state. It is partly for this reason that it is so misleading to refer, as analysts often do, to 'failed' or 'collapsed' states.[116] States like that of Liberia certainly do not conform to Western European or North American norms of good governance, nor are they likely to do so in the foreseeable future. They do, however, have a history and a continued existence, not least because they exist in the minds of their citizens or subjects. Liberians remain conscious of their national identity. A state apparatus of sorts continued to exist even at the height of the civil war, with uniformed policemen and customs officers and civil servants reporting for duty, at least occasionally, even when they had gone for months without pay.

The Liberian state itself could be said to have become a shell in which Liberians continue to live, rather like the looted office buildings in Monrovia which are home to dozens of families who camp in the ruins. In the following chapters, we will look at the history of this edifice with a view to learning more of its true nature.

[116] Zartman, *Collapsed States.*

Part II
AN INQUIRY

5

A NATION LONG FORLORN

When freedom raised her glowing form
On Montserrado's verdant height,
She set within the doom of night,
Midst lowing skies and thunder-storms
The star of Liberty!
And seizing from the waking morn
Its burnished shield of golden flame,
She lifted it in her proud name,
And roused a nation long forlorn
To nobler destiny!

(Edwin J. Barclay, President of Liberia
1930-44, *The Lone Star Forever*)

Settlers and others

It was a group of African-American settlers who founded Monrovia on 'Montserrado's verdant height' – a small hill now topped by an interesting statue of Liberia's founding president J.J. Roberts – in 1822. In the years to come, they were joined by other settlers from America and the West Indies, here and at a couple of other points along the coast, and by slaves from other parts of Africa who, intercepted on the high seas by the British or US navies while being transported as human cargo, were put ashore in Liberia. These last were the original Congos, until very recently regarded as a group separate from the descendants of Americans. In the past few years, those groups of external origin which Liberians used to call 'Americo-Liberians' and 'Congos' have merged into one, and the name 'Congos' is now used more often to denote all Liberians with roots outside West Africa. All of these people, being of African ancestry, were able to claim Liberian citizenship after the establishment of the republic in 1847. People without African ancestry, such as the Lebanese settlers who came in the early twentieth century, are explicitly excluded from Liberian citizenship under the terms of the constitution.

191

These immigrants settled among people whose ancestors had lived in West Africa for as long as they could remember. The Mandingo, professional traders rather than farmers, are the only group other than the descendants of the American settlers themselves who make a virtue out of recalling their origins in other parts. The idea that all of these peoples form a nation, which President Edwin Barclay regarded as 'long forlorn' because it had long been unconscious of its own national destiny, was originally an American import introduced by the settlers living in Monrovia and a couple of other places on the coast, from which it spread. The civil war of 1989-97 has revealed that there is no great popular animosity today against the descendants of the American settlers, who were not singled out for persecution or massacre at any stage of the conflict. On the other hand, the sentiment has grown that the Mandingo, despite the fact that their ancestors have lived in parts of Liberia for at least two centuries, are not real Liberians. At root this is because, unlike those families of American or other settler origin who regard themselves first and foremost as Liberians, many Mandingo sometimes insist that their real homeland lies elsewhere, in Guinea. According to Augustine Konneh, 'in this way a Mandingo to this day can be marginal and consider himself not really Liberian except when it is to his advantage.'[1]

The way in which people have assimilated the idea of Liberian nationhood is a good example of their propensity, now and in the past, to add new ideas to their existing range of cultural resources. Much of West Africa has long been a zone of creolisation *par excellence*, in which different groups of people, often having no strong political centre in the past, have used different languages at the same time and have mixed elements of various languages to form new ones, especially when they are trading with people whose mother tongue they do not understand. They have done the same with religion, often adopting elements of Islam or Christianity, both of which are associated in Liberia with specific forms of political organisation and control of valuable trade-routes, while retaining other spiritual beliefs. It is at least consistent to assimilate political ideologies in a similar way. Liberian nationalism is as much a hybrid as are Liberian Christianity, Liberian Islam and Liberian English. The ideas of a Liberian nation and a Liberian state have been absorbed into a stock of political ideologies and organisational techniques which has been constantly updated.

Some peoples living along the coast – the Vai, the Kru, the Grebo and others – had continuous relations with European and

[1] Konneh, 'Indigenous Entrepreneurs', p.31.

American sailors and traders for quite a long time before 1822.
Other groups living further inland may never have seen a European
or an American before quite recent times, but they too felt the
effects of the Atlantic trade in the form of the foreigners' demand
for local products, notably slaves, and people living in the hinterland
developed decades or centuries ago a taste for the luxury goods
which came from the coast, such as firearms and alcohol. As early
as 1725, a French traveller noted that the people of the coast
'were fond of imitating the Europeans' and that 'they have learnt
of the Europeans to be fond of what comes from abroad'.[2] In
the far north of the country, imported goods were brought not
by Europeans and Americans but by Mandingo and other traders
from the savannah who particularly sought kola nuts from the
forest.[3] The Liberian forest, and the forest areas in what are today
the neighbouring countries of Guinea, Sierra Leone and Côte
d'Ivoire, is rich in natural resources which have historically been
at the frontier of two distinct trading systems, one based further
north in the savannah and dominated by Muslims, the other controlled by merchants arriving by sea, most of them Christians.
The people of the forest have over the centuries sold ivory, kola,
slaves, rubber, wood, gold, diamonds and other local products
in exchange for imported manufactures, salt and other goods.
So significant was this commerce in the development of relations
with outsiders that European traders for centuries routinely referred
to various parts of West Africa as the Gold Coast, the Ivory Coast,
the Slave Coast, the Pepper Coast and, in the case of Liberia,
the Grain Coast, in reference to the forest products on offer there.
Trade was often the cause of war as communities of forest-dwellers
competed to extract products from the forest, some of which they
sold to outsiders for eventual consumption in the Sahel, in Europe,
in North America or further afield; or in what was by far the
most damaging trade, they themselves were forced or induced
to provide slaves for export. For decades or even centuries before
the foundation of the Republic of Liberia, the human population
of the territory was governed by small political entities, often based
on lineages or extended families. Wealthy people sought to acquire
slaves for domestic use or for sale, and to buy imported luxuries
including firearms. This certainly amounted to a distinctive, pre-

[2] Le Chevalier des Marchais, quoted in Carl Burrowes, *The Americo-Liberian Ruling
Class and Other Myths: a critique of political science in the Liberian context*, Philadelphia,
1989, p.63.

[3] Martin Ford '"Pacification" Under Pressure: the political economy of Liberian
intervention in Nimba, 1912-1918', *Liberian Studies Journal*, XIV, 2 (1984), pp.44-63.

modern, social and economic system of the sort which Marxist
historians and anthropologists used to term a mode of production.[4]

On the coast itself, the establishment of permanent settler
colonies at Monrovia and elsewhere after 1822 created struggles
for influence, intimately connected with control of long-distance
trade, in which the settlers competed with the generally Muslim
traders, particularly the Mandingo, whose own trader-princes exercised power over part of the hinterland. Other groups sought
to turn the competition between American settlers, European
traders and Mandingo princes and merchants to their own advantage.
Some forest-dwellers who were seeking to escape the influence
or political control of powerful Mandingo chiefdoms and kingdoms
which were extending their dominion from the savannah towards
the forest saw in the American settlers a source of protection.
As President Arthur Barclay – uncle of the writer of 'The Lone
Star Forever' – recalled in his 1904 inaugural address,[5]

> When we came here in 1822, the country was indeed divided
> among a large number of tribes, but there were signs, not only
> in this territory but along the whole West Coast, of a desire
> to merge the tribal governments into wider political organisa-
> tions which would secure the peace of the country, put a stop
> to incessant raids, devastations, and consequent loss of life and
> property. [...] The more sagacious chiefs saw in our settlement
> the necessary center.

Since slaves were one of the forest products most in demand along
the coast of West Africa until the mid-nineteenth century, there
were constant small-scale wars whose main object was the capture
of slaves for domestic use, for sale to Mandingo merchants for
their own use or for transfer further north, or for sale to the
European and Spanish-Cuban slave-traders who were still operating
along the coast at that date. The American settlers, themselves
the descendants of freed slaves, regarded the ending of the slave
trade as a central part of their national mission. Meanwhile, the
producers of slaves, military entrepreneurs and local notables or
others throughout the forest, desired access to trade goods for
prestige and redistribution to their people but at the same time
endeavoured to avoid becoming subject to powerful corporations
of traders to the extent of being themselves enslaved.[6] Even after

4 Emmanuel Terray, *Une histoire du royaume abron du Gyaman : des origines à la
conquête coloniale*, Paris, 1995, pp.197-212. This text was first written in 1983.

5 Quoted in Nathaniel Richardson, *Liberia's Past and Present*, London, 1959, p.117.

6 Relevant reflections on the working of such a system are in Joseph C. Miller,

the first Americans had established themselves in Monrovia, local potentates – tribal chiefs, in the settler vocabulary – often tried to balance the competing influence of the Mandingo or other traders from inland, the American settlers and Europeans.

After 1822 the American settlers tried to collect customs-dues on the whole coastal import-export trade in the name of their putative national sovereignty, and this was resisted by their competitors. Along the coast many chiefs tried to cultivate exclusive relations with their own foreign trader who could provide them with imported trade goods. These foreigners, 'in most cases were former stewards, pursers and/or mates of steamers or sailing vessels that had been used in the African trade'.[7] Traders arriving by sea during the mid-to-late nineteenth century typically established themselves at some point where they could avoid paying customs-dues to the Liberian government and placed themselves under the protection of a local chief, in many cases marrying one of the chief's daughters or other female dependents, and so gaining entry into the kin-group while signifying acceptance of the leader's authority. Via his new son-in-law, a chief then had his own little trade monopoly. The proclamation of a Liberian republic in 1847 did not immediately alter the conventions of political and commercial exchanges of this sort, although the settlers' aversion to the slave trade and their general insistence on formally recognising only Christian marriages between immigrant families did gradually influence conditions all along the coast.

All over West Africa, the formal declaration of sovereign boundaries as a consequence of colonial partition had a radical effect on politics and trade. French colonial troops pushing inland in the 1880s, for example, met resistance from the great Malinke warlord Almamy Samory Touré, a conqueror and slave-raider whose expeditions led to major population movements and political upheavals.[8] The resulting rise in political violence led to the new colonial administrations redoubling their efforts to 'pacify' the interior, in other words to stop all military activity other than their own, and also increased the number of refugees looking for protection from the new colonial governments. The same effect was felt by the Liberian settlers. In the early 1890s, the entire western part of the hinterland claimed by the Liberian government as its jurisdiction 'was in a state of panic and rout due to the

Way of Death: merchant capitalism and the Angolan slave trade, 1730-1830, Madison, WI, 1988, esp. pp.105-39.

[7] Yancy, *Historical Lights*, p.71.

[8] Person, *Samori, passim.*

invasion of bands of armed horsemen known as the "Sofa" ',[9] raiders
who had formed part of Samory's army, operating over a wide
area and causing some hinterland peoples to seek the protection
of the government in Monrovia. British and French colonial administrations in turn put pressure on Monrovia to pacify the territory
it claimed, obliging it to send its militia on expeditions into the
interior which were little more than predatory raids of their own.
President Arthur Barclay referred to this in his 1904 inaugural
address, observing that 'we made a great initial mistake in the
beginning of our national career. We sought to obtain, and did
succeed in grasping an enormous mass of territory, but we neglected
to conciliate and attach the resident populations to our interest.'[10]
He proposed to rectify this, on the grounds that 'government
must rest on the consent of the governed', and instituted a number
of measures intended to put the territories claimed by Monrovia
on a sounder administrative and political footing in the form of
a system of indirect rule in which district commissioners representing the central government were to work alongside local chiefs.
In 1908 the republic created a new standing army, the ancestor
of the force which was to bring Samuel Doe to power in 1980.

As the colonial partition of Africa in the late nineteenth century
gradually resulted in demonstrable changes in patterns of trade
and government, groups of allies and relatives became separated
by international borders. They were then subject to processes of
ethnographic description and administrative classification by
French, British and Liberian officials operating in a similar way
and for similar reasons. This has led to a considerable confusion
of names. The people generally known in Liberia as Gio, for example, are called Yacouba in Côte d'Ivoire, but may also be called
Dan. The Liberian Krahn are often called Wee by their near-
neighbours the Gio but are known as Guéré in Côte d'Ivoire.[11]
All of these groups, whether in Liberia or elsewhere, were not
centrally organised polities at the time they became subject to
colonial or settler administration by officials who sought to make
some sort of order out of the complexities of local politics and
to acquire a handle by which to assert their control over local
government. This does not mean, however, that all ethnic labels
are colonial 'inventions', a useful concept which is in danger of

---

[9] D'Azevedo, 'A Tribal Reaction to Nationalism', part II, p.43.

[10] Quoted in Richardson, *Past and Present*, p.117.

[11] Holsoe and Lauer, 'Who are the Kran/Guéré?', pp.139-49.

being over-worked.[12] Some ethnic labels, like Mandingo and Vai, are old ones whose meanings have changed as they have been used for purposes of government. Common to all of Liberia's current ethnic labels and forms of local political organisation is that they have been profoundly marked by the exercise of national government.

The formal extension of Liberian power through some sort of regular bureaucratic organisation into what had previously, from the late nineteenth century, been an ill-defined hinterland, was largely the work of President Arthur Barclay (1904-12), himself under pressure from Western governments to extend regular bureaucratic government throughout Liberian territory. Barclay's reforms represented the first systematic attempt by the government of Liberia to impose the political culture and institutions of the settlers on the people of the hinterland. Barclay's efforts were continued by his successors with progressively more potent resources of coercion, control and patronage, with results which have shaped the history of the country. In the intervening decades, this has had a major effect both in the manner in which local communities function and, interestingly enough, on the elite politics of Monrovia.

An earlier chapter sketched the evolution of local social and political entities into those units which Liberians today call 'tribes', formed in the process by which administrators searched for identifiable centres of political authority in local communities, while ambitious local potentates emerged to deliver the services which the central government demanded of them. The self-interested manner in which colonial administrators and ethnographers searched for 'tribes', and the pejorative connotations attached to the word, have caused many Western academics today to recoil from using the word. They generally prefer to speak of 'ethnic groups' in an effort to free themselves from subjective criteria, and they often categorise these ethnic groups by reference to language rather than ancestry. But this is hardly any more satisfactory since Liberia's ethnic groups are in many cases not easily distinguishable from their neighbours by reference to language, as we have noted.[13] All the available labels underestimate the remarkable plasticity and adaptability of clusters of people in West Africa throughout their history, and the degree to which they are capable of assimilating various aspects of collective identity for use in particular

[12] Cf. Eric Hobsbawm and Terence Ranger (eds), *The Invention of Tradition,* Cambridge, 1992.

[13] Above, pp.35-6.

contexts. While the 'tribal' identities imposed by officials from Monrovia or by outside ethnographers certainly have a meaning, it is one which has been added to older meanings without effacing them, in typically Liberian fashion.

It is important to note, then, that tribalism is not an ancient form of organisation which pre-dates the nation-state, but an essentially modern concept which is inherently connected to that of the nation-state. To borrow a useful distinction, the moral codes of ethnicity which bind small communities have deep historical roots, while tribalism is a political resource which enables individuals and factions to pursue their interests in a national state or to castigate their rivals in the same process.[14] As one of the most thoughtful academic writers on Liberia has noted, '"Tribalism", the avowed enemy of national unity, has been a product of Liberian nationalisation itself.'[15]

The politics of stateless societies

Another label sometimes attached by modern writers to the traditional form of various forest communities of modern Guinea, Liberia and Sierra Leone is that of 'stateless societies'. The best available definition is one offered in four points by Robin Horton. Stateless societies, he suggests, have the following features:[16]

1. There is little concentration of authority. It is difficult to point to any individual or limited group of people as the ruler or rulers of the society.
2. Such authority roles as exist affect a rather limited sector of the lives of those subject to them.
3. The wielding of authority as a specialised, full-time occupation is virtually unknown.
4. The unit within which people feel an obligation to settle their disputes according to agreed rules and without resort to force tends to be relatively small.

Before the twentieth century, West Africa contained hundreds of distinct societies corresponding to this definition, with no fixed patterns of centralised government corresponding to the Western

[14] John Lonsdale, 'The Moral Economy of Mau Mau: wealth, poverty and civic virtue in Kikuyu political thought' in Bruce Berman and John Lonsdale, *Unhappy Valley: conflict in Kenya and Africa* (2 vols, London, 1992), vol. II, pp.315-504.

[15] Warren L. D'Azevedo, 'Tribe and Chiefdom on the Windward Coast', *Liberian Studies Journal*, XIV, 2 (1989), p.102.

[16] Horton, 'Stateless Societies', p.87.

notion of statehood. Instead, such societies employed a number
of mechanisms by which decentralised political systems – a group
of kin, bound by moral codes of ethnicity, perhaps no more than
a few dozen or a few hundred strong, under the authority usually
of a patriarch – could combine into larger units for specific purposes. Using the extreme flexibility of lineage-based communities
with no permanent centre, groups of people over a wide area
could quickly form confederations for purposes of common offence
or defence, such as in the powerful Condo confederation which
existed in western Liberia in the early nineteenth century.[17] In
the south-east of Liberia, converts to Christianity played a
prominent part, in political reaction to the inroads of the government of Liberia, in efforts to federate a number of lineages into
a single Grebo kingdom between 1875 and 1890.[18]

This last case is an interesting example of how religious affiliation,
Christian, Muslim or other, could result in the creation of pan-
lineage or pan-ethnic institutions. Religious institutions in all parts
of the country were of notable political and social significance
in the days before the hinterland was conquered by the Republic
of Liberia, and this remained the case even when large numbers
of people became Muslims or Christians. The political aspect of
religion arose from the very nature of people's religious beliefs,
because Liberians of all religious persuasions tended to see themselves, in the words of one ethnographer, 'as inhabiting a world
peopled and controlled by an invisible order of personalised
spiritual beings which interact with humans in a variety of ways
and which must be taken into account at every juncture'.[19] One
of the most important ways in which spirits were believed to become
visible was through the use of masks, which formed a major part
of many religious rituals and institutions. Although the various
traditional religious beliefs and rituals have changed enormously
over the last century, masks are still prominent in Liberian village
life today, particularly in the north and west of the country. Generally carved from wood, masks most commonly function in religious
ritual as expressions of the otherwise invisible spiritual beings which
people believe to influence human society. In south-eastern Liberia,
masks are less often used, but there too they have a function,
chiefly 'within the context of age grades and [are] generally
emblematic of the spirit forces associated with warriors' age sets'.

[17] Svend E. Holsoe, 'The Condo Confederation in Western Liberia', *Liberian Historical Review*, 3, 1 (1966), pp.1-28.

[18] Martin, 'The Dual Legacy', pp.235-6, 258-89.

[19] Siegmann, 'Spirit Manifestation and the Poro Society', p.90.

In central Liberian communities, masks are more directly involved in 'social control by spirit forces'.[20]

The most widespread system of traditional religious belief associated with the use of masks, extending over all the north-west of the country, is the complex of religious societies or sodalities known as Poro (for men) and Sande (for women). Poro and Sande are corporations, controlled in each town by local councils of elders whose identity and whose rituals may not be divulged to outsiders. Some Poro members are also initiates of other, more exclusive societies often associated with some particular skill, such as the ability to cure snake bites. Various arcane aspects of their ritual and organisation have caused Poro and Sande to be labelled by most authors as 'secret societies', but this is a misleading name inasmuch as all adult males and females in many communities are in principle members of either Poro or Sande, making the notion that they are secret rather inaccurate. Secrecy is really an idiom, a means of transmitting esoteric information to initiates more than it is an attempt to exclude the mass of a community from participation.[21] In functional terms, the practice of secrecy enables senior officials of the Poro and Sande to exercise their authority more effectively, as it generally does in all hierarchies. Within the Poro society are high grades whose ritual and membership may not be divulged to people from a lower grade, thus constituting a structure of authority in what were otherwise, at least in the quite recent past, communities with a weak concentration of power in matters of civic government.

In discussing traditional Liberian religious beliefs, it is generally difficult to know whether to use the present or the past tense, for calling a practice 'traditional' does not mean that it forms part of a corpus of belief and action which is unchanging, but is primarily a description of the way many Liberians understand ideas which they have inherited from earlier generations, as opposed to those they know to be recent imports. Some traditional institutions have changed enormously even in living memory, in reaction to the changes in national life which have occurred over the decades, as elders of the Poro will admit. Corporations like the Poro still exist today and are still important in rural areas especially, even though they are less powerful than in the past. Although the Poro system is generally practised in only about half of modern Liberia, the religious traditions of other parts of

[20] *Ibid.*

[21] Beryl L. Bellman, *The Language of Secrecy: symbols and metaphors in Poro ritual*, New Brunswick, 1984.

the country are comparable in some respects. The Grebo, for example, also have secret societies known as *kui* which certainly played an important role in social and political life in the past. One early twentieth-century author wrote that *kui* societies among the Grebo were used to punish what he called wizards and witches,[22] although information is lacking about how exactly these societies functioned a century ago, or even today. It is known, though, that in the nineteenth century, the powers of local chiefs and war-leaders among the Grebo were subject to control by priests known as *bodio*.[23] The Kru also had *bodio*, whose authority was associated with their access to oracles.[24] All over Liberia there were small, exclusive secret societies often based on an association with a particular animal, such as a leopard or a crocodile, which wielded considerable power.

Whether or not specific corporations such as age sets or religious sodalities make use of masks, all tend to make similar assumptions about the nature of power in human societies.[25] Traditionally, all power was thought to derive from the invisible spirits who are believed to inhabit the world, notably those of the forest, the animals and the ancestors, and these spirits could easily enter a living being who then became possessed by them. A person thus possessed actually 'becomes' the spirit temporarily, losing their own personality for a short duration. To illustrate this with a modern analogy, a human body is conceived to be rather like a car which cannot move until it is entered by a driver.[26] The spirit is the driver who can put the human body in motion. A living being is normally occupied by one individual spirit or soul, although this spirit, or rather a component of it, is believed to leave the body for short periods quite often, most obviously in the form of dreams. Conversely, another spirit from the invisible world may temporarily take control of a human body and replace the soul which usually resides there, like someone borrowing a

[22] Sir Harry Johnston, *Liberia*, 2 vols, London, 1906, II, pp.1068-70.

[23] Martin, 'The Dual Legacy', pp.14-24.

[24] Sullivan, 'Settlers in Sinoe County', pp.55-7.

[25] The following is based on numerous works on Liberian religion including: George W. Harley, *Masks as Agents of Social Control in Northeast Liberia*, Cambridge, MA, 1950; Kenneth Little, 'The Political Function of the Poro,' part I, *Africa*, XXXV, 4 (1965), pp.349-365, and part II, *Africa*, XXXVI, 1 (1966), pp.62-72; *Ethnologische Zeitschrift Zürich*, 1 (1980); Bellman, *Language of Secrecy*.

[26] I have borrowed this analogy from Felicitas Goodman, *How About Demons? Possession and exorcism in the modern world*, Bloomington, IN, 1988, pp.1-2.

car from its owner for a short period. It might be the spirit of
a dead ancestor, a spirit of the forest, or even that of an animal.

In Liberia the use of masks is generally associated with the
manifestation of the invisible world of the spirits. This is most
evident in the Poro complex of societies. When Poro priests or
zoes appear in public for certain rituals they wear masks and
camouflage themselves from head to toe to hide their normal
appearance. This is a form of theatre but in many cases that does
not imply any form of levity, although there are separate masked
figures who take part in masquerades intended largely for amuse-
ment. On the contrary, in the past, but even today, the drama
of the masked figure known in Liberian English as the Bush Devil
can be deadly serious since the person who dons the appropriate
mask or costume may, in certain circumstances, be considered
by themselves and others to be possessed by the spirit which dwells
in the mask. How this can happen has been well described by
an ethnographer of the Gio, a group with a rich masking tradition
but without the Poro, when he noted that '[Gio] have the belief
that all the land is possessed by spirits who dwelt there before
human beings came, so the spirits are the real owners of the
land. It is their right to interfere in human behaviour and in
human groups.'[27] He continues:[28]

> To try to understand the relationship between the mask and
> the mask wearer, we should think first about the [Gio] idea
> of spirit. The [Gio] thinkers would say that everything existing
> in this world has some force behind it whch they call *du* and
> we are all just manifestations of our own *du*. They have what
> we can call an alter ego concept, that the *du* of one person
> can move into another body, such as an animal. [...] *Du* is
> like a living being, an entity with a personality that has everything
> except a body. This concept is important for masking.

In a ritual of the Poro or any comparable masking society, a spirit
of the forest which appears at key moments is not a person in
disguise but an invisible being which has taken on physical form
for a while. George Way Harley, an American missionary who
lived for some thirty-four years in Nimba County and made a
close study of the Poro in that area, considered that 'the Poro
may be thought of as an attempt to reduce the all pervading
spirit world to an organisation in which man might contact the

---

27 Eberhard Fischer, 'Masks in a non-Poro Area: the Dan', *Ethnologische Zeitschrift
Zürich*, 1 (1980), p.82.

28 *Ibid.*, p.87.

spirit world and interpret it to the people, where men became spirits, and took on godhead.'[29] He noted that 'these masks combined many elements and ideas. A mask could be a tangible proof of reverence for ancestors, more sacred than the most venerated family portraits. It could be the counterpart of a seal of office, a symbol of authority, the terror of the evil doer, in the presence of which punishment was administered and whose wooden cheeks were rouged with the blood of human sacrifice. A mask corresponded to a holy image or relic in Christianity.'[30]

Because they were considered to be in contact with the spirits which are held to be the real sources of power, or even to be possessed by such spirits, religious officials could have overwhelming social and political influence. The exact manner in which this occurred varied from one part of Liberia to another, with a distinction to be made roughly between the lands on the two sides of the Saint John River, which constitutes a cultural and linguistic boundary approximately dividing the Mande and Mel language families from those of the Kruan language group to the south-east. Mande- and Mel-speakers are characterised by hierarchical chiefdoms and the presence of universal initiation societies, Poro for men and Sande for women. The Kruan peoples are less stratified and do not have universal secret societies.[31] There are further complexities in cases where individuals or whole communities respect some traditional religious practices while also following Muslim or Christian rites, as will shortly be discussed in more detail. The existence in various parts of Liberia of powerful priests, oracles or religious sodalities alongside family heads, patriarchs, clan chiefs or other forms of civic leadership represented a division of the task of regulating the affairs of a community which could be regarded as a system of checks and balances. In this way, stateless societies, while they had no highly centralised systems of government, nevertheless had protocols according to which power could be used (and by reference to which it could be considered as being abused) for the regulation of those human affairs which modern social scientists might regard as political or economic in nature.

Given the power of religious sodalities in pre-republican times, one of the few avenues for a successful political entrepreneur, such as a young man successful in war, to consolidate his power

[29] Quoted in Kenneth Little, 'The Political Function of the Poro', part I, p.355.

[30] Quoted in Galbraith Welch, *The Jet Lighthouse,* London, 1990, pp.170-1.

[31] Mary Moran, 'Liberia' in John Middleton (ed.), *Encyclopedia of Africa South of the Sahara,* 4 vols, New York, 1997, II, p.575.

was himself to assume religious office of some sort, such as by joining a high grade of a secret society, which was not always easy since many of the most prestigious religious offices were hereditary and dominated by men of advanced age. The precise means by which a religious corporation acted as a political check on a civic leader or war-captain could include both co-option and force. In the days before the Liberian government had extended its power to the hinterland, a local chief who was abusing his powers might be publicly humiliated by a masked spirit and consequently lose all authority. If one of the incessant petty wars or raids between towns threatened to get out of hand, it might stop when the main culprit mysteriously died, killed by a leopard ... or perhaps by a human leopard. Human leopards – people possessed by the spirit of a leopard – killed their victims with a multibladed knife which left wounds on the body indistinguishable to the naked eye from those made by a leopard's claws, making it very difficult to know whether a death was the result of an attack by a real leopard or by a person dressed as an animal.[32]

Stateless societies typically have a highly egalitarian ethos. Were a human being, in his or her unmasked workaday form, to acquire great power and to force others to conform to an individual will, this would be highly disruptive. Hence the practice of masking, considered in its purely functional aspect, is a mechanism whereby one individual can wield the power which is inherent in society, even the power of life and death, without being regarded as a disruptive force. Since legitimate authority is deemed to be that emanating from the spirit world, expressed via a mask or through the pronouncements of an oracle, and since the identity of a religious medium is not apparent, it is acceptable to the community of believers.[33] A priest of the Poro may next day reappear in his 'normal' human form as a local blacksmith or farmer, but this ordinary personality is considered to be unconnected with the events of the previous night. Far from being societies without institutions, stateless societies of this sort are ones in which institutions eclipse individuals in importance. In pre-Liberian days, in those communities where chiefs existed as administrators of civic order, they could usually be overruled by priests or religious authorities, so that it was no exaggerration to say that 'the Poro was all of religion, law and politics in one'.[34] A similar role to the council

---

[32] Werner Junge, *African Jungle Doctor: ten years in Liberia*, London, 1952, pp.176-87.

[33] Horton, 'Stateless Societies', pp.110-13.

[34] George Schwab (G.W. Harley, ed.), *Tribes of the Liberian Hinterland*, Cambridge, MA, 1947, pp.286-7.

of *zoes* of a local Poro society could be played in south-east Liberia, where the Poro society did not exist, by the *bodio* or high priest.[35]

One of the features of such 'stateless' societies was that, in the general absence of any highly institutionalised form of civic government other than the religious societies, there was considerable scope for political entrepreneurs, usually young men successful in war, to rise from obscurity to positions of influence through force of personality and the distribution of largesse gained in trade or war. 'These individuals used an alternative base for achieving their positions, usually a combination of special access to economic resources ouside the traditional society – most often European trade goods – and great astuteness in understanding the local political structure and manipulating it to their own purposes.'[36] Small-scale warfare seems to have been common throughout the Liberian hinterland during the nineteenth century, and indeed warfare was an important instrument for the regulation of relations between towns.[37] There are still impressive defensive walls standing to a height of three or four metres in several towns of Lofa County, for example, monuments to the constant small-scale wars of a century or more ago. There are several recorded cases from before 1900 of strangers dominating a given group and even building quite considerable political networks, but there was no institutional means for them to turn these into permanent systems which could be passed on intact to a successor. Political leadership in most regions of the forest before the twentieth century was weak and discontinuous, and decidedly more small-scale, more complex and less rigid than the later attempt to designate 'tribes': discrete entities bound by common central authority in the person of a paramount chief and having a common language and a common body of custom. Whatever their precise origin, local strong men, warlords, chiefs and notables all had to reckon with the authority of the spirits of the forest, which had the ability to punish them.

To a certain extent, even before the institution of republican government over all of Liberia, one avenue for entrepreneurs to build their authority outside the reach of the traditional religious

[35] Sullivan, 'Settlers in Sinoe County', pp.55-7.

[36] Svend E. Holsoe, 'Zolu Duma, Ruler of the Southern Vai, 17??-1828: a problem in historical interpretation', *Liberian Studies Journal*, XV, 2 (1990), p.91. For other examples of political entrepreneurs in different parts of Liberia, see Schröder and Seibel, *Ethnographic Survey of Southeastern Liberia*, p.71; Richard M. Fulton, 'The Kpelle Traditional Political System', *Liberian Studies Journal*, I, 1 (1968), p.15.

[37] Fulton, 'The Kpelle Traditional System', p.15; Martin, 'Dual Legacy', pp.25-6; Sullivan, 'Settlers in Sinoe County', pp.59-61.

system was through conversion to Islam or Christianity. We have mentioned the role of Christian converts in attempts to build a Grebo kingdom in the late nineteenth century, but in general patterns of conversion to Christianity were inextricably linked to the rule of the Liberian government, which set great store by its Christian character. In regard to conversion to Islam, less is known, but it is clear that, certainly before the twentieth century, conversion to Islam in western Liberia especially tended to imply political recognition of the authority of powerful Mandingo trader-princes with family connections further afield.

For outsiders seeking to establish fixed systems of local government amenable to administration from Monrovia, including the district officers, army officers and other officials sent from Monrovia, the stateless societies of the hinterland were frustratingly fluid. Asserting administrative control over them was like trying to eat soup with a fork. Officials attempted to identify people with some form of recognised authority and confirm them as village chiefs or headmen, responsible for carrying out orders from above, whereas traditionally, civic administrators such as these were all subject to the ultimate authority of the spirits of the forest and their mediums. Since the spirits were themselves invisible, and only took human form when they were mediated by a priest or possessed a masked society official, district officers found themselves competing with officers of the secret societies as the ultimate source of authority in local government.

Liberian administration

At the end of the nineteenth century, the hinterland which the government in Monrovia was coming to dominate through its army contained numerous systems of political organisation. In western Liberia alone there were four different types: migrant bands gathered under an individual leader who had no traditional basis of authority; conservative local chiefdoms; expanding chiefdoms gaining control of land and other resources and subjugating village chiefdoms which they then used as local councils to mediate between lineages; and larger confederations of the above. None of them was ethnically homogeneous.[38] In all of them civic authority or political power was largely underpinned, and to some extent controlled, by religious corporations such as Poro societies. In the south-east of the country there was an equal variety of political

---

[38] D'Azevedo, 'Tribe and Chiefdom', pp.103-4.

systems, including acephalous groups, communities governed by prominent age-sets, and federations revolving around prominent individuals or influential priests or secret societies. Patterns of political allegiance were further complicated by the early emergence of Christianity in the area.

Liberian officials seeking to impose their version of order on these societies, and for that matter European administrators in Sierra Leone, Guinea and Côte d'Ivoire faced with similar problems, brought with them a concept of public order quite different from the traditional one. The order publicly enunciated by the True Whig Party was one in which a central government, resting on republican institutions of American inspiration, aspired to uphold a monopoly of violence over a defined territory, and to administer a written code of regulations and laws via a secular and publicly designated hierarchy of officials. This corresponds to the idea of government held by most people in the Western world over the last couple of hundred years.

Seeking to impose this view of public order, during the twentieth century Liberian government officials either formally suppressed all systems of government previously existing in the hinterland or formally incorporated them into systems of indirect rule which, in theory, amounted to a rigorous system of administration whose representatives in the rural areas, the district officers, were subject to central control. In practice, as in so many conquest states, the apparent uniformity of the formal system of government which had its centre in Monrovia was in reality a patchwork structure in which local communities and their leaders reached a variety of accommodations with the centre, in the process of which old institutions of government, such as chieftaincies and religious sodalities, acquired new characteristics and in which schools and churches became engines of assimilation and creators of new social groups.

The government of the Liberian republic aspired to uphold standards of governance similar to those of its colonial neighbours, and republican officials, at least in theory, aspired to modernise the societies they governed. But Liberian governments until the mid-twentieth century hardly had the financial means to realise their ambition of administering their territory in the manner considered by the leading powers of the day to be the hallmark of a sovereign state: policing the frontiers and instituting a national bureaucracy, while also meeting their international financial and diplomatic obligations. (This is to a considerable degree what the World Bank today refers to as 'good governance'.) For much of its history the Republic of Liberia was desperately short of money.

Its impecuniousness caused it to resort to foreign borrowing and this in turn subjected it to pressures from foreign powers – most notably, till the 1930s, Britain and France – which at times seriously threatened its national sovereignty. It was difficult to produce income from direct taxation of the population not only because there was no system of modern mechanised production, but also especially because of the nature of the administration in the hinterland. Citizens of Liberia, relatively few in number and concentrated in Monrovia, could be assessed for tax in a bureaucratic manner, but they also constituted the true electorate and therefore had the means to resist heavy taxation. The bulk of potential tax-payers were living in rural areas of the hinterland where they did not benefit from full rights of citizenship, administered by chiefs, who in turn were supervised by government commissioners with little real entry into local politics.

As early as 1904 President Barclay borrowed from British colonial practice the system of indirect rule, dividing the hinterland into districts administered by commissioners who, till 1914, were often military men using the methods of martial law. Thereafter, official policy tended more towards the appointment of civilians as district commissioners and district officers, who were urged to collaborate with chiefs as far as possible.[39] Some commentators felt that the government in practice had little option in its choice of administrative techniques, given the limits on its resources. In 1932, for example, a delegate of the League of Nations sent to investigate reports that the government was making systematic use of forced labour amounting to virtual slavery, observed that 'the only possible means of governing these tribes, if few Government Commissioners are available, is by supporting a strong Paramount chief over several tribes and holding him responsible for law and order, at the same time giving him such Government assistance as he may require, making it clear to dissident tribes that the Government forces are ready to support the Paramount Chief.'[40] As was also the case in the colonial territories which bordered it, the Liberian government was obliged to create a system of local government by proposing bargains with local potentates it identified in the interior, offering to confirm them as local rulers, often with powers far in excess of those they had previously enjoyed, in return for recognition

[39] Monday B. Akpan, 'The Practice of Indirect Rule in Liberia: the laying of the foundations, 1822-1915' in Hinzen and Kappel (eds), *Dependence, Underdevelopment and Persistent Conflict* pp.79-86.

[40] Dr M.D. Mackenzie's report to Council of League of Nations, 1932, in Richardson, *Past and Present*, p.158.

of Monrovia's sovereignty. The government's instructions to its officials were explicit in insisting that each officially recognised tribe was to be governed by a single paramount chief, elected by a council of clan chiefs, subject to appointment by the President of the Republic. A book of regulations issued by the government in 1949, codifying existing practice, stated that 'For purposes of administration, a tribe shall consist of clans according to tribal traditions, and shall be ruled or governed by a clan chief.' Paramount chiefs were empowered to collect taxes and mobilise labour for public works, receiving ten per cent of the taxes raised. All males subject to tribal administration were liable for communal labour: 'Any traveller requiring carriers shall apply to the Chief of the Section for the desired number which must be promptly supplied', and each carrier was expected to carry up to sixty pounds in weight.[41] As one later commentator observed, 'The alliance between executive branch officials and local traditional rulers was mutually beneficial. On the one hand, chiefs delivered soldiers and voters en bloc to urban leaders.[...]National leaders in turn provided their rural allies with the resources needed to overcome local challenges.'[42]

In many parts of the country, throughout its history the Liberian system of indirect rule bore the stamp of the military means used to establish it in the early twentieth century. It was first established by the Liberian army which had a reputation for brutality and for looting, since its troops largely lived off the land. In 1910 some chiefs in the south-east of the country complained of the activities of the Liberian Frontier Force, which they termed 'this execrable force', and said was 'entirely demoralized, and wherever they have been sent throughout the country – whether to River Cess or in the hinterland – their custom has been to plunder the towns through which they pass and rape their women'.[43] Indeed, the lawless behaviour of the Liberian army was so embarrassing to the government of the United States, as early as 1912, that it linked the offer of a substantial loan in that year to the acceptance of US military personnel, 'drawn from the coloured section of the United States Army', according to a British consul, to serve as officers.[44] This probably had some effect in improving the army's

[41] 'Revised Laws and Administrative Regulations Governing the Hinterland', Dept. of the Interior, 1949, National Documentation Center, Monrovia.

[42] Burrowes, 'Democracy or Disarmament', p.119.

[43] Letter from King Gyude and chiefs of the Grebo to the American Colonization Society, 15 February 1910, quoted in Richardson, *Past and Present*, p.32.

[44] Maugham, *Republic of Liberia*, pp.87-8.

discipline and efficiency, but there is no doubt that it continued to be known for its brutality, to the point that some modern Liberian writers have wondered whether the Liberian army did not inherit the cultural attributes of 'slave raids of an earlier era'.[45] Recruiting the bulk of the troops from the Loma people, who had until the last quarter of the nineteenth century been frequent victims of and participants in the slave trade, the army incorporated many of the military traditions and tactics of the people who formed its recruits, for whom war was a form of social advancement and economic accumulation. A description of a military expedition to put down a rising in the south-east, apparently in 1930, led by President Barclay in person, reveals it to have been a veritable plundering operation, resembling the activities in the same area of the LPC militia some sixty years later.[46] Republican war acquired some of the character of older 'tribal' wars, being an occasion for soldiers to acquire plunder. The gradual evolution of the Liberian army from a citizens' militia into a standing force officered by Americo-Liberians commanding 'native' soldiers, which then assimilated many of the warrior traditions of its rank and file, illustrates how republican institutions of state and Western-style institutions of administration in general assimilated some of the traditions and habits of the persons who manned these same institutions at the lower level.

This last observation is also true of the civil administration, where government devolved upon chiefs at the local level in the hinterland. This system was introduced even in areas, notably the east and south-east, where there was little tradition of strong, institutional chiefdoms. In practice, there were often disputes about which candidate for a local chiefdom the government should recognise, or clan chiefs might object to being made subject to a certain paramount chief. Whereas, in tradition, chiefs had generally been subject to religious institutions, or at least had been required to take decisions in council, religious corporations like Poro and Sande were now declared to be organisations of a non-political nature which may not interfere in the conduct of the administration. Whomever the government recognised as a chief possessed sweeping powers, backed up by the possibility of recourse to the Army, and subject only to the will of the executive branch represented in the first instance by a local district commissioner. The latter, often stationed in remote areas many days' march from Monrovia,

---

[45] Dunn and Tarr, *Liberia: a national polity*, p.89.

[46] Hayman and Preece, *Lighting Up Liberia*, p.29.

had wide powers but had little real grip on local politics unless he could cultivate a good relationship with a local paramount chief.

Behind the rigorous logic of indirect rule lay a multitude of unofficial practices, as both chiefs and district commissioners had recourse to informal means of political control, some of which were improvised, others of which were simply continuations of old practices in a new guise. Chiefs might use powers of levying taxes given to them by the central government primarily to accumulate resources for themselves, often with the complicity of the district commissioners who in theory should prevent such abuses. Central officials sometimes had themselves initiated into secret societies, even when these were illegal, as a way of getting access to the informal fora of local politics. The manipulation of clan disputes, agreements reached in conclave in a secret society or a Masonic lodge, unofficial understandings based on payment of a bribe, the gift of a female concubine or other gratuity: these are all examples of how local government was often conducted as much through informal as formal mechanisms.[47]

The Liberian state

The tendency for formal public administration to develop in parallel, or rather in symbiosis, with networks based on the quasi-traditional authority of chiefs, was common not only in Liberia but also in all the European colonies in Africa which relied on the agency of local collaborators to govern rural areas. This has had a formative influence on African states up to the present day which various authors have noted. One refers to a 'rhizome state', whose underground roots he compares to those of a plant.[48] Another speaks of a 'bifurcated state', separated into an urban sector whose more privileged inhabitants have genuine rights of citizenship and a rural sector subject to quasi-traditional chieftainship and customary law.[49] A third uses the metaphor of a shadow to describe the manner in which the official system of state politics is duplicated by informal methods, often rooted in society itself, which are used by those seeking 'control over elements of society associated with

---

[47] Akpan, 'The Practice of Indirect Rule'.

[48] Jean-François Bayart, *The State in Africa: the politics of the belly,* London, 1993, pp.218-27.

[49] Mahmood Mamdani, *Citizen and Subject: contemporary Africa and the legacy of late colonialism,* Princeton, NJ, 1996, pp.16-23.

the production and reproduction of capital'.[50] These images convey a little of the substance of Liberian administration in the twentieth century, in which a high degree of centralisation nevertheless permitted chiefs and district commissioners to exercise extensive powers of coercion and patronage which they could then use to enhance their standing through the manipulation of informal networks.

In its heyday under President Tubman, the government had a system of rule which penetrated every corner of the country and enabled the Americo-Liberian oligarchy which dominated its higher reaches to enjoy the choicer fruits of power. Chiefs too could derive great benefits from this system as long as they secured the patronage of central government officials, the latter in turn participants in the clientelist politics of Monrovia. Although paramount chiefs received no salary, their right to take a percentage of taxes could earn 'as much as $8,000 in annual commissions. This is more than the annual salary of many officials of the Central Government,' noted a gazeteer in 1956. He went on to note: 'Many Paramount and Clan Chiefs own and operate large coffee, cocoa, oil palm or rubber farms aside from regular subsistence crops.[...] A number of them own cars and beautiful homes in the capital city.'[51] District commissioners also could amass handsome personal fortunes through the use of their office.

The system of indirect rule which was formalised by President Arthur Barclay (1904-12) was instituted largely due to the central government's lack of the financial resources that would have enabled it to take a more direct control of local politics. The financial fortunes of the government were transformed by the Firestone agreement of 1926 and the Open Door economic policy developed by President Tubman under the highly favourable conditions of the long, worldwide, economic boom which followed the Second World War. American and European industrialists were offering high prices for raw materials. The Liberian government, being the representative of a sovereign state, was able to offer them access to its minerals and farmland in return for payment of a royalty or taxes. From the government's point of view, a main attraction of agreements reached with foreign corporations was that these produced income in the form of payments made directly to the central government rather than to local agents of the administration, while foreign concessionaires, having no

---

[50] William Reno, *Corruption and State Politics in Sierra Leone,* Cambridge, 1995, p.12.

[51] Henry B. Cole (ed.), *The Liberian Year Book 1956,* Monrovia, 1956, p.117.

rights of citizenship, could not play a direct role in local politics. Successive heads of state after President Charles King (1920-30), who negotiated the Firestone agreement, found that income from foreign companies especially enabled them to run a political patronage machine on a scale previously impossible. Only the members of the settler oligarchy had real political rights, while natives of the hinterland were subject to chiefs and district officers who often acted as lords in their own districts. This devalued the old republican culture of Monrovia by strengthening the powers of an executive presidency and turned hinterland politics steadily more into the management of ethnic blocks represented by paramount chiefs who were appointed by government. By 1953 President Tubman was ruling that each paramount chief should oversee at least five clan chiefs, and 'they should all be of the same ethnic group'.[52] The highly centralised administration was used to run West Africa's first party-state, probably the most extensive patronage machine the region had ever known until that time. Those with access to government could derive resources both from above, in the form of largesse from the president or his officials, and even more from below, by using the powers granted to them to extract taxes, forced labour and other resources from their subjects. They were also, however, expected to dispense patronage in turn to their own clients, kin and retainers.

Since the legitimacy of paramount chiefs depended on their ability to represent and to govern a tribe (or, at a lower level, a clan or a town), chiefs required a commitment to new notions of tribal authority, splitting older alliances asunder. As young men of talent and ambition could no longer rise to prominence through war, a traditional means of advancement now stigmatised as rebellion and punishable as such, local politics became channelled into intense factional struggles whose objective was formal recognition as a chief.[53] An existing chief was constantly threatened by others who, on one ground or another, attempted to unseat him. 'This pattern of opportunistic factionalism,' the American anthropologist D'Azevedo observed, 'developed into a major mechanism of tribal politics and became an instrument of government control,'[54] since district officers and county superintendents were fully engaged in intrigues to support or unseat a local chief. Nor was it easy for individuals who did not enjoy government favour to make

[52] Decision no.1 of President Tubman, Executive Council of Chiefs of Central Province, Tappita, 10 June 1953, National Documentation Center, Monrovia.

[53] D'Azevedo, 'Tribe and Chiefdom', p.105.

[54] *Ibid.*, p.103.

money through trade, since one of the effects of the Open Door economic policy was to wrest local trade from the hands of 'Liberian and tribal traders' and to transfer it to 'networks of foreign merchants who virtually controlled the entire economy of the country and were able to alienate a large portion of profits through speculation and manipulation of goods'.[55] Needless to say, the foreign merchants – generally Mandingo or Lebanese – who acquired such privileges did so by courting government officials.

In this way identity, whether ethnic, religious or other, became one of the most vital sites in intense struggles for local control.[56] The deadly factional politics of official chieftaincies called for the use of the most base skills of manoeuvre. It is small wonder that, by the 1980s, many observers of the system were to remark on the existence of a 'fast spreading disease called "opportunism" '.[57] The most successful exponents of local politics were those who were appointed to a chieftaincy on the grounds that they represented a given tribe, and it was in their interest to maintain that each clan or tribe had a distinctive culture and ancestry which required autonomous administration. Among the Kpelle, for example, successful chiefs were able to demonstrate their patronage of local language and custom and used the Poro society, seen by the government as a cultural attribute, as a mark of Kpelle ethnicity.[58] In Nimba County too, 'among the Dan and Mano, ethnic identity and leadership were, to a great extent, shaped by government intervention'.[59] Chiefs became cultural brokers, translating the values of 'tribal' society to the Americo-Liberian elite, and *vice versa*. Manipulation of these cultural resources became a matter of considerable political importance since a paramount chief had sweeping powers in the adjudication of local disputes, the collection of tax and the allocation of forced labour, and direct access to more senior government officials up to the president himself. The latter manipulated the politics of chieftaincies in turn, supporting the opposition to any chief who did not conform to his requirements. Some district commissioners built personal fiefs in the hinterland by these means, accumulating money and private estates,[60] and some recruited personal militias of 'armed

55 D'Azevedo, 'A Tribal Reaction', pt. II, p.55.

56 D'Azevedo, 'Tribe and Chiefdom', p.111.

57 George Klay Kieh, quoted in Kappel and Korte, *Human Rights*, p.155.

58 Fulton, 'Political Structures', pp.1218-33.

59 Ford, 'Pacification Under Pressure', p.56.

60 Akpan, 'The Practice of Indirect Rule', pp.90-5.

messengers'.[61] In order to remain in power they had to redistribute some of these resources through local patronage networks, minor versions of the machine run from Monrovia, but also to translate these assets into statements of local cultural values. Public office of any sort gave an opportunity to accumulate wealth. At the same time, continued tenure of public office required the incumbent to maintain political support, or at least a degree of popularity, by distributing wealth to family, friends and hangers-on, who would generally make some sort of moral claim based on the traditional morality of rural life and the extended family.

The most powerful of all Liberian presidents, William Tubman, was in the exceptional position of being able to dispose of high levels of hard-currency income from arrangements with international investors while presiding over a predominantly rural society in thrall to centrally-appointed chiefs who were utterly dependent on presidential favour for their tenure of office. A meticulous manager with a good knowledge of rural Liberia acquired during his youth in the south-eastern town of Harper, Tubman was the first president to tour the country systematically and to hold executive councils in which he would personally listen to the grievances of chiefs against each other or against district officers and deliver instant judgements. He became the centre of a cult of personality unrivalled before or since, which many Liberians to this day consider the model of what a president should be: a father to his people, powerful, stern, generous. The influx of wealth enabled Tubman to build the first extensive system of roads in the rural areas, which brought prestige to the adminstration and also increased the central government's ability to penetrate the hinterland.

The manipulation of ethnic politics was an important link between the countryside and Monrovia. This was possible only because of the ideas of proper behaviour which governed people's social lives. Even today, country people who make their way to Monrovia, or even abroad, are expected to maintain contacts with their area of origin and, on occasion, to intervene on behalf of their families. This pattern seems to be as old as the existence of Monrovia itself. It has certainly provided a medium for political action since early in the twentieth century. Already in 1932 a delegate of the League of Nations, reporting on disturbances in the south-east the previous year which had led to the destruction of forty-four towns, causing 12,000 people to be made homeless, reported that the trouble 'had been instigated by, and was receiving sympathetic

[61] Ford, *Indirect Rule and the Emergence of the 'Big Chief'*, p.28.

support from, political leaders in Monrovia amongst the civilised Krus'. In a pattern which was to become quite familiar later on, he added that 'these agitators, after stirring up the trouble, did not remain with the tribes during the fighting, but retired to the safety of Monrovia.' Kru living in Ghana and Sierra Leone were also reported to have smuggled in weapons for use in the conflict at home.[62]

The increasing use of ethnic manipulation as an instrument of local politics was matched at the national level. National governments tended to use Mandingo, due to their rather particular status and their specialisation in trade, as a counterweight to the Lebanese merchants who had arrived in Liberia, as in other parts of West Africa, in the early twentieth century. Tubman, whose provincial origins put him at odds with some of the grandest families of Monrovia, also awarded trade concessions to prominent Mandingo traders as a way of striking at the interests of certain Americo-Liberian dynasties.[63] Because the Mandingo did not have an acknowledged 'homeland' in Liberia, encouraging them to spread throughout the country in pursuit of trade helped to prevent enterprising tribal chiefs from building business empires for themselves. Tubman's successor, William Tolbert, began his official career in the 1930s as a government disbursement officer, and became close to many Mandingo businessmen to whom he gave government posts after he became president in 1971.[64] By the 1980s, Mandingo owned 'a huge percentage of the shops, stores and transportation in Liberia', in competition with the Lebanese.[65] Doing business in provincial towns and rural areas in many parts of Lofa, Bong and Nimba Counties, Mandingo traders extended credit to local farmers in advance of the harvest, and when the economy of Nimba County went into decline in the 1970s, they still managed to prosper.[66] The political favours which they were accorded by Samuel Doe, added to their commercial privileges, contributed greatly to the anti-Mandingo feeling which flared into violence in 1989.

Attainment of the requisite cultural status was an avenue to success in local politics but was also the means by which a country

[62] Dr M.D. Mackenzie to Council of League of Nations, 1932, printed in Richardson, *Past and Present,* pp.156-8.

[63] Augustine Konneh, 'Mandingo Integration in the Liberian Political Economy', *Liberian Studies Journal,* XVIII, 1 (1993), pp.48-9.

[64] Konneh, 'Citizenship at the Margins', p.151.

[65] Konneh, 'Indigenous Entrepreneurs', pp.8-9.

[66] *Ibid.,* pp.172-3.

boy or girl could better themselves through employment outside their tribal area. Literacy, generally gained through mission education, was a basic qualification for a decent job, but so too were modern manners generally. An American Peace Corps volunteer who was the headmaster of a school in Nimba County in the 1960s noted how his students' main purpose in seeking an education was not so much to acquire practical skills with which they could secure gainful employment as to become 'civilised', as they called it, to accede to the status of a citizen of the Republic, a goal most readily achieved through education.[67]

Children attended school primarily to learn the speech and manners of a burgher, in which patterns of consumption and clothing played an important part.[68] Positions of power and authority in 'traditional' society, dominated by chiefs who claimed to represent a pure tribal culture, were unattractive to members of a younger generation who found in education an alternative source of advancement. This considerably diminished the grip of chiefs and elders generally on rural society. An anthropologist who lived in rural Grand Gedeh County in the 1980s noted that 'power and authority in the hinterland were very localised (covering a community of a few hundred or thousand at most), and also very tenuous and unstable', notably in the case of elders and lineage heads.[69] Migrant labour or military service were the best known avenues for youngsters eager to escape the control of elders. As early as 1927 young men from Nimba County were volunteering for contracts at the Firestone plantation, and a stint there became virtually a rite of passage, permitting a young man to raise the money for a dowry and start a family back in his town of origin.[70] But by the 1980s these avenues were no longer open to many young men or were less attractive than once they had been. The number of school graduates who aspired to paid employment was greater than ever, but the economic crisis of the 1980s made formal jobs hard to acquire. Those who did find paid jobs often preferred to stay in Monrovia rather than return to a rural area where they would be expected to submit to the rule of elders and the moral codes of a small community. By the 1980s in Grand Gedeh, local elders had lost control of marriage, and hence of labour, due

---

[67] David G. Blanchard, 'The Impact of External Domination on the Liberian Mano Economy', (Ph.D. thesis Indiana University, 1973), pp.247-74.

[68] David Brown, 'On the Category "Civilised"'.

[69] Letter from David Brown to the author, 1 December 1996.

[70] Riddell, 'The Gbannah Ma', pp.123-4.

to the decline of local iron smelting in the face of cheaper imported goods and the emergence over decades of a market for migrant labour.[71]

Thus, the longer term effects of the modernisation programme adopted by President Tubman provided greater coercive powers to the miniature despotisms which were the institutions of local government but at the same time, through the provision of greater social mobility and new economic opportunities, undermined the social mechanisms by which elderly men maintained control of rural life. President Tubman himself does not seem to have perceived this as a potential problem, at least not during the early stage of his rule, but to have believed, as many academic commentators did in the 1950s, that the growth of consumption and of a labour market were central elements in the process of modernisation, to be encouraged at all costs. Tubman considered the more conservative cultural values of rural society to be constraints on economic development, and he actively encouraged people to abandon older value systems and to become more acquisitive, believing that a rise in consumption would awaken a desire for accumulation and employment in a virtuous circle. A speech he made to the chiefs and people of Pleebo district is illuminating:[72]

> I think your greatest trouble is that you are too contented with your present condition. You have to become dissatisfied with your present way of living. Can't you see that everybody else is working? Can't you see that people with rubber, coffee, cocoa and oil palm farms are building new houses, living more comfortably and spending more money? [...] Do you want to live under the same conditions as did your great-grandparents, your grandparents or even your parents ten, twenty, fifty or a hundred years ago?

An American schoolteacher working in rural Nimba County in the 1960s noted that the growth of a market economy was resulting in what he called a 'crisis of rising expectations' which he dated particularly to the arrival of a motor road in 1948 and the Lebanese and Mandingo traders who used it to gain access to new rural markets.[73]

The maintenance of hinterland Liberia as a separate jurisdiction became an increasing anomaly during the 1950s as the government

[71] Letter from David Brown to the author, 1 December 1996.

[72] Speech to the chiefs and people of Pleebo, quoted in Smith, *Emancipation of the Hinterland*, p.125.

[73] Blanchard, 'The Impact of External Domination', pp.130-2.

endeavoured to increase the availability of labour for employment on the plantations and other concessions which were generally short of manpower, and in an international context in which former colonies all over West Africa were gaining independence, making Liberia's own internal version of indirect rule look dangerously out of date. The abolition of the hinterland jurisdiction in 1963 and the achievement of a united Liberian administration, in which all were citizens with equal rights in law, also linked the politics of chiefdoms more directly than ever before to national politics. One effect of this which passed little noticed at the time was that it brought the factional struggles which had been so typical of local politics in previous decades, often based on manipulation of what had been officially labelled as tribal culture and ethnicity, into national politics. One observer noted:[74]

> Few have recognized the character of the forces which have been unleashed by President Tubman's Unification Policy or identified them with processes which have been at work in Liberian culture throughout the history of the nation. Old factional struggles inscribed in new administrative practices helped determine the administrative boundaries of the 1960s, and inter-chiefdom rivalries now took on tribal form. Processes of tribal territorial expansion and consolidation, interrupted more than a century ago, have reappeared within the context of national administrative policy and under the banner of national unification.

These were prophetic words indeed. They constituted an early warning of the pressure from the grassroots to open up national politics to people of 'country' origin, which President Tolbert perceived and tried to implement, and of the change which would occur in the style of national politics as a new generation of politicians located constituencies among country people, and as young men and women from country families gained access to new opportunities through education, church membership and wage labour. When a country man became head of state of Liberia for the first time, in the person of Samuel Doe in 1980, it brought the politics of chieftaincy disputes, and rivalries between those social blocs which had been politically defined as tribes, into the national arena. Moreover it did so in the most baleful manner possible, by force of arms and through an institution – the army – which had inherited some of the older traditions of war as a form of social promotion and economic accumulation.

---

[74] D'Azevedo, 'A Tribal Reaction to Nationalism', pt.I, p.1.

6

MEN AND DEVILS

In considering how the growing reach of the Liberian state transformed local politics, and was itself transformed in the process, it is helpful to dwell a little longer on the subject of religious belief. Accordingly, the present chapter concerns what, for want of a better description, we may call the spiritual history of Liberia, as distinct from its political or administrative history.

This is no easy matter to discuss, for a number of reasons. First and foremost among these difficulties is the existence of a gamut of misleading labels attached to various distinctive elements of traditional Liberian religions as a result of the views conveyed by Europeans, Americans and Americo-Liberians, including missionaries, ethnographers, travellers and administrators imbued with a North Atlantic view of what constitutes civilisation, morality and development. A prime example of the imposition of new meanings on native Liberian institutions concerns the masked figure, the spirit of the forest, which is the ultimate authority in Poro ritual. This figure is known in modern Liberian English as the Bush Devil, a name first used, certainly with pejorative intent, by early Christian missionaries.[1] This is misleading because of the negative moral qualities attributed to anything labelled in English as a devil, since the Devil of Christian tradition is the personification of pure evil. The use of the term 'bush devil' implies that this figure incarnates an evil moral quality which is far removed from the character attributed to it by Poro initiates in the past, and even today. To Poro members, although the Bush Devil is certainly redoubtable, and even dangerous, it is not evil. Rather, the spirit of the forest is simply powerful, and its power can be used to inflict punishments which are believed to be in the ultimate interest of the community of believers. It is the guarantor of order.

The same problem is even more clear in literary descriptions of some of the ritual activities associated with traditional Liberian religious practice, most notably in regard to human sacrifice which, according to some texts which we will discuss shortly, was sometimes

[1] Nya Kwiawon Taryor, 'Religions in Liberia', *Liberia-Forum,* 5, 8 (1989), p.6.

used in pre-republican times as a form of communication between mankind and the invisible world. The practice of human sacrifice and of eating human flesh in various contexts in Liberia has often been described by European, American and Americo-Liberian authors as 'cannibalism', reflecting a repugnance in European and American thought attached to such an activity under any circumstances whatever. It is no part of the present argument to suggest that eating human flesh is commendable; it is enough merely to note that this practice has not always had the same associations or meaning for every society in the world as it has had for Europeans, as its quite widespread occurrence in time and space suggests.[2] It is not possible to establish exactly how widespread this practice was in Liberia before the twentieth century, nor even during it, but the evidence suggests that human sacrifice involving the consumption by initiates of human flesh was regarded as one of a range of instruments of religious communication in many parts of pre-republican Liberia. It is important to retrace briefly the history of the practice if we are to understand the reason for the many incidents of human flesh being eaten by fighters during the civil war of 1989-97.

It should be said that the description of politics using an idiom of eating, in which the assimilation of power is described by using the vocabulary of digestion, is actually widespread in Africa. Indeed, it has even formed the basis of a celebrated analysis of African politics as a whole.[3] Of course, this most emphatically should not be taken to mean that all African societies have practised anthropophagy, since the concept of eating may obviously be used as a metaphor only. At least one anthropologist has asserted that the eating of human flesh as a pattern of cultural behaviour has never existed in any human society, even in such well-known cases as the Aztecs of Mexico, arguing that accounts of cannibalism reflect the fear one social group may have of another.[4] Several authors point out that rumours that a person consumes human flesh are easily attached, in former stateless societies such as those of Liberia and Sierra Leone which continue to have a strong egalitarian ethos, to powerful people who are thought to show an excess of selfish individualism. In this view, fear of cannibalism is a form of 'moral panic' which occurs in specific circumstances and is to be understood as a mechanism for the regulation of

[2] P.R. Sanday, *Divine Hunger: cannibalism as a cultural system,* Cambridge, 1986.
[3] Bayart, *The State in Africa.*
[4] W. Arens, *The Man-Eating Myth: anthropology and anthropophagy,* New York, 1979.

power.[5] This is true enough, but it rather coyly evades the question of whether human flesh is ever actually eaten as a form of religious communication in these societies, or whether references to the practice are always metaphorical, a mere form of words. Other scholars, while also acknowledging that rumours of flesh-eating are often a symptom of 'tensions in society' arising from the activities of 'selfish power seekers in antisocial groups', leave little doubt of their belief that among certain groups of those forest peoples of Sierra Leone, Guinea and Liberia who share specific repertoires of religious belief, the eating of human flesh, at least on occasion, has actually occurred, and has been sufficiently sanctioned by custom as to constitute an identifiable practice.[6]

Reports of the consumption of human flesh and human sacrifice in pre-republican times are most often associated with exclusive secret societies. These were exclusive groups of people who were believed to be liable to possession by the spirits of carnivorous animals such as leopards and crocodiles, and who carried out ritual killings while in a state of possession. During the course of the twentieth century, the Liberian government outlawed these societies, but some of them nevertheless continued to function clandestinely, as we shall shortly see. During the mid-twentieth century there were also increasing numbers of reports of the existence of various other occult groups, often said to include national politicians, who were said to partake of human flesh and to practise human sacrifice. In the following paragraphs we will examine in more detail some of the allegations concerning these practices and suggest that the consumption of human flesh indeed occurred as a form of ritual behaviour in the past, at least on occasion, in connection with rituals of human sacrifice, traditionally considered the most potent of all forms of religious sacrifice. The precise conditions under which this occurred, and the people responsible for such sacrifices, changed radically during the twentieth century, to the point that human sacrifice continued to occur, at least occasionally, but became divorced from control by distinct religious hierarchies with widespread support in a given community.

The historical change in this particular religious ritual is closely

[5] Richards, *Fighting for the Rain Forest*, pp.xxiv-v, 80-1; Rosalind Shaw, 'The Politician and the Diviner: divination and the consumption of power in Sierra Leone', *Journal of Religion in Africa*, XXXVI, 1 (1996), pp.30-55.

[6] Arthur Abraham, 'Cannibalism and African Historiography' in A. Abraham (ed.), *Topics in Sierra Leone History: a counter-colonial interpretation*, Freetown, 1976, p.127; Carol MacCormack, 'Human Leopards and Crocodiles: political meanings of categorical anomalies' in Paula Brown and Donald Tuzin (eds), *The Ethnography of Cannibalism*, Washington, 1983, p.53.

associated with the rule of the political and religious elites of the Liberian state who, for a century or more, generally saw themselves as pursuing a mission to improve Liberia by bringing it Christian religion, modern ways of acting and thinking, republican government and economic development. Throughout their history in Africa, the religious attitude of Americo-Liberians has been indissociable from their politics. President Arthur Barclay said as much in his 1904 inaugural address, when he observed that 'every convert from heathenism to the Christian faith in this country is also a political recruit'.[7] As the republican government and long-distance trade networks dominated by Christians and Muslims spread their influence into even the most isolated rural communities, the grip of the national government became deeply implicated in the rural politics of clan and chieftaincy disputes and local religious corporations. Traditional religious institutions such as secret societies, priests and oracles, became sites of struggle for control of local affairs. This occurred in an environment in which the acquisition of power was routinely couched in an idiom of eating, leading to great confusion as to whether powerful people really were eaters of human flesh, or whether this was merely a rumour or a metaphor, devoid of actual substance, attached to any person who acquired great power.

Belief that all power has its origin in the invisible world, where God and spirits dwell, is a constant of Liberian history. What has changed radically during the twentieth century is the means by which individuals may have access to such power. Formerly subject to rules and conventions which assured that rituals were carried out only by the appropriate specialists under controlled conditions, certain potent forms of religious communication, in the course of the twentieth century, came to be used as part of the process by which the republican political elite in Monrovia reached a series of accommodations with the local chiefs who were the mainstays of its system of indirect rule. Religious communication, including human sacrifice, quite simply was privatised.

Poro business is eating business

Perhaps the most important, and certainly the most widespread, of all religious institutions in the Liberian hinterland before 1900 was the Poro.

Poro is often described by Liberians today as a 'bush school',

---

[7] Quoted in Richardson, *Past and Present,* p.122.

a reasonably accurate description. In effect, among the Kpelle, Mano, Loma and several other peoples of north-western Liberia and adjoining parts of Sierra Leone and Guinea nowadays considered to be distinct 'tribes', but formerly more accurately described as congeries of lineages, and also in some areas of Côte d'Ivoire, Poro is a system of initiation for young men.[8] Through Poro, boys at around the age of puberty are initiated into adult society and learn how to act and think as men. Initiation takes place at clearings in the forest which are taboo to outsiders, where boys are said to be eaten by the spirit of the bush, known in Liberian English as the Bush Devil.[9] The young Poro initiate has scars applied to his body in distinctive patterns which are said to be the toothmarks of the spirit which has eaten him. Indeed, the idiom of eating is very marked in Poro, reflected in sayings such as 'Poro business is eating business' or 'Poro is in the stomach'.[10] In the forest, young initiates live in a special village where they are instructed in the ritual knowledge of their community and educated in their duties as men. In particular they are taught the virtues of discipline, courage and obedience, rather like in an old-fashioned English public school. At the end of their period of seclusion, which in the past could last for three or more years but which, by the time the civil war broke out, generally occupied no more than a couple of months in the school holidays, the young men are received back in their towns as newcomers who are deemed to have been reborn. Their old selves 'died' in the bush, eaten by the Bush Devil, the spirit of the forest.

Although today there are men from Poro areas who are not initiated, often when they have had a strict missionary education, it still remains usual for young Kpelle, Loma and others to be initiated in this way, even when they are also practising Christians. As a man grows older, he may spend repeated periods in the Poro bush, for example in connection with the initiation of new generations of youngsters, and may thus rise in seniority. The

---

[8] According to a government ethnographer in 1974, eleven of the sixteen official Liberian tribes had Poro, and a twelfth the Sande only. S. Jangaba M. Johnson, 'The Influence of Islam on Poro and Sande in Western Liberia', paper read to a seminar on African Studies, University of Liberia, 18-19 July 1974.

[9] The following is taken from some of the main works on Poro, including George W. Harley, *Notes on the Poro in Liberia*, Cambridge, MA, 1941; *idem, Masks as Agents of Social Control*; Little, 'The Political Function of the Poro,' parts I and II; *Ethnologische Zeitschrift Zürich*, 1 (1980); Bellman, *The Language of Secrecy*.

[10] Riddell, 'The Gbannah Ma', p.129; Beryl L. Bellman, *Village of Curers and Assassins: on the production of Fala Kpelle cosmological categories*, The Hague, 1975, p.68.

actual control of a local Poro chapter is in the hands of priests known as *zoes*. The office of *zo* appears to be largely hereditary, circulating among certain locally prominent families, notably those whose ancestors made a pact with the earth when they first cultivated it, and whose descendants are considered to be the owners of the land. The earth is clearly of great importance, and when Poro initiates return from the bush they are smeared with white clay, a symbol of contact with the spirit world.[11] Girls are similarly initiated into adult society through the Sande bush, which serves a comparable purpose of education and is run by female *zoes*. It has a less evident political function than the Poro, but is at least as important in governing relations with the spirit world. In the past, before the advent of republican government and Christian education, any person who was not initiated into Poro or Sande, in those parts of Liberia where these were prevalent, was simply not considered part of adult society. According to an author writing on the notion of what constitutes a responsible adult in modern Liberia, 'Men and women who join those societies are perceived to have mastered the arts of communication that facilitate interaction within and without groups and in the adjudication of conflicts.'[12]

Just as the tradition of ethnographic writing has tended to contribute to the formation of tribes by identifying distinct codes of behaviour associated with particular ethnic groups, so too have ethnographers tended to underestimate the tendency for old and new ideas to merge, or for institutions associated with one particular ethnic group to spread their influence to others as a result of social mobility. Christian and Muslim ideas have penetrated the thinking of indigenous religious traditions to the extent that, these days, even Poro officials are often also Christians, and may even hold office as deacons or other church officials. At the end of an interview I had with elders in a town in Lofa County in 1997, some of whom were most probably *zoes*, the old men suggested saying a Christian prayer. When asked if it were not incompatible to be both Christian and a member of the Poro, one replied that Jesus himself was initiated when he was circumcised.[13] Other authors too have noted the ease with which initiates, including *zoes*, may identify Poro as a means of approaching a supreme being,[14]

[11] Harley, *Notes on the Poro,* pp.14, 17.

[12] Al-Hassan Conteh, 'Reflections on Some Concepts of Religion and Medicine in Liberian Society', *Liberian Studies Journal,* XV, 2 (1990), pp.149-50.

[13] Author's interview, Upper Lofa County, 20 December 1997.

[14] Little, 'Political Function of the Poro', part I, pp.354-5.

nowadays easily identified with the Christian God. This combination of Poro and Christian belief, obviously a fairly recent development, illustrates clearly the way in which even the most revered tradition may accommodate novelty and change.

Although republican government and Christian mission have served to diminish the political role of Poro, this process has by no means been one-sided. Successive Liberian governments, while supporting Christian missionary activity, have also given encouragement to Poro and Sande on the grounds that they are a valuable cultural institution which instils discipline and responsibility in young adults. A side-effect of this has been to spread Poro influence to some other parts of Liberia. One ethnographer, noting the growth of a new spirit-being known as Nana among the Gio people, who do not traditionally have Poro or Sande schools, saw the clear influence of Poro in this new cult. The Gio, he noted, 'have rejected Poro for centuries, one has the feeling. They were proud of not having Poro.[...] Only through "Liberian" influence comes the feeling that everyone is afraid of not being of the powerful Poro.' This tendency he called a 'poro-ification' of local religious belief.[15] Similarly, a researcher working in Monrovia in the early 1960s reported that increasing numbers of Bassa people were being initiated into the Poro and Sande societies, a practice which they were said 'to have taken...over recently, from their Kpelle neighbours'.[16] It has become fairly common for people in Monrovia to refer to traditional priests of all types as *zoes,* a word once used almost exclusively for Poro officials. Nevertheless, in the southeast of Liberia, which has never had the institution of Poro, other traditional religious institutions survive, such as the *bodio* priests and *kui* secret society, and various oracles and sodalities of local importance.[17] Although Liberian governments, at least until 1980, always regarded themselves as Christian, and did not encourage the spread of Islam, this religion too has witnessed a growth comparable to that of Christianity. Little is known of the precise reasons which have caused many people from western Liberia especially to convert to Islam in recent decades, but clearly, as with Christian conversion, such factors include the widening of horizons inherent in the process of Liberianisation, opportunities for social and economic advancement offered by access to the networks of trade dominated by Mandingo, almost all of whom are Muslims, and

[15] Fischer, 'Masks in a Non-Poro Area', p.82.

[16] Merran Fraenkel, *Tribe and Class in Monrovia,* London, 1964, p.172.

[17] On *bodio* and *kui* in history, see Martin, 'The Dual Legacy, pp.15-20; Johnston, *Liberia,* II, pp.1068-9.

the influence of models of political organisation derived from Malinke tradition.

In brief, there has occurred what might be called a globalisation – to use a fashionable term – of religious belief generally, in which Christianity and Islam have certainly made many converts, but in which some traditional religious beliefs have also been diffused over wider areas. In addition to Christian priests and preachers, Muslim imams and marabouts, and Poro and Sande *zoes*, modern Liberia also contains various prophets, healers and makers of medicines, often called 'soothsayers' by Liberians, whose powers are believed to come to them individually, often through dreams. Either men or women, these are people who are believed to have a talent or a vocation which will enable them to communicate with the invisible world, especially through dreams or in trance.

One of the results of this intermingling of ideas over the whole national territory is that it is difficult to determine the exact figures for religious affiliation. A 1986 census reported that 75 per cent of Liberians were adherents of traditional religion, 15 per cent were Christians and 10 per cent Muslims.[18] These figures are provisional inasmuch as they take no account of the number of people professing allegiance to several different religious institutions simultaneously, such as Poro initiates who are also practising Christians. Even people who do not consider themselves Christian have been greatly influenced by Christian beliefs which they have incorporated into the existing repertoire of religious thought. Nor do these census figures give any idea of the great variety of traditional religious institutions, nor of the extent of adherence to the various Christian denominations or Muslim Sufi brotherhoods. Within Christianity there are a variety of independent or spiritual churches which exist alongside the older generation of missionary churches of European or American origin, or newer international denominations like the Aladura churches of Nigerian origin. Increasingly the churches in Monrovia especially are of the pentecostal and charismatic varieties, which have grown rapidly in recent years.[19]

In view of the great variety of religious forms, it is perhaps hazardous to make general statements about exactly what Liberians believe or how their religious institutions function. Nevertheless, it is helpful to observe that there are some features which are widespread in different parts of the country and across different institutions, such as the tendency for people to combine older

[18] Taryor, 'Religions in Liberia', p.3.

[19] Gifford, *Christianity and Politics in Doe's Liberia.*

with newer religious practices, the use of masks by various traditional religious corporations especially among communities which have the Poro and Sande societies, and the multiplicity of esoteric societies of a religious nature both inside and outside the Poro cultural area and of brotherhoods or sodalities inside Christianity or Islam. As with the description of ethnic groups in an earlier chapter,[20] it would require excessive length to attempt an exhaustive survey of the religious practices of each area of Liberia, and in any case such an undertaking would tend to suggest that Liberian society is divided into watertight compartments defined by ethnicity or religion, whereas in fact the tendency for people to maintain plural religious allegiances is more striking. For this reason, we will dwell at most length on the specific beliefs associated with just one religious institution, the Poro, since it is the most important traditional religious institution and has been the subject of the most extensive descriptions over quite a long period. Sande and Poro beliefs and ritual contain elements which are to be found in other Liberian religious systems. It is to be hoped that this will help in clarifying some ideas about how Liberian religious thought more generally has changed during the twentieth century.

It has been noted already that the description, common in the ethnographic literature, of Poro and Sande as 'secret societies' is inaccurate in some respects.[21] Poro and Sande are schools in which boys and girls are initiated into adult society under the aegis of elders who control the rituals and other elements of their instruction and are strictly bound not to reveal details of their instruction to non-members. It is this last feature of the societies which suggests secrecy, but since, in principle, every man and woman in the communities where Poro and Sande exist has been initiated, it is rather unhelpful to label them 'secret societies', however hard it is to avoid the term. For present purposes it is important to make a distinction between Poro and Sande and a large number of more exclusive sodalities which have also existed in recent Liberian history and which may more correctly be described as 'secret societies', since they are elite groups whose membership and rituals may not be divulged even to other members of the communities in which they exist. Secret societies in the fullest sense of the term include a wide variety of corporations which cultivate esoteric spiritual knowledge, including snake societies which specialise in curing snakebite, societies which are

---

[20] Chapter 1.

[21] Above, p.200.

believed to exercise control over thunder and lightning, and societies such as human leopards and crocodiles whose members are believed to be possessed by the spirits of wild animals.

A first point to note is that secret societies of this last sort exist in many parts of Liberia, including in areas which have Poro and Sande but also in regions such as the south-east which do not. The fact that traditional secret societies have existed in all parts of Liberia, certainly until very recently, may in fact give some clue as to their historical origin. According to a leading historian of the Malinke, Yves Person, the various Poro traditions probably originated under the old Mali empire in a region in present-day Guinea. The decline of Mali and its successor states in the sixteenth century, amid conditions of widespread political and social upheaval, seems to have been the cause of some of the migrations in which the ancestors of some groups of modern Liberians first arrived in the territory. There they displaced or settled among groups who were already living in the forest. The Mano, Mende, Loma, Kissi, Kpelle and others all appear to have been subjects of the Mali emperors, and all have the Poro, which they brought with them in the flight from the collapse of Mali. The more exclusive secret societies of probably the oldest Liberian people, the Kru, are considered by Person to be of different origin.[22]

It appears, then, that immigrants coming from medieval Mali to the territory of modern Liberia, bringing with them the institutions of Poro and Sande, encountered groups living in the forest with their own traditions of secret societies. A certain degree of mutual assimilation occurred in the process, with religious institutions and various forms of civic government having a notable effect on each other. This may suggest that the habit of assimilating new religious beliefs into old ones predates the arrival of Christianity. The fact that the ruling dynasty of medieval Mali was Muslim, but that most of its subjects were not, has had a marked effect on how the various peoples of the forest and those of the savannah, most notably the Malinke, regard one another. Liberian Mandingo claim actually to be distant descendants of the rulers of medieval Mali, and in pursuit of this claim to high status they profess Islam and do not have the Poro, although they are regarded as experts in certain types of esoteric knowledge. These attitudes continue to have important consequences to this day. During the civil war of 1989-97, the Mandingo-led militia, Ulimo-K, tried hard to obliterate the Poro society from areas which it overran in Upper Lofa County, desecrating forest groves, looting masks and other

[22] Person, *Samori*, I, pp.63-4.

ritual objects, and humiliating and brutalising the *zoes* or priests of the Poro. So much was this resented by the Kpelle and Loma farmers of the area that some *zoes*, living in refugee camps in Guinea, in 1993-4 sponsored the organisation of their own militia, the Lofa Defense Force.

The association of Poro with the earth and the forest, and that of some secret societies with the spirits of wild animals, no doubt arises from people's sensitivity to the environment in which they have lived over generations and in which their thinking has been formed. A British colonial official in Sierra Leone, which shares many of the cultural repertoires of northern Liberia, commenting on the effect on human culture of life in a physical environment which he found 'uncanny', wrote: 'The bush seemed to me pervaded with something supernatural, a spirit which was striving to bridge the animal and the human. Some of the weird spirit of their surroundings has, I think, entered into the people, and accounts for their weird customs.'[23] Stripped of the unacceptable supposition that unfamiliar customs are 'weird', and that the forest is 'uncanny', this is no more than an assertion that people's culture over a long period is formed largely by their experience of their natural surroundings. This certainly seems to be the case in the evolution of Liberian thinking, where the forest is the home to a great variety of flora and fauna and is in some respects a dangerous environment as well as a fertile one. We must, however, add the important qualification that describing Liberian thought as sensitive to its natural environment should not be mistaken for the sentimentality of many nature-lovers in modern Europe and America. Rural Liberians are indeed sensitive to nature but will kill any animal unblinkingly, and relish eating most sorts of game as well. No delicacy is more appreciated, also by city-dwellers, than 'bush-meat', the flesh of a wild animal. Even at the present time, in many rural areas of Liberia there are few domesticated animals to be seen. All meat is hunted. Big animals eat little animals.

For people who believe that the spirit world is real and that it may be entered by humans quite easily, or conversely that spirits may enter humans, a period spent secluded in the forest, such as in the Poro or Sande bush during initiation, makes a deep impression. The veteran American missionary George Way Harley, probably the most knowledgeable of all foreign writers on Poro, was surely correct in observing that Poro initiates in older times

[23] W. Branford Griffith, preface to Sir K.J. Beatty, *Human Leopards*, New York, 1978, p.viii.

during their years in the bush school 'lived in fear of death and no doubt felt that they were very close to the spirit world, perhaps actually in it'.[24] There, they were 'in close contact with the spirits...if not actually residing in the realm of the unseen'.[25] According to Harley, during their period in the bush in earlier times, initiates might eat human flesh. Boys who had been executed for offending the laws of the Poro society or who died of other causes during their period of seclusion might have their vital organs eaten by others. This was a way both of offering a sacrifice to the Bush Devil and of ensuring the continuity of the spirit of the victims, since a part of their life essence was deemed to enter into those who ate their hearts or other organs. The victims simply failed to return from their seclusion in the forest, and their families would be told that the Bush Devil had eaten them.[26] As Harley also notes, where transgressors of the Poro law were killed, the victim might be thought of, not as a wrongdoer, but 'as a sacrifice to law and order'.[27]

Poro rituals articulate a view of power as morally ambiguous, a source of both life and death, just as eating itself is a fundamentally ambiguous activity, being essential for life but also implying the death of another being. In a philosophy where animals, like everything else, are believed to have souls, the everyday act of eating merely to sustain life has important implications for, as Elias Canetti has noted, 'everything which is eaten is the food of power'.[28] Since eating meat implies the destruction of animals (and even eating vegetables has a similar implication, if all things are thought to have souls), it connects the acquisition of power with the process of destruction, so central to the principle of all religious sacrifice.[29] Eating irreversibly transforms the thing eaten, which is thereby obliterated, but which may also gain an enhanced status due to the transferral of power to an individual or a social group, such as in the act of sacrifice.[30]

Several commentators affirm that *zoes* of the Poro belong to formal grades of increasing seniority which require particular forms

---

[24] George W. Harley, *Native African Medicine, with Special Reference to its Practice in the Mano Tribe of Liberia,* London, 1970, p.128.

[25] Harley, *Notes on the Poro,* p.3.

[26] Harley, *Native African Medicine,* p.132.

[27] *Ibid.,* p.131.

[28] Elias Canetti, *Crowds and Power,* London, 1987, p.257.

[29] H. Hubert and M. Mauss, *Mélanges d'histoire des religions,* Paris, 1929, p.xiv.

[30] MacCormack, 'Human Leopards and Crocodiles', p.56.

of entry, including, in older times, human sacrifice.[31] Entry to
the rank of a very senior *zo* required the candidate to sacrifice
his own son, according to Harley.[32] If this was indeed so, it would
be consistent with the idea that, since human sacrifice was held
to be the supreme form of sacrifice, it was appropriate for entry
to the most powerful grades of Poro. However, we should not
allow these remarks by George Way Harley to pass without further
comment, for Harley, while a fine researcher on the Poro, was
also a Christian missionary and a qualified medical doctor who
abhorred certain of the practices of the Poro. He recorded what
he could learn of the Poro and of other secret societies during
the years he lived in Nimba County from 1926 to 1960, when
these institutions had already been greatly influenced by the
Liberian government. As a Christian appalled by the notion of
human sacrifice, he may well have over-estimated the frequency
with which such sacrifices and the ritual consumption of human
flesh occurred in earlier Poro ceremonies – if, that is, we are to
accept that they actually occurred at all. No author believes that
Poro existed solely or even principally to perform human sacrifices;
all agree that it uses the idiom of eating to express the re-emergence
of boys as men as a result of initiation. What can hardly be doubted
in Harley's writings is that many of his informants told him of
people being killed and their flesh eaten in the forest in years
gone by, and these oral accounts led him to believe that such
sacrifices had taken place at least sometimes in earlier years, perhaps
only a decade before he went to live in Nimba County.

Other foreigners who visited Liberia in the 1920s were similarly
sure that such things had existed very recently, such as the British
traveller who noted, concerning what she called 'cannibalism':
'of its previous almost general practice before the opening up
of the Guinea Coast I think there is no doubt in any knowledgeable
mind', an opinion she based largely on discussions with Liberian
officials.[33] Although it is impossible to determine precisely how
frequently human sacrifice may have been practised, it was clearly
spoken of as a principle associated with access to great power,
including at the higher reaches of Poro. It is no small wonder,

---

[31] Bellman, *The Language of Secrecy*, p.47; Konneh, 'Indigenous Entrepreneurs',
p.23; Riddell, 'The Gbannah Ma', pp.129-30; Patrick Joseph Harrington, 'Secret
Societies and the Church: an evaluation of the Poro and Sande secret societies
and the missionary among the Mano of Liberia', (Ph.D. thesis, Gregorian University,
Rome, 1975), pp.17-18.

[32] Harley, *Native African Medicine*, p.133.

[33] Lady Dorothy Mills, *Through Liberia*, London, 1926, p.112.

then, that a Christian like Harley should have concluded that, at the heart of the Poro mystery, there is 'frightfulness'. Since what Harley called 'frightfulness', by which he appears to have meant human sacrifice, was also associated with a power which was morally ambivalent, he went on to say that 'it was overcome by a frightfulness more terrible still, until the all-highest could sit and say, "I am what I am".'[34] This assumption that power is what it is, inherently neither good nor evil, is still prevalent in Liberia, where senior *zoes* are regarded to this day as having aspects both of a curer and a potential agent of death.[35]

The durability of older beliefs in the spiritual nature of animals and even things is supported by numerous sources. A foreigner living in Nimba County in the 1960s recorded that the Mano villagers there believed in the material and spiritual nature of things and people. He was told that human beings have three spirits: one is the spirit which may wander freely during dreams; another is the 'essence' of a person, which becomes an ancestor spirit at death; and a third is the 'breath of life' which causes a person to draw breath, and which dies when breathing ceases.[36] Similar beliefs in the existence of multiple souls, some of which are held to survive the death of the physical body, are in no way peculiar to Liberia but are quite widespread throughout West Africa.[37] It is interesting, in this regard, to recall the belief of Samuel Doe's tormentors, on the night of his death, that he was trying to make a part of himself disappear and escape by blowing on his body.[38]

While early writers on the Poro believed that among its rituals were human sacrifice and the consumption of human flesh, these practices were most closely associated with more exclusive secret societies, most particularly the human leopard societies which formerly existed throughout much of modern-day Sierra Leone and Liberia. There are few accounts of leopard societies from before 1900, by which time they were already changing under the influence of colonial government in Sierra Leone and Guinea or of republican government in Liberia itself. Hence, in addition to the usual difficulties attendant on interpreting evidence on

[34] Harley, *Notes on the Poro*, p.32.

[35] Bellman, *Village of Curers and Assassins*, p.63, n.17.

[36] Blanchard, 'The Impact of External Domination', pp.73-5.

[37] Cf. Peter Sarpong, *Ghana in Retrospect: some aspects of Ghanaian culture*, Tema, 1974, pp.37-9.

[38] Above, pp.10-11.

African institutions or customs written by colonial or Americo-
Liberian officials and ethnographers, there is also a risk of attributing to the leopard societies of an earlier period characteristics
which they acquired only as a result of their interaction with colonial
government.

Some of the fullest early accounts of human leopards were
those gathered by a British colonial commission of inquiry in Sierra
Leone, which found evidence of the existence of secret societies
dating back to the 1850s. Interestingly, the commission thought
that leopard societies were of rather recent creation, suggesting
that their more lethal activities might be some sort of response
to colonial rule.[39] The societies it investigated were formed of
'men of mature age, past their prime' who met in secret conclave
and regularly killed human victims in a form of sacrifice. They
then ate the flesh of their victims, with a view to 'increasing their
virile powers'. This act of eating bound them together and was
in keeping with their identity as leopards.[40] In any event, 'the
prime object of the Human Leopard Society was to secure human
fat wherewith to anoint the Borfima,' the name of a cult object
kept by each such society.[41] Another colonial account from Sierra
Leone, from 1901, similarly reported that members of a leopard
society had to kill a relative to obtain human fat to 'feed' their
cult object.[42] A modern Sierra Leonean historian agrees that reports
of human sacrifice from this period, accompanied by the consumption by initiates of human flesh, arose from the activities
of leopard societies seeking medicine for their fetish.[43] To judge
from these descriptions and others of similar societies in Liberia,[44]
it seems that at the centre of a particular leopard society was
a ritual object which required to be 'fed' with blood or fat from
a sacrifice. This gave power to the cult object and, hence, to the
society's members. Whereas a less powerful object, such as a mask
or one of the portable miniatures known as *ma*, could be fed
with animal blood or even with spittle, a leopard fetish demanded
the blood of a member of the society which owned it, who was
required to supply the sacrifice of a blood relative, in other words
a member of his own family. A German medical doctor who saw

[39] Beatty, *Human Leopards*, p.4.

[40] *Ibid.*, p.vii.

[41] *Ibid.*, pp.v, 3-4.

[42] T.J. Alldridge, quoted in Furbay, *Top Hats*, p.123.

[43] Abraham, 'Cannibalism and African Historiography', p.126.

[44] Sibley and Westermann, *Liberia*, pp.179-80.

the cult object of a leopard society in the 1940s described it as 'a lump of black wax about the size of a child's head, wrapped in cloths and bits of leopard-skin'. At its core was vegetable and animal matter. He was told that the appearance of cracks in the wax covering was taken as a sign that the fetish required 'feeding' with blood, and that this tended to occur in the dry season.[45] The idea that objects which contain a powerful spirit require to be fed, like humans, is not a peculiarity of Liberia, but is recorded in some other parts of West Africa, too.[46]

Unlike Poro and Sande, membership of leopard societies was restricted to the most senior members of a community. A British official writing on human leopards in Sierra Leone opined that they did not apparently form 'an organised society in the ordinary acceptance of the term'. 'At most,' he thought, 'it is a temporary binding together of a few individuals of like disposition to effect a common object, but in any case these individuals must have the means of identifying each other wherever they may happen to be.' Among the Mende they were mostly 'persons of between middle age and old age'.[47] Two anthropologists who studied the Kpelle of Liberia in the 1920s found that 'in the strongholds of the [leopard] society all the men of importance in the community are sometimes compelled to become members'.[48] It was, they thought, little different from 'ordinary secret societies among the West African natives except in its utilization of human beings in its fetish worship'. The main purpose of eating human flesh was to 'feed the charm', thereby 'bringing strength to the members or protection to the community'.[49] This last remark is of particular interest as it suggests that, despite their occasional lethal activities, leopard societies were regarded as socially valuable. Their elite character implied the possession both of great esoteric knowledge and of great power, including the power of life and death, which could be used for the greater good of the community in which they existed. It certainly appears that, in their 'classical' form, meaning, in the present context, that which they had before the submission of hinterland societies to the Liberian government, the most powerful religious societies were regarded as a source of protection at the same time as they were known to take human

---

[45] Junge, *African Jungle Doctor*, p.185.

[46] Cf. R.S. Rattray, *Ashanti*, London and Kumasi, 1923, pp.111-12.

[47] F.W.H. Migeod, *A View of Sierra Leone*, London, 1926, pp.227-8.

[48] Sibley and Westermann, *Liberia*, p.180.

[49] *Ibid.*, p.181.

life. The Kwa-iru society among the Grebo of south-eastern Liberia, for example, acted as 'a kind of police' on behalf of the village assembly.[50]

In pre-republican times, the elders who generally controlled religious corporations also had economic privileges which enabled them to regulate commercial exchanges in their communities. A researcher in Nimba County in 1967-8 met some old men who said that they had taken part in trade expeditions taking kola nuts from the forest to exchange them for salt and trade goods with the Mandingo in the days before either French or Liberian forces had entered the area. They said that the trade was 'conducted by members of the Leopard and Crocodile societies', both elite societies. 'The stated fee for joining these societies was the sacrifice of a member of one's own domestic group in a cannibalistic feast; the ability to make such a sacrifice symbolized one's access to sufficient labour to mount a trading expedition.'[51] The researcher, an American, grappling with this sensitive issue adds later: 'While there is no sure way of verifying the occurrence of such cannibalistic feasts, I was able to talk with several old men who were reputed to have been members of one or the other of these societies many years ago, and they all vouched for the practice of such rites.'[52] We may note in passing the recurrence of a highly pejorative vocabulary by outside researchers, such as reference to 'cannibalistic feasts' to designate what appear to have been religious rituals involving human sacrifices and the consumption of human flesh. More interesting in the above description is the fact that oral traditions record the role played by elite secret societies in regulating trade in older times, a point confirmed by a modern Liberian scholar.[53]

The most powerful medicines, which included those requiring human blood for their maintenance, were of special use in time of war. During the small-scale, seasonal campaigns which occurred regularly in many parts of Liberia before the twentieth century, and whose principal aim was the acquisition of slaves and plunder, *zoes* and other religious specialists were solicited by warriors to provide them with powerful war medicine. Many war medicines were made from human body-parts.[54] According to two anthro-

---

50 Johnston, *Liberia*, II, p.1070.

51 Riddell, 'The Gbannah Ma', pp.129-30.

52 *Ibid.*, p.140, n.3.

53 Konneh, 'Indigenous Entrepreneurs', pp.22-3.

54 Schwab, *Tribes*, pp.232-4; Harley, *Native African Medicine*, p.3.

pologists among the Kpelle in the 1920s, 'warriors become brave by eating parts of the body of an enemy, by drinking his blood...or by using his skull as a drinking bowl.'[55] Wars were common, and were often carried out primarily for enrichment, but their duration could be controlled by the religious influence of secret societies, not least to prevent them from destabilising whole communities. The control of peace and war was thus also connected to the relations between generations, as young men were expected to seek prestige and wealth through war, but might then find their power limited by a secret society dominated by elders.

Where an elite society such as a leopard society existed in a Poro area, it is not clear exactly what was the relationship of this elite group to the Poro. There is agreement among all sources that the Poro lodges have always included a number of higher degrees or more specialised societies from which ordinary members are excluded. Some authors maintain that high degrees of Poro before the twentieth century were identical with the leopard societies in those same areas,[56] although other sources make no mention of this. However, since in such an area every single male human leopard would also be a member of Poro, the distinction may be a rather pedantic one. What is clear is that the language of the secret societies, the idiom of eating, was identical to the language of Poro.

There are further similarities between the leopards and other secret societies and less exclusive institutions such as Poro, whatever the institutional connection between them may or may not have been in the past. In both cases, respect for them was based in part on fear. This is not surprising, for fear is a component of respect for any form of public order whatever, in any part of the world.

Secret societies under Liberian administration

The power of life and death attributed to the most powerful religious institutions of pre-republican times reflected their role as pillars of social and political order in the communities of rural Liberia before the twentieth century. It was for this reason that the Liberian government, as its soldiers and administrators occupied the hinterland, and as new market forces penetrated towns and villages,

[55] Sibley and Westermann, *Liberia,* p.207.

[56] Beatty, *Human Leopards,* p.20; Harrington, 'Secret Societies and the Church', pp.17-18; Fulton, 'Political Structures', p.1228.

had to develop a policy for dealing with these institutions, just as it had towards chiefs.

The Americo-Liberian rulers, imbued with a Christian mission to eradicate what they saw as the satanic, superstitious and backward practices associated with traditional religion, were disposed to distrust the secret societies which they knew to exist in the rural areas which they aspired to govern. In 1912 the government banned by law the leopard society and many similar societies and instituted draconian punishments for members.[57] Although the text of this legislation has not been discovered, it appears to have been sweeping. A later administrative code, which consolidated a number of regulations and laws dealing with hinterland affairs, specified that illegal societies included the human leopard society, the Neegee, Susha, Toya, Kela, Uama-yama societies, and 'all secret societies of a political nature'. Membership of such societies was punishable by twenty years' imprisonment.[58]

Despite the existence of this legislation, there is no doubt that human leopards and crocodiles and similar secret societies continued to exist in many areas after 1912. A British traveller in Nimba County during the 1920s spoke to several men and women, some of them quite young, who had been condemned to long prison terms for leopard activities, and she saw parts of their costumes. Two of them admitted to her having eaten human flesh.[59] Some authors have interpreted the underground continuation of the secret societies as 'a reaction to the threats to traditional life by the pacification of the interior by the Liberian government',[60] a form of self-defence on the part of local communities threatened by national government. It is the case that secret societies were associated with both political and commercial interests, so that their members were threatened by the government's reorganisation of chiefdoms as well as by its propensity to grant trade privileges to Mandingo, almost invariably Muslims who tended to remain outside traditional secret societies. One modern author has described how Muslim teachers and traders made inroads into the economic monopolies previously held by senior *zoes*, such as

[57] S. Henry Cordor, *The Study of Africa: an introductory course in African studies for Liberian schools*, Monrovia, 1979, p.12.

[58] Article 69, 'Revised Laws and Administrative Regulations Governing the Hinterland', Government of Liberia, Department of the Interior, 1949, National Documentation Center, Monrovia.

[59] Mills, *Through Liberia*, pp.118-21. There are photographs of leopard prisoners facing pp. 170 and 172.

[60] Fulton, 'Political Structures', p.1228.

in the kola trade. He records that in the 1930s, a marabout named al-Hajj Muhammed Tunis introduced the Tijaniyya brotherhood of Sufi Islam to Liberia and 'helped abolish the dreaded Leopard society'. This was particularly effective among the Vai, many of whom converted to Islam.[61] The Tijaniyya have continued to make inroads in western Liberia, not least as a consequence of the persecution of Poro and other traditional institutions by the government of Ahmed Sékou Touré in neighbouring Guinea in the 1960s and 1970s.[62]

While the intrusion of both republican government and wider market forces often represented a threat to the power of local notables, some were able to turn the process to their advantage, such as those people who succeeded in having themselves appointed as paramount chiefs and who developed an interest in collaborating with the central government in the official system of indirect rule. An individual prepared to use fully the considerable powers at the disposition of a paramount chief might find that membership of a secret society added substantially to the range of coercive instruments available, due to the ability of societies to commit killings without recourse to any judicial organ. In such cases, a secret society came to represent less a council of local elders than the entourage of a local despot. The position of the secret societies was thus as ambiguous as that of the government-organised chiefdoms themselves, being rooted in local tradition but also liable to domination by ambitious individuals using their position to gather formidable power. Evidence of the ambiguous position of the secret societies, or rather of their leading members, may be gleaned from many reports gathered from the 1920s onwards. A Belgian administrator with long experience of similar societies in the Congo, who did comparative research in Liberia and recorded the opinion of a Liberian administrator on the activities of human leopards in the future Nimba County in 1926-7, thought that the extension of settler government had transformed leopard societies into 'political instruments' wielded by 'a veritable gang of killers'. By the 1930s many, he thought, were acting for personal gain rather than on behalf of any wider community.[63]

It would be inaccurate to assert that the leopard societies were politicised as a result of Liberian conquest, since these associations

[61] Konneh, 'Indigenous Entrepreneurs', p.106.

[62] Augustine Konneh, *Religion, Commerce and the Integration of the Mandingo in Liberia,* Lanham, MD, 1996, p.74.

[63] Paul-Ernest Joset, *Les sociétés secrètes des hommes-léopards en Afrique noire,* Paris, 1955, pp.113, 158-9, 161, 178-86.

had always been both political and religious in nature. Rather, they became increasingly motivated by factional rather than communal interest as incorporation into a system of indirect rule created opportunities for individual political entrepreneurs to shake off the traditional checks and balances which required chiefs to reach their decisions in council. This is a crucial point since the powers wielded by the *zoes* of the Poro, and even more so by elite societies given to human sacrifice, were held to be exercised properly when they were used on behalf of an entire community, exactly as European governments during the same period reserved the right to take human lives, in the form of judicial punishment or formal war, for the greater good of the nation. Hence, if human leopards became more violent during the twentieth century, and more self-interested, it was a reflection of the fact that local government in general had tended to lose many of the checks and balances which it had previously contained and to become more despotic.

   That the traditional secret societies survived in many areas, albeit with a notably different character, was partly because their very secrecy made them so difficult to suppress. There is no doubt of the rigour, or even brutality, of the government's early attempts to destroy the secret societies entirely. President Edwin Barclay (1930-44) seems to have been particularly severe in his policy against the human leopards, sending informers into the rural areas to report on them, although in the event these officials sometimes became recruits to the secret societies themselves. An African-American League of Nations official who visited Liberia in 1930 recorded:[64]

> This strange, ferocious society had killed and consumed hundreds of individuals, raided towns, and even, on occasion, had brought human flesh to the market for sale. At first, in the effort to check the outrages, Barclay tried sounding out natives to locate the mainsprings of the movement, but when these investigators had tasted the flesh, they too became addicts. Finally, Barclay had the whole society rounded up, and some 600 were brought in, all of which could not be executed, naturally. Barclay picked the sixteen ring leaders and ordered them shot; some others he put in prison virtually for life.

Barclay organised military expeditions in which dozens of human leopards were killed, such as that commanded by Colonel Elwood Davis, an African-American officer commissioned in the Liberian

---

[64] Charles S. Johnson, *Bitter Canaan: the story of the Negro Republic*, New Brunswick and Oxford, 1989, p.169.

army. The English writer Graham Greene, travelling in Liberia in the mid-1930s, recorded a meeting with him in which Davis claimed to have 'court-martialled and shot fifty members of the Leopard Society in a village near Grand Bassa'.[65]

Some leopard societies were able to survive this repression, however, precisely because they had the support of some of those very same paramount chiefs who were also pillars of government policy in the hinterland. Ten years after Colonel Davis's campaigns, an ethnographer writing in the 1940s described the leopard societies among the Loma people as 'virtually a gangster organisation', to which initiates had to provide a human sacrifice,[66] and went on to state that in Nimba County it had become 'a convenient tool for chiefs, most of whom were members', to perpetuate their power independently of the central government. The same author quoted a former district commissioner who said that the chiefs used the leopard society to '[get] rid of all persons they considered undesirable, like possible competitors, and did whatever else they chose. With its assistance they had the land in a reign of terror.'[67] A chief could respect government regulations by day, and, disguised as a leopard or possessed by the spirit of a leopard, murder his enemies at night.

As it became clear that the government's 1912 ban on secret societies was not fully effective, the government developed a more nuanced approach towards traditional religious sodalities, making a distinction between the human leopards, which it continued to regard officially as illegal, and the Poro and Sande schools, which it encouraged as vehicles for the transmission of tribal culture and exempted from the ban. George Way Harley, who first came to Liberia in 1926, noted that the Poro and Sande had been 'completely suppressed' by the Liberian government at an earlier period, but later revived 'in a very modified and emasculated form' on account of their 'disciplinary function', but shorn of what the American missionary habitually called their 'frightfulness'.[68] Harley had a high regard for the institution of Poro in its new form but considered the leopard society, on the other hand, as a 'degradation' of its former self, apparently a reference to the

[65] Graham Greene, *Journey Without Maps*, London, 1948, pp.161, 186-93.

[66] Schwab, *Tribes*, p.297.

[67] *Ibid.*, p.299.

[68] Harley, *Masks as an Agent of Social Control*, p.vi; R. Earle Anderson, *Liberia: America's African friend*, Chapel Hill, NC, 1952, pp.50, 92. Anderson makes clear that Harley is his source for his information.

growing propensity of its members to engage in murders for purely
factional benefit.[69] We may note, however, that the fact that leopard
societies were being increasingly used by cliques of local notables
to advance their factional interests in local politics does not imply
that their religious aspect had diminished. On the contrary, just
as officials of Poro, on donning the mask of a spirit, were thought
to be actually possessed by that spirit, so it was with the human
leopards. An Austrian woman travelling in the area in the 1930s
noted that 'it is believed that during sleep the souls of people
with magic powers can leave their bodies and wander about doing
evil. The soul may enter into the body of a leopard and attack
people or animals in the village by night. No ordinary leopard
is so bloodthirsty as these human leopards.'[70] Such attacks, she
said, were particularly feared in Western Liberia, home of the
Poro.[71]

Moreover this religious aspect was increasingly tolerated by the
government's own judiciary and executive. One of the most detailed
written accounts of a killing by a human leopard from the 1940s
was by a German missionary doctor who, performing an autopsy
on the victim of a supposed leopard attack, came to the conclusion
that the wounds had in fact been caused by humans who had
neatly excised the liver from the body. The doctor reported the
case to the minister of the interior in Monrovia, who indicated
that no further investigation was necessary. The local army commander of the area where the killing had taken place was none
other than the same Colonel Elwood Davis who had told Graham
Greene ten years earlier how he had made war on the human
leopards in Grand Bassa County.[72] In this account from the early
1940s, Davis, by now a serious alcoholic, was unwilling to act against
the human leopards. Eventually, when the case was brought to
trial, it was established in open court that killings had indeed
been carried out by members of a local leopard society which
was discovered to have been introduced by a Christian missionary
from Grand Bassa County, one Mr Cane, who had himself been
initiated as a leopard in his youth. He was now the possessor
of a powerful cult object which required regular anointing with
human blood. At his trial Cane pleaded in his defence that it
was not he who was responsible for these deaths, but the spirit

---

[69] Harley, *Native African Medicine*, p.140.

[70] Etta Donner, *Hinterland Liberia*, London and Glasgow, 1939, p.2.

[71] *Ibid.*, p.164.

[72] Junge, *African Jungle Doctor*, p.192.

of the leopard which possessed him. This was accepted by the court, which simply banished Cane to Grand Bassa County.[73]

A second eye-witness description from the same period, revealing the extent to which government-appointed chiefs were central to the politics of leopard societies in at least some cases, was written by a Catholic missionary who lived in what is now Lofa County in 1948-9 at a time when several ritual killings attributed to a local leopard society took place. These murders were said to have been carried out in order to provide powerful medicine for the local chiefs. 'It is commonly said,' the American Father Milligan wrote, 'that members of this society are solemnly pledged to the killing of one human being each year.'[74] Eventually, thirty people were arrested on suspicion of conspiring to obtain human beings for sacrifice and taken to Monrovia for trial. The prosecution was eventually dropped and the suspected ring leader of the human leopards, one Mbombo Yalla, paramount chief of the Gbandi, was reinstated by President Tubman. Yalla returned to his chiefdom displaying an utter contempt for his accusers. He sang a song which was translated to Father Milligan as follows:[75]

You people are all in my stomach;
I have power to do with you anything I like;
I can even kill you if I want to, and will if you don't do as I say.

Those secret societies most closely associated with human sacrifice, like the Neegee or water-leopards, the alligators and the human leopards, remained banned by law even if, as we have seen, government officials of both the executive and judiciary became increasingly tolerant of them or even complicit in their activities. The Poro and Sande societies, on the other hand, by this time were not only exempt from the interdiction on secret societies but were actively encouraged by a government which saw in them a useful institution of social control. This was a point of view widely shared by foreign observers too, sometimes even by Christian missionaries. 'When the rapid changes that are taking place in the hinterland at last allow the coming generations to erode its authority,' a missionary anthropologist wrote concerning the Poro in 1947, 'the effect must be most serious, unless some other factor can be brought in to replace the high disciplinary influence it

---

[73] *Ibid.*, pp.176-87.

[74] Ralph T. Milligan, *Bolahun,* New York, 1989, p.27.

[75] *Ibid.*, pp.163-5.

once exercised.'[76] As late as 1975, a missionary among the Mano wrote, 'it is only during the last fifteen years that Western-type civilization has penetrated to this region,' surely a rather un-historical perspective. More pertinent was his observation that 'the Poro and Sande societies continue to play an important role in moulding individuals to social norms, maintaining adherence to traditional values and in providing stability in what is a fragile and somewhat fragmented society.'[77] This description, we may note in passing, concerns an area which was to be at the heart of the NPFL rising in 1989-90.

The revived Poro and Sande, from the 1920s increasingly patronised by the government in the service of indirect rule, were constituted quite differently from their earlier incarnations in cer-tain key respects. A succinct description of the change which had taken place was given by President Tubman when he addressed a Council of Chiefs in the Central Province, in 1953. He told them:[78]

> There appears to be a tendency of some of the *Zoes* of the Poro Society to overshadow the [government-appointed] Tribal authority as well as Government and become the most powerful force in the Nation. In no case can this be tolerated. The Poro may operate, but it must operate as a private institution and not as a Tribal or Government institution. This refers also to the Razor Society, Black Deer Head and any other tribal in-stitution.

The government's view of Poro and similar societies which were encouraged to operate as 'a private institution', but must not chal-lenge the 'tribal authority' represented by government-recognised chiefs, says much about how the True Whig Party government was prepared to make use of almost any institutions which it found useful to its vision of a centralised national government ruling through a system of indirect rule in the hinterland. The government no doubt acted thus for purely pragmatic reasons, but its willingness to countenance at least some secret societies could only encourage, this time in matters of religious thought, the marked Liberian tendency towards assimilation.

---

[76] Schwab, *Tribes,* pp.286-7.

[77] Harrington, 'Secret Societies and the Church', pp.5-6.

[78] Minutes of the Executive Council of Chiefs of the Central Province, Tappita, 10 June 1953, Decision no.14, National Documentation Center, Monrovia.

The political assimilation of religious ritual

The most prestigious of the American families who settled in West Africa in the early nineteenth century tended to be Presbyterians, Baptists, Methodists and Episcopalians, but over the years a great number of different Christian denominations have made their appearance in Liberia, including African initiated churches like the popular Aladura churches which originated in Nigeria. Liberia contains dozens of different denominations or strains of Christianity, most of which have assimilated various aspects of traditional African beliefs or rituals into their doctrine to varying degrees. There are many members of the Poro, the Sande and similar societies who also attend church regularly, there are Muslims who practice traditional sacrifices, and there are quite a few people who are members of two or more churches simultaneously. 'Many, if not most, Christians in Liberia either hold dual memberships in their Church of birth or confirmation and the Church of the Lord Aladura,' according to the Methodist Bishop Arthur Kulah, 'where the doctrines and practices of the Christian Church and the African Traditional Religions are held concurrently, or their Church and the African Traditional Religions.'[79] Many Liberians evidently do not consider this sort of plural religious allegiance to be inconsistent, although in recent years there are increasing numbers of pentecostalist Christians who reject all aspects of traditional religion on the grounds that any religious ritual without a clear biblical basis is the work of Satan. There has also been an upsurge of Islamic reform, such as the substantial advances made by the puritanical Ahmadiyya movement among Muslims in the 1960s and '70s.[80] Certain tendencies and certain types of moral dilemma which can arise among adherents to Christianity appear also to occur in similar circumstances among Muslims, since Christianity and Islam both have some common features which can bring them into fundamental conflict with traditional religious thought at various points.

The many people who attend different churches, sometimes in combination with traditional practices, or who combine Muslim prayers with performance of indigenous rituals, clearly do so because they believe they can obtain a range of benefits by using a wide variety of religious techniques. For example, one man who attended an Aladura church, a well known type of church which

[79] Arthur F. Kulah, *Theological Education in Liberia: problems and opportunities,* Lithonia, GA, 1994, p.102.

[80] Konneh, 'Indigenous Entrepreneurs', p.66.

uses significant elements of traditional African ritual practices, explained to Bishop Kulah, 'I go to the prophet church because the prophet can tell me what will happen to me in the future. The prophet makes sacrifice for me when I get bad luck. He gives me holy water to drink when my stomach hurts. He is able to drive the evil spirits from my house.'[81]

Multiple religious allegiance like this generally poses no difficulty to the many Liberians who find it a sensible approach, but a fundamental problem can arise when a person who is a Christian or a Muslim and is also a follower of traditional religion is faced with certain types of moral choice which are ultimately theological in nature but which can also have important political aspects. At its most common, this can concern the question of whether, for example, it is appropriate for a practising Christian also to offer animal sacrifices to the ancestors. Some churches believe this to be acceptable, but many would claim it to be unChristian and possibly diabolical. The fundamental dilemma which this poses can become most acute for people who acquire high status in life.

This may be illustrated by a specific example, that of Yakpawolo Kollie, the son of a chief who was initiated into Poro at the age of ten, probably around 1945. Since he was to inherit the chieftaincy from his father, Kollie underwent further training from the elders of his village. He also attended a Methodist mission school, and at a certain stage he adopted the *kwi* (Western) name James Paye, given to him when he was baptised. At school and church, Paye was told that he should not take part in traditional rituals such as those of the Poro society, the harvest festival, sacrifice and prayer to the ancestors, and that polygamy was sinful; but these, he had been brought up to believe and taught in the Poro bush, were 'the pillars upon which his society rests'. Painful though it was, Paye accepted the conditions set out by his Christian instructors and qualified to study in America, where he earned a Ph.D. in political science. About a year after his return from the United States, Paye was elected to be a senator for his county. This was probably in the 1960s or 1970s. What occurred next is described by Bishop Kulah:[82]

> Immediately after his election, several of James' Christian and non-Christian friends and relatives told him that to be an effective senator he needed charms and amulets to protect him from

[81] Quoted in Kulah, *Theological Education*, p.80.
[82] *Ibid.*, p.77.

all harm and danger. James was also told that he must make sacrifice, even if it meant the taking of someone's life, in order to purify him for the jobs ahead. James' dilemma was that he could not dismiss those proposals, because in his dreams James was [i.e. had become] his deceased grandfather not only confirming those proposals, but instructing new ones.

Senator Paye, then, found that the moral requirements of the Western cultural style, necessary for advancement in Liberian society and politics, were ultimately incompatible with those of his family, as was made clear to him by the spirit of his late grandfather, which possessed him. The higher he rose in his career, the more acute the dilemma became. In the end it hinged on human sacrifice. In this context it is useful to note that, despite the biblical command 'thou shalt not kill', orthodox Christianity is not opposed to the taking of human life under certain conditions, such as in time of war. What is absolutely contrary to Christian doctrine is the notion of human sacrifice, since an essential belief of Christianity is that one human being was executed 2,000 years ago in a human sacrifice so perfect that it is never to be repeated, only commemorated. In orthodox Christian thought, the human sacrifice practised by leopard societies in an attempt to communicate with God is impious because it has been made unnecessary by the sacrifice of Christ, as at least one foreign missionary in Liberia has noted.[83]

Intrinsic to this religious contradiction is also a moral one. Christianity and Islam are dualistic religions, in which good and evil are represented as absolute contrasts, personified by God and Satan. This is not the case with traditional Liberian religious thought. In the theology of Poro, for example, the spirit of the forest is held to be powerful and capable of both cruelty and beneficence. The high priests of the society, the *zoes*, are pillars of public order but may also be required to perform human sacrifices, traditionally of their own relatives or children, in order to keep this order intact. Such sacrifices, while terrifying, are not held to be evil as long as they are carried out in the right way and for the proper purpose. The question arises as to who precisely may decide which of these purposes is morally correct or socially permissible. Two early European writers familiar with the Poro complex noted that the Kpelle with whom they discussed the matter considered the supreme being to be just and good. The authors concluded that, in the view of their interlocutors, 'God is the

[83] Junge, *African Jungle Doctor,* p.186.

source of the moral law, but not of moral actions; these latter receive their stimulus and character from the teachings in the Poro-bush.'[84] For the proper moral order to be upheld, therefore, depended not on the will of the supreme being, but on the performance of traditional religious rituals in the right manner since it was these which gave form and shape to moral law. Harley, despite his detestation of the 'frightfulness' which he identified in the Poro's earlier practice of human sacrifice, recognised that 'the spirits of the ancestors are the personification of good.[...] The central figure in the Poro is in the last analysis, a personification of the ancestors.'[85]

However, the balance of power in traditional religious institutions was upset as a result of the manner in which the Liberian republic co-opted local government in the twentieth century. Members of leopard societies, for example (or, more accurately, people who were believed to have been entered by the spirit of a leopard), came to operate in a context in which they may fairly be suspected of being more concerned with their individual or factional interest than with the welfare of a wider community. The Liberian conquest of the hinterland did not actually destroy local institutions of power so much as reach a series of understandings with them. It was a process of reciprocal assimilation,[86] in which people who succeeded in being recognised by the government as tribal chiefs gained great power and wealth through access to the resources of the Liberian state, on the one hand, while Americo-Liberian politicians and officials, on the other, gained entry to local politics. One way in which officials from Monrovia could gain influence in local politics was by joining secret societies which not only gave them access to conclaves of local notables but also strengthened the perception that they had access to powerful spiritual resources, to add to the Christian churches and the Masonic craft which settler families already dominated. Normally, entry to a high grade of a society like Poro would require long years of apprenticeship, which politicians and officials hardly had time for. One short cut to immediate high-level entry was through human sacrifice, regarded as an instrument for achieving great power, traditionally necessary only in very specific circumstances and requiring sacrifice of a close relative. But an outsider, such as a politician, could use this technique to gain instant entry to an elite secret society.

[84] Sibley and Westermann, *Liberia,* p.193.

[85] Quoted in Esther Warner, *Trial by Sasswood,* Oxford, 1970 (first published 1955), p.117.

[86] The phrase is from Bayart, *The State in Africa,* pp.150-79.

Instead of providing his own son or daughter, he could, through simple access to the mechanism of the market, provide another human victim instead.

We do not know whether the Honourable James Paye, Ph.D., of the Liberian Senate, whose fearful dilemma we have described, chose to forgo making a human sacrifice, in which case he is likely to have declined in the esteem of some of his supporters, or whether he did so at the expense of his Christian principles, thus advancing his career. However there is abundant evidence that at least some Liberian politicians, faced with a choice as cruel as that facing James Paye, opted to make a human sacrifice, as we shall examine next. This has become an important part of modern Liberian political culture, although not one which is openly discussed. An essential element of the many Liberian religious sodalities is, after all, secrecy: *ifa mo*, 'do not speak it'.[87]

Ritual killing and modern politics

Perhaps the most distinctive characteristic of the Poro society, in comparison with the religious institutions of those areas of Liberia which do not have the Poro, is its diffusion over a wide area and the apparent recognition by members of local lodges that they share some form of common bond with other Poro members, even when the latter employ rather different forms of Poro. Authors who have studied the Poro society are divided on the question of precisely how many different degrees of membership it contained in older times, and how centralised it was. The general consensus seems to be that before the twentieth century each village had an autonomous society, but that senior *zoes* were able to associate over wider areas. Only Harley went as far as to opine that there existed a supreme council of Poro, and seemed to think that this was an ancient feature of the society, although most other authors have questioned this finding.[88]

Interestingly, a Liberian government expert, Varney Fahnbulleh, a specialist on tribal affairs at the Internal Affairs Department, told a visiting anthropologist in the 1960s that the Liberian government itself had worked to centralise Poro. He said that as 'a part of the process of gaining more control in the hinterland the government sponsored the first "national" Poro organisation by bringing in a super-*zo* figure who sat on the top of a sacred mountain

[87] Bellman, *Village of Curers and Assassins*, p.68.

[88] Harley, *Masks as Agents of Social Control*, p.vii.

and demanded loyalty from all the local Poro lodges'.[89] Unfortunately,
we do not know the name of this mountain, but it appears to
have been Mount Gibi, which seems to have developed as an
important ritual site with the approval of the government.[90]

Varney Fahnbulleh's testimony supports the view that, after an
early period in which the government tried to suppress the secret
societies, it came to see them, officially or otherwise, rather as
institutions to be infiltrated and adapted for the government's
own purposes, mainly because they were so central to the fabric
of rural society. Such a sequence of events certainly conforms
to the little which is known of the relationship between Americo-
Liberian politicians and the secret societies. President King (1920-30)
is said to have been the first Liberian president ever invited to
a Poro graduation ceremony. After King was obliged to resign
the presidency, he was widely believed to have used occult powers
to cause a bolt of lightning to strike the house of his successor
on the day of his inauguration.[91] He was also rumoured to have
been a member of the more exclusive Alligator Society.[92] 'When
the League of Nations Commission was appointed to inquire into
Liberian conditions, Mr King and several members of his cabinet
– so it was believed in Monrovia – had sacrificed a goat. After the
sacrifice, which should traditionally have been a human one, a
boatload of young Krus had been drowned close to the beach
at Monrovia, and it was generally felt that the alligator was dis-
satisfied with the goat,' Graham Greene recorded.[93] Greene, who
had an interview with President Edwin Barclay, thought that the
government had put up only 'the feeblest of resistance' to secret
societies and that Americo-Liberian politicians 'could not properly
resist' the secret societies 'because they *believed*'.[94] Certainly, leaders
of the True Whig Party after Barclay joined traditional societies
quite routinely, just as they also had leading positions in various
Christian churches. President Tubman was declared to be the head
of all Poro societies and his wife was initiated into the Sande
society. He was at the same time the head of the Masonic craft
and a prominent Methodist. Tubman made the Poro and Sande
subject to regulation by the state bureaucracy, through an act

[89] Fulton, 'The Kpelle Traditional Political System', p.18
[90] Cf. the anecdotes in Hayman and Preece, *Lighting Up Liberia,* pp.131, 141-3.
[91] Furbay, *Top Hats,* pp.127-8.
[92] Crocodiles are commonly referred to as alligators in Liberia.
[93] Greene, *Journey without Maps,* p.161.
[94] *Ibid.* The emphasis is Greene's.

of the legislature in 1952 which explicitly provided for the appointment of an assistant secretary of the interior to compile ethnographic information and 'supervise matters pertaining to the Poro, Sande and other societies in the tribal areas'.[95] The government actively defended the Poro, such as in 1958 when a group of Christians in Lofa, 'said to be encouraged by missionaries, desecrated the Poro bush, destroying masks and other ritual objects, and exposing them to public, including female, view. The missionaries involved were fined $600 each and imprisoned for one year.'[96] Tubman's successor, William Tolbert, was both a *zo* and president of the World Baptist Alliance. With Samuel Doe, insecure in office as he undoubtedly was, the cultivation of various religious groups patronised by his predecessors took on an almost obsessive quality. Not only did Doe join the Poro society and have himself proclaimed the head of a supreme council of *zoes,* but he was always interested to hear of new marabouts and prophets whom he would invite for an interview, imprisoning those he believed to be imposters or charlatans.[97] After his assumption of power, Doe ostentatiously began to attend church regularly for the first time in his life, and 'chose no other church than Tolbert's church, the Baptist church. Not only that, in the church he also took the seat reserved specially for Tolbert,' noted one resident of Monrovia.[98] Sometimes he attended the mosque as well.

More recently still, Charles Taylor has been initiated into a high degree of Poro, apparently in late 1996 or early 1997. This became publicly known when he married his second wife at St John's Methodist Church in Gbarnga on 28 January 1997. While making his marriage vows he gave one of his names as Dahkpanah, a title used for *zoes* of the Poro society.[99] Taylor's initiation into the society shortly before his wedding is reported to have been masterminded by one Isaac Cisco, the chief native investigator at the Ministry of Internal Affairs.[100] One leading NPFL official claims that a special form of Poro initiation has been developed for politicians, which takes only one day to complete and which requires the absolute minimum of scars, just a couple of nicks

---

[95] Kenneth Best, *Cultural Policy in Liberia,* Paris, 1974, p.28.

[96] Fraenkel, *Tribe and Class,* p.172.

[97] Sawyer, *Effective Immediately,* p.29.

[98] Brehun, *War of Horror,* p.25.

[99] *The Inquirer,* 31 January 1997.

[100] *Bassa Voice* (Monrovia), 6 February 1997.

with a razor under the arm where they will not be seen.[101] Certainly, Charles Taylor showed particular concern to cultivate *zoes* from the start of the war, and during his election campaign in 1997 he donated minibuses emblazoned with his name to the National Council of Zoes, Chiefs and Elders.

While the Poro and Sande societies have functioned openly, and even received official encouragement, since the 1920s, the more exclusive of the traditional secret societies have remained illegal. Nevertheless, the archives of the Liberian government itself contain many reports indicating the continued existence of secret societies given to human sacrifice, or at least of groups of people wishing to acquire human body-parts for ritual purposes. In 1957, for example, the superintendent of Maryland County reported that a child had been found dead 'with parts cut from the body'. The missing parts were the tips of one finger on each hand, both ears, and part of the genitals. The superintendent instructed the local chief to use what he called the 'country custom' – probably the traditional trial by ordeal called sasswood – to find out who was responsible.[102] During Tubman's presidency reports of ritual killings began to circulate in Monrovia. During late 1954 an opposition newspaper carried several reports that people were being abducted and killed by candidates for political office in forthcoming elections. Two leading politicians of the True Whig Party were persistently named as being connected with these deaths, which were said to have as their purpose the acquisition of power through human sacrifice. Former President Edwin Barclay, who had engineered the succession for his protégé William Tubman but who had become disenchanted with his style of government and was now campaigning against him, circulated a petition of protest which he submitted to the President.[103] Tubman's reply was scathing, but he admitted the existence of rumours 'alleging that dangerous people called "heartmen" were walking at nights to capture and murder innocent persons, and to extract their hearts' and that Monrovia was 'horrified and terrorised'.[104]

Throughout the years of the True Whig Party ascendancy, there

[101] Author's interview with John T. Richardson, Monrovia, 8 April 1997.

[102] W. Fred Gibson, superintendent of Maryland County, to Paramount Chief of Nymowe chiefdom, Hedo Hodo, 8 June 1957, and Gibson to Tubman, 12 June 1957, National Documentation Center, Monrovia.

[103] Wreh, *The Love of Liberty*, pp.70-5.

[104] 'Special Message of William V.S. Tubman, President of Liberia, to the Extraordinary Session of the 43rd Legislature of Liberia', 13 June 1955, National Documentation Center, Monrovia.

were regular rumours and reports of this sort. An American travelling through Nimba in the 1950s found that her Liberian employee was afraid of becoming a victim of ritual killing. She told the man that he should not worry because the secret societies 'are not so strong in Africa as they used to be'; but he replied: 'It is still the old days in Africa, Ma. The secret societies are not less strong; they are only more secret.'[105] Ten years later, a Peace Corps volunteer in Lofa County recorded that 'the Leopard Society is by no means an extinct sect'.[106] But increasingly, reports of ritual killings were associated less with the traditional secret societies, such as the human leopards, than with so-called 'heartmen', defined by one modern Liberian newspaper as 'groups of organised killers often contracted by political aspirants and businessmen to kill people and extract their body parts to perform rituals'.[107] Heartmen are said to supply hearts to 'juju men to make their clients succeed in life for high jobs in government or in private employment or for protection against enemies'.[108] Modern heartmen, then, are not considered to be officials of any traditional society, but appear to be freelance killers who specialise in procuring corpses or human organs for those who require them, particularly business people and politicians in search of wealth and power, who may belong to an outlawed secret society or may simply contact an independent occult practicioner who claims to be able to confer power on his or her clients, in return for payment, through the manipulation of spiritual forces requiring human blood or human body parts.[109]

Before 1980 such matters were rumoured far more often than they were formally investigated. This is hardly surprising because the practice of ritual killing by members of the political elite, even if it was no more than a rumour, struck at the heart of the True Whig Party's claim to exercise hegemony in Liberia. The Americo-Liberian settlers generally derived their prestige and their elevated social position from their claim to represent a superior civilisation, which was Christian and technically advanced. Any suspicion that True Whig Party rule in fact reposed in part on the manipulation of forces which an orthodox Christian would

[105] Warner, *Trial by Sasswood*, pp.132-3.

[106] Marvin H. Unger, *Pawpaw, Foofoo, and Juju: recollections of a Peace Corps volunteer*, New York, 1968, p.73.

[107] *National Chronicle*, 13 March 1997.

[108] *New Democrat*, 2, 158 (31 October-2 November 1995).

[109] Conteh, 'Reflections on Religion and Medicine', p.149.

be obliged to regard as evil, and therefore Satanic in origin, would
have serious implications for the ideological and even cosmological
claims on which settler rule was ultimately based. The mere existence of such rumours reflects the degree to which the hinterland
and settler elites were commonly supposed to have assimilated
one another, contrary to the fundamental tenet of Americo-
Liberian ideology which proclaimed that the settlers owed their
position to their leading role in introducing a 'civilisation' based
on American values.

The exact nature of those associations which can be demonstrated to have carried out ritual killings since the mid-twentieth
century is not easy to discern, but it appears most likely that rural
leopard and crocodile societies of a recognisably traditional type
grew weaker as the power of central government increased. This
would be compatible with the evidence that cults devoted to the
acquisition of power through human sacrifice and the consumption
of human flesh were growing in importance not in the rural areas,
but in Monrovia itself, the seat of the central government and
the locus of national power. Hence, when a suspected leopard
society was suppressed in what is now Lofa County in 1948, a
local missionary recorded reports that 'the Leopard Society...head-
quarters are in the city of Monrovia itself'.[110] An African-American
working with the Peace Corps in Maryland County in the 1960s
reported the common view that the main organisers of human
sacrifice were not traditional village societies but Americo-Liberians,
including one convicted by a court in 1965. The American recalled
that they 'killed tribal people to satisfy conditions established by
"witch doctors", related to the purging of sins to gain some
economic or political advantage'.[111] Some people said that True
Whig Party officials used their own secret society, freemasonry,
to collect human parts during election campaigns.[112] The most
notorious case of ritual killing used for political purposes ever
to be made public, and in some ways the most revealing, concerned
Allen Yancy and James Anderson, sons of leading officials of the True
Whig Party who were sentenced to death with five others in 1979
after being convicted of a ritual murder. Not only was the evidence
against them overwhelming, but Yancy admitted even in private

[110] Milligan, *Bolahun*, p.27.
[111] Carl Meacham, 'Peace Corps Service in Liberia, 1965-66: reflections of an
African-American volunteer', *Liberian Studies Journal*, XV, 1 (1990), pp.100, 103.
[112] Tipoteh, *Democracy*, pp.127-8.

that he was guilty as charged.[113] The Yancy and Anderson families were leaders of the wing of the True Whig Party which was opposed to President Tolbert's reforms, and both families were from Maryland, Tubman's old fief, rather than Monrovia. It seems that Tolbert signed their death warrants in an attempt both to act against this practice and to weaken the opposition within his own party.

Tolbert's successor, Samuel Doe, seems himself to have believed that human sacrifice could be a means of obtaining spiritual power. Charles Taylor, to name but one, was convinced that the Statue of the Unknown Soldier erected by Doe in 1981 to commemorate his coup, and which was destroyed in the battle of Monrovia in April 1996, was sanctified with a human sacrifice.[114] There are eye-witness accounts of Doe's soldiers eating parts of Thomas Quiwonkpa's body in 1985.[115] Throughout the late 1980s, cases of ritual killings came before the law courts: in 1985, for example, six people, including a former senior official of Doe's party, were sentenced to death for a ritual killing in Maryland.[116] In the three subsequent years, at least twelve people were hanged after conviction, and thirty-five presumed victims of ritual killings were identified, also in Maryland.[117] Doe's defence minister, Gray Allison, was convicted of a similar offence in August 1989, and while his trial was certainly politically motivated, few doubt that he was guilty as charged.[118] There were regular reports of similar court cases involving less senior figures, such as four members of an independent church arrested in 1988 on suspicion of 'killing, cooking and eating a child'.[119] Although most reports do not imply that such groups were traditional secret societies, one article does suggest that the Neegee, 'a secret society that is linked with deals in human parts and human sacrifice for the achievement of various mundane activities', was still in existence despite being illegal since 1912.[120] Even if we were to maintain that the vast majority of

[113] Personal communication by former minister in the Tolbert Government, Monrovia, 27 March 1997.

[114] Huband, *The Liberian Civil War*, p.92. Many people in Monrovia also make this allegation.

[115] Above, p.60.

[116] Amnesty International, quoted in Kappel and Korte, *Human Rights Violations*, p.161.

[117] Quoted in Médecins sans Frontières, internal document.

[118] Kappel and Korte, *Human Rights Violations*, pp.223-5.

[119] Paul Gifford, 'Liberia's Never-die Christians', *Journal of Modern African Studies*, 30, 2 (1992), p.352.

[120] Conteh, 'Reflections on Religion and Medicine', p.149.

reports such as these are mere rumour or calumny, still there remain a few instances, such as the Yancy and Anderson case mentioned above, in which evidence was tested in court and the accused freely admitted the charges.

It is striking in the pattern of human sacrifice which may be discerned after the 1940s, particularly those cases which were said to involve politicians, that members of such cults do not appear to have sacrificed their own kin, which was traditionally thought to be the most effective of all forms of sacrifice, but simply to have paid heartmen for victims. Human sacrifice, in other words, had become fully subject to market principles. The attitudes of national politicians towards such practices had come a long way since the government had outlawed secret societies in 1912, and since the ferocious campaigns against human leopards in the 1920s and '30s. Senior officials had discovered that entering secret conclaves of this sort gave them access to sites of political influence in the rural areas. Thereafter, it appears, some prominent Americo-Liberians went on to establish cults of their own, making private cults of human sacrifice a feature of elite Liberian life.

In short, it seems that there has been a mutual assimilation of the Christianity professed by Liberia's governing elite and of traditional religious beliefs, and that this has accompanied the mutual political assimilation which took place over the same period. Doubtless these theological and sociological tendencies are intimately related. It is no doubt a wild exaggeration to suspect all rich or powerful people of using such methods, as many Liberians today do. There is, for example, no hard evidence that ritual killings were ever carried out in order to secure advancement in the Masonic craft as so many Liberians believe, perhaps because they have assumed that Freemasons practised ritual killing in the same way as members of certain indigenous secret societies. The fact remains, though, that the evidence that people were killed during the twentieth century for purposes of human sacrifice is so strong as to be overwhelming, although precisely how frequent such killings have been is impossible to determine.

In general, it is perhaps unsurprising that the government of Liberia, for all the public attachment of prominent individuals to orthodox Christian doctrine, should have been sanguine about the popular tendency to assimilate Christian beliefs into the range of existing religious belief since the end result, certainly until quite recently, was a view of natural authority which placed an extreme emphasis on submission to duly constituted authority. Some of the oldest churches, notably the Baptists, Presbyterians, Methodists and Episcopalians, were dominated by leading settler families to the extent that prominent politicians often combined tenure of public office with senior positions in the churches. The Christianity preached in Liberia until only a few years ago was often of a type which modern Liberian intellectuals and churchmen trace back to the historical experiences of the American slaves who actually introduced the religion to the country in the nineteenth century. Even until the 1970s, this was a lugubrious creed in which God was represented as an all-powerful, stern and paternal master who would unfailingly detect and punish the failings of mankind. God, in fact, was a bit like President Tubman.

Many commentators, Liberian and foreign,[121] agree that the type of Christianity taught and preached for so many years played an important role in forging the political culture which has served Liberians so badly. One writer, Moses Nagbe, attributes this attitude to the early missionaries who, he claims, offered clothes, food and money to attract people, sapping their self-reliance and in-stilling in them a culture of dependence. Describing himself as something of an agnostic, he noted:[122]

> There is a popular belief that Liberia was founded as a Christian nation, therefore, all Liberians need to do is bow heads, fold hands and legs, and God will do the rest. When some of those who hold power break laws openly, for example, most Liberians maintain, directly or indirectly, that God will think, talk or act for Liberia. [...] The Liberian politician sees God as the economic trouble-shooter. [...] God, he believes, will pull a magic formula and all will be improved, without touching his weakness in spending.

This analysis is shared by many people. One former government minister, for example, agrees that Liberians have developed 'an eschatological belief that God or a spirit brother would solve their problems'.[123] Since Liberia is a land created by God – so the reasoning goes – and is under God's protection, politicians and others can engage in the most blatantly self-interested behaviour and ignore the longer-term implications of their actions, since every-thing is in the safe hand of the Almighty. The emergence of a vision of a stern and omnipotent God who will forever preserve Liberia, provided only that Liberians acknowledge His power, is

---

[121] Gifford, *Christianity and Politics in Doe's Liberia,* esp. pp.140-2.

[122] K. Moses Nagbe, 'Liberia: a land of the magic God', *Daily Observer,* 10, 76 (12 June 1990).

[123] S. Byron Tarr, 'The Ecomog Initiative' in 'Liberia: a Liberian perspective', *Issue,* XXI, i-ii (1993), pp.78-9.

Men and Devils

surely connected with the growth of a veritable cult of the presidency which one critic referred to as 'a superman cult of the presidency on the verge of deification'.[124] This particular view of the disposition of God towards His people in Liberia has not so much encouraged a sense of individual responsibility for the whole of society as a conviction that society will endure whatever individuals may do.

It is unfair to assert, as some critics have done, that the theological vision of an all-powerful God who will always preserve Liberia is the result only of the type of Christianity taught by generations of missionaries, since it also reflects the influence of traditional religion, and notably the virtues of obedience and self-discipline inculcated through traditional initiation rituals and especially by the Poro. One might add, as other factors which contributed to the culture of political acquiescence which reached its apogee under President Tubman, the economic effect of royalties and loans paid by foreign governments and corporations directly to the Liberian government and the construction of a highly centralised patronage system incorporating the technique of indirect rule through quasi-traditional chiefs. All of these combined to produce, in the minds of Liberians, particular views about authority and legitimacy which were expressed largely in a religious idiom.

The existence of such views of power and authority gives preachers and priests an important political role, not only on account of their perceived function as intermediaries with the invisible world but as influential actors in the formation of public opinion and potential recruiters of political support, in Monrovia especially. It is no surprise to learn that politicians devote great attention to popular preachers of all types, seeking their allegiance and paying great heed to their views. During the war of 1989-97 some preachers are said to have jockeyed for political favour, writing 'secret letters to rebel leaders pledging their support' or giving honours to corrupt officials.[125]

There are many examples of how the interaction of religion and politics articulated by public rumour and religious sermons may be used by politicians to great effect, some of which have been mentioned at various points of the chronicle of the Liberian war contained in the first part of the present book. One such

---

[124] Albert Porte, quoted in S. Henry Cordor, *Facing the Realities of the Liberian Nation: problems and prospects of a West African society*, Iowa City, 1980, p.83.

[125] Column by religious correspondent Gibson Jerue, *The Inquirer*, 5, 45 (23 March 1995), p.4.

illustration may be taken from the events of early December 1996 in Monrovia. Inhabitants of the city had been traumatised by the orgy of killing and plundering which had taken place just eight months earlier, on 6 April. In late November 1996, rumours began spreading, especially from pulpits, that three days of darkness would begin on Sunday, 8 December. People were in deep foreboding and believed this to be a prophecy of a new battle. The Ecomog commander General Malu took these rumours very seriously, knowing that in this febrile atmosphere such prophecies of disaster could themselves provoke an incident. On 7 December he ordered Ecomog armoured vehicles to deploy across Monrovia in a massive display of force. On the day of the impending darkness, with all of Monrovia in a state of extreme anxiety, Charles Taylor invited the press to see him turning on the lights on a Christmas tree which he had erected, and his beaming face was across the front pages reflecting the light of Christmas. This was more than a brilliant stroke of public relations: it was a highly effective demonstration by Charles Taylor that he was a master of the cosmic forces which Liberians often believe to lie behind the daily round of political events.

War, power and the spiritual order

One Liberian newspaper noted that heartmen were 'a nationwide plague until the war when it became unnecessary for one to even hide to kill for killing was the tool of the trade'.[126] At least some observers, then, see an element of continuity in the exercise of violence in peace and war, in the sense that activities which had previously been carried out by heartmen or other specialists in secret, could now be carried out openly by combatants in the civil war.

There is certainly abundant evidence that religious beliefs in the broadest sense have affected the way in which fighters have behaved. We may recall that early accounts of the NPFL, at a time when its rank and file were largely young Gio men and women from rural Nimba County, describe them being initiated through quasi-traditional rituals. Some smeared their faces with a white clay they called *leh*, a practice associated with people in contact with the spirit world, such as in Poro rituals.[127] A similar observation applies to many other practices which foreign observers have found

---

[126] *New Democrat*, 2, 158 (31 October-2 November 1995).

[127] Above, p.113.

particularly puzzling or bizarre in the Liberian war. Transvestitism is often taken as a demonstration of the strength of a warrior, containing an element of wildness, an ability to transcend established genres. Among the Gola, 'gender ambiguity and androgyny' are said to be 'potential qualities of all living things as well as spirit entities. Cross-sex impersonations and role exchanges occur in a number of Gola rites, and gender transformation or ambisexuality is a facility of wild animals of the bush and of all nature spirits.'[128] Some sources claim that such cross-dressing is traditionally used as a sign of liminal status during the passage from boyhood to manhood,[129] in which case its use by adolescents setting out on the essentially adult business of making war is not surprising. A foreign correspondent visiting the capital of Ulimo-K at the height of the war was told that 'combining male and female attributes is considered a powerful charm'.[130] The widespread adoption by fighters of war-names is also indicative of a change of status as they assume a new, warlike personality. The tactics used by fighters in the 1990s often also have a basis in the traditional search by warriors to obtain the strongest possible war medicine, which often contains human body parts.[131]

Some Liberians, when asked why male fighters during the civil war dressed in female clothing and adorned themselves with various objects, reply simply that this was done to frighten people. Others say that these are techniques traditionally used in war. Both observations are true enough but fall short of a fully satisfactory explanation insofar as they imply that the civil war was of a purely traditional sort. In effect, some of the trappings and some of the military tactics retained from older ways of waging war were used in the 1990s, but, crucially, the traditional limits placed upon war had been removed. The wars of the Liberian hinterland before the twentieth century were generally small-scale, seasonal, and primarily intended to acquire plunder or slaves. The principal mechanisms of control were religious in nature, making military entrepreneurs subject to the authority of various religious institutions. Only exceptional individuals, outsiders like Samory Touré, could escape these controls. The contrast between that situation

---

[128] Warren L. D'Azevedo, 'Gola Womanhood and the Limits of Masculine Omnipotence' in Thomas D. Blakeley, Walter E.A. van Beek and Dennis L. Thomson (eds), *Religion in Africa,* London and Portsmouth, NH, 1994, p.361, n. 9; cf. Moran, 'Warriors or Soldiers?'

[129] Bellman, *Language of Secrecy,* p.111.

[130] Steve Weizman, 'Into Battle with Guns and Magic', *Guardian,* 14 July 1994.

[131] Cf. Schwab, *Tribes,* pp.232-4.

and the events of the 1990s suggests the value of examining the ritual control of violence during the civil war, or rather the lack of such control, if we are to understand why the war happened in the way it did.

At the beginning of the war, the NPFL showed itself intent on acquiring some religious support by drafting in all manner of ritual experts. There was no need for them to be at all traditional or even to be Liberian. When asked why people had to be imported from Côte d'Ivoire and other parts of West Africa to innoculate fighters against bullets and supply them with other war medicine, when there were plenty of Liberian *zoes* available to do the job, a senior aide to Charles Taylor replied that this was because the young NPFL fighters had no confidence in the ability of their local *zoes*, old men from their own towns and villages for whom they had little respect.[132] Although almost all the fighters believed that it was possible to obtain spiritual medicine which would make them invulnerable to bullets and successful in battle, they were at the same time contemptuous of those individuals who, according to the traditional values of their home areas, should have been able to provide them with this. We have noted that throughout recent decades, under pressure from the government and the churches, Poro and similar traditional authorities have lost power as control of political life passed into the hands of officials appointed by the state. At the same time, many of the powers and privileges of the traditional secret societies, including the perceived ability to acquire spiritual power through sacrifice, were effectively privatised. Human sacrifice was practised no longer by *zoes* but by heartmen, freelance vendors of human body parts, for the use of individual clients. One consequence, which became clear during the war, was that many young people have ceased to believe that traditional secret societies and their officials can make war medicine, a skill which is thought to require great power. On the other hand, the same young fighters still believe as strongly as ever in the possibility of such spiritual power: what was lacking during the war was a ready source. This was the reason for bringing in foreign experts, who supposedly had access to exotic forms of power.

Only the most exceptional *zoes* were regarded by the irreverent young NPFL fighters as having really impressive power. A good illustration is the case of Singbe, who was a *zo* living before the war near Mount Gibi in Margibi County, a place with a national reputation as a centre of spiritual power, and possibly the place

[132] Author's interview with John T. Richardson, Monrovia, 8 April 1997.

of residence of the *zoes* whom the government had once attempted to establish as the central administrators for all Liberian Poro societies.[133] To judge from descriptions, Singbe was probably a polio victim whose physical deformity added to his mystique, since garbled reports of his powers may have led people who had never seen him, but only heard of him, to assume that he was a dwarf, regarded as a particularly powerful being. One later newspaper article described him as 'the mysterious handicapped CO Singbe' who 'emerged in the early days of the Liberian war'.[134] Mount Gibi was said to be guarded by strange animals and dwarfs, and its summit could be approached only by senior *zoes*. The NPFL forces who first arrived in this area in 1990 regarded the mountain with trepidation, but some young fighters, being contemptuous of traditional *zoes*, ventured onto its slopes anyway. They did not return, allegedly because of the mysterious powers wielded by Singbe. The 'much talked about' Singbe was able to organise a local militia to fight against the NPFL by means of 'magical military operations'.[135] The most fantastic reports of his powers circulated. He was said to be able to tie people up from long distance and to be invulnerable to bullets. Reports of his exploits even reached the press in Sierra Leone, where one Freetown newspaper described him as 'a powerful spiritual dwarf', capable of killing eighteen NPFL fighters in one attack.[136] Charles Taylor, impressed by such reports, promptly persuaded Singbe to accept a post as an NPFL general and put a pick-up truck at his disposal, which greatly enhanced Singbe's mobility, adding to the stories of his amazing powers. He is reported to have died in 1992 during a skirmish with Ulimo.[137] There were many other reports of fighters using spiritual forces on a major scale, such as when the NPFL's advance into Grand Gedeh in 1990 was stopped by a river in flood. The AFL defenders of the area, many of them Krahn, were widely held to have achieved this with the use of 'African science'. However, the secret of how the AFL had achieved this is said to have been treacherously revealed to the NPFL by Oldman Toe, a prominent traditional priest who had held a grudge against Samuel Doe since

133 Above, p.250.

134 *Bassa Voice* (Monrovia), 6 February 1997.

135 *The News,* 28 April 1992, which also contains a picture of Singbe.

136 *The National* (Freetown), 11 April 1991.

137 Letter from Bart Witteveen to the author, 15 September 1997.

1981, when his son, the youngest member of the PRC junta to have taken power with Doe, had been executed.[138]

Fighters in every militia, while often being unimpressed by traditional priests other than the most prestigious ones like Singbe and Oldman Toe, needed power to help them win military victories. They had been brought up in a society in which power, by nature invisible, was expressed in an idiom of eating. They had been led to believe that the eating of human hearts and drinking of human blood could endow power, since the spiritual essence of the victim was imparted to the eaters, a principle in regular practice through the use of animal sacrifices. Thus, the fact that fighters ate human flesh on many occasions during the war, was not a consequence of physical hunger so much as a means of intimidating their enemies and acquiring the power to win victories, an idea clearly derived from older rituals of sacrifice. Some people assert that fighters were encouraged to carry out such practices by their ritual specialists, while others may have simply improvised their behaviour on the basis of a received belief that this would make them powerful. They often referred to the human heart using mechanical images, calling it 'the engine' or 'the main machine'. During the third battle of Monrovia on 6 April 1996, one Liberian newspaper wrote, 'our reporters on both sides saw fighters engaging in cannibalism and sorcery. In some instances, the fighters would kill and butcher the chest and extract the heart and later eat it. According to the fighters, "to eat the heart of a strong man at the front makes us strong too".'[139] Even the usually cautious US State Department was moved to observe that 'Fighters – whether AFL, LPC or one of the ULIMO sub-factions – also targeted their enemies, fighters and civilians alike, removed their victims' body parts and ate them in front of civilians.'[140]

Interviewed in April 1996 by Liberian journalists who asked them about such activities, some fighters 'confirmed that the war was being fought by "men" and not "boys", meaning that sorcery was used'.[141] This is an interesting juxtaposition of ideas since it implies that, for the fighters, the manipulation of spiritual power, including through eating human flesh, was not only likely to give them a greater chance of success but was also one of the signs

[138] Youboty, *Liberian Civil War*, pp.342-3.
[139] Throble Suah, 'In Pursuit of One Man', *The Inquirer*, April-July 1996, pp.2-4.
[140] US Department of State, *Liberia Country Report on Human Rights Practices for 1996*, Washington, DC, 1997.
[141] Suah, 'In Pursuit of One Man', *The Inquirer*, April-July 1996, pp.2-4.

of adulthood. Since many of the fighters were young, often barely teenagers, it suggests that they regarded the battle as tantamount to an initiation into adult life, as no doubt many teenagers would, all over the world, if they were required to fight in a war. It is not particularly surprising to learn that adolescent boys consider that to have fought and killed makes them into real men. It is, however, illuminating to discover that they believe the use of esoteric techniques including the consumption of human flesh, to be a part of this transition. This is certainly not a universal human belief but does have a grounding in Liberian history.

Nor was it just teenage fighters who held the idea that they could have access to spiritual power through the consumption of human flesh, or at least by a ritual use of human body parts. Even Christian ministers may be suspected of engaging in such practices, as was the Reverend Jimmie Dugbe, who in 1995 was indicted by a grand jury on suspicion of attempting to kidnap a five-year-old girl to kill her 'as a sacrifice for him to retain his position as General Superintendent of the Assembly of God Mission Church'.[142] Most interesting is the allegation concerning Charles Taylor himself made by his former defence minister, Tom Woewiyu, after he had defected from the NPFL in 1994. 'We saw a lot,' said Woewiyu, describing his time as Taylor's right-hand man, 'including the formation of a group of cannibals called Top 20. Taylor is a member of this group. Human sacrifices, under the direction of his uncle Jensen Taylor, take place in Taylor's house.'[143] A group of sixteen NPFL generals and fourteen Special Force commandos made similar allegations concerning Taylor. They issued a formal statement affirming that 'we...stand in readiness to testify Taylor's ritualistic killings of our peers'.[144] True or not, such claims were widely believed.

The abundant evidence that fighters and others who lived through the war believed that power might be obtained from spiritual sources, and the observation that their behaviour included elements which are part of traditional religious practices, does not mean that the act of fighting was some sort of cultic behaviour. The main purposes of fighting were to gain wealth and prestige or to take revenge. But in order to achieve these goals, power

[142] Taryunon Nyenon and Gibson Jerue, 'Rev. Dugbe Ordered Detained', *The Inquirer*, 5, 32 (1 March 1995).

[143] Interview with anonymous source [later revealed as Tom Woewiyu], 'Jackson Doe's Death', *New Democrat*, 1, 30 (23-29 June 1994).

[144] Statement dated 16 November 1995, copy of original document, in 'Taylor's Generals Drop Arms', *New Democrat*, 2, 167 (30 November-5 December 1995), p.4.

was necessary, and it was here that some fighters had recourse
to what they believed to be sure techniques, such as acquiring
the strength of others through eating their vital organs or drinking
their blood. During the war the practice was vulgarised to the
extent that what had once been an esoteric practice performed
by officers of elite sodalities with deep roots in society, now became
the standby of adolescents drunk on cane juice or high on amphetamines and marijuana. All that they required was a gun.

At this point it may be helpful to summarise the argument so
far. Both the more exclusive traditional secret societies in Liberia,
and more widespread institutions like Poro, employ an idiom of
eating. According to some older accounts, Poro, human leopards
and some other secret societies actually made use of human sacrifice
in their initiation rites in the past. A sceptic might argue that
this cannot be proved since there are few reliable accounts from
before the mid-twentieth century, and hence, the idea of eating
parts of a sacrificial human victim could be no more than a
metaphor. That seems unlikely to this author, since the weight
of evidence suggests that human flesh really was eaten in some
religious rituals, as well as in war, before the twentieth century.
This may be debated. What can be demonstrated more convincingly, however, is that during the twentieth century, a process
occurred by which the institutions and political culture of the
Liberian republic and those of various rural secret societies were
assimilated by one another, as the power of the central government
penetrated the hinterland and vice versa, as people of rural origin
penetrated the institutions of national power, culminating in the
overthrow of the True Whig government by Samuel Doe and his
colleagues in 1980. In this process, the earlier constitutions of
both the republican institutions and the secret societies were eroded
from within. In both cases there was a tendency for the institutional
checks and balances which prevented the abuse of power to fall
into decay. What was subverted was not just the legal constitution
of the Republic of Liberia, but also the spiritual constitution of
the secret societies, Islam and the churches alike. Power, whether
local or national, was increasingly unregulated other than by factional intrigue.

One consequence of the centralisation of power and of its con-
testation by intense factional manoeuvre was an inflation in the
vocabulary by which power was expressed and understood, including that of sacrifice and eating. The practice of human sacrifice
was taken out of the hands of officials of traditional secret societies

and used by heartmen, independent commercial entrepreneurs who obtained human organs and sold them for monetary gain to those who believed that they could acquire wealth and power by their ritual use and even consumption. In fact, it was privatised.

Human sacrifice, including the eating of sacrificial flesh, appears to have occurred in national politics with increasing frequency from the mid-twentieth century. Related practices certainly took place during the war of 1989-97. It is emphatically not the argument here that such beliefs caused the war. It could be better said that the war occurred because the way in which the Liberian republic had evolved had left many people with acute feelings of political and economic frustration, and a conjuncture of circumstances, including such factors as the policy of foreign states, produced a context in which war could occur. Many Liberians hungered for power to rectify their situation. And since hunger for power was commonly represented as being capable of fulfilment by the consumption of the vital organs of others, combatants in the war have on occasion had recourse to this practice in a literal, not a metaphorical, form.

No doubt there were many fighters in the war who never took part in such sacrifices. It could be argued that, even if this practice did occur during the war, it remained a marginal one and therefore that too much importance should not be placed on it. The point of the argument in this book, however, is that studying evidence of religious change in Liberia for clues as to the changing distribution of power, so often perceived to stem from the invisible world, helps us to determine why the Liberian war happened in the way it did.

The psychology of transformation

Not surprisingly, many former fighters who have carried out such atrocious actions admit to having troubling dreams. Some display obsessive behaviour, like the ex-fighter who shaved her head because of her shame at having killed a woman and her baby, or the one who, having gone insane with the guilt of participating in the murder of his own father, simply killed chickens for no reason.[145] In one rehabilitation centre a former fighter with the AFL said in 1992: 'I dream about all the people I killed. The ones I saw face to face just before I killed them. I dreamed I saw them all in a room, sitting round a table. There are 43 of

---

[145] Personal communication by church source, Yekepa, 24 December 1997.

them. I am there too. But nobody is talking. Nothing happens, and nobody talks'. Another former child soldier said the ghosts he saw 'are all wearing white gowns, and white hats', but he couldn't see their faces because they were white too.[146] The dreams of ex-fighters are of particular interest because of the great importance attached to dreams in Liberia and indeed throughout Africa, where they are commonly believed to be, not a purely subjective phenomenon, nor the product of the unconscious, as in Freudian psychology, but messages from a spirit world which has a real and objective existence.

It is not possible to say how far a small sample of individual dreams is representative of those of a wider community, but it is nonetheless instructive to study the contents of combatants' or ex-combatants' dreams where they have been recorded. Some people troubled by disturbing dreams of the war proclaim themselves to have found solace by being reborn in Christ. This is an interesting idea since rebirth in Christ both promises a new life and also echoes traditional ideas of rebirth, such as when boys are 'eaten' by the Bush Devil on being initiated into the Poro society. An interesting case is that of Mohammed Fofanah, the thirty-two-year-old son of the imam of a leading Monrovia mosque, who converted to Christianity and changed his name to Christian Fofanah because of a dream in which he had seen the Koran burning his hands. During the war, using the war-name Gorbachev, Fofanah had killed a large number of people while fighting, first for the AFL, and later for Ulimo-K. He had become an alcoholic and a chain smoker. He believed that by being born again in Christ he could overcome these traumas.[147] A similar conversion is that of the well-known LPC fighter Joshua Milton Blahyi, better known as General Butt Naked, who led a brigade which fought naked in the belief that this would protect them against bullets. During the momentous battle of Monrovia in April 1996, in which he played a leading role, Blahyi underwent a profound religious experience which he believed was tantamount to being born again in Christ. Later he travelled to Israel, and returned to establish his own Christian ministry in a popular area of Monrovia. Similarly, the former military chief of the LPC, Ruth 'Attila' Milton, told the congregation at the Second Providence Baptist church in Monrovia in 1997 that she too had been born again in Christ. God

---

[146] Mark Huband, 'Ghosts of Civil War Haunt Liberia's Child Soldiers', *Guardian*, 13 April 1992.

[147] J. Adasco Bundor, 'Imam's Son Embraces Christ', *Concord Times*, 1, 10 (20-22 December 1995).

had saved her life in the war when she had been surrounded by NPFL fighters, she told them. She fell asleep, 'and had a dream in which she was advised not to be scared and that her life would be saved'. She had thrown away her amulets and was now born again in Christ.[148]

It appears that Christian teaching is particularly attractive to any ex-fighter who wishes to make a radical break with his or her past, perhaps because of the Christian belief that the Holy Spirit is universal in nature and can enter anybody to provide instant transformation. One eleven-year-old former fighter, for example, having been 'born again' in Christ, said he had 'taken an oath never to kill again. I'm now a complete born-again Christian and a child of God.'[149] Certainly, a number of former fighters, including such leading figures as Blahyi, Milton and Armah Youlo, claim to have become born-again Christians. It is noteworthy that born-again Christians like Blahyi, reflecting on the awful experience of the war, are attracted by the Christian belief that all evil is the work of the Devil. This enables them to consign the actions they themselves took during the war, now considered evil in the light of their new Christian faith, to the work of another self, the one who 'died' when they were born again in Christ. That old self, they now believe, was actually an agent of Satan. Looking back, some of these converts are appalled by the actions which they took in their earlier life. Blahyi, for example, claims to have taken part in his first human sacrifice at the age of eleven, and to have repeated it every new moon for the next fourteen years. While he was a fighter with the LPC, he recalls, 'for us, killing became a form of fun. I met Satan regularly and talked to him.' He concludes that 'the devil is alive. [His power] works. People all over the world should pray for Liberia.'[150] There are no known examples of people converting to Islam for comparable reasons, and further research would be required to investigate whether Muslim theology has played a role similar to that of Christianity in providing succour to former fighters. Some Liberian Christians express scepticism concerning certain claims of rebirth in Christ, such as in the case of the former minister Oscar Quiah, who placed an advert in a newspaper claiming that he was now born

[148] *National Chronicle,* 20 February 1997.

[149] Charles Osagie-Usman, 'Mission of Revenge', *West Africa,* 3984 (7 February 1994), p.205.

[150] Interview by Joshua M. Blahyi with Ross Herbert of the South African *Star* newspaper. I am grateful to Ross Herbert for making the notes of this interview available in a letter dated 1 September 1997.

again in Christ, asserting that 'for seven years, Liberia was overtaken by demonic spirits'.[151]

There may well be a substantial number of charlatans, opportunists or misfits who claim to be born again, or who set up businesses as prophets and preachers, but this does not detract from the earnestness with which many Liberians who have suffered trauma as victims, as perpetrators, or as both, are now searching for spiritual order and healing. As Harley noted of Mano religion, traditional Liberian religious thought is intensely logical in the sense that 'it is almost a part of [Mano] religion to demand a cause for every effect'.[152] Many people, according to this standard, tend to see in the horror of the war evidence of profound disorder in the spirit world. Consequently, the prime task both for their personal well-being as well as for that of society at large is to re-establish some sort of order in the spirit world. Because of this conviction that the spirit world is the real locus of power, and in that sense the material world is merely a reflection of these deeper forces, the discourses of various preachers and healers and their clients can be read as a commentary on the history of Liberia in the twentieth century. There is broad agreement among Liberian religious thinkers that the occurrence of the war is *prima facie* evidence of grave spiritual disorder. Other than this, there is little agreement. Various people have their own analysis and their own opinions as to how to solve Liberia's spiritual crisis. Generally speaking, the range of opinions may be roughly divided into two sorts: there are those who advocate a return to tradition on the grounds that ancestral customs which once gave order and stability to rural society have been devalued and abandoned, and there are those who argue the opposite, namely that the use or abuse of religious tradition was one of the root causes of the war.

Concerning the first group, that is of people who argue the necessity of a return to tradition, we may cite the case of an acting chief of the Kissi who lamented that 'there was a time when we sent our children to the [Poro] bush, where they learned to respect their elders. With the war, we cannot send our children to the bush. [...] We have no jails for our bad children. We have no forest where we can send bad children. We have to live with them.'[153] He was clearly implying that the existence of a generation of wild and uncontrollable youngsters was the consequence of a lack of

[151] Advert in *The Inquirer,* 29 January 1997.

[152] Harley, *Native African Medicine,* p.15.

[153] Quoted in Jeffrey Goldberg, 'A War Without Purpose in a Country Without Identity', *New York Times Magazine,* 22 January 1995, p.39.

traditional education through initiation into a bush school. A former vice-president of Liberia, Peter Naigow, agreed that the rebuilding of society would require a mobilisation of traditional leaders, among others. 'We must get the *zoes*, the chiefs, the church people, and everybody involved at the village, town, district and clan levels.'[154] Kekura Kpoto, a leading politician and senior member of the Poro, in 1995 organised a mass sacrifice to the ancestors, featuring seven cows, fifty bags of rice, and soup. Five thousand people participated in the event in a Monrovia sports stadium. The food was distributed to displaced people. The event was condemned by some Christians, but generally applauded by Muslims.[155] Kpoto is also known to have canvassed support for the launch of a political party based on membership of Poro. There is no doubt that there has been a distinct revival of Poro in some rural areas since the war, mainly as a result of the absence of central government. For example, the paramount chiefs and elders of ten districts in Lofa County, appealing for peace between Ulimo-K and the LDF in 1995, the latter a militia closely connected to the Poro, warned that 'anyone who does not comply...will be declared an enemy of the people of Lofa, and we the chiefs and elders of Lofa County will ensure that he faces the full weight of our traditional rules', this last being a clear threat of capital punishment.[156]

Such attempts to restore traditional religious practices are strenuously opposed by the new generation of Christian evangelicals. In their analysis, the war was caused not by the abandonment of tradition, but, on the contrary, by people diluting the purity of the Christian gospel with ancestral beliefs which they take to be the work of Satan. Born-again Christians pronounce themselves absolutely opposed to all forms of amulets and traditional medicines. Evangelist Amos K. Amoson told his congregation that 'some people in the church are pretending to be true believers, but have medicine under their coats, medicine tied around their waist and are also using human blood to wash their faces.' He added that 'the throat that you cut in the darkness to get the blood out for position or riches, God sees you.'[157] One group of itinerant preachers in Monrovia known as the Street Preachers

---

154 Interview with Dr Peter Naigow, *West Africa*, 3879 (20 January 1992), pp.102-3.

155 *New Democrat*, 2, 125 (6-11 July 1995), p.14.

156 'First Resolution on Resolving the Conflict in Lofa Co.', *The Inquirer*, 5, 81 (16 May 1995), p.8.

157 *The News*, 19-20 March 1997.

specifically takes issue with those who recommend making sacrifices to appease the ancestors and 'who believe the war will end if the ancestors forgive us for our evils'. These sacrifices they regard as simply 'an act of the Devil'.[158] Many pentecostalists like these appear to have a particular regard for the Book of Revelation, and some at least firmly believe that the millennium which it describes is close at hand. This is perhaps understandable for anyone who has lived through Liberia's war.

For Christians like these, the war is a sign that Liberians must choose between God and Satan, and for them this means rejecting all aspects of traditional religion, as was made clear by one preacher who said he had had a vision of the Angel Gabriel who told Liberians that 'God has seen your plight and has delivered you from the demons and devils of war which have roamed your nation since 1979.' Moreover, this divine punishment was because of the use of blood sacrifice, contrary to Christian teaching. The Angel told him that God had allowed 'evil powers to invade our country' because 'when ritualistic killings became a way of life for every ordinary Liberian, God was obliged to withdraw His hand of protection for a while'.[159] There is little information available about developments in Islam during the war. It would be interesting to know, for example, whether the 'purified' Islamic movements which were in evidence in the 1960s and '70s are still growing in popularity. It is clear that, in some parts of the country, young people easily express dislike of all Mandingo,[160] and it is possible that this contributes to a wider suspicion of Islam.

In between the conservatives who call for a return to traditional values, and those Christians who call for a radical rejection of all ancestral beliefs, are the so-called 'healing churches', such as that run by Mother Fanta Turay, a convert from Islam. Worshippers at Mother Turay's church in Monrovia dress in white and make use of exorcism to cast out evil spirits. Mother Turay admits that some people accuse her of 'dealing' or using diabolic powers, which she firmly denies.[161] Such churches are very popular in Monrovia, probably because they devote so much time and energy to spiritual healing, using techniques which people recognise and

[158] Charles Jackson, 'Challenging the Ancestors', *New Democrat*, 2, 12 (11-13 July 1995), p.14.

[159] Amos Bryant, 'A Message for Liberia', *Daily Observer*, 11, 15 (29 December 1995), pp.5-6.

[160] Konneh, 'Indigenous Entrepreneurs', pp.174-5.

[161] Charles Jackson, 'People of the "Holy Ghost" ', *New Democrat*, 1, 2 (10-17 November 1995), p.10.

a spiritual vocabulary which is widely understood. Certainly, healing of the type undertaken by the spiritual churches can be effective, but it can also be worse than useless when carried out by insensitive or unskilled practicioners or simple charlatans. The psychiatrist Dr Grant has complained about the number of patients he has seen who have been victims of incompetent or brutal 'healing' methods by spiritual healers. Some people being treated by self-professed healers were confined for up to six days without food or water and in chains, 'the weight of which would sometimes require a D-8 tractor to lift up', he wrote scathingly.[162]

In general, it is clear that religious beliefs and allegiance are changing at great speed. A worrying new spiritual threat in Monrovia is the snake men who have made their appearance only since the beginning of the war, said to have been introduced by Ecomog soldiers from Nigeria. These appear to have no connection to traditional Liberian snake societies but to be a new import, although it is notable that even eighty years ago, in Sierra Leone there was 'a widespread and old belief among the Mende that certain persons are Boa-men...who kill young children by supernatural means'.[163] The modern snake-men, very often Nigerians, are said to transform themselves into snakes particularly when having sex with women, whom they will first make unconscious and then penetrate in their animal guise. A woman who has had sex with a snake man wakes up unaware of what has happened, but will die soon afterwards. It is possible that this belief is connected with the spread of AIDS, but there is no doubt of the general supposition that Nigeria is a centre of enormous and generally malevolent spiritual power. Nigerian heartmen are popularly rumoured to have kidnapped all of Monrovia's hunchbacks for sacrificial purposes, since it is supposed that their humps contain human fat, of great value for anointing objects which will thereby gain power. It is known that there are some immensely rich Nigerians, some of whom occasionally visit Monrovia in their private aircraft on business, and their wealth is widely assumed, by pentecostalists especially, to be Satanic in origin. Any Liberian who has visited Nigeria risks being suspected of having been initiated into some Satanic sect. The particular power of Satan, in Christian eyes, is his ability to endow people with worldly power and wealth in return for their everlasting souls. Not surprisingly, some born-again Christians suspect Charles Taylor of being a Satanist, like

[162] Edward Snoh Grant, 'Please Stop the "Church Prophets"', *New Democrat*, 1, 9 (3-9 February 1994), p.21.

[163] Migeod, *A View of Sierra Leone*, p.225.

the preacher, a former LPC fighter, who says that 'you see Charles Taylor and you see the Devil in his eyes.'[164]

Central to the experience of those who have undergone profound religious conversions as a result of the war, or the far greater number who consider the causes of the war to be partly religious in nature, is a question concerning the moral value of power. As a result of the changes they have experienced in the twentieth century, Liberians have become uncertain as to the circumstances in which power may be used for morally legitimate purposes, and those in which its use is illegitimate. Lay people are uncertain about this, and, if they look for specialist advice, they are faced with a bewildering variety of often self-proclaimed spiritual experts offering their opinion, and their services, from bishops and imams to heartmen. Whereas Liberians traditionally believe that power from the spiritual world is necessary for life itself, nowadays they must choose from a wide array of spiritual services on offer. Each particular school or variant of religious thought has its own moral implications, which help to form the overall moral climate of Liberian society. Every functioning person must make moral choices, and the more powerful a person is, the more difficult are the choices involving degrees of good and evil she or he must make. If the power of leaders is not to be abused, as it surely has been in Liberia, then society needs to reach some consensus about what constitute common interests, who may represent these, and under what circumstances, if at all, they are justified in taking human life for the greater good of the community. All of these things have become utterly opaque in Liberia as a result of the great confusion which has arisen about the connection between religious worship of various forms and the associated moral values. For example, there are those who consider traditional religious customs like Poro to be good, because they have served Liberian communities for generations in the past and are associated with the ancestors, and there are Christians who consider that such customs are precisely the cause of Liberia's problems. There are Christians who make common cause with Muslims, and other Christians who regard Muslims as dangerous agents of Satan. Many pentecostalists and born-again Christians refer to spiritual healers such as Ma Turay, whose church was described in an earlier paragraph, as 'Sixes', a reference to 666, the mark of the Beast in the Book of Revelation.

Religious debates such as these, then, represent more than just differing views on the correct form of worship, but also differing

164 Confidential interview.

perceptions of morality. Orthodox Christianity and Islam offer
dualistic views, in which good and evil are absolute. A seeker for
truth is encouraged to choose good in place of evil, even if in
practice human beings may fail in their attempts to do this. In
the traditional religious thought of Liberia, there is no absolute
good or evil but, instead, an ambivalent power which is given
moral meaning through ritual action. Power is a-moral, or rather
it becomes moral only through its application, which may be for
the common good of a community or for personal gain at the
expense of others. In the traditional religious thought of Liberia,
a prime means of acquiring spiritual power is through sacrifice,
a potent means of communication with the invisible world in many
religions. Sacrifices need to be made regularly to secure access
to power which can be used for social or antisocial purposes depend-
ing on circumstances. Power itself is morally neutral but is not
to be acquired lightly. To achieve great power in a secret society,
initiates in the past are said to have been required to sacrifice
their own child, the closest one can approach to self-sacrifice
without actually perishing. However repulsive this might seem to
a modern reader, the practice has an undeniable logic: the access
to great power offered by membership of a powerful secret society
cannot be undertaken easily or without giving something of oneself
in return, like an entry-fee. Offering a blood relative brings the
initiate closer to the invisible world and ensures that only the
most single-minded people will enter. It was precisely this principle
that was breached during the twentieth century by politicians in
search of instant power who did not offer their own children
but simply bought victims on the market.

What people think of these theological ideas nowadays, particularly in the wake of the civil war, may be glimpsed by the
debates on aspects of traditional belief and morality which figure
in the remarkable essays reflecting on these matters sometimes
published in Liberian newspapers. Several essayists agree that one
of the most shocking aspects of the war has been the disrespect
shown by the fighters to the conventions which have governed
Liberian society in the past. One writer, a certain Benjamin Brown,
begins his essay with a long and graphic account of the stories
told to him as a child of the astonishing powers possessed by
great *zoes* who could make rain fall, could fly at supersonic speed
and make themselves invulnerable to bullets. They can consult
with the dead in their graves and cause trees to blossom or die.
They can even cause a whole village to disappear temporarily to
evade a tax collector. Not all *zoes* have these marvellous abilities,
since some are more powerful than others, Brown tells us. It is

the task of *zoes* to ensure that local government is in safe hands, that chiefs are tough, prudent and far-sighted, and that their wives have sufficient spiritual power to defend themselves against all sorts of intrigue and witchcraft. The author is aware that nearly all his readers will be familiar with such stories, 'things you probably knew before reading this article'. The question Brown then asks is: what happened to all these powerful *zoes* during the war? Villages have been burned and the *zoes* themselves turned out of their houses, brutalised and humiliated. Sande and Poro bushes, 'places that are reservoirs of major tribal secrets' have been ransacked, 'and the secrets dashed on Broad Street for the observation of the uninitiated'. The greatest damage of all is the exposure to public view and to ridicule of the secrets which are at the heart of the esoteric societies. He concludes: 'The Liberia we all own and cherish is perishing. Where are the *zoes*?'[165]

A similar article is written in a more mystical form by a writer who records a dream in which he met one of the 'mythical African dwarfs...the type my grandfather used to tell us about'. The dwarf reveals himself to be a guardian of the forest and the messenger of a high god called DenDen. The dwarf leads him to a meeting of spirits in their traditional visible form of masked dancers. The dreamer notices that everyone in the town is masked. This he finds very strange, for if everyone becomes a masked dancer, who will beat the drum to which the spirits must dance? The dwarf then accuses the dreamer of being a desecrator of the sacred head of DenDen. The dwarf launches a furious tirade against the dreamer, accusing him of being one of the Liberians who have brought war on themselves, defiling religion and all the principles of their ancestors. They have killed the young, the innocent and the weak. But their greatest crime is to have desecrated the sacred deity. Particularly shocking was the public display of secrets by mere boys:[166]

Your fighters donned our sacred masks and comically displayed our hidden secrets for all uninitiates to see. At God Bless You gate, your fighters placed the masked head of DenDen upon a pole beside a decayed skull! From that day you killed all of the masked devils. No more are we revered. Because of you, we can no longer dwell among humanfolk but must linger in the ethereal world in the Forest of DenDen, doomed to ignominy.

[165] Benjamin T. Brown, 'Liberia Perishes. Where are the Zoes?', *Heritage,* 17-24 December 1996, p.8.

[166] M.V. Passewe, 'The Dream', *The News,* 8-9 January 1997.

Who will beat the *sangba* when masked devils play? Who will ever revere DenDen when the dust of your senseless war settles?

Because of these outrages, the dwarf concludes, the spirits have decided to wage war on the people. However, because the spirits are benevolent and do not bear grudges, they will refrain from attacking the people and simply leave them to their fate, unless Liberians cease their war. The alternative is spelled out plainly:

If the war doesn't stop, your people will become the servants of their neighbouring brothers. Your wives will tote water and break wood for bread forever in distant homelands. And your children will become merchants of war for bread alone!

The meaning of the two texts is plain. The great sacrilege of the war is to have exposed the secrets of the masking societies to public view, as a result of which the spirits are unable to take visible form and to operate for the benefit of Liberia, whose fate will be subjugation by others and war carried out purely for loot, with no further aim.

What is perhaps most difficult to grasp in these essays is the significance attached to secrecy and unmasking. It is useful in this regard to consider a penetrating essay by Elias Canetti on the great significance for human societies of what he calls 'transformation'. As he notes, it is 'the talent for transformation which has given man so much power over all other creatures', but which is also 'one of the great mysteries'.[167] Humans are intensely conscious of their powers of transformation as they progress through life from one stage or condition to another, from childhood to adulthood and death. All human beings and all human societies have the ability to transform in some respect or other, even if it is only the fundamental human trait of adopting different moods or assuming different aspects of the infinite variety of a human personality, or the transformation from birth, through childhood and puberty, to adulthood and inevitable death.

Liberians generally believe that a great many types of transformation are possible. People may transform themselves into spirits, for example during sleep. They may also transform themselves into animals, as the Human Leopards do. A person may be possessed by the spirit of another person, or that of a devil, and supposedly be transformed into that other person. Unlikely

---

[167] Canetti, *Crowds and Power*, p.389. The following is based on his arguments on pp. 389-445.

as all of these may sound, the evidence suggests that many Liberians believe them all to be possible.

Since transformation of one sort or another is so important to all human existence, the prohibitions placed upon it are one of the main constituents of any social and religious order. No hierarchy can be maintained without prohibitions which regulate the movement of members from one class to another, and which prevent members of a lower class from believing themselves equal or related to members of a higher class. Hence, all hierarchies arrange forms of initiation for people passing from one class or category to another, and it is quite commonplace to consider – as in Poro – that a person 'dies' in one class to be reborn in another. In Liberia, these initiations are traditionally carried out through religion, which also inculcates a deeply internalised discipline.

Of all the many formal systems used by human societies to educate children and to define individual character, religion is one of the most important. This is certainly the case in Liberia. A useful point here is that made by the philosopher Michel Foucault in his studies on the relationship between the discipline exercised by individuals to define and control their own personality, which he calls 'techniques of the self', and the formation of political regimes. In investigating the manner in which specific political systems have functioned, Foucault writes of a quality which he calls 'governmentality', defined as 'the meeting-point between the techniques of domination exercised over others and techniques of the self'.[168] If governmentality is produced, as Foucault suggests, by the meeting of these different forms of discipline – those imposed from within, and those imposed from without – then it becomes clearer how specific notions of the ways in which humans can transform themselves spiritually, psychologically and socially acquire a political meaning. If we apply this insight to Liberia, it is apparent that, in a country with a tradition of stateless societies, religious institutions like Poro have been particularly important since they fulfil crucial social and political roles for a whole community by instilling certain values in initiates during their period in the bush. Only in the twentieth century did hinterland societies come under the authority of a continuous form of political organisation in the shape of the republican state of Liberia which, as we have seen, actually upheld its rule with a highly coercive regime of clientelism. This has been instrumental in forming Liberia's governmentality.

[168] Michel Foucault, *Dits et Ecrits, 1954-1988,* 4 vols, Paris, 1994, IV, p.785.

As Canetti points out, the two best articulated forms of power known to the older human civilisations are differentiated by their contrasting relationships with transformation: one is the power of the master-transformer, who can assume any shape at will, whether that of an animal or that of the spirit of a dead person, such as the trickster who is so prominent in West African folklore and whose power depends on the many shapes he can assume. He assumes real power as a shaman who may summon spirits, who may communicate with them, or who may fly like a bird, without changing his physical location. Powerful *zoes* are presumed to have such powers. The second type is the precise opposite of the shaman. It is the static figure of the divine king, to whom all self-transformation is forbidden since he is a fount of commands which transform others. This second type of power has had a decisive influence on the modern conception of power as an entity as nearly as possible fixed and static, which itself does not transform but may regulate the transformation of others.[169]

In many respects the Bush Devil of the Poro or the *bodio* among the Grebo and Kru resemble the figure of the divine king.[170] The Bush Devil is always the same, since his mask is unchanging and shows only a fixed expression. The Bush Devil itself does not age or die although, we may note, it can survive only if it is fed with blood from sacrifices, usually of animals. At the same time, the masked Bush Devil is the fount of commands which may transform others. It turns boys into men and girls into women. The Bush Devil and its counsellors may also be the source of medicines which can allow hunters and warriors to transform, to turn themselves into animals to escape their enemies or hunt their prey. The Bush Devil can supply medicines which transform bullets into water. But behind the mask of the Bush Devil there is a dangerous mystery since the identity of the being behind it cannot be seen. So, while the mask always covers a dangerous and unknown power, it is itself a precisely known quantity. When the mask is worn during ceremonies, it can be reassuring since if one behaves in a familiar and recognised manner in a planned ritual, the reaction of the masked figure can be predicted. Once the correct attitude to the mask has been learned, it acts as a protector against the dangerous power contained within itself.

The act of exposing the masks of secret societies to public ridicule, as happened in the war, is thus tantamount to destroying

169 Canetti, *Crowds and Power*, p.442.
170 Martin, 'Dual Legacy', p.16.

the possibility of communication with the spirits since it is impossible for them to assume visible form, as they do by entering a mask. It also makes the masks useless as ritual objects; they become simply pieces of carved wood. They are no longer able to act as a guarantor of social transformations. Once the Bush Devil has been unmasked, he can no longer serve to keep people in their proper places in society, to prevent individuals from transforming in ways which are dangerous to others and to ensure orderly progress from one phase of life to another, such as from childhood to adulthood. This is a disturbing prospect when it is the mainstay of social order. According to the dream of DenDen, the fate for Liberia if it does not cease war is to be enslaved and to know war as a brutal search for bread alone.

One of the most common ways in which outsiders have considered the history of Africa during the twentieth century is as a contrast between tradition and modernity, two terms in need of greater clarification if they are to have much explanatory power. Earlier generations of foreigners were inclined to believe that tradition in Africa was unchanging, a point of view which can no longer be seriously held. Tradition, it has been noted, is more a mode of considering historical change than an actual corpus of knowledge. Quite what modernity means is a subject on which numerous books have been written, but in Liberian history it could be said to include the experience of the submission of rural communities to a national government making use of bureaucratic techniques of organisation, the spread of a money economy, the weakening of the authority of elders within lineages, the growth of cities, enhanced possibilities of long-distance communication, and the influence of the universal religious ideas of Islam and Christianity.

Most studies have, in the conventional Western idiom, considered these processes of change in terms of economic and political development. Many Liberians, including the leading figures in the war, seem to believe rather that the specific political and economic arrangements made by human beings are subject to the will of God or other denizens of an invisible world. The power of the invisible world can be obtained by humans in a process of negotiation, for example by priests or other officials using rituals. This aspect of negotiation, precisely because it is visible, provides a medium for the study of religious ideas. During the twentieth century, the access to this power by small communities, officiated by priests, oracles or *zoes* with local roots, regulated by custom, was privatised as wealthy politicians and businessmen simply bought their way into the system as a way of enhancing their power over Liberia.

The exhibition of great power is widely taken as a sign that a person has been privileged by the spirit world, and, in these circumstances, it is perhaps comprehensible that 75 per cent of Liberian voters should have considered Charles Taylor as the obvious choice as President of the Republic in July 1997. Perhaps it was true, as he insistently claimed, that God intended him to be President of Liberia. In any event, voters appear to have made their choice for him less out of any sentimental affection, and certainly not out of naivety, but largely out of a recognition that he was powerful.[171]

---

[171] Elizabeth Ohene, 'Chosen by God?', *Focus on Africa*, 8, 4 (1997), pp.21-4.

7

FALSE PROPHETS

*Beware of false prophets, which come to you in sheep's clothing, but
inwardly they are ravening wolves.*   (Matthew VII:15)

Politicians

'Shut your mouth! I don't want to hear anything about your
politicians and their revolutions,' replied an old man in a refugee
camp when he was asked his opinions on politics. 'It's your
politicians and their politics that bring us into exile today. What
good have we poor illiterate people got from your big book and
politics? Is it not only death and hardship?'[1]
   This seems to be a point of view widely held, especially by
Liberians old enough to remember the coup of 1980 and the
promises which various politicians made about the liberation of
the country people of Liberia. For there is a remarkable continuity
between the leading actors of those years and those of the civil
war, when some politicians became warlords or managers working
with various armed factions, while others worked with Ecomog,
effectively fronting for Nigerian interests. 'Most of the players in
the civil war were also actively involved in the pre-coup "reform
years" [1971-80],' one Liberian writer has noted, 'and so the war
is in many ways a continuation of the power struggles among
the political elites that began then. Doe was the only new major
national politician to rise to prominence in the post-coup period.
All others belonged to political networks that had been established
during the Tolbert regime.'[2] In terms of the elite actors, then,
Liberia's civil war resembled nothing so much as the continuation
of party politics by other means, with a remarkable lack of new
ideas or new personalities emerging from the turmoil.

---

[1] Sherman Seequeh, 'Our Political Crisis: revolutions or holocaust?' *Heritage*, 5-12
November 1996, p.9.
[2] Jarrett, 'Civil War', pp.39-40.

Some of the politicians and technocrats who rose to national prominence in the 1970s and who have proved so durable are no doubt decent enough people in some respects, but their choice of career dictates that they must always be as close as possible to the centre of power. This applies even if they are working in the private sector or with a non-governmental organisation. The role of the state in Liberian public life is such that anyone who has chosen a living as a politician or senior manager (careers dominated by 'book men'), is likely to depend largely on the quality of their contacts in government if they are to prosper or even survive. This requires continued occupation of at least a corner of the political field, which in turn necessitates having a talent for the factional manoeuvre which is the very stuff of Liberian politics. The upper levels of the Liberian state, as of many African states, are composed of personal networks formed by people such as these. One critic, even before the war, noted:[3]

> Our country is infested with scores of marauders, fix it men and women and gravy-seekers of all seasons. These mercenaries have no principles: they are prepared to 'sing the praises' of any regime that will give them unbridled access to the public coffers. [...] These highway robbers used so-called 'patriotism and being apolitical technocrats' as a facade to plunder the national treasury.

Some of the most 'heartless and conscienceless opportunists,' he went on to say, were former 'so-called "progressives and agents of change" '. This is a reference to the progressive politicians who in the 1970s, when they were campaigning against President Tolbert and the True Whig Party, liked to wear African shirts and sandals made from rubber car-tyres to demonstrate their solidarity with the poor. 'Strangely,' another critic wrote, 'when these supposedly "ethnically dressed" PA[L] officials assumed their respective positions in the new government, they disposed of these attires. They were replaced with Western styled designer suits.'[4] He might have added that many of the progressives sported military fatigues in between their African shirt period and their designer suits phase. The soldiers of the PRC – soon dubbed People Repeating Corruption by the Monrovia rumour mill – were also quick to adopt expensive Western suits. 'They became vicious in their pursuit

---

[3] George Klay Kieh, Jr, quoted in Kappel and Korte, *Human Rights Violations*, p.155.

[4] Dolo, *Democracy Versus Dictatorship*, p.57.

of those things that Traditional African Politics (Liberian version) bestows upon its patrons: wine, wealth, women and weapons.'[5] There can be little doubting the strength of the popular contempt for politicians. But, inglorious though their record is, it would be both unfair and superficial to attribute the horrors of the civil war solely to the greed or selfishness of an elite, since the attitudes of politicians are not totally disconnected from those of other Liberians, and the venality which politicians bring to their unending search for position is no more than a reflection of a popular attitude which expects patrons to provide money and jobs for their clients lower down the social scale. An exiled Liberian points out that 'former public officials or civil servants who do not have booties [sic] to show for their period of service are ridiculed and decried as failures. They are scorned and bad mouthed, simply because they failed to do the "cultural thing": to exploit the public coffers.'[6] Many other writers echo the theme that, since the entire society expects to receive largesse from a president or other patron, this will inevitably lead even politicians of good character into corruption. 'If even the Angel Gabriel became president of Liberia, he would within five years – or less – become totally and irrevocably corrupted,' wrote the late Henry Andrews, one of the very few former ministers to be widely respected for his integrity.[7]

According to Amos Sawyer, also a leading politician, most of the defects of Liberia's government originated in the way the Republic of Liberia was constituted a century and more ago. 'The idea of Liberia was flawed in conception, design and implementation,' he writes. 'The ethos of this nation is rooted in the psychological defense and compensatory mechanisms which its architects created and zealously fostered, in order to come to terms with the violence done to their self-esteem in racist America...and on the other hand with the survival imperatives on a new frontier'. According to Sawyer, these origins caused the Liberian elite before 1980 to behave with the utmost arrogance, instilling a deep inferiority complex in Liberians of non-settler origin.[8] It is certainly the case that the ruling oligarchy of settler families for well over a century regarded indigenous Liberians from a position of

---

[5] *Ibid.*, p.58.

[6] *Ibid.*, p.12.

[7] Andrews, *Cry, Liberia, Cry!*, p.70.

[8] Amos Sawyer, quoted in Bill Frank Enoanyi, 'A New Beginning', *Heritage*, 24-29 October 1996.

superiority and with a contempt which, if anything, increased over the years. They expected country people to become *kwi* ('civilised') by speaking English, getting an education, becoming Christian and adopting American consumption patterns.

While it is no doubt accurate to assert that the arrogance of Liberia's ruling elite was connected to the foreign origin of the settlers who dominated the country's government for so long, and to their assumption that they possessed a superior culture, this alone hardly explains all the forms of political activity which developed under the rule of the True Whig Party. In understanding the growth of a vast government patronage machine, and the development of a spirit of factionalism allied to an exaggerated cult of the presidency, it is more helpful to consider the way in which the national government based in Monrovia reached a series of accommodations with local potentates in the system of indirect rule. Factional conflicts of a sort which had once been confined to a chief's council of elders became more widespread as the political reach of Monrovia was extended into rural families and lineages, to the point that the civil war itself can legitimately be seen as the greatest and most tragic of all expressions of political factionalism. Throughout the period of True Whig Party rule, country people were able to enhance their social status by attaching themselves to an Americo-Liberian patron and rising in his service. So pervasive was this practice that even before the 1980 coup, the Liberian elite was actually far less ethnically exclusive than has often been supposed. There had been such extensive inter-action, political, social and sexual, between people of settler and 'tribal' origin that the governing elite was already thoroughly in-filtrated by people of country origin who had risen up the greasy pole of patronage, if not to the top position, then at least to the upper reaches. By the same token, many of the progressive politicians and 'book men' who championed the cause of the 'tribal' population before 1980, sporting their African shirts and rubber sandals, were actually people from settler families, like Sawyer, Matthews and Tipoteh, the latter of whom adopted a 'tribal' name in preference to his given name of Rudolf Roberts. In this sense, the style of Liberian government which had evolved by the 1980s was less exclusively the product of settler arrogance than critics such as Amos Sawyer have believed, and may more accurately be seen as the consequence of interaction between settler and country families. The degree to which Americo-Liberian and hinterland political traditions had fused was perhaps difficult to appreciate before 1980, but the subsequent years provide a longer perspective.

There is no doubt that the military coup of 1980 was initially popular among many Liberians, particularly those of 'country' origin who had been victims of discrimination under the True Whig Party. They anticipated favourable treatment from a government led by a genuine country man, Samuel Doe, and staffed by progressive politicians whose rhetoric committed them to improving the lot of the ordinary woman or man. In view of the dismal record of the progressive politicians in government, and the culmination of the 1980s in a terrible war, it is no small wonder that many older Liberians feel such a sense of betrayal, disillusioned by politics and politicians of every sort.

A conflict of generations

Younger Liberians, especially those who have come of age in the war, often have views and attitudes significantly different from those of their elders. One obvious difference is that young Liberians today are generally far less respectful of their elders than would have been thought proper in the past. They also tend to be far more individualist generally, a trait which many Liberians regard with some alarm. 'I believe African communalism is largely dated,' writes Moses Nagbe, a university lecturer and novelist. 'Collectivism has largely fallen victim to individualism. [...] It is has also brought in a lot of sophisticated crimes that seek to place materialistic urge at the podium, emphasising individual glory over community well-being.'[9] When Nagbe was a refugee on the *Bulk Challenge,* a rusty hulk of a ship which for weeks plied the coast of West Africa while it took 4,000 Monrovians to safety in April 1996, he was shocked by the attitude of many of the youngsters on board, with their 'wild music, wild language, wild attitudes'. These were adolescents who had grown up during the war, and who had adopted the trappings of adulthood very early in life. They wanted to own consumer goods, many of them had children of their own already, and they took pleasure in being served instead of serving others. They had no respect for age. They were seekers of instant gratification. Of the people of this age-set on the ship, Nagbe thought 40 per cent were 'agile and uncontrollable', 35 per cent 'agile and fairly controllable', and only 25 per cent 'agile and controllable'.[10]

It would be wrong to suppose that there was ever a time in

[9] Nagbe, *Bulk Challenge,* p.104.

[10] *Ibid.* pp.53-4.

which Liberians were overwhelmingly communal in nature, as older
people like to think when they contemplate the past. But even
taking account of nostalgia, and of the tendency of an older generation to be shocked by the ways of youth, it is clear that the war
created new expectations among the young, as wars often do.
Perhaps the most significant aspect of this change is the tendency
for young Liberians to develop new ideas about the moral ties
they have to others. It is the disrespect for age shown by youth
today which so often shocks older Liberians, and the combination
of this lack of respect with the pursuit of material success which
is traditionally regarded as one of the proper attributes of age.
Young people like those whom Moses Nagbe saw on the *Bulk
Challenge* – the boys in their basketball boots and dark glasses, the
girls in jeans – are now to be found all over Liberia. They believe
that they can acquire the good things in life through aggressiveness
but, above all, by a good fortune which has its origin in the invisible
world. They seek to acquire what Liberians call 'power', not power
in the conventional political sense, but the ability to prosper, from
which all else will follow.

One Liberian politician noted during the war how warlords
had become role models for young people. Such leaders, he wrote,
are 'encased in an aura of glamour which may be likened to
the modern-day "jet-set" '. A warlord was 'glorified and popularised,
and given respectability and acceptability bordering on worship
by the masses'. The warlords who constituted such formidable
models of political entrepreneurship were emulated by young
Liberians, he claimed. 'This "rags-to-riches" fairy tale is a Liberian
(and African) reality; this recognition and glorification, and this
romanticism of a "rebel leader", a "warlord", transmit powerfully
convincing socio-political and economic signals to our young men
and women, the less informed, the under-privileged, and the dis-
advantaged.'[11] These are perceptive remarks, although it is rather
ironic that they come from the pen of Bai Gbala, himself a notorious
accomplice of warlords: in his student days in America an associate
of Charles Taylor, and later a leading supporter of Samuel Doe.

The regard for material success which writers such as these
identify in young Liberians, especially those who have been fighters
themselves, combined with a refusal to be subject to their elders,
has clear historical antecedents in the perennial quest by the young
to rise in status in societies where authority is associated with age.
Young men in every generation in Liberia have struggled to acquire

[11] Bai M. Gbala, 'The Legacy of a Rebel Leader', *New Democrat Weekly Review*, 1,
2 (10-17 November 1995).

the wealth needed to marry and start a family, thus beginning
the social ascent towards becoming elders themselves. The growth
of the economy in the boom years of the 1950s and '60s, resulting
in a 'sizeable transfer of labour from the subsistence sector to
the concessions',[12] marked a modest social revolution as young
men, and even women, were able to obtain salaried employment
and to gain some financial independence from their elders. These
conditions turned out to be unsustainable, as salaried employment
became scarcer in the conditions of the late 1970s and 1980s.
The first wave of fighters which attacked Monrovia in July 1990
was dominated by young men and women from rural Nimba County
who demonstrated a very ambiguous attitude towards the city and
its wealth. While they castigated their fellow country people for
living in the city and being seduced by its soft ways, and while
they punished mercilessly those they considered corrupt, at the
same time the fighters were anxious to gorge themselves with
plunder. Many a fighter 'took up arms to get his or her share
of the national pie by force', in the words of one Liberian author.[13]
Combatants also sought social prestige, as another observer recognised when he wrote that 'the kids, men, and women we saw
during the war carrying AK-47s and sporting wigs, wedding gowns,
lipstick and the like; and hanging on the doors of cars they had
seized, for show, were kids, men, who wanted to be seen as "somebody".'[14] The war was an opportunity to prove themselves and
to make enough money to embark on adult life. Far from this
being unprecedented, it was behaviour often condoned by older
Liberians living in the rural areas, during the first few months
of the war at least, according to a local journalist who wrote that
young fighters went on looting expeditions with the approval of
their elders, 'parental accomplices', who had been 'blindfolded
by looted materials and money often brought home from the
frontline by those kids'.[15] The indulgence with which parents in
Nimba County regarded the children who joined the NPFL in
1990 may not have lasted for long, but recalling its existence does
serve to put into perspective the notion of a young generation
run completely wild. A possible explanation for the difference
between the attitudes of parents and their children, however, may
be found in a change over the course of time in what people

[12] Dorjahn and Isaac, *Essays on Economic Anthropology,* p.6.

[13] Wilton Sankawulo, *What My Country Needs Today,* Monrovia, 1995, p.46.

[14] Enoanyi, *Uncle Sam's Stepchild,* p.86.

[15] Quoted in Cruise O'Brien, 'A Lost Generation?', p.70.

realistically expected to be the rewards of political allegiance. In the boom years of the 1950s and '60s, even people of quite lowly status in society could reasonably expect that their fortunes would rise over time if they remained steadfast in their loyalty to a political patron. With the economic difficulties experienced after the mid-1970s, the resources available to major politicians declined, while the population growth rate and the greater number of school graduates meant that there was more competition for such resources. This enhanced competition may have encouraged opportunistic switches of political allegiance. Perhaps one might add that expectations of social advancement are not governed solely by a purely mathematical relationship between a quantity of money and the numbers of people competing for it, but also by the growth of a spirit of ambition, of dissatisfaction with the status quo, which the rhetoric of economic development had done so much to instil.[16]

The dislike or envy of Monrovia which was so evident among country people at the beginning of the war has a surprisingly long history. As early as 1898, the leader of a rising on the Kru coast declared that 'the people in Monrovia don't care how the bush people live so long as they can make money. We gave their fathers bread and they give us the lash of whips in return. Let us march.'[17] An American observer in the 1940s, noting the existence of an undercurrent of resentment in the rural areas, predicted that 'the roar of their rage will swell until it will reach the gates of Monrovia, like the trumpet blasts which tumbled down the walls of Jericho.'[18] An old man recalling at a later period the regime of forced labour administered by the Liberian army gave a graphic account of how recalcitrants were flogged and given heavy stones to carry. 'Why? To punish our people – we were under martial law.[...] We get no power, no power.'[19]

Nevertheless, the observation that there existed a deep and enduring resentment in the rural areas, directed at the wealth and power concentrated in Liberia's capital city, and that this became more acute in the 1970s and 1980s as a result of demographic and economic change, still leaves many questions unanswered about the origins of the war. Attributing the cause

---

16 See above, p.218.

17 Quoted in Hayman and Preece, *Lighting Up Liberia*, p.161.

18 *Ibid.*

19 Quoted in David Brown, 'Recollections of Early Liberia', *West Africa*, 3328 (11 May 1981), p.1020.

of the civil war to a long-simmering discontent suggests no more
than that what happened was bound to happen. This is certainly
not the case. History could have turned out very differently if
the generation of 'progressive' politicians had not chosen to throw
in their lot with an upstart military regime in 1980, or if Charles
Taylor had not decided to oppose Nigeria from the very start
of the war, leading to a seven-year contest with Ecomog, or if
he had not decided to launch an invasion of Sierra Leone, or
if the US had intervened in June 1990. These were all actions
or inactions stemming from individual decisions. They were by
no means historical inevitabilities. They collectively turned what
might have been little more than a standard West African coup
into a devastating war and a threat to regional stability.

Moreover, the specific way in which the armed factions fought
cannot be attributed only to the wildness of a generation of youths
frustrated by a lack of economic opportunity. The maintenance
of political control over a long period through manipulation of
social networks was surely a prime reason why the war was fought
on such a broad social front. The economic frustration of the
young explains in some measure the fighters' preoccupation with
looting, but it cannot serve as a full explanation for the extent
of the practice. The tactics and style of fighting were clearly derived
in part from older traditions of warfare, as is most obvious in
the combatants' choice of attire in the first phase of the war.
Making war for economic gain is also a deeply traditional activity
in Liberia. Accounts of the seasonal nineteenth-century campaigns
which modern Liberians refer to as 'tribal wars' indicate that warfare
was a prime form of economic activity, even a veritable mode
of production. In Nimba County, from which so many of the
earliest NPFL fighters came, rural communities until the twentieth
century were composed of lineages engaged in subsistence farming
and hunting, with cash crops like kola being the monopoly of
elders.[20] Armed raiding, 'petty cannibalistic warfare' in Harley's
phrase,[21] was a means for young men to acquire wealth and to
rise in status and power and was a form of factional struggle between
rival families and towns. Such wars, and the entrepreneurs who
waged them successfully, were kept under institutional control by
the Poro and similar religious institutions. After the hinterland
had been conquered by Liberian government forces in the early
twentieth century, warfare of this sort was no longer possible since

---

[20] Martin Ford, '"Pacification" Under Pressure', pp.44-63.
[21] Harley, *Native African Medicine*, p.3.

it was now stigmatised as rebellion. Nevertheless, it is apparent that in many rural areas the older ideas concerning the proper purpose of war did not disappear during the twentieth century. It is clear that the many Krahn country men who rose in the army or the government under Samuel Doe regarded the power they wielded largely as an opportunity to loot, which they were able to do with impunity thanks to their control of the state apparatus. Perhaps they were not so different from the True Whig Party politicians who, although infinitely more sophisticated than Doe and more elegant in their way of doing business, also saw politics as primarily an avenue for enrichment. Doe himself once described politicians as follows:[22]

> If you mind us politicians, we will leave you all. All we want are your votes, and finish with you; that's all we do. We play with the people's brains, convince them and confuse them. After we've finished talking politics, you know what we look for? We want to eat.

The tendency to regard political activity, the exercise of violence and the accumulation of wealth as related activities is thus deeply rooted in Liberian history. In some sense, these three activities are related in all societies: what differs crucially is the institutional arrangements made to regulate them. The many Liberian politicians who have advocated overthrowing oppressive governments by force, such as opponents of Tolbert and Doe quite routinely did, were either unaware of the fragility of these institutional controls or paid no heed to the matter. Amos Sawyer was one of the few people who seems to have perceived at an early stage that events which he had witnessed at first hand might have opened a Pandora's box of violence. He realised, in retrospect, the role which the 1979 rice riots had played in legitimising looting as a political act.[23] After Doe had come to power and his men had set up an organised system of looting, Sawyer warned, accurately enough, that 'The military dictatorship...will only be dislodged by another armed band and Liberia will continue a hopeless downward spiral under a series of armed gangs.'[24] Sawyer continued nonetheless to advocate the use of violence to excise what he called 'the essential core of tyrannical autocracy'.[25]

---

[22] Quoted in Michael Schatzberg, 'Power, Legitimacy and "Democratization" in Africa', *Africa*, 63, 4 (1993), p.447.

[23] Sawyer, *Effective Immediately*, p.5.

[24] *Ibid.*, p.36.

[25] Sawyer, *Emergence of Autocracy*, p.313.

Culture and imagination

Pointing out that Liberia's civil war has roots deep in the country's history and in received attitudes towards politics and the exercise of violence does not mean that it was inevitable. It is worth making the point once more, since there is such frequent misunderstanding of the matter, that African societies are not unchanging ensembles, doomed always to perpetuate themselves as they are, but stores of historical experience from which people derive many of the repertoires of actions which constitute culture. People are not programmed by the history of their communities to act in specific ways only, although the patterns which they see around them and the principles in which they are educated as children no doubt have a formative effect. The past offers a huge variety of principles and keys to action, some of which flatly contradict one another, and people in every generation are free to reject what comes from the past and to invent or borrow new ways of doing things. All that is required is the will to do so.

Many Liberians, thinking about the war, have concluded that it stemmed from deep-rooted ideas and attitudes which must change if the country is to revive. This is what Henry Andrews meant when he said that 'Liberia will change only by our minds',[26] or through what another writer calls a 'national psyche conversion'.[27] These and other analysts emphasise the need for Liberians to adopt above all a different attitude towards power and a new moral rigour in tenure of public office. To this list of requirements might be added that, if despotism is to be avoided in future, Liberians will also have to find a new means of bestowing legitimacy on those who hold power, and possibly to heal the deep-seated feelings of inferiority which many authors believe to exist in many people of 'country' origin.

Byron Tarr, the former finance minister in the Interim Government, considers that this is at bottom a problem which derives from the lack of 'a critical intellectual tradition',[28] although it should be said that a lively and critical intellectual tradition certainly existed in the nineteenth century and arguably until the 1920s.[29] It is this lack of intellectual independence, according to Tarr,

[26] Andrews, *Cry, Liberia, Cry!*, p.70.

[27] Dolo, *Democracy Versus Dictatorship*, p.12.

[28] Tarr, 'Founding the LAP', p.44.

[29] Cf. Joseph Guannu, *The Perennial Problems of Liberian History*, Monrovia, 1989, p.1; Cordor, *Facing the Realities*, pp.12-13.

292   *False Prophets*

which has produced in Liberians the practice of assimilating new ideas uncritically:[30]

> Without a critical intellectual tradition, the culture failed to question concurrent adherence to Western, Eastern and African cultures. For example, no incongruity was perceived to exist between the concurrent practice of fundamental Christianity, aspects of traditional secret societies, voodoo and witchcraft. Not only did status derive from membership in all, higher status was conferred by concurrent leadership of all. In this society in which nothing was sacred because there is no legacy, conspicuous consumption has become the right of the privileged few, and the aspiration of the subjugated many.

This point requires some comment. The practice of assimilating new ideas and institutions by incorporation rather than displacement has deep roots in the traditional philosophies of rural Liberian communities. Tarr is certainly correct in identifying the exact manner in which different intellectual and cultural traditions have been assimilated as a key weakness of Liberian public culture. However, it would not be correct therefore to assume that those individuals most highly trained in the critical intellectual traditions and disciplines of the West, such as those with diplomas from American universities, have acquired a cultural repertoire better fitted for effective government than their less educated brothers and sisters. On the contrary, educated people have played a leading role in developing the economy of plunder which has characterised Liberian public life for most of the twentieth century.

The central point is to know whether or not the common West African practice of assimilating new ideas into older ones, which might be called 'cultural creolisation', is itself the root of Liberia's failure of development, as Byron Tarr has suggested. In considering this matter, it could be said in the first place that there is no evidence that the addition of new elements to a given cultural repertoire is in itself a harmful practice since it is also a source of adaptation and renewal, so vital in an era of social and political change as rapid as that experienced by West Africa in the twentieth century. Liberians do not assimilate new ideas uncritically. Rather, the evidence suggests that they, like other West Africans, have assimilated new ideas from East and West, as Tarr puts it, primarily when they believe this is in their interest. What is perhaps most distinctive about the way the assimilation of new ideas and practices has occurred in recent Liberian history is the degree to which

[30] Tarr, 'Founding the LAP', pp.44-5.

it has been associated with coercion. The creation of highly despotic paramount chieftaincies and the forced development of labour mobility by imposing hut tax and recruiting forced labourers are examples of coercive measures imposed on rural populations in the twentieth century by the central government. These and other harsh administrative requirements were accompanied by the proclamation of new ideas or cultural practices which rural populations were urged to assimilate.

But why exactly did successive True Whig Party governments exercise such a coercive type of government in the hinterland? The radical critics of the True Whig Party who emerged in the 1960s and 1970s tended to suppose that it was because the Americo-Liberian stalwarts of the ruling party, having ties of family and interest to the US, were particularly disposed to act as collaborators with foreign interests such as the US government and the Firestone Company.[31] It was tempting to believe that Liberia's ills stemmed from the existence of a form of black colonialism. This thesis takes no account of the mutual assimilation of Americo-Liberian and indigenous practices which, behind the rhetoric of True Whig Party rule, actually took place during the twentieth century, reflected in the concurrent allegiance to various religious systems mentioned by Byron Tarr in his analysis. Nor does the black colonialism thesis take account of the degree of coercion implied by almost any truly national policy whatever in a country like Liberia which included in its borders a great number of political communities who had never constituted a nation before the idea was imported from America. It should also be said that the oppressive measures adopted by the Liberian government as it acquired power in the hinterland were to a large extent forced on it by external pressure, since until the 1930s Liberia's very sovereignty was under threat from European powers which required the government to impose an internationally acceptable form of administration on the territories it claimed as its own, which meant in effect suppressing independent potentates and outlawing practices such as slavery and human sacrifice. The government tried to avoid European pressure by allying itself with the US, which played a growing role as a patron from 1912 onwards and particularly after negotiation of the Firestone contract in 1926. This gave the US

[31] Influential in propagating this point of view was Liebenow, *The Evolution of Privilege,* and *Idem, Liberia: the quest for democracy,* Bloomington, IN, 1987. Various works by MOJA officials such as Sawyer and Tipoteh are also illustrative. Cf. D. Elwood Dunn, 'Liberia Reconsidered: a review', *Canadian Journal of African Studies,* 21, 2 (1987), pp.259-62.

government a vested interest in protecting the independence of Liberia and also transformed the finances of the Liberian executive branch by providing it with regular payment of dollar royalties in place of the paltry receipts from local taxes and tariffs. The transformation of government finances under President King (1920-30) freed the president from dependence on the legislative branch and was at the origin of a growth of the power of the president into the grotesque cult of later times. It is no coincidence that it was accompanied by a decline in the influence of independent intellectual critics, the most persuasive of the observations made by Byron Tarr. It is impossible to say how Liberia would have evolved if it had been governed by a group of people other than the True Whig Party in the early twentieth century. What can be said with slightly more confidence is that there were powerful forces in the world, the very same ones which led to Africa's colonisation, which insisted that any African regime they recognised should be one able and willing to deliver certain conditions including the suppression of slavery and practices judged to be unacceptable, such as human sacrifice, combined with the respect of international borders and of international legal obligations including in financial matters.

The Liberian tradition of flattering those in power, then, comes less from the habit of assimilating new ideas of diverse origin than from the manner in which successive Liberian presidents have inserted their government in international political and commercial relations and used the resources at their disposal to construct a vast patronage system. Over time, these material factors produced patterns of government and behaviour which came to be regarded as normal, and various groups developed a vested interest in their perpetuation. Even the victims of oppression could find ideological justification for the way they were treated. For example, an American who lived in Nimba County in the 1960s, outraged that country people submitted so meekly to all manner of injustices, noted that '[Mano people] grant the Liberian legal order legitimacy on traditional grounds. The Liberian order is considered legitimate by the tribesmen because it is imposed by persons occupying positions of authority according to traditional rules of selection.' He added that Mano people tended to believe that people of settler origin possessed very strong spiritual powers.[32] People may submit without protest to even the most repressive systems or institutions if they believe that these are rooted in reason and nature, which in the Liberian case meant in religious

---

[32] Blanchard, 'The Impact of External Domination', p.172.

cosmology.[33] All human beings adopt certain techniques which they use to define themselves, which determine who they are, and it is as at the point where these subjective techniques combine with the techniques employed in a society for dominating others that the 'governmentality' of that society is formed and evolves.[34] Hence, people's ideas of such matters as personal and public morality, identity and power are created in the imagination. It is from the imagination that Liberians derive the idea that all power has its origins in the spirit world. Imagination, we should add at once, is not to be understood as meaning that which is unreal, but rather to designate a realm in which the real and unreal are indistinguishable.[35] Since all people create ideas about abstract matters and relationships of cause and effect in their imagination, Liberians are not exceptional in this regard. The difference between Liberia and any other society is only the precise way in which this occurs as a result of Liberia's particular history of governmentality.

Just as imagination is a characteristic of all humans, so too the range of transformations available to humans is unique, including the ability to effect radical changes of mood or emotion and to change appearance through disguise or masking. As we have seen, many Liberians believe that humans can acquire the power to perform transformations which to a Western reader appear quite impossible, such as to become invisible or to turn from a human into an animal. They also believe that profound transformations may be performed by the act of eating. Anything which is eaten is irreversibly transformed,[36] and when the substance consumed is considered inherently powerful – such as a human heart – the eater also is transformed into a more powerful being. No matter how unlikely or even revolting this may seem, the fact remains that it is clearly what many Liberians believe.

Since we have said that all beliefs are created in the imagination, it is relevant to ask how people come to acquire specific beliefs such as these, and how one belief may supersede or be replaced by another. It is not very helpful to begin with the proposition that since the idea that power can be eaten is obviously absurd, it is therefore destined to be replaced by other, more rational

---

[33] Cf. Mary Douglas, *How Institutions Think*, Syracuse, NY, 1986, p.55.

[34] Foucault, *Dits et écrits*, vol.IV, pp.223, 785.

[35] A definition coined by Gilles Deleuze. Quoted in Jean-François Bayart, *L'illusion identitaire*, Paris, 1996, p.138.

[36] MacCormack, 'Human Leopards and Crocodiles', p.56.

beliefs. As a leading sociologist of religion puts it, 'there are too many examples of modern people believing the most dreadful nonsense to suppose that people change from one set of beliefs to another just because the second lot are better ideas. The history of the human ability to believe very strongly in things that turn out not to be true suggests that whether something is true and whether it becomes widely accepted are two very different questions.'[37] A more relevant question, then, is why certain beliefs current in a given society come to be considered unconvincing in the course of time, and lose currency in favour of newer, more compelling ones. This is an unending process in all human societies, inseparable from history itself.

If a society is reasonably stable, in the sense of being able to reproduce itself in a broadly predictable manner, then its fundamental beliefs may be deemed satisfactory and there is no obvious reason for people to jettison them in favour of others. Indeed, abandoning them might be far more dangerous, since it could destabilise the established order. Ideas about what is good and bad, or proper and improper conduct, help to maintain any established order but may vary from time to time or place to place. To take a relevant example, to judge from the available evidence, many rural Liberians a century or more ago believed that it was not improper or immoral for a person to make war for economic reasons. The ritual control of violence upheld by the secret societies or other religious institutions enabled civic authorities, such as chiefs and patriarchs, to forbid and to prosecute acts of violence committed outside the bounds of ritual control or, in other words, to maintain a control of violence which is one of the defining characteristics of a coherent political order. The violence associated with some beliefs or conventions sanctioned by social acceptance is not at all unusual, since all public order is dependent on a system in which the use of violence is subject to a socially legitimated control.

The evidence suggests that, before the twentieth century, in many parts of rural Liberia people believed a number of things which today appear wrong or absurd to Western readers, but which were satisfactory to the people who held these ideas. At least on the basis of the rather poor information we have about these societies at that time, we may say that many people in Liberia's nineteenth-century hinterland believed it was possible for a person to transform into an animal such as a leopard and it was possible

[37] Steve Bruce, *Religion in the Modern World: from cathedrals to cults*, Oxford, 1996, p.38.

to derive strength from a powerful being by eating the essence of that being, especially the heart. They also believed that a masked figure, the spirit of the forest, was a channel of superhuman power. Such things appeared convincing largely, no doubt, because those who controlled the performance of these actions were the people who wielded power in society. In the last hundred years Liberians have been exposed to the influence of people who affirm that many of the beliefs and practices which Liberians have had in the past are wrong (like human sacrifice) or even impossible (like transformation into an animal). Most importantly, they have been subject to a government which informed them that it was wrong to make war without official sanction and punished them severely if they did so, and they have been exposed to orthodox Christian and Muslim thought which holds that eating human flesh is an abomination. Exposure to these influences has not only affected the repertoire of Liberian beliefs, but it has also changed the moral value which Liberians attach to certain activities. Whereas traditional Liberian thinking tended to regard the invisible world as morally neutral, and considered moral value to be attached to spiritual forces only in the process of channelling them into some practical use, Christianity and Islam are both dualistic systems, in which God is the fount of all good, never of evil. Hence one of the effects of both Christian and Muslim influence is that Liberians, whatever religious allegiance they declare, have come to accept quite widely that whatever is morally wrong to the point of being evil is actually the work of an identifiable being, Satan, who is himself invisible but who is very real, and who may recruit human agents. This he does through certain ceremonies or other rituals. God, equally invisible and equally real, also recruits human agents and punishes offenders.

During the course of the twentieth century people have been exposed to acute dilemmas as they are solicited by various authorities, political and religious, urging them to regard certain courses of action as right or wrong. Often it is possible to satisfy conflicting requirements, but on occasion the injunctions are impossibly contradictory, or the authorities which issue them are themselves ambiguous. A good example is the dilemma described earlier, of Senator James Paye Ph.D., who was told by his Christian pastor that he should not engage in human sacrifice but who was expected as a senior chief to do so in order to exercise power.[38] Liberians of every class have been faced with similar choices about which institutions they should respect, and which moral values

[38] See pp.246-9.

to apply. Today this tension is clear in the debates which are raging over the proper means for people to find spiritual healing, between advocates of a return to tradition and those, such as the more radical Christian pentecostalists, who maintain that all ancestral religious practices are evil.

After a century of rapid and profound change, not only is there considerable confusion about what precisely constitutes good and evil, including in such important matters as taking human life for religious purposes or making war, but when people look to the various authorities who should be able to pronounce on such matters, they find that these are in a state of equal disarray. In modern Western thought, the identification of that which is morally virtuous, and thus to be encouraged, and that which is pernicious, to be condemned, is only partially the role of the state. A state is expected to promulgate laws which outlaw certain practices which are held to be morally undesirable and to prescribe certain codes of correct behaviour, for example in commercial transactions. When the state pronounces on matters of personal morality, it cannot be sure of persuading the population which it governs of the correctness of its view, and public administrators often proceed cautiously in such matters since the political consequences which can follow the state's outlawing of a moral practice which the mainstream of society regards as not deserving of condemnation can be profound. A good example of this concerns the law enacted by the Republic of Liberia in 1912 to outlaw traditional secret societies. The state promulgated this law on the grounds that some secret societies were associated with certain patterns of behaviour, notably in regard to human sacrifice, which it believed to be immoral, and which it henceforth classified as criminal. The ban on secret societies was less than totally effective. Furthermore, since the societies which had been made illegal were highly political in nature, they actually became part of the mechanism of local government which the state subsumed into the apparatus of the state through the practice of indirect rule, although this was done surreptitiously.

If the state promulgates a moral code which is not acceptable to society at large, or to important elements of it, this can lead to the spread of practices of subterfuge as people practise in secret types of behaviour which they are not allowed to admit in public. This can lead to extremes of deception and evasion which become part of the political culture. No less an authority than Samuel Doe sometimes used to argue that Liberia's problems arose from the fact that people tried to deceive God by pretending to do what He wanted but in reality doing something different. The result was what Doe considered the typically Liberian vices of lack of sincerity, lack of commitment and lack of patriotism.[39] Doe himself was a fine example of deception in action for, while being the president of the Republic and therefore a man of great power and high status, he was also a trickster and self-transformer of renown, believed to be able to fly and disappear at will. Who was to know whether he was ever what he claimed to be, or whether anything he said was the truth or a lie?

The attempt by the state to enforce new moral codes by law was a conspicuous characteristic of government in Liberia, and of colonial government elsewhere in Africa, during the earlier twentieth century.[40] This tendency has survived the demise of colonial government in much of Africa. Colonial programmes of imposing change on rural societies were little different in essence from the modern rhetoric of economic and political development which has dominated African public discourse since the 1950s. In the Liberian case certainly, and quite clearly in many other African states also, this attempt by the apparatus of the state to impose a new moral order on society has, to say the least, been less than fully effective. Precisely because moral ideas are made in the imagination and circulated in society at large, they are not easily enforceable, particularly in countries like Liberia whose historical experience of the existence of a bureaucratic state which aspires to promulgate rational, written codes of law is superficial. Religious institutions have been far more effective in propagating new moral ideas both through their religious activities as such and, in the case of the Christian churches, through the prominent role they have played in the promotion of education. Both Christianity and Islam in Liberia have tended to assimilate non-Christian ideas and practices and have been associated with various forms of economic self-advancement, while orthodox Christianity in particular gained a strong political influence due to the number of prominent Americo-Liberians who occupied both political and religious office simultaneously. We may recall that Presidents King, Tubman, Tolbert and Doe are all reported or known to have been members of secret societies and also Christians, with President Tolbert being no less than the president of the World Baptist Alliance. Their influence as religious leaders was constantly mixed with the requirements of their politics. It is small wonder that the mainstream Protestant churches in Liberia which were so closely

[39] Quoted in Youboty, *Liberian Civil War*, p.391.
[40] Cf. Lucy Mair, *African Kingdoms*, Oxford, 1977, pp.36-7.

associated with True Whig Party rule, such as the Baptists, Methodists and Episcopalians, tended to emphasise the Old Testament vision of God as a stern father who demanded obedience.

However, both Christianity itself, and the republican government with which it was associated from its inception, also contain within them the seeds of a particular concept of liberation. Broadly, the Christian. notion of liberation proposes that man, by following the way of Jesus, can liberate himself from evil and actually overcome death by a supreme transformation. Every human being has the possibility of following this path, according to Christian teaching, but it is also related to a view of history as a process which will lead to the end of the world in a series of climactic events foretold in the New Testament Book of Revelation. This mystical vision predicts the reign of the Anti-Christ, and the coming of the millennium, when peace and harmony will reign for a thousand years.

Concepts of freedom and liberation which bore a strongly Christian character were central to the thinking of Liberia's founding fathers from the moment they landed in West Africa in 1822. The American settlers gave the country its name and its motto, 'The love of liberty brought us here'. Whatever one may think of their particular view of liberation, or of the manner in which they applied it, it is interesting to note its effect on societies which do not appear to have had any previous notion of liberation comparable to that of the Americo-Liberians. There is no trace of the concept of liberation in what is known of the religious or political thought of Liberians outside the Christian coastal settlements before the twentieth century. Clearly, people in the Liberian hinterland before the twentieth century could and did conceive of struggling, and even fighting, in order to improve their social and economic position, or to throw off oppressive rule, as the numerous risings of resistance against the imposition of republican government up to the 1930s testify, although it is interesting to note that some of the most important of these were led by people who had converted to Christianity.[41] But fighting to advance one's material self-interest is quite different from the concept of liberation as it has gained ground in the twentieth century in Liberia.

A New Testament theology which emphasises the power of the individual to achieve liberation from sin through Jesus Christ became more popular both in the mainstream churches and in the

---

[41] Martin, 'Dual Legacy', pp.235-6, 258-89.

independent churches[42] at the same time as a new generation
of politicians, the progressives of the 1970s, began to argue the
ideologies of political liberation and revolution, which in their
case meant taking power by the use or threat of force in order
to liberate the country people from True Whig Party rule. The
legacy of the progressives' idea of liberation may be identified
in the claim made by Charles Taylor, himself generally considered
one of the generation of progressives, to have effected a revolution
after launching the 1989 rising which started Liberia's civil war.
Revolutionary thought is clearly to be seen in the names of organisations like Ulimo, which claims to be devoted to the liberation
of the people, and in the habit of the myriad fighters and looters
of referring to themselves as 'freedom fighters'.

An originally Christian concept of liberation, then, appears to
have become absorbed into the political vocabulary of Liberia
as a result of a long historical process inseparable from the
Liberianisation of the hinterland. After Presidents Tubman and
Tolbert had opened up the national political arena to a greater
extent to people from rural areas, the Christian notion of liberation
through religion became assimilated into the more secular ideas
of revolution then fashionable among young intellectuals and thus
became an instrument in the unending process of factional struggle.
The political use of the notion of liberation, much vaunted by
the generation of progressive politicians and by Samuel Doe when
he claimed to have liberated the country people (through a body
called, tellingly, the People's Redemption Council, also a reference
to a Christian notion), is quite different from the notion of fighting
to remove an unacceptable government, which is a widespread
human propensity, or of making war to get rich, which was common
in Liberian political thought before the twentieth century and
which has been revived in the 1990s. The rhetoric of political
liberation used in Liberia from the 1970s onwards uses concepts
of originally Christian origin, transferred from a mystical to a
material context, allied to Marxist and other secular ideas, to
promise a climactic transformation, the creation of a new country
and a new politics through an act of political revolution.

Needless to say, there are few Liberians who would in fact regard
their experience of the last twenty years as a political liberation,
and there is little prospect of this coming about in the foreseeable
future. On the contrary, eight years of civil war, following on the
Doe years which many Liberians would consider almost an opening
phase of the war, have brought enormous suffering. So total has

[42] Gifford, *Christianity and Politics in Doe's Liberia*.

False Prophets

this catastrophe been that Liberians need to re-examine all sorts of ways of doing things which they had previously taken for granted. It is not only the political and social order which have been disturbed, but also the religious order, or to be more precise that realm of consciousness known as the imagination, where the real and unreal fuse, and where ideas of truth, good and evil precipitate.

The fact that many people are convinced that the war is a reflection of the disposition of invisible cosmic forces places a particular burden of responsibility on Liberia's spiritual leaders, most of whom would most probably agree that the war is to some extent the result of a breakdown of spiritual order. The most prominent Christian and Muslim leaders have an outstanding record of working for peace throughout the war, notably through the Inter-Faith Mediation Committee, internationally recognised for its work. Many individual Christian and Muslim members of this committee have shown considerable physical courage in pursuing this work. However, laudable though the work of these leaders may be, the spiritual anarchy of Liberia today is so deep as to be hardly touched by even the most dedicated work for peace.

The teachers and religious ideologues who have most success in propagating their ideas are those who are able to use to full extent popular cultural repertoires of the spirit world, for example by reference to good and evil spirits and the power of dreams. They are rarely to be found in the mainstream Christian churches. For this reason, some of the more staid of the old missionary churches have come to consider that their most pressing need is to evolve techniques which are effective in the key site of struggle, namely the imagination.

One of the most thoughtful observations is that of the Methodist Bishop Arthur Kulah, who appreciates the power of the spiritual techniques used by traditional religion and by many spiritual churches as well as by many Muslim clerics, but which are frequently spurned by the mainstream Christian churches, including his own. He argues that the older and wealthier missionary churches must learn to use techniques valued in traditional Liberian society such as 'dream interpretations, making sacrifices, healing, handling fear, and dealing with the concept of the exercise of power and the place of freedom'.[43] They should teach 'the theology of witchcraft, fear, dreams and human sacrifice', with a view, of course, to eradicating evil wherever they find it.[44]

---

[43] Kulah, *Theological Education,* p.26.
[44] *Ibid.,* p.41.

The esoteric notion of governing the invisible world of the imagination through such techniques as those recommended by Bishop Kulah is not divorced from the government of the visible or material world. On the contrary, in traditional Liberian thought the two are inseparable, as Harley noted when he asserted that the people of Ganta whom he knew so well had 'no concept of the natural, no recognition of natural laws' in contradistinction to the supernatural.[45] They were far more inclined to reason in terms of cause and effect, seeking a logical explanation for events and visible phenomena by reference to a range of entities and powers they believed to exist, visible and invisible. In this context, transformations which a European might think of as personal or purely psychological, such as between different emotions or states of mind in an individual, may also have social importance. A major role of any public authority is to regulate transformations in society, one of which is the type of social transformation which occurs when people move from one social or economic class to another. This has been a conspicuous occurrence in the Liberian war, as it is in most wars. Many participants in the Liberian war were young people who aspired to a higher social status, which they attempted to wrest by force of arms. There was no authority which could prevent them from taking this course, and a plethora of warlords to urge them on and supply them with weapons. It would appear also that during the war many women changed their social and economic status substantially, which may in time result in specific adjustments to the social order.

In a stable and peaceful society, transformations both of the individual (such as in the passage from childhood to adulthood) and of groups (such as rapid changes in economic and social status) are regulated by public authorities which can be either religious or secular in nature or both. The Liberian state has lost much of the power to regulate social transformations which it formerly had, and this places a particular onus on religious institutions. The transformation of the national psyche which leading commentators believe to be at the heart of Liberia's needs is taking place in the religious sphere. The older hierarchies have been immensely disturbed. Many people brought up to revere the power of the masked spirits believe this to have been destroyed by their public unmasking and desecration during the war. Nevertheless, it would be a mistake to underestimate the durability of the secret societies, especially Poro, which has endured for centuries and has a formidable ability to adapt. The public exposure of

[45] Harley, *Native African Medicine*, p.15.

the secrets of Poro and other societies, and the scenes of public consumption of human flesh during the war which shocked so many Liberians, have certainly made inroads into the culture of submissiveness to authority which intellectuals have also identified as a fundamental Liberian problem by exploding a fundamental principle of Poro, which is silence. Some of the leading remakers of the imaginative order are the Christian preachers and churches which have mushroomed since the 1970s. Muslim clerics appear less successful than their Christian counterparts in penetrating the public imagination, but this is a tentative finding on a subject which certainly requires further research.

Some implications for the wider world

This book has attempted to discover why the civil war occurred in Liberia, and why it happened in the way it did. The war was a struggle by rival warlords for control of a state which had come under new ownership in 1980. The most important actors in the war were politicians and technocrats who had emerged in the 1970s, when True Whig Party rule was crumbling, unable to adjust to the emergence of new social groups or to maintain its patronage networks under adverse economic conditions. The state which the warlords fought to control was highly centralised, but it had incorporated in the course of time various local systems of power, very often in the form of kinship networks, which were subsumed in the system of indirect rule. This complex structure, characterised by its combination of formal and informal methods of operation, made little provision for rational power-sharing. At every level, tenants of public office were limited in their ability to act principally by the constraints imposed by those above them in a patronage system, rarely by those below them, unless it was through some form of subterfuge. The ways in which people at all levels thought about power was rooted in religious ideology.

It was noted in the introduction to this book that concentrating on the development of a conflict in any one country – in this case, Liberia – risks obscuring any similarities or connections which may exist with other parts of the world, creating an impression that Africa today is the victim of a series of unrelated conflicts in countries such as Rwanda, Sierra Leone, Somalia and others. In fact, there are clear similarities between what has happened in Liberia in the last century or more and developments elsewhere in the world. All over Africa, and in other parts of the former colonial world, the imposition of an apparatus of government built on the European model subsumed indigenous systems in forms of indirect rule, whether or not these were openly labelled as such. In the process, European or American-style organs of government became inculturated, infused with techniques and moral codes which arose out of local history. The foreign and the native combined in a process of assimilation.[46] All over Africa and in many other parts of the world, older systems of moral economy rooted in small rural communities have been combined with ideas introduced from elsewhere, including by Christian missionaries and secular technocrats or planners who often make a rigid distinction between what is real and what is a product of the imagination. Too many social engineers have ignored the fact that a political order is actually made in the imagination.

All over Africa too, entrepreneurial young men, and occasionally women, have sought to turn the Western concept of liberation into political form, often by force of arms. To mention only a few near-neighbours of Liberia: Guinea, Benin, Togo, Ghana, and Burkina Faso are all governed by military men who have transformed themselves, with varying degrees of success, into politicians, generally claiming to have liberated their people in the process. In each case these presidents originally took power by force of arms. Nigeria, for most of its history, has also been governed by military men, although they no longer claim to have liberated anyone at all. Moreover, Côte d'Ivoire, Guinea and Sierra Leone all contain populations which share many of the cultural repertoires of Liberian Gio, Mano, Grebo, Krahn, Kissi, Loma, Mandingo, Mende and other peoples who live on both sides of an international border. The psychological inferiority which, according to thoughtful Liberians, their countrymen have suffered as a result of the requirement that they become *kwi* or 'civilised', as it was called in Liberia, also has its equivalent elsewhere. Everywhere in Africa, over several generations, people have been told that their way of doing things is wrong, and that they must become developed. Social and economic changes similar to those which produced the generation of political radicals and warlords in Liberia have had comparable effects elsewhere in West Africa, for example in the radical populism of Jerry Rawlings of Ghana and Thomas Sankara of Burkina Faso, two leaders who caught the imagination of many young West Africans in the 1980s.

While Rawlings and Sankara have ceased to represent an ideological threat to the older established heads of state (the former has grown older and less radical, and the latter was murdered

---

[46] Cf. Jean-François Bayart, 'L'historicité de l'Etat importé' in J.-F. Bayart (ed.), *La greffe de l'Etat*, Paris, 1996, pp.11-39.

by a friend and colleague), the social forces from which they drew
their initial support have not gone away. The conditions of life
and the prospects of future employment facing school graduates,
for example, are generally worse in most of West Africa today
than they were when these two young officers first came to power.
It is not only in Liberia that frustrated school-leavers or drop-outs
have resorted to arms to get what they see as their deserts.[47]
Hundreds of thousands of young men especially, unable to find
suitable employment at home, and often with some education,
have gone abroad in search of work and fortune. Included in
this much larger number of exiles and emigrants are a small number
of former military men who had tried their hands in coups but
failed, like survivors of the more than twenty coup attempts in
Ghana between 1982 and 1986, and some radical intellectuals or
simple adventurers. In the late 1980s a significant number of these
congregated in Libya. Here, Colonel Gadaffi, smarting from his
defeat in Chad, was determined to find allies who would project
Libyan influence into West Africa. It was precisely from this reservoir
of radicals and adventurers gathered in Libya that Charles Taylor
drew the core of his original military force in 1989. From early
on in his campaign it was known that he had with him dissidents
and revolutionaries from Gambia, Sierra Leone, Ghana, Nigeria
and elsewhere. In time, some of his associates were to launch
new rebellions or coups in both Gambia and Sierra Leone. The
outbreak of war in Guinea-Bissau in 1998 may have provided yet
another theatre for adventurers, revolutionaries and fortune-
seekers from a dozen African countries. So Nigeria's President
Babangida was correct in seeing at an early stage the threat to
order throughout West Africa posed by the NPFL invasion of
Liberia. He recognised that there was nothing exceptional about
Liberia, and that something comparable could have occurred almost anywhere in the region. 'Today it is Liberia,' Babangida told
his fellow-heads of state at an ECOWAS summit in Abuja in 1992.
'Tomorrow it could be any one of the countries represented here.'[48]

Changes in the international order mean that West African
governments can no longer rely on the same degree of protection
from outside as they once could. Up to 1990 Liberia was an
American protégé, and it was unthinkable that the US would allow
a full-scale civil war to occur there. One of the most respected

[47] Cf. Bazenguissa-Ganga, 'The Spread of Political Violence in Congo-Brazzaville'.

[48] Quoted in Ademola Adeleke, 'The Politics and Diplomacy of Peacekeeping in
West Africa: the Ecowas operation', *Journal of Modern African Studies*, 33, 4 (1995),
p.588.

and mild-mannered of Liberian analysts, looking back on this, could not contain his anger on reading one of many statements from Washington absolving the US from any part in the Liberian crisis:[49]

> The United States has hardly gotten anything right on Liberia in the last ten years. Let's start with their funnelling of some 500 million US dollars in arms and military support to the Doe regime in spite of its flagrant violations of human rights. Then note their disgusting pronouncement that the 1985 election results were not bad by African standards. Now observe their childishly simplistic analysis that what was happening in Liberia in 1990 was purely a Liberian affair. Marvel at their cruel and inhumane decision to sit with two thousand heavily armed marines just offshore while Liberians were being massacred like sheep and the city was going up in flames in 1990.

The US assistant secretary of state in the Bush administration, Herman Cohen, using less emotive language, agreed with at least some elements of this analysis. 'We missed an opportunity in Liberia,' he noted at the end of his term of office. 'We did not intervene either diplomatically or militarily.[...] We deployed a large marine amphibious force near Liberia to evacuate US citizens. [...] A modest intervention at that point to end the fighting in Monrovia could have avoided the prolonged conflict.'[50] US policy on Africa, which has so often veered between a ruthless pursuit of short-term interest and naive crusades, like the Somalia fiasco of 1992-3, has been fixed in the former mode when it comes to Liberia. So it was Nigeria which in 1990 took up the challenge to try to impose itself as a regional hegemon, which it has not succeeded in doing in Liberia, since it failed to prevent Charles Taylor from gaining power, and he has resumed a distinctly anti-Nigerian stance since becoming head of state in 1997.

The Liberian war was the first emergency in Africa after the end of the Cold War. The conjuncture of circumstances which led the US government to decide to abstain from intervention coincided with the exposure of foreign journalists to a dramaturgy of war which they found incomprehensible. The costumes of the transvestite warriors, their casual brutality, and the display of ghastly trophies such as human skulls, seemed to many Western reporters

---

[49] G. Henry Andrews, 'United States and France, You Can't Be Serious', *New Democrat*, 2, 105 (27 April-2 May 1995), p.7.

[50] Quoted in Ramcharan, 'Cooperation Between the UN and Regional/Sub-Regional Organizations', p.5.

to come from a well of cultural representations of which they had no knowledge. This was an accurate perception inasmuch as many of these symbols were indeed taken from a traditional cultural repertoire. The best foreign journalists concentrated on reporting verifiable facts. Rather more journalists, engaging in a brand of pop anthropology, reverted to a cultural repertoire of their own, a limited stock of ancient clichés about Africa. After the August 1990 invasion of Kuwait by Iraq, the Liberian war rapidly became forgotten. When it did come into the headlines, briefly during the second and third battles of Monrovia in October 1992 and April 1996, it was presented in the world's media in the form of a further peek into this particular Heart of Darkness. 'Do you know why there are so many journalists here? I don't,' one warlord asked Kenneth Best, a leading Liberian editor. 'Because the world likes to see Africans killing each other,' was Best's cynical reply. 'People get a kick out of it.'[51] Meanwhile, further wars in the Balkans especially and in Chechnya, Somalia, Rwanda and elsewhere have all fuelled the perception in the West that a new wave of wars in the old third world or on the fringes of the first world are comprehensible only as throwbacks to an age-old way of doing things, a clash of civilisations, or an identity crisis.[52]

It is true that questions of identity are not completely irrelevant to the Liberian war, although, since the ethnic pogroms of 1990, fighting has rarely taken the form of ethnic rivalry. It is far more accurate to identify the key clashes of ideas as being those stemming from a crisis of moral beliefs and of related concepts such as the legitimacy of authority and power. But these are subjects which journalists are generally unwilling to explore and which Western diplomats too would prefer not to consider, not least because, these days, they are generally content to leave Africa to the Africans.

In these circumstances, younger Africans in particular, in a continent where half of the population is under the age of eighteen, are searching for a means of resolving their everyday and their existential problems in a great variety of ways, common to many of which is the enduring conviction that power has its roots in the invisible world.[53] If all religion is concerned with a perceived invisible world of God or gods and spirits, mankind has found a great number of ways of conceiving and expressing this relationship. All of these have implications for the ways in which people

[51] Quoted in Huband, *The Liberian Civil War*, p.122.

[52] Cf. above, pp.17-20.

[53] Stephen Ellis and Gerrie ter Haar, 'Politics and Religion in Sub-Saharan Africa', *Journal of Modern African Studies*, 36, 2 (1998), pp.175-201.

construe the fundamental questions of human life: What is a person? What is life, exactly, and what is death? What is the sense of history, and what is the place of an individual life in the cosmic order? Why does misfortune occur to some people and not others? It is not only the young, the ignorant or the naive who believe in the importance of religion in Liberia. Most of the main players in the country's recent history have publicly referred to God as the ultimate author of their fate and the arbiter of events – Samuel Doe, Prince Johnson, Roosevelt Johnson, Charles Taylor and others have all done so.[54] There is every reason to believe that this belief in divine power is not just a figure of speech, but a deeply-held conviction. At the same time, warlords such as these are violent, ruthless men, who combine a belief in God's omnipotence with a sense of self-seeking and personal enterprise which has few moral limits, as their careers show. They are able to attract support from others who appear to know equally few moral bounds. Most Liberian warlords seem to believe that God has a destiny for each of them, but that what this destiny may be is a matter to be discovered less by any institutionalised system of religious communication than by recourse to a veritable free market, an infinite variety of intermediaries including marabouts, soothsayers, *zoes,* priests and heartmen whose perceived expertise may be purchased with dollars. They are able to act in this way because of the lack of institutional controls on religion, a product of Liberia's history in the twentieth century.

Many Africans appear to believe, like the Liberian warlords, that God is the ultimate arbiter of their destiny and the source of all power. This leaves them with the great problem of how to gain access to power from the invisible world when there are so many intermediaries proposing their services. How are people to choose amid such a bewildering variety of prophets and priests, all claiming to have privileged means of communication with the invisible world? It is as though the disorder of the visible world mirrors some confusing developments in the invisible one, in which case the highest priority is to restore some sort of stability to that sphere.

The family tree

Some readers will no doubt wonder how those Liberians who have survived such terrible times have the psychological resilience to

---

[54] E.g. Gifford, *Christianity and Politics in Doe's Liberia,* pp.140-2; Roosevelt Johnson interview with Ben Asante in *West Africa,* 4147 (28 April 1997), pp.681-2; Youboty, *Liberian Civil War,* p.449.

get on with their lives. Many live in dire poverty, and others are so traumatised or find it so difficult to make sense of what they have lived through that they at times appear capable of some sort of collective madness. Almost any sort of manifestation of the imagination could appear in these circumstances, such as a millennarian religious movement. Perhaps it is useful to add at this point that the present book, since it concerns a war, inevitably gives a rather one-sided view of the lives of millions of people, and to that extent risks misrepresenting the condition of Liberia as a whole. Although the war has affected all Liberians to some degree, there are many who have never been victims of assault, many are still able to have some sort of normal family life, and it is quite possible that many, if asked, would say that they are happy.

It is interesting to compare this with what a modern historian wrote in answer to a question concerning how people survived in early modern England, at a difficult period of their history, when poverty and sudden and early death were commonplace and they lived under a brutal political regime. People found solace above all in the rhythms of social life, 'in the sense of belonging to a place and to a community of people'. For people 'are attached to places, as they are attached to families and friends. When these loyalties come together, one has the most tenacious cement possible for human society.'[55] Liberian society too survives in such a way.

As in other countries of West Africa, Liberian society may be compared to a spider's web:[56]

> In web-like societies, social control is fragmented between different centres. The whole can be seen as a web where no single strand of social control holds the societal fabric together. It is rather held together by a network of strands. In web-like societies, although social control is fragmented and heterogeneous, this does not mean that people are not governed – they most certainly are. But the allocation of values are [sic] not centralised in the state. Numerous systems of justice, allocation and social control operate simultaneously.

These web-like relationships give people the psychological strength to survive, and also serve as channels for economic distribution. However, one of the great weaknesses of pre-war Liberia was the

55 W.G. Hoskins, *The Age of Plunder: the England of Henry VIII, 1500-1547*, London, 1976, p.48.
56 Piet Human and André Zaaiman (eds), *Managing Towards Self-Reliance: effectiveness of organisations in Africa*, Dakar, 1995, pp.37-8.

culture of dependency, whereby each person expects to receive money from their social relationships. This is common throughout West Africa but took a very extreme form in Liberia as a result of the vast patronage system perfected by President Tubman, a form of government which Presidents Doe and Taylor aspired to emulate. This is certainly not an economically productive system since it penalises individual enterprise. Here too the religious imagination is crucial, and future scholars of Africa may do well to return to some of the classic texts of history and sociology on the importance of definitions of the religious and the profane in creating a capitalist system of production.[57]

Young Liberians today are still part of the great web of society, but many want to move a comfortable distance away from their relatives in order to start a business or earn money whose profits they can use for themselves rather than to support an endless string of social parasites. This does not imply an end to family life or kin relations, but underlines the strength of the Liberian proverb: 'the family tree can bend but it cannot break'.

[57] E.g. Weber, *The Protestant Ethic;* R.H. Tawney, *Religion and the Rise of Capitalism: a historical study,* Harmondsworth, 1975.

ANNEXES

A

CASUALTIES OF THE LIBERIAN WAR, 1989-97

It will never be possible to establish with much precision how many Liberians died as a direct result of violence during the war, considered as having started on 24 December 1989 and ended with the election of Charles Taylor to the presidency on 19 July 1997. There are indications that some highly inflated figures have been widely circulated.

As with many wars, in between bouts of widespread killing, there were periods of months, or in some parts of the country years, when violence was restricted to a few isolated incidents. Some parts of Liberia actually witnessed very little combat, such as large parts of Nimba County which, after the first three months of heavy fighting in rural Nimba, were under NPFL administration for the remainder of the war. However, even in these areas there was widespread looting, sometimes associated with violence, as unpaid fighters plundered the cities, towns and villages where they were stationed. Other areas, most notably the Tubmanburg area of Bomi County, Upper Lofa County, and some areas of the south-east, were subject to years of violence as factions attacked and counter-attacked one another. Many casualties, and possibly even some significant massacres in these areas, have certainly gone unrecorded. However, with the exception of a few major battles, and a few organised massacres, factions generally preferred not to face each other in large-scale combat and saw little reason to kill non-combatants on a massive scale. Their main aim was to intimidate and to loot, and this was often achieved by committing individual acts of exemplary atrocity and terror. While these were often bestial in the extreme, the number of victims they produced was less than in, for example, campaigns of genocide or wars which make extensive use of heavy artillery and aircraft.

The first phase of the war lasted almost exactly a year, from December 1989 to the stabilisation of Monrovia under Ecomog

Field Commander General Dogonyaro. An Ecomog press officer reckoned that almost 300,000 people were killed in this period, but this is clearly an unacceptably high estimate.[1] The Catholic church reckoned that 'a conservative estimate' was 75,000-100,000 people killed by November 1990,[2] although other church sources put the figure lower, at 50,000 dead.[3] Church and other humanitarian sources may have been inclined to exaggerate the statistics out of a desire to alert the international public to the gravity of the situation. If we enumerate the major massacres which are known to have taken place during this period, several thousand people certainly lost their lives in Nimba County in the first period of the war, as the NPFL established itself and the AFL attempted to put down the insurrection, and probably at least a couple of thousand were killed in the battle for Monrovia in July-August 1990, including 600 people massacred at St Peter's Church, Sinkor, on 29-30 July. Hundreds of people were massacred when the NPFL occupied Buchanan in May 1990 and at Bakedu, a Mandingo town where the NPFL killed some 500 people after occupying Lofa County in July 1990. The NPFL itself estimated that the war had cost 13,000 deaths by September 1990.[4] Allowing for the many single killings or smaller massacres elsewhere, the figure given by one American journalist, who had visited Liberia on several occasions before the war and who had a good record of accuracy, that 20-25,000 people were killed in the first year of the war seems credible.[5]

After General Dogonyaro had stabilised Monrovia in late 1990, and his successors as Ecomog Field Commander had installed a ceasefire, the number of casualties subsided. Throughout 1991 many foreign correspondents continued to use figures of 15-20,000 dead throughout the whole war to date.[6] One journalist may have accounted for the discrepancy between these lower figures and the higher ones used by the churches by suggesting there had been 60,000 deaths in total, of which 40,000 were from starvation.[7]

[1] Agetua, *Operation Liberty*, p.19.
[2] Justice and Peace Commission, *The Liberian Crisis*, Monrovia, 1994, p.26.
[3] Undated clipping from *One World*, journal of the World Council of Churches.
[4] *The Patriot* (May-June 1991), p.9.
[5] Berkeley, 'Repression and Slaughter', p.129.
[6] E.g. Agence France-Presse published in the *Times* (London), 2 July 1991 gives 15,000 dead; *West Africa*, 3827 (7 January 1991), p.3149, gives 15-20,000; the *New York Times*, 4 October 1991, gives 20,000.
[7] Report by Cindy Shiner in *Africa News*, 9-22 January 1992.

The latter figure seems very high, as more detailed estimates reckon that about fifty people were dying a day of starvation in Monrovia in July-August 1990,[8] which would imply some 3,000 deaths from starvation in the city for those two months. Outside Monrovia, in the rural areas, food was easier to obtain.

After 1990, some sort of functioning economy was restored throughout the country, some rural areas recommenced agricultural production, and international aid organisations began distributing food relief. Nevertheless, there were certainly periods when there were many deaths from hunger and disease. In mid-1993 for example, as a result of Ecomog's enforcement of an economic embargo on areas run by the NPFL, Unicef reckoned that 500 children were dying every week from hunger, and that 200,000 people faced starvation.[9] The International Committee of the Red Cross also said that hundreds were dying every week in the centre and north of the country.[10] There was large-scale starvation in the Tubmanburg area in 1996, and no doubt many other pockets of extreme hunger in various parts of the country at certain periods of the war, such as at Zwedru in Grand Gedeh, where in late 1995 people were living on leaves and fruit.[11]

At least 3,000 more people were to die in a second battle for Monrovia in October 1992,[12] and thousands more in the fighting which followed, as well as in the campaign by Ulimo which entered Liberia from Sierra Leone during 1992. Nevertheless, the total number of deaths as a direct result of violence remained probably under 40-50,000 by March 1993, when the UN Secretary-General produced a figure of 150,000 casualties related to the war.[13] The Reuters press agency was correct in pointing out at the time that this figure was 'far higher than previous UN estimates'.[14] Since the UN figure referred to 'casualties' rather than deaths, it is possible that the UN estimate took account of those who had been wounded, or that it included people dying from hunger and disease. In fact, it would be impossible to make any accurate

8 According to Médecins sans Frontières, reported in *West Africa,* 3819 (5 November 1990), p.2796.

9 Quoted in *Daily Telegraph* (London), 2 September 1993.

10 Reuters despatch, 12 August 1993.

11 Cindy Shiner, 'Hungry Children Keep the Peace', *Guardian,* 11 November 1995.

12 Reuters despatch, Abuja, 8 November 1992.

13 Report of UN secretary-general to the Security Council on Liberia, S/25402, 12 March 1993.

14 Reuters despatch, Monrovia, 17 July 1993.

estimate of those dying of illness as a result of the war since this would presumably require comparing the death-rate from disease in the pre-war period with those dying from disease during the war, for which the available statistics are not adequate. The UN itself may not have given great thought to these distinctions, as in September 1993 the Secretary-General referred to more than 150,000 people having been 'killed in the fighting' in Liberia,[15] perhaps a slip of the pen when reproducing his estimate of casualties made five months earlier.

The figure of 150,000 has been used since March 1993 as a measure of deaths in the Liberian war, overlooking the fact that the original estimate was for 'casualties' only. Curiously, from 1993 until 1997 commentators often continued to refer to 150,000 war dead from year to year despite the continuing hostilities. Some humanitarian organisations by 1997 had updated the figure to 200,000, presumably to take account of fatalities after 1993. In the period 1993-7 there was indeed some heavy fighting. The feud within Ulimo, the LPC campaigns in the south-east and the anti-NPFL offensive launched in late 1994 by a coalition of forces with Ecomog backing must have caused together several thousand deaths. There were also some substantial individual massacres, most notably the 600 people killed at Carter Camp in June 1993. In addition, between 3,000 and 6,000 people are estimated to have been killed in the third battle of Monrovia in April 1996.

Ecomog is not known to have produced complete figures on the number of dead suffered by its own forces. During the first phase of deployment, up to January 1991, Ecomog announced that it had sustained sixty casualties of which forty-four were Nigerians. Twenty-seven Nigerians were listed as killed in action, including eight soldiers who had poisoned themselves by drinking butane which they had mistaken for alcohol.[16] Field Commander Dogonyaro dismissed as 'malicious' claims in the Nigerian press of 700 Nigerian military deaths.[17] The French researcher François Prkic has obtained Nigerian military documents indicating some 950 Ecomog deaths in the first two weeks of Operation Octopus in November 1992, and estimates total Ecomog deaths during the whole war as 2,000 Nigerian soldiers and 700-800 Ghanaians.[18]

Charles Taylor, who now has a vested interest in minimising

---

[15] Reuters despatch, New York, 10 September 1993.

[16] Agetua, *Operation Liberty*, p.105.

[17] *African Concord* (Lagos), 21 January 1991.

[18] Prkic, 'Le Ghana dans la gestion de la crise libérienne'.

the brutality of the war which he did so much to initiate, claimed on one occasion in 1998 that the war resulted in some 30-50,000 deaths,[19] and in another interview he put the number lower still, at 20,000.[20] Both estimates seem too low.

Even if we assume an estimate of the order of 20-30,000 deaths in the period 1993-7, added to the total of 40-50,000 for the earlier period this leaves a total of some 60-80,000 deaths directly caused by the war in the whole period 1989-97. This is no more than an order of magnitude. Nevertheless, it does indicate that the figures of 150,000 to 200,000 commonly used for war deaths over the whole 1989-1997 period are a very high estimate, and are probably the result of a misunderstanding of a casualty figure first used by the UN.

[19] Interview with Aad van den Heuvel, 'President in Afrika', Nederland 1 TV, 29 July 1998.
[20] Anderson, 'The Devil they Know', p.38.

B

PRINCIPAL CHARACTERS

SOME OF THE MAIN PROTAGONISTS IN THE PERIOD
OF LIBERIA'S CIVIL WAR

Boley, George E.S.	Born 1949, Putu Chiefdom, Grand Gedeh County. Ph.D., University of Akron, Ohio, 1977. 1979: imprisoned in connection with political activities for Progressive People's Party. 1980: released after 12 April coup and made Minister of State for presidential affairs under PRC. 1991: established Liberia Peace Council. 1993-4: LPC became an armed force.
Doe, Samuel K.	Born Tuzon, Grand Gedeh County, c. 1951. Rose to rank of master sergeant in Liberian army. 1980: participated in overthrow of President Tolbert and was named co-chairman of People's Redemption Council and head of state. 1985: elected president of Liberia in rigged election; defeated coup attempt by Thomas Quiwonkpa. September 1990: murdered by Prince Johnson.
Johnson, Elmer	From a leading Americo-Liberian family. Studied at Boston University, US. 1980: joined US marines, took part in 1983 invasion of Grenada. 1984: participated in coup attempt against Samuel Doe; wounded. 1990: commanded NPFL first battalion and was NPFL chief strategist. June 1990: killed.
Johnson, Prince Y.	Born Nimba County, 1952. 1971: joined Armed Forces of Liberia, rising to rank of lieutenant. Trained in United States.

Became aide to General Thomas Quiwon-kpa. 1983: deserted after flight of Quiwon-kpa. Participated in 1985 coup attempt. 1987: participated in death of Thomas Sankara in Burkina Faso. Joins NPFL. 1989: commanded Special Forces of NPFL in invasion of Liberia. July 1990: established Independent National Patriotic Front of Liberia. September 1990: murder of Samuel Doe. October 1992: supported NPFL attack known as Operation Octopus but later changed sides and fought with Ecomog. 1993: left Liberia for exile in Nigeria.

Johnson, Roosevelt

Born Maryland County, Krahn mother. A schoolteacher, he became an official of the Ministry of Finance. 1991: emerged as leading military official of Ulimo in Sierra Leone. June 1992: deputy field commander of Ulimo: escaped assass-ination by pro-Kromah faction in Ulimo. 1994: emerged as military commander of wing of Ulimo known as Ulimo-J. December 1995: allied with Charles Taylor to contest disarmament to Ecomog. April 1996: government attempt to arrest Johnson led to third battle of Monrovia. Late 1997: minister in Liberian government

Kromah, Alhaji G.V.

Born Monrovia, 1953, from a prominent Mandingo family originating in Lofa County. Attended Koranic school and Catholic school from age 11. 1976: BA in law, University of Liberia. 1977: employed in office of the vice-president. 1979: appointed assistant Minister of Information. 1982: director-general Liberian Broadcasting Service. 1984: Minister of Information. 1989: called for Mandingo to support government of Samuel Doe. 1991: formed Movement for Redemption of Muslims in Conakry. Later merged into Ulimo. 1994: emerged as leader of Ulimo-K.

Sawyer, Amos

Born 1945, Sinoe County. 1973: Ph.D. from Northwestern University, USA.

	Lecturer at University of Liberia and political activist with MOJA. 1979: candidate for mayor of Monrovia. 1981: chairman of National Constitution Drafting Commission. 1990-4: president of Interim Government of National Unity.
Taylor, Charles Mac-Arthur 'Ghankay'	Born Arthington, 1948. 1972: travels to USA. Graduates with BSc from Bentley College, Massachusetts. Becomes chairman of the board of the Union of Liberian Associations in the Americas. 1980: returns to Liberia and becomes senior official of the PRC government. 1983: flees to USA, allegedly having embezzled $900,000. Imprisoned in USA pending extradition. 1985: escapes from prison, travels to Ghana. 1986: detained in Ghana, released and travels to Burkina Faso. 1989: initiates Liberian civil war. 1990: emerges as leader of NPFL. 19 July 1997: elected president of Liberia.

BIBLIOGRAPHY

A NOTE ON SOURCES

In writing this book, I have relied heavily on the Liberian press and on my own interviews with participants and observers. My reliance on the press in particular requires a note of explanation.

There were generally half a dozen or so newspapers published in Monrovia at any one time during the civil war. Many were irregular, and few managed to appear for more than a few months or a couple of years due to financial pressures. Some papers were the official organs of one or another party or faction, but more often newspapers purported to be independent. Like all newspapers anywhere in the world, they could be influenced by one or other political party, and they were susceptible to printing highly partial accounts of events. Liberian intellectuals sometimes lament these propensities of their own press and attribute them to the poor quality of the country's journalists and the inadequacy of their training.[1]

My point of view differs from this. There is no doubt that Liberian journalists by and large do not observe the same conventions as their colleagues in the United States or Europe, but the articles they publish in the local press are nonetheless crucial sources for Liberian history. They should be used and interpreted in a manner slightly different from the European or American press, such as the *New York Times* or the *Washington Post*, which are also useful sources but need to be handled and interpreted in their own way. Unlike the main Western newspapers, some Monrovia newspaper journalists and editors openly accept articles in return for cash, opening their columns to whomever pays for the privilege. Others are said to accept payment from politicians in return for writing favourable stories. Both practices are contrary to the principles taught in schools of journalism, but this does not mean that Liberian newspapers cannot be taken seriously. On the contrary, they are essential sources of information since they reflect a wide range of public and political opinion, at least in Monrovia.

[1] Sankawulo, *What My Country Needs Today*, pp.35-7.

321

It does, however, mean that they must be read critically, since their aim is not to reflect a balanced point of view but to give the public the news which the individual editor feels the public needs and wants, couched in terms the public will understand. Liberian newspapers are to some extent best understood as written forms of *radio trottoir,* as I have argued elsewhere.[2] For the foreign analyst, the key challenge is to understand the nature of this particular information culture, which I have tried to do in making such extensive use of Liberian press sources.

A similar caveat applies to interviews. Individuals naturally remember things differently and recount their experiences in the light of their own standpoint and interests. It is helpful to compare accounts of similar events by two or more different people, but there is a great deal which is agreed upon.

I have modified phonetic spellings and corrected typographical and minor grammatical errors in quotations wherever appropriate.

ARCHIVES

A Center for National Documents and Records Agency was established by an act of the legislature in November 1977. It stored some 24 million pages of documents in the National Archives Building. It also exercised a supervisory role in the preservation of records in all government ministries, agencies and public corporations and had branches in four of the 13 political sub-divisions of Liberia.

In 1990, the National Archives building was badly damaged and comprehensively looted in the first battle of Monrovia. The building is today a hollow shell. An estimated 60 per cent of the documents were destroyed. The remaining records were transported, apparently in conditions which have had an adverse effect on the conservation of the archives, to their current repository in the National Documentation Center situated in the centre of Monrovia in the Law library on Ashmun Street. There appears to be no system of classification, but nevertheless it is possible to retrieve some documents of great historical value.

The Justice and Peace Commission of the National Catholic Secretariat in Monrovia is Liberia's leading human rights organisation. It has an extensive collection of local newspapers which, although looted and vandalised in the third battle of Monrovia

---

[2] Stephen Ellis, 'Tuning in to Pavement Radio', *African Affairs,* 88, 352 (1989), pp.321-30.

in April 1996, still constitutes a valuable collection. In addition the Justice and Peace Commission occasionally produces useful documents and reports of its own which can be obtained from the office.

Various other non-governmental agencies have useful archives which are not open to public consultation in principle, but copies of which may occasionally be obtained.

UNPUBLISHED SOURCES

Akingbade, Harrison Oladunjoye, 'The Role of the Military in the History of Liberia, 1822-1947' (Ph.D. thesis, Howard University, 1977).

Anon., 'Case Study of Grand Gedeh County', notes by a Liberian informant communicated by Bart Witteveen, 14 September 1997.

Blanchard, David G., 'The Impact of External Domination on the Liberian Mano Economy' (Ph.D. thesis, Indiana University, 1973).

Cole, Robert E., 'The Liberian Elite as a Barrier to Economic Development' (Ph.D. thesis, Northwestern University, 1967).

Greenwood, Ralph, 'The Presidency of William V.S. Tubman, President of Liberia, 1944-71' (Ph.D. thesis, Northern Arizona University, 1993).

Harrington, Patrick Joseph, 'Secret Societies and the Church: an evaluation of the Poro and Sande secret societies and the missionary among the Mano of Liberia' (Ph.D. thesis, Gregorian University, Rome, 1975).

Jarrett, Max Bankole, 'Civil War in Liberia: a manipulation of chaos?' (M.A. thesis, School of Oriental and African Studies, University of London, 1996).

Johnson, S. Jangaba M., 'The Influence of Islam on Poro and Sande in Western Liberia', seminar on African Studies, University of Liberia, 18-19 July 1974.

Konneh, Augustine, 'Indigenous Entrepreneurs and Capitalists: the role of the Mandingo in the economic development of modern-day Liberia' (Ph.D. thesis, Indiana University, 1992).

Liberty, Clarence E. Zamba, 'Growth of the Liberian State: an analysis of its historiography' (Ph.D. thesis, Stanford University, 1977).

Martin, Jane, 'The Dual Legacy: government authority and mission influence among the Glebo of Eastern Liberia, 1834-1910' (Ph.D. thesis, Boston University), 1968.

Prkic, François, 'Le Ghana dans la gestion de la crise libérienne', paper presented at a conference on Ghana, Centre d'étude d'Afrique noire, Bordeaux, 29-30 May 1998.

———, 'The Economy of the Liberian Conflict', paper presented at a conference on Defence, Economics and Security in Mediterranean and Sub-Saharan Countries, Lisbon, 5-6 June 1998.

Republic of Liberia, 'Report of the Armed Forces of Liberia (AFL) on the June 6, 1993, Carter Camp Massacre in Harbel', Ministry of Defense, Monrovia, 1993.

Republic of Liberia, 'AFL Reaction to the Wako Commission Report', submitted to the UN Secretary General by Lieut.-Gen. J. Hezekiah Bowen, AFL Chief of Staff, Monrovia, 1993.

Sullivan, Jo Mary, 'Settlers in Sinoe County, Liberia, and their Relations with the Kru, c.1835-1920' (Ph.D. thesis, Boston University, 1978).

Tokpa, Alaric K., 'Class Conflict and Military Intervention in Liberian Politics' (M.Phil. thesis, University of Ghana, Legon, 1990).

United Nations, 'The Carter Camp Massacre: Results of an Investigation by the Panel of Inquiry...', New York, 10 September 1993.

PUBLISHED SOURCES

Periodicals. In addition to a range of Liberian and other newspapers, I have relied heavily on *West Africa* magazine, published weekly in London, which was the most useful journal of record throughout the period. Key articles, especially interviews with the leading actors, are included in the list of published works below. Other articles from newspapers and periodicals are generally not referred to in the following bibliography since full details are included in the footnotes to the text.

Books and published reports. The following bibliography is divided into two parts, one consisting of books and articles directly concerning Liberian history or the civil war, the other consisting of general and comparative material. Included are all the works cited in the text plus a small number of others considered sufficiently important.

On Liberia and the Liberian civil war

Abdullah, Ibrahim, 'Bush Path to Destruction: the origin and character of the Revolutionary United Front (RUF/SL)', *Africa Development*, XXII, 3-4 (1997), pp.45-76.

————, 'Bush Path to Destruction: the origin and character of the Revolutionary United Front/Sierra Leone', *Journal of Modern African Studies*, 36, 2 (1998), pp.203-35.

Adeleke, Ademola, 'The Politics and Diplomacy of Peacekeeping in West Africa: the Ecowas operation', *Journal of Modern African Studies*, 33, 4 (1995), pp.128-64.

Africa Watch, *Liberia: Flight from Terror: testimony of abuses in Nimba County* (New York, 1990). Reprinted in the *Liberian Studies Journal*, XV, 1 (1990), pp.142-61.

————, *Liberia: a human rights disaster*, New York, 1990. Reprinted in *Liberian Studies Journal*, XVI, 1 (1991), pp.129-59.

————, *Liberia: the cycle of abuse: Human rights violations since the November ceasefire,* New York. Reprinted in *Liberian Studies Journal,* XVII, 1 (1992), pp.128-64.

——, *Liberia: waging war to keep the peace. The ECOMOG intervention and human rights,* New York, 1993. Reprinted in *Liberian Studies Journal,* XVIII, 2 (1993), pp.278-318.

Agetua, Nkem, *Operation Liberty: the story of Major General Joshua Nimyel Dogonyaro,* Hona Communications, Lagos, 1992.

Akpan, Monday B., 'The Practice of Indirect Rule in Liberia: the laying of the foundations, 1822-1915' in Eckhard Hinzen and Robert Kappel (eds), *Dependence, Underdevelopment and Persistent Conflict: on the political economy of Liberia,* Bremen, 1980, pp.57-168.

Anderson, Jon Lee, 'The Devil They Know', *New Yorker,* 27 July 1998, pp.34-43.

Anderson, R. Earle, *Liberia: America's African friend,* University of North Carolina Press, Chapel Hill, NC, 1952.

Andrews, G. Henry, *Cry, Liberia, Cry!,* Vantage Press, New York, 1993.

Aning, Emmanuel Kwesi, *Managing Regional Security in West Africa: Ecowas, Ecomog and Liberia,* CDR Working Papers, Centre for Development Research, Copenhagen, 1994.

——, 'Ghana, Ecowas and the Liberian Crisis: an analysis of Ghana's role in Liberia', *Liberian Studies Journal,* XXI, 2 (1996), pp.259-99.

Armon, Jeremy, and Andy Carl (eds), 'The Liberian Peace Process 1990-1996', *Accord: an International Review of Peace Initiatives,* 1 (1996), Conciliation Resources, London.

Azikiwe, Nnamdi, *Liberia in World Politics,* Arthur H. Stockwell, London, 1934.

Bah, Mohammad Alpha, 'The Status of Muslims in Sierra Leone and Liberia', *Journal: Institute of Muslim Minority Affairs,* 12, 2 (1991), pp.464-81.

Banks, Philip, and S. Byron Tarr, 'A Negotiated Settlement: our only way out. A rejoinder', *Liberian Studies Journal,* XVIII, 2 (1993), pp.265-77.

Barrett, Lindsay, *Report on Liberia,* Pan-African Communications Services, Monrovia, 1993. A collection of articles published in *West Africa* magazine.

——, 'General Quainoo and Liberia's Crisis', *West Africa,* 4014 (5 September 1994), pp.1545-6.

Bellman, Beryl L., *Village of Curers and Assassins: on the production of Fala Kpelle cosmological categories,* Mouton, The Hague, 1975.

——, *The Language of Secrecy: symbols and metaphors in Poro ritual,* Rutgers University Press, New Brunswick, NJ, 1984.

Berkeley, Bill, 'Liberia: between repression and slaughter', *Atlantic Monthly,* 270, 6 (Dec.1992), pp.52-64. Reprinted in *Liberian Studies Journal,* XVIII, 1 (1993), pp.127-39.

Best, Kenneth, *Cultural Policy in Liberia,* UNESCO, Studies and documents on cultural policies, Unesco Press, Paris, 1974.

Boley, George E.S., *Liberia: the rise and fall of the First Republic,* Macmillan, London, 1983.

Brehun, Leonard, *Liberia: the war of horror*, Adwinsa publications, Accra, 1991.

Brown, David, 'On the Category "Civilised" in Liberia and Elsewhere', *Journal of Modern African Studies*, 20, 2 (1982), pp.287-303.

——, 'Warfare, Oracles and Iron: a case study of production among the pre-colonial Klowe, in the light of some recent Marxist analyses', *Africa*, 54, 2 (1984), pp.29-47.

Burrowes, Carl Patrick, *The Americo-Liberian Ruling Class and Other Myths: a critique of political science in the Liberian context*, Occasional paper no.3, department of African-American Studies, Temple University, Philadelphia, PA, 1989.

——, 'Democracy or Disarmament: some second thoughts on Amos Sawyer and contemporary "politicians"', *Liberian Studies Journal*, XX, 1 (1995), pp.117-25.

Chaudhuri, J. Pal, 'Liberia under Military Rule (1980-85)' in Kappel, Korte and Mascher (eds), *Liberia: underdevelopment and political rule in a peripheral society*, pp.47-68.

Clapham, Christopher, 'The Politics of Failure: clientelism, political instability and national integration in Liberia and Sierra Leone' in Christopher Clapham (ed.), *Private Patronage and Public Power: political clientelism in the modern state*, Frances Pinter, London, 1982, pp.76-92.

Clower, Robert W., George Dalton, Mitchell Harwitz and A.A. Walters, *Growth without Development: an economic survey of Liberia*, Northwestern University Press, Evanston, IL, 1966.

Cole, Henry B. (ed.), *The Liberian Year Book 1956*, Liberian Review, Monrovia, 1956.

Conteh, Al-Hassan, 'Reflections on some Concepts of Religion and Medicine in Liberian Society', *Liberian Studies Journal*, XV, 2 (1990), pp.145-57.

Corby, Richard A., 'Manding Traders and Clerics: the development of Islam in Liberia to the 1870s', *Liberian Studies Journal*, XIII, 1 (1988), pp.42-66.

Cordor, S. Henry, *The Study of Africa: an introductory course in African studies for Liberian schools*, Liberian Literary and Educational publications, Monrovia, 1979.

——, *Facing the Realities of the Liberian Nation: problems and prospects of a West African society*, University of Iowa Press, Iowa City, 1980.

Daniels, Anthony, *Monrovia Mon Amour*, John Murray, London, 1992.

Davis, Ronald, *Ethnohistorical Studies on the Kru Coast*, Liberian Studies Monograph no.5, University of Delaware, Newark, Delaware, 1976.

D'Azevedo, Warren L., 'A Tribal Reaction to Nationalism', published in four parts: *Liberian Studies Journal*, I, 2 (1969), pp.1-22; II, 1 (1969), pp.43-63; II, 2 (1970), pp.99-115; III, 1 (1970-1), pp.1-19.

——, 'Tribe and Chiefdom on the Windward Coast', *Liberian Studies Journal*, XIV, 2 (1989), pp.90-116.

——, 'Phantoms of the Hinterland: the Mandingo "presence" in early Liberian accounts', *Liberian Studies Journal*, XIX, 2 (1994), pp.197-242.

——, 'Gola Womanhood and the Limits of Masculine Omnipotence' in Thomas D. Blakeley, Walter E.A. van Beek and Dennis L. Thomson (eds), *Religion in Africa*, Vol.4 of the monograph series of the David M. Kennedy Center for Institutional Studies at Brigham Young University, James Currey, London, and Heinemann, Portsmouth, NH, 1994, pp.343-62.

De Montclos, Marc-Antoine, 'Libéria: des prédateurs aux ramasseurs de miettes' in François Jean and Jean-Christophe Rufin (eds), *Economie des guerres civiles*, Hachette, Paris, 1996, pp.269-97.

De Saint-Exupéry, Patrick, and Sophie Roquelle, 'La "montagne de fer" que convoite l'Elysée', *Le Figaro* (Paris), 8 January 1992.

Dennis, Benjamin, *The Gbandes: a people of the Liberian hinterland*, Nelson-Hall, Chicago, 1972.

Dixon, W. Nah, *In Search of a Leader*, Monrovia, 1993.

Dolo, Emmanuel, *Democracy Versus Dictatorship: the quest for freedom and justice in Africa's oldest republic, Liberia*, University Press of America, Lanham, MD, and London, 1996.

Donner, Etta, 'Togba, a Women's Society in Liberia', *Africa*, XI, i (1938), pp.109-11.

———, *Hinterland Liberia*, Blackie and Sons, London and Glasgow, 1939. Originally published in German.

Dorjahn, Vernon R., and Barry L. Isaac (eds), *Essays on the Economic Anthropology of Liberia and Sierra Leone*, Institute for Liberian Studies, Philadelphia, PA, 1979.

Dunn, D. Elwood, 'Liberia Reconsidered: a review', *Canadian Journal of African Studies*, 21, 2 (1987), pp.259-62.

———, *Liberia*, World Bibliographical Series, 157, Clio Press, Oxford, Santa Barbara, Denver, 1995.

———, and Svend E. Holsoe, *Historical Dictionary of Liberia*, African historical dictionaries no.38, Scarecrow Press, Metuchen, NJ, and London, 1985.

———, and S. Byron Tarr, *Liberia: a national polity in transition*, Scarecrow Press, Metuchen, NJ and London, 1988.

Ellis, Stephen, 'Liberia 1989-1994: a study of ethnic and spiritual violence', *African Affairs*, 94, 375 (1995), pp.165-97.

Enoanyi, Bill Frank, *Behold Uncle Sam's Step-Child*, SanMar publications, Sacramento, CA, 1991.

Ethnologische Zeitschrift Zürich, I (1980), Peter Lang, Bern. Special number on masks in Liberia.

Fahnbulleh, H. Boima, *In Whose Interest? Disarmament and the international community in the resolution of the Liberian civil war*, Barrett Communications Company, Monrovia, 1994.

Fischer, Eberhard, 'Masks in a non-Poro Area: the Dan', *Ethnologische Zeitschrift Zürich*, 1 (1980), pp.80-8.

Fleischman, Janet, 'An Uncivil War,' *Africa Report*, 38, 3 (May-June 1993), pp.56-9.

———, 'Human Rights and the Civil War in Liberia', *Liberian Studies Journal*, XIX, 2 (1994), pp.173-82.

Ford, Martin, '"Pacification" under Pressure: the political economy of

328   *Bibliography*

Liberian intervention in Nimba, 1912-1918', *Liberian Studies Journal,*
XIV, 2 (1984), pp.44-63.
———, 'Nimba's Conquest, Mandingo Trade and the "Rashomon Effect"',
Liberia-Forum, 5, 8 (1989), pp.18-31.
———, *Indirect Rule and the Emergence of the 'Big Chief' in Liberia's Central
Province, 1918-1944,* Liberia Working Group papers no.7, Liberia Work-
ing Group, Bremen, 1992.
Fraenkel, Merran, *Tribe and Class in Monrovia,* Oxford University Press,
London, 1964.
Fulton, Richard M., 'The Kpelle Traditional Political System', *Liberian
Studies Journal,* I, 1 (1968), pp.1-19.
———, 'The Political Structures and Functions of Poro in Kpelle Society',
American Anthropologist, 74 (1972), pp.1218-33.
Furbay, Elizabeth D., *Top Hats and Tom-Toms,* Ziff-Davis, Chicago and
New York, 1943.
Gbala, Bai M., 'Gbala on Ulimo's Ethnic Feud', *New Democrat,* 1, 30 (23-9
April 1994).
Gershoni, Yekutiel, 'From Ecowas to Ecomog. The Liberian crisis and
the struggle for political hegemony in West Africa', *Liberian Studies
Journal,* XVIII,1 (1993), pp.21-43.
Gifford, Paul, 'Liberia's Never-die Christians', *Journal of Modern African
Studies,* 30, 2 (1992), p.349-58.
———, *Christianity and Politics in Doe's Liberia,* Cambridge University Press,
1993.
Goldberg, Jeffrey, 'A War without Purpose in a Country without Identity',
New York Times, 22 January 1995, section 6, pp.36-9.
Goodridge, Reginald B., 'Sovereignty on Auction', *Liberian Diaspora,* III,
2 (June 1991), pp.10-12.
Grant, Edward Snoh, 'Something Verging on Criminality', *New Democrat,*
2, 156 (24-6 October 1995).
Greene, Graham, *Journey Without Maps,* Pan edn, London, 1948. First
published 1936.
Guannu, Joseph S., *Liberian History up to 1847,* 2nd edn, private publication,
Smithtown, NY, 1983.
———, *The Perennial Problems of Liberian History,* occasional paper, Liberian
Observer Corporation, Monrovia, 1989.
Gunther, John, *Inside Africa,* Harper, New York 1953.
Harley, George Way, *Notes on the Poro in Liberia,* Papers of the Peabody
Museum, XIX, 2, Peabody Museum, Cambridge, MA, 1941.
———, *Masks as Agents of Social Control in Northeast Liberia,* Peabody Museum,
Cambridge, MA, 1950.
———, *Native African Medicine, with special reference to its practice in the
Mano tribe of Liberia,* new impression, Frank Cass, London, 1970. First
published 1941.
Hayman, Arthur, and Harold Preece, *Lighting Up Liberia,* Creative Age
Press, New York, 1943.
Hinzen, Eckhard, and Robert Kappel (eds), *Dependence, Underdevelopment*

and *Persistent Conflict: on the political economy of Liberia,* Übersee-Museum, Bremen, 1980.

Hlophe, Stephen S., *Class, Ethnicity and Politics in Liberia,* University Press of America, Washington, DC, 1979.

Holsoe, Svend E., 'The Condo Confederation in Western Liberia', *Liberian Historical Review,* 3, 1 (1966), pp.1-28.

———, 'Zolu Duma, Ruler of the Southern Vai, 17??-1828: a problem in historical interpretation', *Liberian Studies Journal,* XV, 2 (1990), pp.91-108.

———, Warren L. D'Azevedo and John Gay, 'Chiefdom and Clan Maps of Western Liberia, *Liberian Studies Journal,* I, 2 (1969), pp.22-39.

——— and J.J. Lauer, 'Who are the Kran/Guéré and the Gio/Yacouba? Ethnic identifications along the Liberia-Ivory Coast border', *African Studies Review,* 19, 1 (1976), pp.139-49.

Horton, S. Augustu P., *Liberia's Underdevelopment – in spite of the struggle,* University Press of America, Lanham, MD, and London, 1994.

Huband, Mark, *The Liberian Civil War,* Frank Cass, London, 1998.

Human Rights Watch – Africa, *Easy Prey: child soldiers in Liberia* (New York, 1994).

———, *Human Rights Abuses by the Liberian Peace Council and the Need for International Oversight.* Reprinted in *Liberian Studies Journal,* XX, 1 (1995), pp.162-71.

Inegbedion, E. John, 'Ecomog in Comparative Perspective' in Timothy G. Shaw and Julius Emeka Okolo (eds), *The Political Economy of Foreign Policy in Ecowas,* Macmillan, London, 1994, pp.218-44.

Iweze, Cyril, 'Nigeria in Liberia: the military operations of Ecomog' in Vogt and Ekoko, *Nigeria in International Peace-Keeping,* pp.216-44.

Johnson, Charles S., *Bitter Canaan: the story of the Negro Republic,* Transaction Books, New Brunswick, NJ, 1989.

Johnson, Prince Yormie (ghost-written by Wilton Sankawulo), *The Gun That Liberates Should Not Rule,* Monrovia, 1991.

Johnson, Roosevelt, interview in *West Africa,* 4147 and 4148 (28 April, 5 May 1997), pp.681-2, 715-7.

Johnston, Sir Harry, *Liberia,* 2 vols, Hutchinson, London, 1906.

Joset, Paul-Ernest, *Les sociétés secrètes des hommes-léopards en Afrique noire,* Payot, Paris, 1955.

Junge, Werner, *African Jungle Doctor: ten years in Liberia,* Harrap, London, 1952.

Justice and Peace Commission, *The Liberian Crisis,* National Catholic Secretariat, Monrovia, 1994.

Kamara, Tom, 'Charles Taylor: the true story', *New African* (London), July 1991.

Kappel, Robert, 'Resistance of the Liberian People: problems of the ignored facts' in Hinzen and Kappel (eds), *Dependence, Underdevelopment and Persistent Conflict,* pp.169-96.

———, and Werner Korte (eds.), *Human Rights Violations in Liberia, 1980-1990: a documentation,* Liberia Working Group, Bremen, 1990.

———, Werner Korte and R. Friedegund Mascher (eds), *Liberia: under-*

development and political rule in a peripheral society, Institut für Afrikakunde, Hamburg, 1986.

Kieh, George Klay, 'Merchants of Repression: an assessment of United States military assistance to Liberia', *Liberia-Forum*, V, 9 (1989), pp.50-61.

———, 'Combatants, Patrons, Peacemakers and the Liberian Civil Conflict', *Studies in Conflict and Terrorism*, 15 (1992), pp.125-43.

Kimble, Frank, 'The United States-Liberia Operational Experts Project', *Liberian Studies Journal*, XV, 1 (1990), pp.1-12.

Knoll, Arthur, 'Harvey S. Firestone's Liberian Investment (1922-1932)', *Liberian Studies Journal*, XIV, 1 (1989), pp.13-33.

Konneh, Augustine, 'Mandingo Integration in the Liberian Political Economy', *Liberian Studies Journal*, XVIII, 1 (1993), pp.44-62.

———, 'Citizenship at the Margins: status, ambiguity and the Mandingo of Liberia', *African Studies Review*, 39, 2 (1996), pp.141-54.

———, *Religion, Commerce and the Integration of the Mandingo in Liberia*, University Press of America, Lanham, MD, and London, 1996.

Korte, Werner, *Ethnische Tradition und militärische Intervention in Afrika. Essay über den Putsch von 1980 in Liberia*, Bremer Afrika-Studien, Bd 10, Lit Verlag, Münster, 1995.

Korvah, Paul Degein, *The History of the Loma People*, O Books, Oakland, CA, 1995.

Kromah, Alhaji G.V., interview in *West Africa*, 4082 (15 January 1996), pp.65-7.

Kulah, Arthur F., *Theological Education in Liberia: problems and opportunities*, SCP/Third World Literature Publishing House, Lithonia, GA, 1994.

'Last Moments of Doe', *West Africa*, 3815 (15 October 1990), pp.2650-2.

Lawyers' Committee for Human Rights, *Liberia: a promise betrayed*, New York, 1986.

Le Roy, Marcel, *Au pays du Niamou. Aux confins du Libéria*, Editions Contemporaines, Paris, 1951.

Liebenow, J. Gus, *Liberia: the evolution of privilege*, Cornell University Press, Ithaca, NY, 1969.

———, *Liberia: the quest for democracy*, Indiana University Press, Bloomington, 1987.

Little, Kenneth, 'The Political Function of the Poro,' part I, *Africa*, XXXV, iv (1965), pp.349-65, and part II, *Africa*, XXXVI, i (1966), pp.62-72.

Lowenkopf, Martin, 'Liberia: putting the state back together' in Zartman (ed.), *Collapsed States*, pp.91-108.

Lumumba-Kasongo, Tukumbi, 'Social Movements and the Quest for Democracy in Liberia: MOJA and its transformation into a political party' in Mahmood Mamdani and Ernest Wamba-dia-Wamba (eds), *African Studies in Social Movements and Democracy*, Codesria, Dakar, 1995, pp.409-61.

McEvoy, Frederick D., 'Understanding Ethnic Realities among the Grebo and Kru Peoples of West Africa', *Africa*, 47, 1 (1977), pp.62-80.

Magyar, Karl P., and Earl Conteh-Morgan (eds), *Peacekeeping in Africa: Ecomog in Liberia* (St Martin's Press, New York, and Macmillan, London, 1998.

Maugham, R.F.C., *The Republic of Liberia*, Geo. Allen & Unwin, London, 1920.

Meacham, Carl, 'Peace Corps Service in Liberia, 1965-66: reflections of an African-American volunteer', *Liberian Studies Journal*, XV, 1 (1990), pp.85-107.

Milligan, Ralph T., *Bolahun*, Vantage Press, New York, 1989.

Mills, Lady Dorothy, *Through Liberia*, Duckworth, London, 1926.

Moran, Mary, 'Warriors or Soldiers? Masculinity and ritual transvestism in the Liberian civil war' in Constance R. Sutton (ed.), *Feminism, Nationalism and Militarism*, Association for Feminist Anthropology/ American Anthropological Association, Arlington VA, 1995, pp.73-88.

———, 'Liberia', in John Middleton (ed.), *Encyclopedia of Africa South of the Sahara*, 4 vols, Charles Scribner's Sons, New York, 1997, II, pp.568-76.

Mortimer, Robert A., 'Senegal's Role in Ecomog: the francophone dimension in the Liberian crisis', *Journal of Modern African Studies*, 34, 2 (1996), pp.293-306.

Murphy, W.P., 'Secret Knowledge as Property and Power in Kpelle Society: elders versus youth', *Africa*, 50, 2 (1980), pp.193-207.

Nagbe, K. Moses, *Bulk Challenge*, Champion publications, Cape Coast, Ghana, 1996.

Naigow, Peter, interview in *West Africa*, 3879 (20 January 1992), pp.102-3.

Njoh, Joseph, *Through The Liberian Storm*, Minerva, London, 1996.

Nwokedi, Emeka, *Regional Integration and Regional Security: Ecomog, Nigeria and the Liberian crisis*, Travaux et documents no.35, Centre d'étude d'Afrique noire, Bordeaux, 1992.

Ogunleye, Bayo, *Behind Rebel Line: anatomy of Charles Taylor's hostage camps*, Delta, Enugu, 1995.

Ohene, Elizabeth, 'Chosen by God?', *Focus on Africa*, 8, 4 (1997), pp.21-4.

Omonijo, Mobolade, *Doe: the Liberian tragedy*, Sahel Publishing, Ikeja, Nigeria, 1990.

Osaghae, Eghosa E., *Ethnicity, Class and the Struggle for State Power in Liberia*, Codesria, monograph series 1/96, Dakar, 1996.

Outram, Quentin, ' "It's Terminal Either Way". An analysis of armed conflict in Liberia, 1989-1996', *Review of African Political Economy*, 24, 73 (1997), pp.355-72.

Quainoo, Arnold, interview in the *Daily Graphic* (Accra), 11 May 1991.

———, interview in 'General Quainoo and Liberia's Crisis', *West Africa*, 4014 (5 September 1994), pp.1545-6.

Ramcharan, B.G., 'Cooperation between the UN and Regional/Sub-Regional Organizations in Internal Conflicts: the case of Liberia', in *African Yearbook of International Law* (ed. Abdulqawi Yusuf), annual publication, 4 (1996), Kluwer Law International, The Hague, 1997, pp.3-17.

Reno, William, 'Foreign Firms and the Financing of Charles Taylor's NPFL', *Liberian Studies Journal*, XVIII, 2 (1993), pp.175-87.

———, 'The Reinvention of an African Patrimonial State: Charles Taylor's Liberia', *Third World Quarterly*, 16, 1 (1995), pp.109-20.

————, *Warlord Politics and African States,* Lynne Rienner, Boulder, CO, 1998.

Republic of Liberia, Bureau of Folkways, *Traditional History and Folklore of the Glebo Tribe,* Department of the Interior, Monrovia, 1957.

————, *The Harbel Area Massacres (at Carter Camp and Camp A). White Paper of the Interim Government of National Unity on the Matter,* Ministry of Foreign Affairs, Monrovia, 21 June 1993.

Richardson, Nathaniel, *Liberia's Past and Present,* Diplomatic Press, London, 1959.

Riddell, James C., 'The Gbannah Ma (Mano) in Two Economies: dynamics of finite-labour economics', in Dorjahn and Isaac, *Essays on the Economic Anthropology of Liberia and Sierra Leone,* pp.121-40.

Ruiz, Hiram A., *Uprooted Liberians: casualties of a brutal war,* US Committee for Refugees, Washington DC, 1992.

Sankawulo, Wilton, *What My Country Needs Today,* Institute for Liberian Languages, Monrovia, 1995.

Sawyer, Amos, *Effective Immediately: dictatorship in Liberia 1980-6: a personal perspective,* Liberia Working Group paper no.5, Bremen, 1987.

————, 'Proprietary Authority and Local Administration in Liberia', in James S. Wunsch and Dele Olowu (eds), *The Failure of the Centralized State: institutions and self-governance in Africa,* Westview Press, Boulder, CO, 1990, pp.148-73.

————, *The Emergence of Autocracy in Liberia: tragedy and challenge,* Institute for Contemporary Studies, San Francisco, 1992.

Schroeder, Günter, *Eine Verborgene Dimension Gesellschaftlicher Wirklichkeit,* paper no.6, Liberia Working Group, Bremen, 1988.

————, and Werner Korte, 'Samuel K. Doe, the People's Redemption Council and Power: preliminary remarks on the anatomy and social psychology of a coup d'état', *Liberia-Forum,* 2, 3 (1986), pp.3-25.

Schröder, Günter, and Dieter Seibel, *Ethnographic Survey of Southeastern Liberia: the Liberian Kran and the Sapo,* Liberian Studies Association in America, monograph series no. 3, Newark, Delaware, 1974.

Schuster, Lynda, 'The Final Days of Dr Doe', *Granta,* 48 (London, 1994), pp.41-95.

Schwab, George (George W. Harley, ed.), *Tribes of the Liberian Hinterland,* Peabody Museum, Cambridge, MA, 1947.

Sessay, Max Ahmadu, 'Politics and Society in post-War Liberia', *Journal of Modern African Studies,* 34, 3 (1996), pp.395-420.

Sibley, James, and D. Westermann, *Liberia – old and new,* James Clarke, London, n.d.

Siegmann, William C., 'Spirit Manifestation and the Poro Society', *Ethnologische Zeitschrift Zürich,* I (1980), pp.89-95.

Sisay, Hassan B., *Big Powers and Small Nations: a case study of United States-Liberian relations,* University Press of America, Lanham, MD, and London, 1985.

Smith, Robert A., *The Emancipation of the Hinterland,* The Star Magazine and Advertising Services, Monrovia, 1964.

Stakeman, Randolph, *The Cultural Politics of Religious Change: a study of the Sanoyea Kpelle in Liberia*, Edwin Mellen Press, Lewiston, NY, 1986.

Tarr, S. Byron, 'Founding the Liberia Action Party', *Liberian Studies Journal*, XV, 1 (1990), pp.13-47.

——, 'The Ecomog Initiative in Liberia: a Liberian perspective', *Issue: a Journal of Opinion*, XXI, 1-2 (1993), pp.74-83.

Taryor, Nya Kwiawon (ed.), *Justice, Justice: a cry of my people*, Strugglers' Community Press, Chicago, 1985.

——, 'Religions in Liberia', *Liberia-Forum*, 5, 8 (1989), p.3-17.

Taylor, Charles, interview with Baffour Ankomah, *Ghanaian Chronicle* (Accra), 12-18 Oct. 1992.

Tipoteh, Togba-Nah, *Democracy: the call of the Liberian people*, Tofters Tryckeri, Sweden, 1981.

Tokpa, Henrique F., 'Cuttington University College during the Liberian Civil War: an administrator's experience', *Liberian Studies Journal*, XVI, 1 (1991), pp.79-94.

Twe, Boikai S., 'A Perspective on Psychological Disorders of Liberia', *Liberian Studies Journal*, XIX, 1 (1994), pp.41-8.

Twaddell, William H., testimony to Africa sub-committee of the US House of Representatives, 1996, reproduced in *The Inquirer* (Monrovia), 5, 55 (13 August 1996), pp.2-4.

Umoden, Gabriel (ed.), *The Liberian Crisis: a photographic expedition*, Gabumo Publishing, Lagos, 1992.

Unger, Marvin H., *Pawpaw, Foofoo, and Juju: recollections of a Peace Corps volunteer*, Citadel Press, New York, 1968.

United Nations, *Report of UN Secretary-General to the Security Council on Liberia*, periodic publications, New York. Reports 3-5 are printed in the *Liberian Studies Journal*.

United States Department of State, Human Rights Report for 1990, reprinted in *Liberian Studies Journal*, XVI, 1 (1991), pp.116-28.

US Department of State, *Liberia Country Report on Human Rights Practices for 1996*, released by the Bureau of Democracy, Human Rights, and Labor, January 30, 1997. Available on internet site: http://www. state.gov/www/global/human_rights/1996_hrp_report/liberia.html

Unoke, Ewa, *The Untold Story of the Liberian War*, IBIC, Enugu, 1993.

Van den Boom, Dirk, *Bürgerkrieg in Liberia. Chronologie – protagonisten – prognose*, Studien zür Politikwissenschaft Bd 80, Lit Verlag, Münster, 1993.

Vogt, Margaret A., 'Nigeria's Participation in the Ecowas Monitoring Group – Ecomog', *Nigerian Journal of International Affairs*, 17, 1 (1991), pp.101-22.

—— and A.E. Ekoko (eds), *Nigeria in International Peace-Keeping, 1960-1992*, Malthouse Press, Lagos, 1993.

Warner, Esther, *Trial by Sasswood*, Pergamon Press, Oxford, 1970. First published 1955.

Welch, Galbraith, *The Jet Lighthouse*, Museum Press, London, 1990. First published 1960.

Weller, Marc (ed.), *Regional Peace-Keeping and International Enforcement:*

the Liberian crisis, Cambridge International Documents Series, Cambridge University Press, 1994.

Wold, Joseph Conrad, *God's Impatience in Liberia*, William B. Eerdemans, Grand Rapids, MI, 1968.

Wonkeryor, Edward L., *Liberia Military Dictatorship: a fiasco 'revolution'*, Strugglers' Community Press, Chicago, 1985.

Woewiyu, Tom, anonymous interview, 'Jackson Doe's death', *New Democrat*, 1, 30 (23-29 June 1994).

———, 'Transcript of Statement by Hon. Tom Woewiyu, Minister of Labor, Liberia National Transitional Government, Delivered in Monrovia July 19, 1994', *Liberian Studies Journal*, XIX, 2 (1994), pp.342-7.

———, interview in *New Democrat* (Monrovia), 1, 41 (1-7 September 1994).

Wreh, Tuan, *The Love of Liberty...: the rule of President William V.S. Tubman in Liberia, 1944-1971*, C. Hurst & Co., London, 1976.

Yancy, Ernest Jerome, *Historical Lights of Liberia's Yesterday and Today*, 3rd edn, Around the World Press, Tel Aviv, 1967.

Yankah, Kwesi, and Lazarus D. Maayang, 'Charles Taylor: dark days in Ghana', *Uhuru* (Accra), 3 (1990), pp.39-42.

Youboty, James, *Liberian Civil War: a graphic account*, Parkside Impressions, Philadelphia, PA, 1993.

General and comparative

Abraham, Arthur, 'Cannibalism and African historiography' in Arthur Abraham (ed.), *Topics in Sierra Leone History: a counter-colonial interpretation*, Leone Publishers, Freetown, 1976, pp.12-30.

Africa Development, XXII, 3-4 (1997), special issue on 'Lumpen Culture and Political Violence: the Sierra Leone civil war', edited by Ibrahim Abdullah and Yusuf Bangura.

Agir Ici-Survie, *Jacques Chirac et la Françafrique. Retour à la case Foccart?*, Harmattan, Paris, 1995.

Arens, W., *The Man-Eating Myth: anthropology and anthropophagy*, Oxford University Press, New York, 1979.

Azikiwe, Nnamdi, *My Odyssey: an autobiography*, C. Hurst & Co., London, 1970.

Bayart, Jean-François, *The State in Africa: the politics of the belly*, Longman, Harlow and New York, 1993. French edn 1989.

———, *L'illusion identitaire*, Fayard, Paris, 1996.

———, 'L'historicité de l'Etat importé', in J.-F. Bayart (ed.), *La greffe de l'Etat*, Karthala, Paris, 1996, pp.11-39.

———, Stephen Ellis and Béatrice Hibou, *The Criminalization of the State in Africa*, James Currey, Oxford, and Heinemann, Portsmouth NH, 1999. French language edn 1997.

Bazenguissa-Ganga, Rémy, 'The Spread of Political Violence in Congo-Brazzaville', *African Affairs*, 98, 390 (1999), pp.37-54.

Beatty, Sir K.J., *Human Leopards*, reprint, AMS Press, New York, 1978. First published 1915, with foreword by Sir Branford Griffith.

Boahen, A. Adu, *African Perspectives on Colonialism*, Johns Hopkins University Press, Baltimore, MD, 1987.

Brown, Paula, and Donald Tuzin (eds), *The Ethnography of Cannibalism*, Society for Psychological Anthropology, Washington, DC, 1983.

Bruce, Steve, *Religion in the Modern World: from cathedrals to cults*, Oxford University Press, 1996.

Bullock, Alan, and Oliver Stallybrass (eds), *The Fontana Dictionary of Modern Thought*, Fontana, London, 1977.

Cain, Peter, and A.G. Hopkins, *British Imperialism: innovation and expansion, 1688-1914*, Longman, London and New York, 1993.

Canetti, Elias, *Crowds and Power*, Penguin, London, 1987. First German edn., 1960.

Chartier, Roger, *Au bord de la falaise. L'histoire entre certitudes et inquiétude*, Albin Michel, Paris, 1998.

Clapham, Christopher, *Africa and the International System: the politics of state survival*, Cambridge University Press, 1996.

Cruise O'Brien, Donal, 'A Lost Generation? Youth identity and state decay in West Africa', in Richard Werbner and Terence Ranger (eds), *Postcolonial Identities in Africa*, Zed Books, London, 1996, pp.55-74.

Diagne, Abdoulaye, 'Les travaux de recherche sur l'UMOA: un aperçu', *Africa Development*, XVI, 3-4 (1991), pp.5-26.

Douglas, Mary, *How Institutions Think*, Syracuse University Press, Syracuse, NY, 1986.

Doza, Bernard, *Liberté confisquée : le complot franco-africain*, Bibli-Europe, Paris, no date.

El-Kenz, Ali, 'Youth and Violence', in Stephen Ellis (ed.), *Africa Now*, Netherlands' Ministry of Development Cooperation, James Currey and Heinemann, The Hague, London and Portsmouth, NH, 1996, pp.42-57.

Ellis, Stephen, 'Tuning in to Pavement Radio', *African Affairs*, 88, 352 (1989), pp.321-30.

———, 'Africa and International Corruption: the strange case of South Africa and Seychelles', *African Affairs*, 95, 379 (1996), pp.165-96.

———, and Gerrie ter Haar, 'Politics and Religion in Sub-Saharan Africa', *Journal of Modern African Studies*, 36, 2 (1998), pp.175-201.

Fage, J.D., *A History of West Africa*, 4th edn, Cambridge University Press, 1969.

Farah, Nuruddin, 'Highway to Hell', *Transition*, 70 (1996), pp.60-71.

Foucault, Michel, *Dits et Ecrits, 1954-1988*, 4 vols, Gallimard, Paris, 1994.

Gaisseau, Pierre Dominique, *Forêt sacrée. Magie et rites secrets des Toma*, Albin Michel, Paris, 1953.

Geertz, Clifford, 'Religion as a Cultural System' in Michael Banton (ed.), *Anthropological Approaches to the Study of Religion*, ASA monograph no.3, Association of Social Anthropologists, Tavistock Publications, London, 1966, pp.1-46.

Gifford, Paul, *African Christianity: its public role*, C. Hurst & Co., London, 1998.

Gombeaud, Jean-Louis, Corinne Moutet and Stephen Smith, *La guerre du cacao. Histoire secrète d'un embargo*, Calmann-Lévy, Paris, 1990.

Goodman, Felicitas, *How About Demons? Possession and exorcism in the modern world*, Indiana University Press, Bloomington, 1988.

Grégoire, Emmanuel, 'Les chemins de la contrebande : étude des réseaux commerciaux en pays hausa', *Cahiers d'études africaines*, 124, XXXI, 4 (1991), pp.509-32.

Hobsbawm, Eric, *Age of Extremes: the short twentieth century, 1914-1991*, Michael Joseph, London, 1994.

———, and Terence Ranger (eds), *The Invention of Tradition*, Cambridge University Press, 1992. (Original publication 1983).

Horton, Robin, 'Stateless Societies in the History of West Africa' in J.F. Ade Ajayi and Michael Crowder (eds), *History of West Africa*, 2 vols, 3rd edn, Longman, Harlow, 1985, I, pp.87-128.

———, *Patterns of Thought in Africa and the West: essays in magic, religion and science*, paperback edn, Cambridge University Press, 1997.

Hoskins, W.G., *The Age of Plunder: the England of Henry VIII, 1500-1547*, Longman, London, 1976.

Hubert, H., and M. Mauss, *Mélanges d'histoire des religions*, 2nd edn, Félix Alcan, Paris, 1929.

Hughes, Arnold, 'The Attempted Gambian Coup d'État of 27 July 1981' in A. Hughes (ed.), *The Gambia: studies in society and politics*, African Studies series no.3, Centre of West African Studies, University of Birmingham, 1991, pp.92-106.

Human, Piet, and André Zaaiman (eds), *Managing Towards Self-Reliance: effectiveness of organisations in Africa*, Phoenix Publishing, with Gorée Institute, Dakar, 1995.

Huntington, Samuel, 'The Clash of Civilizations?', *Foreign Affairs*, 72, 3 (1993), pp.22-49.

———, *The Clash of Civilizations and the Remaking of World Order*, Simon & Schuster, New York, 1996.

Kaplan, Robert, *Balkan Ghosts: a journey through history*, Macmillan, London, 1993.

———, 'The Coming Anarchy: how scarcity, crime, overpopulation and disease are rapidly destroying the social fabric of our planet', *Atlantic Monthly*, February 1994, pp.44-76.

———, *The Ends of the Earth: a journey at the dawn of the 21st century*, Random House, New York, 1996.

Kasfir, Sidney L. (ed.), *West African Masks and Cultural Systems*, Annales, 126, Musée royale de l'Afrique centrale, Tervuren, 1988, introduction pp.1-17.

Lacey, Robert, *Little Man: Meyer Lansky and the gangster life*, Arrow books, London, 1991.

Lonsdale, John, 'The Moral Economy of Mau Mau: wealth, poverty and civic virtue in Kikuyu political thought', in Bruce Berman and John Lonsdale, *Unhappy Valley: conflict in Kenya and Africa* (2 vols, James Currey, London; Ohio University Press, Athens, OH; East African Publishing, Nairobi, 1992), II, pp.315-504.

MacCormack, Carol, 'Human Leopards and Crocodiles: political meanings of categorical anomalies' in Brown and Tuzin (eds), *The Ethnography of Cannibalism*, pp.51-60.

Mair, Lucy, *African Kingdoms*, Oxford University Press, 1977.

Mamadou, Ousmane Samba, 'The CFAF Devaluation, Naira Parallel Exchange Rate and Niger's Competitiveness', *Journal of African Economies*, 6, 1 (1997), pp.85-111.

Mamdani, Mahmood, *Citizen and Subject: contemporary Africa and the legacy of late colonialism*, Princeton University Press, 1996.

Migeod, F.W.H., *A View of Sierra Leone*, Kegan Paul, Trench, Trubner, London, 1926.

Miller, Joseph C., *Way of Death: merchant capitalism and the Angolan slave trade, 1730-1830*, University of Wisconsin Press, Madison, WI, 1988.

Minear, Larry, Colin Scott and Thomas Weiss, *The News Media, Civil War, and Humanitarian Action*, Lynne Rienner, Boulder, CO, and London, 1996.

Misser, François, and Olivier Vallée, *Les gemmocraties : l'économie politique du diamant africain*, Desclée de Brouwer, Paris, 1997.

Observatoire géopolitique des drogues, *Atlas mondial des drogues*, Presses Universitaires de France, Paris, 1996.

Person, Yves, *Samori. Une révolution dyula*, 3 vols, IFAN, Dakar, 1968, 1975.

———, *Cartes historiques de l'Afrique Manding*, Centre de Recherche Africaine, Paris, 1990.

Prunier, Gérard, *The Rwanda Crisis, 1959-1994: history of a genocide*, C. Hurst & Co., London, 1995.

Rashid, Ishmail, 'Subaltern Reactions: lumpen, students and the left', *Africa Development*, XXII, 3-4 (1997), pp.19-44.

Rattray, R.S., *Ashanti*, Oxford University Press, London, and Basel Mission Book Depot, Kumasi, 1923.

Reno, William, *Corruption and State Politics in Sierra Leone*, Cambridge University Press, 1995.

Richards, Paul, *Fighting for the Rain Forest: war, youth and resources in Sierra Leone*, International African Institute in association with James Currey and Heinemann, London and Portsmouth, NH, 1996.

Richburg, Keith B., *Out of America: a black man confronts Africa*, Basic Books, New York, 1997.

Robinson, Ronald E., 'Non-European Foundations of European Imperialism: sketch for a theory of collaboration' in William Roger Louis (ed.), *Imperialism: the Robinson and Gallagher controversy*, New Viewpoints, New York, 1976, pp.128-52.

Rufin, Jean-Christophe, *L'empire et les nouveaux barbares*, J.-C. Lattès, Paris, 1991.

Sanday, P.R., *Divine Hunger: cannibalism as a cultural system*, Cambridge University Press, 1986.

Sarpong, Peter, *Ghana in Retrospect: some aspects of Ghanaian culture*, Ghana Publishing Corporation, Tema, 1974.

Schatzberg, Michael, 'Power, Legitimacy and "Democratization" in Africa', *Africa*, 63, 4 (1993), pp.445-61.

Shaw, Rosalind, 'The Politician and the Diviner: divination and the consumption of power in Sierra Leone', *Journal of Religion in Africa*, XXXVI, 1 (1996), pp.30-55.

Silberzahn, Claude, with Jean Guesnil, *Au coeur du secret. 1500 jours aux commandes de la DGSE, 1989-1993*, Fayard, Paris, 1995.

Tawney, R.H., *Religion and the Rise of Capitalism: a historical study*, Penguin, Harmondsworth, 1975 (first published 1926).

Terray, Emmanuel, *Une histoire du royaume abron du Gyaman. Des origines à la conquête coloniale*, Karthala, Paris, 1995.

United States Department of State, Bureau for International Narcotics and Law Enforcement Affairs, *International Narcotics Control Strategy Report*, Washington, DC, annual.

Van Creveld, Martin, *The Transformation of War*, Free Press, New York, 1991.

Van de Walle, Nicolas, 'The Decline of the Franc Zone: monetary politics in Francophone Africa', *African Affairs*, 90, 360 (1991), pp.383-406.

Vansina, Jan, *Paths in the Rainforests*, University of Wisconsin Press, Madison, 1990.

Weber, Max, *The Protestant Ethic and the Spirit of Capitalism*, Routledge, London and New York, 1992 (German original 1904-5, rev. edn 1920-1).

————, (Max Rheinstein, ed.), *Max Weber on Law in Economy and Society*, 20th century Legal Philosophy Series, VI, Harvard University Press, Cambridge, MA, 1954.

Wilks, Ivor, 'Space, Time and "Human Sacrifice" ' in I. Wilks, *Forests of Gold: essays on the Akan and the Kingdom of Asante*, Ohio University Press, Athens OH, 1993, pp.215-40.

Woodward, Bob, *Veil: the secret wars of the CIA, 1981-1987*, Pocket Books, New York, 1987.

Yeebo, Zaya, *Ghana: the struggle for popular power*, New Beacon Books, London, 1991.

Zartman, I. William (ed.), *Collapsed States: the disintegration and restoration of legitimate authority*, Lynne Rienner, Boulder CO, 1995.

INDEX